BATTLE OF BANNOCKBURN

Frontispiece, Scotland, vol. two.

SCOTLAND

BY

SIR WALTER SCOTT, Bart.

WITH A SUPPLEMENTARY CHAPTER OF RECENT EVENTS
By MAYO W. HAZELTINE

ILLUSTRATED

VOLUME II

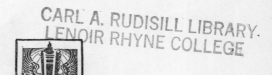

NEW YORK
PETER FENELON COLLIER & SON
MCM

CONTENTS

CHAPTER XXV

CHAPTER XXVI

CHAPTER XXVII

CHAPTER XXVIII

CHAPTER XXIX

CHAPTER XXX

CHAPTER XXXI

CHAPTER XXXII

CHAPTER XXXIII

CHAPTER XXXIV

CHAPTER XXXV

CHAPTER XXXVI

CHAPTER XXXVII

CHAPTER XXXVIII

CHAPTER XXXIX

CHAPTER XL

CHAPTER XLI

LIST OF ILLUSTRATIONS

SCOTLAND

VOL. II.

HISTORY OF SCOTLAND

CHAPTER XXV

Disadvantages of the Protestants—They receive Supplies of Treasure from England: a large Sum of which is intercepted by the Earl of Bothwell—The Protestants are repulsed from Leith, and retire to Stirling much discouraged—They recover Courage at the Exhortation of John Knox; and send Lethington to the Court of England—Aid is granted to the Reformers by Elizabeth—A Detachment of the French ravage the Coast of Fife—The Protestant Gentlemen skirmish with them—Critical Arrival of the English Fleet—The French retreat

THE lords of the congregation were not long in discovering that in the task of besieging a fortified town like Leith, defended by veteran and disciplined troops, they had greatly overrated their own strength. The town, being open to the sea, could not easily be reduced by famine; and the insurgents, however brave in the battlefield, were far inferior to the French in the attack and defence of fortified places. Brantome gives us reason to believe that the talents of the general of the French were of the first order, and affirms that it was sufficient to gain a high name in arms to have assisted at the siege of Leith.

But the Scottish nobles labored under other disadvantages besides inferiority in military skill. A still greater difficulty arose from the want of money to pay and maintain an army in the field, without which the feudal array of the reformed chiefs was sure to crumble to pieces anew in the space of a month or two. Meantime the necessary suspension of hostilities gave the queen an opportunity of disuniting the league of the reformed party by tampering with its leaders individ-

(13)

ually, and several who had been proof against the regent's threats were found not inaccessible to her promises. To guard against such pressing evils, the lords of the congregation resolved upon invoking the assistance of England, the only neighbor of power and wealth whose alliance or countenance could counterpoise that of France.

The cause of the reformation had been espoused and defended by Queen Elizabeth, whose right to the crown and whose title to legitimacy depended upon her father Henry's having disowned the authority of the Church of Rome. Indeed, if she herself had not seen her danger from the queen of Scots' title being set up in preference to her own, the princes of Lorraine had, with arrogance peculiar to their house, called her attention to the subject by making open pretence to the throne of England in behalf of their niece, Mary of Scotland. Money had been struck in France bearing the arms of England; proclamations had been made in the names of Francis and Mary, as king and queen of that country, as well as of France and Scotland; and an open and avowed claim to the crown of England was brought forward in Queen Mary's behalf by every mode short of a direct challenge of Elizabeth's title. The English Catholics were known to be favorable to these views. It was natural, therefore, that Elizabeth, whose birth and title of succession were thus openly impugned by the princes of Lorraine, should foster and encourage those Scottish insurgents who were in arms to dispossess their sister, the queen-regent, of the government of Scotland. Accordingly, though accustomed to act with great economy, she was readily induced to advance considerable sums to the lords of the congregation, by which assistance, in 1559, they were enabled to form the siege of Leith.

Their undertaking was, at first, very unfortunate. A large sum of the subsidy furnished by Queen Elizabeth fell into the hands of the Earl of Bothwell, whose ill-omened name now first appears in history, and who had adopted the faction of the queen-mother. Two skirmishes, in which the Protestants were defeated, filled the besiegers with consternation: they renounced their enterprise precipitately, and retreated from Edinburgh to Stirling with fallen hopes and an army diminished by desertion. But Knox encouraged them by his fulminations from the pulpit: he sternly upbraided the hearers with their confidence in the arm of flesh, and promised them victory as soon as they should humble themselves to acknowledge the power of the Divine Disposer of events. The severe minister reminded them of the former errors of some among them, of the selfish views of others, of the want of concord among their leaders, the deficiency of zeal among the followers, and charged on their own faults and follies those losses which men of more timorous spirit ascribed to the superiority of the enemy. The eloquence of this extraordinary and undaunted preacher was calculated to work on the stubborn and rough men to whom it was addressed. The lords of the congregation resumed their purpose of resistance to the last, and resolved to despatch William Maitland of Lethington, one of the most distinguished statesmen of his time, to show the queen of England the pressure of the circumstances under which they labored, and to demonstrate the necessity of assisting them in their defence, unless she would be content to see the Protestant party in Scotland utterly destroyed. The negotiator selected on this occasion had recently held the office of secretary to the queen; but as he dissented from the counsels which were transmitted to her from Paris, and had remonstrated with firmness against the measures to which she was instigated by attachment to her faith and family, he incurred the hatred and suspicion of the French to such a degree that he considered his life in danger from their resentment. Under such personal apprehension he fled from Leith to join the lords of the congregation at Stirling; for although he professed the reformed faith, he was never believed to be deeply animated with religious zeal. The great reputation which Lethington enjoyed as a statesman did not exceed his real abilities; and his judicious remonstrances easily per-

suaded the sagacious Elizabeth to grant the succors required
by his constituents.

It was the marked attribute of this great princess's administration, that, slow and cautious in adopting steps of
importance, she was equally prompt and determined in the
execution of them; and she took her measures on this occasion with her characteristic wisdom and activity.

In the meantime the queen-regent of Scotland, who had
received some additional assistance from France, and was
in expectation of a much larger force, resolved to press the
moment of advantage before the power of England could
be put in motion. A body of French infantry, and a considerable party of horse, amounting altogether to about four
thousand men, were sent into Fife, the most civilized part
of Scotland, and where the inhabitants were most devoted
to the Protestant faith, to punish the rebellious, and to destroy the power of the barons of that district. The invaders
passed by the bridge of Stirling, and then marched eastward
along the coast of the Firth of Forth, burning and wasting
the villages and gentlemen's houses with which the shores
were thickly studded. This was not done without much
resistance and retaliation. The prior of Saint Andrew's,
Lord Ruthven, Kirkcaldy of Grainge, a gentleman of Fife
distinguished for his pre-eminent courage in an age when
courage was a universal attribute, with other active leaders
of the congregation, attended upon the motions of the French
detachment, limited their forays, skirmished with them on
every occasion, and conducted their resistance with such
zeal and activity that though in number only five or six
hundred men, they gained occasional advantages, and maintained by their zeal and courage, even in these arduous circumstances, the character of their country and the spirit
of their party. The two armies continued for several days
to move along the coast; the flames of towns and villages
marking the progress of the French, and the sudden and
vigorous charges of the Protestants interrupting from time
to time the work of devastation, when the sight of a gallant

navy of ships of war sailing up the Firth of Forth attracted the attention of both parties. D'Oysel, the French general, concluded that they were the fleet expected from France, and in that belief made his soldiers fire a general salute. But he was soon painfully undeceived by the capture of two of his own transports, which sailed along the shore to supply his men with provisions, and presently after this act of decisive violence the fleet showed English colors.

It was now the turn of the French to fly, as the invading detachment must otherwise have stood in considerable danger of being cut off from their friends on the southern side of the Forth. So that, instead of marching onward to Saint Andrew's and Dundee, both which towns had been especially devoted to plunder and destruction, d'Oysel attempted a retreat to Stirling, by a dangerous march in the opposite direction. The Scots had broken down a bridge over the Devon, hoping to intercept the enemy's return; but the French, well acquainted with the duties of the engineer, threw over a temporary bridge, composed of the roof or timbers of a church, which afforded them the means of passage. They effected with difficulty their retreat to Stirling, and from thence to Lothian. The critical arrival of the English fleet being considered as an especial interference of Providence in the Protestant cause, gave new courage to the lords of the congregation, who assembled forces on every side. The English land army, amounting to six thousand men, under Lord Grey de Wilton, now entered Scotland, agreeably to the engagement of Elizabeth, and united their forces with those of the Protestants. The French troops retired into Leith, and prepared to make good their defence, in hopes of receiving succor from France. The town was instantly blockaded by the English fleet on the side of the sea, and beleaguered on the landward side by the united armies of Scotland and England.

In 1560, the eyes of all Britain were bent on this siege of Leith, which the English and Scottish, now for the first time united in a common cause carried on with the utmost

perseverance, while the French defended themselves with
such skill and determination as was worthy the character
they bore of being the best troops in Europe. They were,
indeed, defeated at the Hawkhill, near Loch End, where
the Scottish cavalry charged them with great fury, and
gained considerable advantage; but the garrison of Leith
shortly after avenged themselves by a successful sally, in
which they killed double the number they had lost at the
Hawkhill. On this occasion it became evident that the English, who had not lately been engaged in any great national
war, had in some degree lost the habit of discipline. The
attack on the besiegers found their lines carelessly watched;
and the ground where they opened their trenches being
unfit for the purpose, argued inexperience on the part of
the engineers.

The loss which they had sustained taught the English
greater vigilance and caution; but so intimately were the
French acquainted with defensive war that the siege advanced very slowly. At length a breach was effected and an
assault both terrible and persevering was made on the town.
The ladders, however, which were prepared for the occasion
proved too short for the purpose, and the besiegers were
finally repulsed with great loss. The English were at first
depressed by this repulse; but they were encouraged to continue the siege by the Duke of Norfolk, commanding in the
northern counties of England with the title of lieutenant.
He sent a reinforcement of two thousand men, with an assurance that the besiegers should not lack men so long
as there were any remaining between Tweed and Trent.
The siege was renewed more closely than ever, with reliance rather on famine than force for reducing the place.
But the garrison endured without murmur the extremity
of privation to which they were reduced, and continued to
maintain the defence of Leith with the most undaunted
firmness.

While the affairs of Scotland were in this unpropitious
condition, Mary of Guise, whose misrule had been the cause

of these civil hostilities, died in the castle of Edinburgh. That strong fortress had remained during the civil war under the charge of the Lord Erskine, who remained neutral between the parties, and would admit neither of them in any numbers into the important national citadel. But when the siege of Leith was about to commence, the queen-regent, weak in health and broken in spirits, and unable to partake in the dangers and hardships to which the town was about to be exposed, requested to be received into the castle of Edinburgh for the safety of her person. This was readily granted by the Lord Erskine, on condition that she should be attended by a train so limited as to excite no apprehension for the security of the place. Here her disease, which was of a dropsical nature, gradually increased, aggravated, no doubt, by mental distress, arising out of the difficulties which multiplied around her.

On her death-bed she desired an interview with the prior of Saint Andrew's and some of the lords of the congregation, and expressed her sorrow for having listened to the councils which had brought the country to the pass in which it now stood. Having thus confessed her own errors, she pressed on them the necessity of keeping in view their duty to their infant sovereign. She heard with respect the admonitions of Willox, a Protestant divine of eminence, not, as we may suppose, with any idea of renouncing her own faith, but to give a sign of the candor toward those of a different persuasion, from which, in her life, she had too often departed. In these melancholy circumstances died Mary of Guise, of whom it was justly said that her talents and virtues were her own; her errors and faults the effect of her deference to the advice of others, and especially of her aspiring brothers.

Her death was speedily followed by proposals of peace from France. The ambitious views of the House of Lorraine had engaged France in a war not only with Scotland but with all Britain; and their sister's death deprived them of that interest in the Scottish government which Bothwell,

Seton, and a very few other Scotsmen of influence hitherto
acknowledged. Leith was now reduced to the last extremity,
and must be either effectually reinforced or surrendered.
The position of affairs in France afforded strong reasons
against detaching any considerable force for relief of the
town.

The enterprise of Amboise had opened to view a deep
and extended conspiracy against the power of the House of
Lorraine; and though it was discovered and prevented for
the time, yet its elements existed all over France, and a
single spark might unexpectedly extend a conflagration over
the whole. It was, therefore, a point not of prudence only
but necessity on the part of the French government, instead
of sending fresh troops to Scotland, to make such an accommodation with the nobles of the kingdom as would permit
them to withdraw the veteran troops who were cooped up
in Leith, in order to their being employed in more pressing
service at home.

In managing a difficult negotiation, where France was
confessedly the weaker party, the princess of Lorraine employed Monluc, bishop of Valence, and the Sieur de Randan,
men of consummate talent. Cecil, and Wotton, dean of
Canterbury, were present at the conferences, on the part
of England. The removal of the foreign troops was quickly
agreed on; for the French government now desired their
presence at home as much as the Scots wished their absence.
The fortified places of Leith, Dunbar and Inch Keith were
to be surrendered, and the fortifications destroyed. It was
made a condition that no foreign forces should be introduced
into Scotland without consent of parliament. The administration of government was vested in a council of twelve persons, of whom seven were to be named by the king and
queen, and the other five by parliament. An indemnity
was stipulated for whatever violences had been committed
by either party during the civil war. On the matter of religion, it was declared that the estates should report to the
king and queen their opinion on that matter; and it was

agreed that the parliament should be convoked without further summons.

A treaty was at the same time made between France and England, by which Francis and Mary recognized in the fullest manner the claim of Elizabeth to the English crown, and agreed that Mary, in time to come, should neither assume the title nor bear the arms of England. By this pacification, which was called the Treaty of Edinburgh, the civil wars of Scotland were conducted to a termination highly favorable to the cause of the Protestant religion, and very different from what seemed at first probable.

CHAPTER XXVI

Petition to the Scottish Parliament on the Part of the Reformers—
The Parliament abolish the Roman Catholic Form of Worship,
and prohibit the Celebration of the Mass under severe Penalties
—The Change of Religion meets no Opposition from the Catholic Bishops and Prelates; but gives great Offence to Francis
and Mary, who receive an Envoy from Parliament very coldly
—The Church Government of Scotland is arranged on a Calvinistic and Presbyterian Model—The Clergy are meanly provided for, the Nobles retaining the greater Part of the Spoils of
the Catholic Church—Debates on this Subject—Character of the
Presbyterian Church of Scotland—Destruction of the Ecclesiastical Buildings—Queen Mary returns to Scotland; her Reception at Edinburgh—Intolerant Zeal of the Reformers, expressed
in Pageants and by Riots, and by the vehement Exhortations of
John Knox—These Disturbances appeased by the Moderation
of Lord James Stewart, Prior of Saint Andrew's—Transactions
with England—Correspondence between the Queens

THE Scottish parliament met on August 1, 1560. They
had never assembled in such numbers, or had affairs
of such weight before them; but the most pressing
and important business was a petition from the principal
Protestants, comprehending the chief lords of the congregation, desiring and urging the parliament to adopt a formal
manifesto against the errors and corruptions of the Church
of Rome, the exorbitance of its power and wealth, and its
oppressive restrictions on the liberty of conscience. The
parliament, with little hesitation, adopted the declaration,
that the domination of the Church of Rome was a usurpation over the liberties and consciences of Christian men; and
to make their grounds of dissent from his doctrines still more
evident, they promulgated a confession of faith, in which
they renounced, in the most express terms, all the tenets

by which the Church of Rome is distinguished from other
Christian churches, and disowned the whole authority of
the Roman pontiffs and the hierarchy of their church. The
entire system of ecclesiastical government, both in doctrine
and practice, which had existed for so many centuries, and
been held inviolably sacred, was by these enactments utterly
overthrown, and one altogether new adopted in its stead.
The worship of Rome, so long that of the kingdom and of all
Europe, was at once denounced as idolatrous; and, following
one of Rome's worst tenets, secular punishments were menaced against those who continued to worship according to
the manner of their fathers. The celebration of mass was
punished in the first instance by banishment, in the second
by a forfeiture of goods and corporal punishment, in the
third by death itself.

It is remarkable that the acts of parliament authorizing
these great and radical changes in the religion and church
government of the country passed without the slightest opposition on the part of the Roman Catholic churchmen,
bishops, and mitred abbots, who had still retained seats in
the Scottish parliament. They were confounded and over-
awed by the unanimity with which the nobility, gentry, and
burgesses united in these innovations. As their zeal for the
peculiarities of their faith certainly assumed no self-denying
form, it is probable no one ecclesiastic might care to draw
upon himself, as an individual, the popular hatred, and perhaps the popular vengeance, likely to attend on any one who
opposed the general demand for reform; and all might hope
that the propositions approved in parliament had every
chance of falling to the ground by the king and queen refusing their consent.

Neither did they in that respect calculate falsely. Sir
James Sandilands, Lord Saint John, being sent to announce
the proceedings of this reforming parliament to Francis and
Mary, was very coldly received at the court of France, and
the ratification of its statutes which he sought to obtain was
positively refused. The princes of Lorraine, on the other

hand, by their insolent carriage toward the envoy, by their
general expressions of resentment, by the levy of troops, and
their employing Lord Seton and other active agents in Scotland to draw together those who still favored the Catholic
cause, intimated their purpose that the war should be re-
kindled in Scotland in the next spring, by the invasion of a
French fleet and army.   But these intentions were cut short
by the sudden death of Francis II., who had acted as much
under the influence of his beautiful wife as she herself, their
niece, had under that of the princes of Lorraine.   Charles
IX., the brother and successor of Francis, was entirely governed by the councils of his mother, who, jealous of the
ascendency which Mary had acquired over her deceased
husband, avenged herself, now that she had the power in
her hands, by so many marks of slight and contempt, that
the younger queen-dowager, overwhelmed with the reverse
of fortune, retired entirely from the court, and took up her
residence in solitude at Rheims.

The Scottish Protestants were rejoiced at the timely
change which destroyed all possibility of their plans of
reformation being disturbed by the power of France, and
proceeded with full assurance of success to complete the
model of their church government.   The tenets of the celebrated Calvin, respecting ecclesiastical rule, were selected,
probably because they were considered most diametrically
opposite to those of Rome.   This form of church government had been established in the city of Geneva, where
John Knox and other reformed teachers pursued their theological studies, and it was earnestly recommended by them
to the imitation of their countrymen

This modification of the reformed religion differed in its
religious tenets but little from that of the Lutherans, and
still less from that which was finally adopted in England.

But the Presbyterian system was, in its church government, widely distinguished from that of all countries which,
renouncing the religious doctrines of the Roman clergy, had
retained their hierarchy, whether in whole or in part.   In-

vented in a republican country, the Presbyterian government was entirely unconnected with and independent of the civil government of the State, and owned no earthly head. The Church was governed in the extreme resort by the general assembly of the Church, being a convocation of the clergy by representation, together with a certain number of the laity, admitted to sit and vote with them, as representing the Christian community, under the name of lay elders. In the original sketch of the Scottish Church discipline, provision was made for certain persons named superintendents, who were intrusted, as their name implies, with the spiritual power of bishops. A digest of the forms of the Church, called the Book of Discipline, was willingly received and subscribed to by the leaders of the congregation, the lay reformers offering no objection to anything which the preachers proposed, whether respecting the doctrines of the Church or the forms by which it was to be governed.

But though the clergy and laity went thus far hand in hand, there was a point at which their views and interests parted. This was upon the mode in which the revenue of the Church of Rome should be disposed of. No less than one-half of the land in the kingdom of Scotland, and that by much the more valuable, had, one way or other, been engrossed by the popish clergy; and the lay nobles, outstripped by them in wealth, and often in court favor, envied their large revenues at least as much as they abhorred their doctrines and disliked their persons. The hope of engrossing the principal share in so rich a plunder was probably looked forward to by the nobles as a compensation for the destruction of the old form of church government, which presented so many good places of retreat for sons, legitimate or natural, and near relations otherwise not easily provided for in so poor a country. Having seen this source of influence destroyed, they were desirous in exchange to secure the funds out of which it had arisen; and their surprise and displeasure were great when the Presbyterian clergy preferred their claim for a share. Many of the aristocracy had

already secured portions of the patrimony of the Church by
feus, leases, and other modes of alienation exercised by the
Catholic clergy, who, being still in lawful possession of the
lands, were easily induced to sell or otherwise dispose of
them to their lay friends; and without meaning to bring
a charge of self-intended greediness against the whole body
of Scottish laymen, distinguished as promoters of the reformation, we may fairly say that there was a large majority
whose zeal for their own interest equalled at least that which
they felt for the Protestant doctrines.

Thus determined on their own private views, it was with
the utmost reluctance the Scottish statesmen were induced
to listen to a proposal, framed on a report of the reformed
clergy, that the church revenues should be divided into three
shares or portions, to be applied: 1. To the decent support
of the clergy; 2, to the encouragement of learning, by the
foundation of schools and colleges; and, 3, to the support
of the poor of the realm.   Maitland of Lethington asked,
with a sneer, whether the nobility of Scotland were now to
turn hod-bearers, to toil at the building of the kirk.   Knox
answered, with his characteristic determination, that he who
felt dishonored in aiding to build the house of God would
do well to look to the security of the foundations of his own.
But the nobles finally voted the plan to be a "devout imagination, a well-meant but visionary system, which could not
possibly be carried into execution."   At a later period the
parliament were in a manner shamed into making some
appointment for the clergy, payable out of the tithes which
either remained in the hands of the bishops and abbots of
the Scottish Church, or had fallen into the hands of lay
impropriators.

By this arrangement the bishops, abbots, etc., were
allowed to subsist as an order of proprietors, although
deprived of all ecclesiastical dignity or office in the reformed church; and their possession of the church revenues afforded the means by which the ecclesiastical possessions were transmitted to the lay nobility by sale, lease,

and other modes of alienation. The general regulation of parliament bore, that the church property, whether in the hands of the bishops or of lay titulars, as the lay impropriators were called, should be liable to be taxed to the extent of one-third of their amount, for the support of the Protestant clergy; and a committee was appointed to *modify*, as it was called, the especial stipends payable in every individual case, reserving by far the greater proportion of the fund in reversion to the prelatic possessor or lay titular. The obvious selfishness of these enactments gave just offence to the clergy. John Knox, deeply incensed at the avarice of the nobility, pronounced from the pulpit of Edinburgh, that two parts of the church revenue were bestowed on the devil, and a third divided between God and the devil. A hundred marks Scottish (not six pounds sterling) was the usual allowance modified to the minister of a parish: some parishes were endowed with a stipend of thrice that amount; and the whole sum allowed for the maintenance of the national Church, consisting of a thousand parishes, was about three thousand five hundred pounds a year, which paltry endowments were besides irregularly paid, and very much begrudged. When it is considered how liberal the ancient kings and governors of Scotland had been to the Church of Rome, it appears that in this point, as in all others of doctrine and discipline, the Scottish reformers had held a line of conduct diametrically opposite to that pursued by their Catholic ancestors.

This unkindly parsimony toward themselves was the more acutely felt by the Protestant preachers, as the principal lords of the congregation, and the Lord James of Saint Andrew's himself, were the persons by whom these miserable stipends were modified. "Who would have thought," said the ardent Knox, "that when Joseph ruled in Egypt, his brethren would have come down thither for corn, and returned with their sacks empty? Men would have thought that Pharaoh's storehouse would have been emptied ere the sons of Jacob were placed in risk of starving for hunger."

Wisheart of Pittarrow, a zealous reformer, was appointed comptroller, to levy and pay the allotted stipends; but as the poor ministers complained to heaven and earth that they were not able to obtain payment even of the small pittance allowed them, it became a common phrase to bless the good laird of Pittarrow as a sincere professor, but bid the devil receive the comptroller as a greedy extortioner.

Such were the original regulations of the Presbyterian Church of Scotland, which has now subsisted, with short interruptions, for more than three centuries, and set an example, with few exceptions, of zealous good men actually submitting to that indigence which had been only talked of by the monks and friars, and laboring in their important duties for conscience' sake, not for gain. Their morals are equal to those of any church in the world, and superior to most. As in the usual course of their studies they are early transferred from the university to the pulpit, the Scottish Church has not produced so many deep scholars or profound divines as those of the sister kingdom, whose colleges and fellowships afford room and opportunity for study till the years of full intellect are attained. On the other hand, few instances occur in which a Scottish minister does not possess a scholar-like portion both of profane learning and theological science. In the earlier days of the Church the Presbyterian clergy were hurried into some extremes, from their ardent desire to oppose diametrically their doctrines and practice to those of Rome, when it had been better to have conformed to the ancient practices. Because the Catholic Church demanded a splendid ritual, prescribed special forms of prayer, and occupied superb temples, the Scottish kirk neglected the decencies of worship, and the solemn attitude of devotion which all men assume in the closet; and the vulgar audience reprobated the preachers who showed so much anxiety to discharge their office as to commit their discourses to writing previous to delivering them. Because the Catholic priests easily granted absolution for such offences as their hearers brought in secret to the confessional, the kirk insisted upon performance of public and personal penance, even in cases which were liable to harden the feelings of the criminal, to offend the delicacy of the congregation, and to lead to worse consequences. Instead of the worldly pomp and circumstance which the Church of Rome assembled around her, the reformed preachers could only obtain eminence by observing an austere system of morals themselves, and exacting the same from others—a practice which in extreme cases might occasionally lead to hypocrisy and spiritual tyranny. Lastly, as they disclaimed all connection with the State, the Scottish divines could not be charged, like the papist clergymen, with seeking the applause of monarchs, and a high place in courts; but they cannot in the early ages of the Church be acquitted of interfering with the civil government in cases where they pretended that religion was connected with it (a connection easily discovered, if the preacher desired to find it), and so dedicating to politics the time and reasoning which were due to religion. The current of ages, however, and the general change of manners, have in a great measure removed those errors, imputable to the Scottish Church, and incidental to every human institution, which arose from superabundant zeal; and it is hoped and believed that, while some excesses have been corrected and restrained, it is, as a national church establishment, still animated by the more refined and purer qualities of fervid devotion.

The fabric of the Roman Church having now been destroyed, unless in so far as its ruins afforded refuge to abbots *in commendam*, lay impropriators, and other titles given to such nobles as had enriched themselves at the expense of the establishment, the reformers were resolved to destroy those splendid monuments of ancient devotion, which, in their eyes, had incurred condemnation from having been the scene of a false or idolatrous worship. The work was intrusted to the agents of the zealots among the party, who found ready assistance everywhere from a disorderly rabble, to whom devastation was in itself a pleasure. The basest

covetousness actuated their superiors, who frequently lent
their countenance to the destructive proceedings for the sake
of the paltry gain which could be derived from the sale of
the sacred vessels, bells, lead, timber, and whatever of the
other materials could be turned to profit. Thus, by the blind
fury of the poor, and the sordid avarice of the higher classes,
"abbeys, cathedrals, churches, libraries, records, and even
the sepulchres of the dead," says the eloquent Robertson,
"perished in one common ruin." It is said John Knox himself justified this unlimited destruction by the noted saying,
"Pull down the nests, and the rooks will fly off!" an expression, the politic meaning of which could only apply to
the cloisters of the monks and friars. Other ill-instructed
preachers gave encouragement to devastation, by quoting
the examples afforded in the Old Testament of the destruction of places in which idolatrous rites had been used: a
manifest misapplication of Scripture, and one which, pushed
to its conclusion, would have seemed to warrant an exter-
minating war against those who adhered to the old religion,
as well as against the destruction of sacred buildings.

The only rational cause assigned for this havoc was, that
so long as ancient shrines, images long venerated, relics
averred to have wrought miracles, and similar objects of
superstitious worship, were left in the eyes of the people,
they might have proved the means of occasioning a relapse
to the ancient faith. But thus far the object might have
been obtained by following the example of the reformers in
England, who defaced altars, removed images, and burned
the relics of popery, to show that there was no power in
them to help themselves, but spared for a better and more
rational course of worship the noble edifices in which they
were installed. In scourging the buyers and sellers out of
the temple, no violence was menaced against the sacred
edifice itself, though it had incurred profanation.

The ruin of the Scottish ecclesiastical buildings was, however, almost universal. The citizens of Glasgow alone set
an example of rational moderation in Scotland. The me-

chanics of that city, under command of their deacon, took arms to resist the destruction of their venerable cathedral, at the same time offering their permission and assistance to destroy whatever could be made the object of idolatrous worship, but insisting that the edifice itself should be left uninjured; and, notwithstanding their having succeeded in saving this ancient fabric, we have never heard that popery has regained its footing in the ancient diocese of Saint Mungo.

Having thus entirely new-modelled the system of church government and of national worship, the parliament of Scotland resolved to recall from France the descendant of their monarchs, whose connection with that country was broken off by the death of her husband; naturally supposing that Mary, alone, and unsupported by French power, could not be suspected of meditating any interruption to the new order of religious affairs so unanimously adopted by her subjects.

With this view, the lord prior of St. Andrew's, the queen's illegitimate brother, and a principal agent in all the great changes which had taken place since the commencement of the regency of Mary of Guise, was despatched to Paris to negotiate the return of his royal sister. The Catholics of Scotland sent an ambassador on their own part: this was Lesley, bishop of Ross, celebrated for his fidelity to Mary during her afflictions, and known as a historian of credit and eminence. He made a secret proposal, on the part of the Catholics, that the young queen should land in the north of Scotland, and place herself under the guardianship of the Earl of Huntley, who, it was boasted, would conduct her in triumph to the capital at the head of an army of twenty thousand men, and restore, by force of arms, the ancient form of religion. Mary refused to listen to advice which must have made her return to her kingdom a signal for civil war, and acquiesced in the proposals delivered by the prior of St. Andrew's, on the part of the parliament. The young queen took this prudent step with the advice of her uncles of Guise, who, fallen from the towering hopes they had

formerly entertained, were now chiefly desirous to place
her in her native kingdom, without opposition or civil war,
in which the proposals of the bishop of Ross must have
immediately plunged her.

In 1561, Mary set sail for the country in which she was
to assume a crown entwined with many thorns. Elizabeth
had refused her a safe-conduct; and it is said that the English ships of war had orders to intercept her. The widowed queen of France took a lingering and painful farewell
of the fair country over which she had so lately reigned,
with expressions of the deepest sorrow. A mist hid her
galleys from the English fleet; and she arrived safely at
Leith on the 19th of August, in the aforesaid year.

Her subjects crowded to the beach to welcome her with
acclamations; but the preparations made for her reception
had been too hasty to cover over the nakedness and poverty
of the land. The queen, scarcely nineteen years old, wept
when she saw the wretched hackneys, still more miserably
accoutred, which were provided to carry her and her ladies
to Holyrood, and compared them in her thoughts to the fair
palfreys with brilliant housings which had waited her commands in France. Upon her landing, her subjects, softened
with the recollection of her early misfortunes, charmed with
the excellence of her mien, the delicacy of her unrivalled
beauty, the vigor of her blooming years, and the acuteness
of her wit, were almost enraptured with joy. Some part of
the reception afforded by their loyal zeal was well meant,
but certainly ill chosen. Two or three hundred violinists,
apparently amateur performers, held a concert all night below her windows, and prevented her getting an hour's sleep
after the fatigues of the sea. Mary, though suffering under
the effects of this dire serenade, professed to receive the compliment of these "honest men of the town of Edinburgh" as
it was intended, and even ventured to hint a wish that the
concert might be repeated.

The circumstance of the queen differing from the greater
part of her subjects in religion was not, however, forgotten;

and it seems very early to have been considered as a crime on the part of Queen Mary, by the more zealous of her Protestant subjects, that she did not at once, and forever, relinquish the Catholic religion, in which she had been bred up, and against which, in all probability, she had never heard a single word of argument till the first moment she touched Scottish ground. It seems to have occurred to no one that a sincere conversion could only be the result of argument and instruction, and that a hasty change of her early faith could only have indicated that the young queen was altogether indifferent on a subject so serious.

Her zealous subjects, whose hatred to popery had become a passion, tried the effect of reproaches and menaces upon the young queen, without waiting for the slower course of argument and persuasion. Pageants were presented before her, calculated to throw dishonor and reproach on the religion which she professed; and shows, made for the ostensible purpose of honoring the queen, were so conducted as to cast derision on the Catholic worship. As Mary made her solemn entry into Edinburgh, she was conducted under a triumphal arch, when a boy came out of a hole, as it were from heaven, and presented to her a Bible, a psalter, and the keys of the gates, with some verses, now lost, but which we may be sure were of a Protestant tendency. The rest of the pageant exhibited a terrible personification of the vengeance of God upon idolaters; and Korah, Dathan, and Abiram, were represented as destroyed in the time of their idolatrous sacrifice. The devisers of this expressive and well-chosen emblem, intended to have had a priest burned on the altar (in effigy, it is to be hoped), in the act of elevating the Host; but the Earl of Huntley prevented that completion of the pageant. These are the reports of Randolph, envoy of England, who was present on the occasion, and who seems to have felt that by such proceedings the Protestants were acting too precipitately and overshooting their own purpose.

These were but innuendoes of the dislike felt toward the

queen's religion: the following incidents showed plainly that
the more violent reformers were determined that their sovereign should not enjoy that toleration for which they themselves had, not many years since, been humble petitioners.
The prior of St. Andrew's, when he went over to France,
had been warned by the preachers that to permit the im-
portation of one mass into the kingdom of Scotland would
be more fatal than an army of ten thousand men. It is
probable, however, that he did not hesitate to promise that
the queen should have the free exercise of her religion,
and she prepared accordingly to take advantage of the
stipulation.

But when, on the Sunday after Mary's landing, preparations were made to say mass in the royal chapel, the reformers said to each other, "Shall that idol the mass again take
place within this kingdom?—it shall not." The young master of Lindsey, showing in youth the fierceness of spirit
which animated him in after life, called out, in the courtyard of the royal palace, that "the idolatrous priest should
die the death according to God's law." The prior of St.
Andrew's with great difficulty appeased the tumult, and
protected the priests, whose blood would otherwise have
been mingled with their sacrifice. But unwilling to avow
an intention so unpopular he was obliged to dissemble with
the reformers; and while he allowed that he stood with his
sword drawn at the door of the chapel, he pretended that
he did not do so to protect the priest, but to prevent any
Scottish man from entering to witness or partake in the
idolatrous ceremony.

It was immediately after this riot, and the display of the
insulting and offensive pageant before mentioned, that the
young queen had the first of her celebrated interviews with
John Knox, in which he knocked at her heart so rudely as
to cause her to shed tears. The stern apostle of presbytery
was indeed unsparing of rebuke, without sufficiently recollecting that previous conviction is necessary before reproof
can work repentance; and that, unless he had possessed pow-

ers of inspiration, or the gift of working miracles, he could not have, by mere assertion, converted a Catholic from the doctrines, however false, which she had believed in from her earliest childhood.   Even Randolph, the English envoy, says of him, "I commend better the success of his doctrine and preachings than the manner of them, though I acknowledge his doctrine to be sound.   His daily prayer for her is, that God will turn her heart, now obstinate against God and his truth; and if his holy will be otherwise that he will strengthen the hearts and hands of the chosen and elect stoutly to withstand the rage of tyrants."   Such orisons were little likely to conciliate the sovereign who was the object of them.   Yet Knox afterward expressed remorse that he had dealt too favorably with the queen, and had not been more vehement in opposing the mass at its first setting up; according to the opinion of those who thought that a sovereign may and ought to be resisted in an idolatrous form of worship, or, in other words, excluded from the tolerance which her subjects claim as their dearest privilege.

Tumults arose at Stirling on the same score of the queen's private worship: but though Mary felt the injury, and expressed her sense of it by weeping and sorrowing, yet she wisely passed it over, and trusted to the influence of the prior, her brother, who, by his great interest among the wiser sort of the reformers, by proclamations banishing the monks and friars, and other popular steps in favor of the reformed religion, procured a reluctant connivance at the celebration of the Catholic rites in the chapel royal.   Mary, indeed, employed her brother as her first minister in all affairs, and especially in restoring quiet on the borders, where he executed many freebooters, and left England no cause of complaint.

The intercourse of Mary with that country had always stood upon a delicate and doubtful footing.   Elizabeth was desirous that the Treaty of Edinburgh, in 1560, which ended the war of the reformation, should be formally ratified, particularly in respect of that article by which the queen of

Scotland and her late husband had agreed to lay down, and never again to assume, the royal titles or arms of England. If Mary had complied with this clause without restriction, it would have been a virtual resignation of her right of succession to England through her grandmother, Margaret, daughter of Henry VII.; a sacrifice which Queen Elizabeth was in no respect entitled to demand, nor Queen Mary disposed to grant. Lethington offered to ratify the clause of renunciation, if it were limited to Elizabeth's lifetime, which was all that was or could have been intended by the original treaty. But on the point of her successor Elizabeth was always desirous to preserve an affected obscurity; and to insist on entertaining any discussion involving that topic was to give her at all times the highest offence. Her ministers, therefore, were pertinacious in demanding that Queen Mary should resign, in general terms, all right whatever to the crown of England, without restriction either as to time or circumstances. While their envoys were engaged in these discussions, the two queens preserved a personal correspondence, in which high-flown and flighty professions of friendship and sisterly affection served to cloak, as is usual in such cases, the want of cordiality and sincerity which pervaded the intercourse of two jealous females, each suspicious of the other.

CHAPTER XXVII

Insanity of the Earl of Arran—Lord James Stewart created Earl of
Mar—The Grant offends the Earl of Huntley—Breach of the
Peace by his Son Sir John Gordon—The Queen makes a Progress to the North, where she is coldly received, and Inverness
Castle is held out against her—The Earldom of Murray is conferred on Lord James, instead of that of Mar—Huntley rebels—
Battle of Corrichie—Suitors for Mary's Hand—She determines
to consult Elizabeth—The Queen of England behaves with In-
sincerity; recommends the Earl of Leicester—The Scots cast
their eyes on Henry Darnley—His Mother's Claims on the Succession of England—Henry Darnley comes to Scotland, and
renders himself personally agreeable to Queen Mary—Her Character at this Period of her Life—Her Love of more private
Society—The Rise of Rizzio at the Scottish Court—He becomes
French Secretary to the Queen, and a Favorite—Elizabeth's
Displeasure at the proposed Match of Mary and Darnley—She
intrigues with the Protestant Party in Scotland—The Earl of
Murray leaves the Party of the Queen, and joins that of the
Reformed Nobles and Clergymen—Desperate Plots of the Earls
of Darnley and Murray against each other: both fail—The
Queen and Darnley are Married—Murray and the Duke of
Chatelherault take up Arms—The Queen gathers an Army,
drives the Insurgents from Place to Place, and finally compels
them to retreat into England—They are ill received by Elizabeth, who disowns them and their Cause—Mary endeavors
to obtain some Toleration for the persecuted Catholics—She
accedes to the Catholic League of Bayonne

THE young queen of Scotland conducted herself with
great wisdom and popularity in the management
of public business. She treated gravely of affairs
of State with her council, with whom she held frequent
sittings. Hunting, hawking, and other sports, filled up the
day; and music and dancing were the usual amusements
of the evening. These sports, however, gave additional

offence and scandal to the Protestant preachers, men of
ascetic and self-denying habits, who accounted such pleasures, if not positively sinful in themselves, as at least the
ready inlets to sin, and who did not, in writing or preaching on such vanities, altogether place their pens or tongues
under the guidance of that charity which thinketh no evil.
Still the majority of her subjects made allowance for their
queen's youth, gayety, and beauty, and, so long as she discharged her duty to her subjects in a grave and princely
manner, did not blame her for endeavoring to enliven the
court of her native kingdom with some shadow of the festivities which had surrounded her while on the throne of
France.

In 1562 the young Earl of Arran, son of the Duke of
Chatelherault, formerly governor of the kingdom, lodged
an account of a plot, whereby the Earl of Bothwell and
the Hamiltons had resolved to change the administration,
by murdering the prior of St. Andrew's and Lethington.
But this information was attended with no important consequences, the poor young nobleman who made it having
shown symptoms of lunacy.　He was afterward placed
under confinement in the castle of Edinburgh, and, as will
presently appear, was finally made the victim of unjust and
cruel confiscation and oppression.

A more serious convulsion took place in the same year.
The Earl of Huntley has been mentioned as one of the few
Scottish nobles who still professed the Catholic religion.
The family, having been always loyal, had been liberally
remunerated for their fidelity by former monarchs, and
their estates, jurisdictions, and superiorities in the north
of Scotland were almost as extensive as those which the
great Earls of Douglas had possessed in the south.　Their
power, however, was less influential, its sources being more
distant from the court.　The present earl had expected, from
similarity of faith, to have an especial share in the favor of
Queen Mary; and, disappointed to find her regard engrossed
by her brother, Lord James the Prior, he viewed that states-

man with jealous and envious eyes. About this time it happened that the queen conferred upon her brother the earldom of Mar and the lands belonging to it. This very natural liberality toward so near a relative increased the resentment of Huntley, who had occupied some possessions belonging to this estate without challenge, and now foresaw that the Lord James, in virtue of the royal grant, would insist on resuming them. Moreover, considering his high court favor, the new Earl of Mar's settlement in the north was likely to diminish Huntley's importance, and innovate upon his supremacy in these provinces. In the earldom of Mar the lord prior of St. Andrew's had gained a great point, though it was only a part of what his ambition aimed at; for he raised his hopes to the far more wealthy earldom of Murray, also possessed by Huntley, since the year 1548, in virtue of a grant from the crown. Thus Huntley was exposed, in fact, to the hazard of a much greater patrimonial loss than he at first apprehended.

While such causes of discontent occurred between these two powerful nobles, one of those instances of feudal violence took place which are so frequent in Scottish history, and so often the prelude to acts of open rebellion. In 1562, Sir John Gordon, the third son of the Earl of Huntley, engaged in a fray with Lord Ogilvy in the streets of Edinburgh, and dangerously wounded him. The queen caused both the offenders to be strictly confined, and was supposed, at the instigation of her brother Mar, to have been peculiarly rigorous in the case of young Gordon. This was a new subject of offence; and Sir John Gordon, escaping out of prison, hastened to his father's domains with loud complaints of ill usage and threats of revenge.

During this altercation the queen had determined on a royal progress to the north. It has been strongly averred that the new Earl of Mar had proposed this expedition for his own purposes. If by this it be only meant that he desired the benefit of the royal presence and countenance to enable him to enter on the estate of Mar, or, if possible, on the earldom of Murray in lieu of it, the suspicion may be very just. But there is room for positively denying that he had any thoughts of using violence against Huntley, since he brought with him, into the province where his enemy was all-powerful, only a very moderate body of southland forces.

The queen made a fatiguing, cold, and laborious journey, and was received with little courtesy in the north, where the effects of Huntley's displeasure against her brother and minister were sufficiently visible. Instead of being hailed with dutiful acclamations by crowds of submissive and faithful subjects, the aspect of the inhabitants was doubtful if not absolutely hostile, and her little troop of attendants were fain to observe the regular duties of watch and ward against surprise. Her retinue of soldiers was indeed so small that it became necessary every man in her train, ambassadors and others, should keep watch in succession; and the queen, instead of showing female affright at the grim front of war, lamented, with the spirit of her warlike fathers, that her sex prevented her mounting guard in turn, and forbade her to parade with jack and steel-cap, a broadsword and a Glasgow buckler. When she arrived at Inverness, the castle was held out against her by the Gordons. But the garrison, proving inadequate to defend it, were forced to surrender, and the captain who had refused admission to his sovereign deservedly suffered the pains of death.

In the meantime, Mar had accomplished the point which he had long struggled for, and prevailed upon the queen to grant him the earldom of Murray instead of that of Mar, to which it was now said to be discovered that Lord Erskine possessed a legal right, prior to that granted to Lord James Stewart. This new arrangement in favor of the queen's brother was the signal for open hostility.

The Earl of Huntley, incensed at the recall of the royal gift of 1548 in his favor, now conceived that the ruin of his house was resolved upon, and determined to take up arms. He summoned together his vassals, and menaced an attack upon the new Earl of Murray and the forces who escorted the sovereign's person.

The queen, in the meantime, proceeded to Darnoway, the principal messuage of the earldom of Murray; and having put her brother in possession of the honors and estates belonging to that great lordship, she summoned the neighboring barons and clans to join her array, and protect her against Huntley and his army. They brought their men to the queen accordingly, and the Earl of Murray led them against the Gordons, who were posted near Corrichie. Huntley had but seven or eight hundred men, but reckoned on his interest among the northern barons, who had ostensibly joined Murray, but who, in reality, neither loved his person nor were willing to endure his power.

The Earl of Murray drew up on a rising ground the small phalanx of southland men in whom he could confide, and commanded the northern clans, whose faith he doubted, to commence the attack on the Gordons, October 28, 1562. They did so, but with no desire of making a serious impression; and recoiling from the charge came running back with their antagonist close behind them on Murray's band of spearmen, who received both fliers and pursuers with levelled lances. The onset of the Gordons, made in the Highland fashion, with drawn swords and disordered ranks, was unequal to the task of breaking so firm a battalion. The assailants retired in disorder; and the instant they did so the neighboring clans, who had begun the fight, anxious to secure the favor of the victors, turned their swords upon the repulsed party, and endeavored to atone for their former flight by making slaughter among those before whom they had just retreated.

The consequences of the loss of this battle of Corrichie were most disastrous to the family of Huntley. The earl himself, thrown from his horse, and too unwieldy to rise from the ground, was smothered in the retreat. His body, brought to town on a pair of panniers, was afterward produced in parliament, where a doom of forfeiture was pro-

nounced against him.   His son, Sir John Gordon, condemned
to be beheaded, was butchered at Aberdeen by an unskilful
executioner.   The doom of forfeiture was pronounced against
this powerful family, and was not reversed until the 19th
of April, 1567.   It was supposed that the Earl of Huntley's
purpose, had he possessed himself of the queen's person, was
to have united her in marriage with one of his sons; but
as there is no evidence to prove such a charge, we cannot
extend his guilt beyond his avowed designs against Murray,
his feudal enemy.

Excepting the battle of Corrichie, the reign of Queen
Mary had hitherto passed with great tranquillity, and, setting
aside the suspicions of the clergy and their more zealous followers, with great contentment to her subjects.   The Scots
became naturally desirous that the race of their monarchs
should be prolonged by their young queen forming a suitable match.   This being generally promulgated, a beauty
with a kingdom for her dower was not likely to want wooers.
The Archduke Charles, third son of the emperor, the infant
Don Carlos, then heir of the Spanish monarchy, and the Duke
of Anjou, brother of her late husband, preferred suit for
Mary's hand; but as all these princes were Catholics and
foreigners, the alliances they proposed would have once
more revived the jealousies for her freedom in Church and
State which Scotland had entertained, and would probably
have again involved the country in an intestine war, as well
as in a quarrel with England.

This event was the more to be dreaded, because the clergy
and the more zealous among the reformers had pressed upon
the government the necessity of demanding the queen's
assent to the alterations in the Church, and the modern
institutions which had supplanted the ancient ecclesiastical
system.   The Earl of Murray (by which title we must hereafter term the Lord James Stewart, hitherto called the prior
of St. Andrew's), was, on the contrary, of opinion that the
Protestants ought to temporize with the queen, allow for
the prejudices of her education, and wait until further con-

viction should open her eyes to the excellence of the reformed religion; and so warm grew the discussion between John Knox and the earl on this subject that the former renounced Murray's friendship, and a coldness between them ensued which continued for two years.

In these delicate circumstances Mary saw the necessity of paying attention, in her choice of a husband, to the opinions and even to the prejudices of the reformers, and perceived no mode of doing this so certain as by consulting Queen Elizabeth, whose opinions were not likely to be disputed by the Scottish Protestants. Another powerful reason of state strongly recommended that Elizabeth should be advised with upon this occasion. The right which Mary possessed to the English succession was of a kind which Elizabeth, if she pleased, might find means of setting aside by assent of her parliament; and she might probably do so, should her kinswoman form a union with a foreign or Catholic prince. On the contrary, there were hopes that, if Mary should agree to be guided by her advice, Elizabeth might acknowledge the queen of Scotland, allied to a husband of her own choosing, as the lawful heir of the English throne. Sir James Melville, an accomplished diplomatist, was sent to procure, if possible, some information upon Elizabeth's intentions in this important affair.

It may be said of Elizabeth, that if ever there was a monarch whose conduct seemed, according to the speech of the old heathen, to be governed alternately by two souls of a very different disposition and character, the supposition might be applied to her. Possessing more than masculine wisdom, magnanimity, and fortitude on most occasions, she betrayed, at some unhappy moments, even more than female weakness and malignity. Happy would it have been for both queens had Mary's request for counsel and assistance reached Elizabeth while she was under the influence of her better planet. The English sovereign might then, with candor and good faith, have availed herself of the opportunity to conciliate the genuine friendship and to acquire the

gratitude of her youthful relation, by guiding her to such
a match as would have best suited the interests and assured
the amity of the sister nations. Unfortunately, Elizabeth
remembered with too much acuteness Mary's offensive
pretensions to the crown of England, pretensions which
were founded on the defect of her own title and the illegiti-
macy of her birth, and she already regarded the queen of
Scotland rather as a rival to be subdued than a friend to be
conciliated. Besides, as a votaress of celibacy, Queen Elizabeth was not greatly disposed to forward any marriage,
more especially that of a princess who stood to her in the
painful relation of a kinswoman possessing a claim to her
throne, and a neighbor of her own sex and rank, between
whom and herself comparisons must needs be frequently
drawn with respect to wit, beauty, and accomplishments.
The line of conduct prompted by these jealous feelings impelled Queen Elizabeth to embrace the opportunity, afforded
by Mary's desiring her opinion upon her marriage, to cross,
baffle, and disconcert any negotiations which might be entered into on that topic. For this purpose, after observing a
great deal of oracular mystery, in order to protract matters,
Elizabeth gave it as her advice that Mary would do well to
choose for her husband the Earl of Leicester, as a person on
whom she herself would willingly have conferred her own
hand, but for her resolution to live and die a maiden queen.

The Earl of Leicester, as is well known, stood toward
Elizabeth in the relation of a handsome and aspiring favorite. His claims, those of personal appearance excepted,
were of a very ordinary character, yet the queen had conferred upon him the highest offices of the state, and it was
shrewdly suspected had favored him with a larger share of
her own affections than she would willingly have acknowledged. It is evident that by proposing this nobleman as a
husband for Mary, Elizabeth could have no other view than
to involve the queen of Scotland in a matrimonial treaty,
which, while it might divert her mind from any other match,
could never be brought to a satisfactory conclusion.

The queen of Scots listened with approbation to Elizabeth's advice, as far as it recommended to her to honor with her choice a subject and a native of Britain, so as neither to excite the resentment of England nor the suspicions of her own subjects, by again engaging in a foreign connection. But many very reasonable considerations directed her thoughts to a person different from Leicester, a subject of her own, and a near relation to Queen Elizabeth. There were circumstances in the favored party's connection and descent which rendered the selection highly expedient.

The person on whom the choice of Mary fell was Henry Stewart, Lord Darnley, eldest son of the Earl of Lennox, at this time an exile in England. Matthew, the father of Darnley, was himself the son and successor of that Lennox who was slain fighting against the allied forces of Hamilton and Douglas, near Kirkliston, on the 4th of September, 1526. Earl Matthew had been devotedly desirous of forwarding the proposed match between Edward VI. and Mary, while the latter was yet in infancy; and when the rest of the nobility entirely deserted what was called the English party he continued attached to his engagements with Henry VIII., and rather than renounce them fled to England, under a certainty of being attainted, and placed himself under that monarch's protection. Henry was grateful, and did what he could to compensate Lennox for the evils of banishment and the loss of his Scottish estates. He bestowed on the exiled earl the fine manor of Temple Newsome, near Leeds, and the hand of his own niece. This lady was daughter of King Henry's sister Margaret, queen-dowager of Scotland, by her second husband, the Earl of Angus, and was mother of the reigning Queen Mary. It will be remembered that the queen-dowager was delivered of Lady Margaret Douglas during the time that her husband and she were expelled from Scotland. Lady Margaret was, therefore, a native Englishwoman.

Now, on the failure of Henry VIII.'s issue, those circumstances of genealogy and birth tended to establish in Lady

Margaret Douglas a claim to the English throne, which, according to the notion of the times, was capable of being placed in competition with those of the queen of Scotland. This will appear more plainly from the following considerations.

Queen Mary claimed the throne of England, failing Queen Elizabeth and her heirs, as grand-niece of Henry VIII., by her mother, the same Queen Margaret. Lady Lennox was that queen's full niece, and one degree nearer in blood to the reigning queen than was Mary herself. Besides, the Countess of Lennox had the great advantage over the queen of Scotland that she was a native Englishwoman, and it was at least possible that the English lawyers, in case of a contest for the crown, might give the native of the soil a preference over the alien. This rendered the getting rid of Lady Margaret Lennox's pretensions of the greatest importance to Queen Mary, considering her prospects of the English succession; and it seemed so obviously desirable to unite both these titles by a marriage between Henry Darnley and the young queen of Scots, that a suspicion of it appears to have flashed across the mind of Elizabeth herself. After pointing out to Melville the various excellences which distinguished her favorite Leicester, whom she pretended to recommend to Mary's choice, she added, pointing to Henry Darnley, "Yet you prefer to him that long lad yonder." This betrayed a suspicion which Elizabeth was little disposed to see realized, that there were, even thus early, thoughts of a match between Mary and Henry Darnley. It does not, however, appear to have been deep-rooted; for, upon Lennox applying to the queen of England for leave to go to Scotland under pretence of his wife having a claim as heir female on the earldom of Angus, her royal license for the journey seems to have been willingly granted. The truth, probably, was, that Elizabeth was too confident of her power to perplex any negotiation for marriage which Mary might enter into, both by her influence over the queen of Scotland herself, which she probably overestimated, and by the interest which her

intrigues had maintained among the nobility of that kingdom. In this view, her permitting Darnley to appear as a
suitor might serve only to embroil a transaction which she
did not desire to terminate.

Receiving the permission of Elizabeth, the Earl of Lennox returned to Scotland after twenty years' absence, where
he was most favorably received. He did not indeed succeed
in making good his wife's claims on the earldom of Angus,
which as a male fief was in the grasp of the Earl of Morton,
who managed it in behalf of his nephew Archibald Douglas;
but great favor was shown him by the queen, his claims on
Angus were compensated by gifts from the crown, and he
himself was restored in blood and estate against the forfeiture
by which he was attainted.

In a few months afterward Henry, Lord Darnley, the
earl's only son, set sail for Scotland, with Elizabeth's permission, and about the 16th February, 1564–5, he waited
upon Queen Mary, at Wemys Castle; a most unfortunate
meeting, as it proved, both for Mary and himself. There
was nothing in Darnley's appearance which could raise any
personal objection on the queen's part to weigh the policy
which strongly recommended to her as a husband the high-
born young nobleman who possessed, through his mother,
a title to the succession of England which might stand in
competition with her own. On the contrary, Henry, Lord
Darnley, though of uncommon stature, was well made in
proportion, possessed courteous manners and a noble mien,
gained the eye and the heart of the queen by the showy
accomplishments of dancing, tilting, hunting, and the like,
and won the goodwill of her retinue by liberality, which
large remittances received from his mother enabled him to
maintain. He was at length emboldened by Mary's own
smiles, and the general favor with which he had been received at court, to propose love to his sovereign; and though
he at first received a modest repulse, he came in course of a
little time to be favorably listened to.

With the purpose better to judge of the events which

follow, we must take here a short review of the queen's personal character and behavior, adopting for our guide Sir James Melville, one who had the best opportunities of knowing her, who was himself at once a sound Protestant and an accomplished courtier, and whose memoirs, now freed from all suspicion of interpolation, may be justly compared with the most valuable materials which British history affords.[1]

Queen Mary, since her arrival from France, had behaved herself after a manner so princely, honorably, and discreetly, that her reputation was spread abroad in all countries; and she was at the same time so courteous and affable, that, excepting the Protestant preachers, whose judgment concerning a papist sovereign cannot be supposed unprejudiced, she had gained the universal love and approbation of her subjects.   Unimpeachable in her public conduct, this accomplished princess loved to retire into something like private society, but always with the honorable attendance of her ladies, and accessible to the ambassadors who resided at her court.   When Randolph, the English envoy, pressed matters of state upon her at such a moment, "I see," she said, "you are weary of this reception.   You had better preserve your diplomatic gravity, and return to Edinburgh, and keep all your weighty conversation till the queen return there; for I promise you I do not know myself what is now become of her, or when she will return to her throne and canopy of state."

It would seem that Mary herself was conscious of her tendency to this easy pleasantry, and had an apprehension that it might, in an unguarded moment, be carried too far. Indeed, something of this kind occurred in the case of one Chastellar, a French cavalier, half poet, half courtier, and entire madman.   The queen used to amuse herself with this adventurer's eccentricity, by which ill-judged familiarity he was encouraged to conceal himself one night in her apart-

---

[1] See the late beautiful and correct edition printed from the original by the Bannatyne Club.

ment. Being detected, he was dismissed with severe censure, which did not hinder a man of such ill-regulated understanding from renewing his attempt, for which he was tried and executed. His death suited his extravagant character. He refused ghostly consolation, prepared himself for his end with the verses of Ronsard, a French poet; and as he knelt down to the block exclaimed, as his last words, "Farewell to the most beautiful and most cruel queen that ever lived."

While Mary was in prosperity, nothing discreditable to her arose from Chastellar's insane conduct, yet, considering the fatal issue, it must have given her much pain, and may have been the cause of the injunction which she laid upon Melville. Under this anxiety, she amiably represented to him her youth and turn to cheerfulness, and imposed upon him the delicate task, that should she at any time forget herself, and be hurried into any impropriety of speech or behavior, he must interpose his admonition to reform the same. Melville would willingly have shifted this office upon the Earl of Murray and Lethington, by whom Mary's state affairs were managed; but the queen compelled him to accept the office of her monitor, as she could, she said, endure rebuke more willingly from a disinterested friend than from her immediate ministers.

There was at this time in the court of Mary a man named David Rizzio, or Riccio, a native of Turin, a person of poor parentage, who had been, however, well educated, and, among other accomplishments, was an excellent musician. He came to Scotland in the train of an ambassador from Savoy; but his assistance being found useful to fill a part in the queen's private concerts, he left the envoy's service for that of Mary. Rizzio's knowledge of languages recommended him to the queen, who employed him in conducting her foreign correspondence; and finding him apt, intelligent, and useful, upon the departure of her French secretary she promoted the Piedmontese to that confidential office. This situation, of course, procured him easy and frequent access to her presence and to her ear. The familiarity with which

the queen naturally received him, as a man of little consequence, whose talents served, and whose accomplishments
amused her, excited the resentment of the fierce nobility of
Scotland. They observed with indignation that the foreign
secretary, in virtue of his office, presented all papers to be
signed by her majesty; and some of them would shoulder
him, and frown on him, when they met him in the presence
chamber. Others who had suits at court made the same
observations, but, acting upon different principles, addressed
themselves to the secretary for the furtherance of their business; and Rizzio became rich from the gifts that flowed in
upon him.

Yet the poor secretary felt himself surrounded by enemies, and bewailed his condition to Melville as one of envy
and danger. Melville, with his usual good sense, counselled
him to decline making any ostentation of his credit with the
queen, and to avoid showing any possession of her ear by
forbearing to speak with her apart in the presence of her
nobility. But Rizzio afterward told Melville that the queen
desired him to wait upon her with his usual freedom. The
sensible and faithful Melville then mentioned to the queen
herself the conversation which had taken place, and the
envy which her favor to Rizzio was drawing upon a man
whose understanding was not very well able to endure it.
The queen took no offence at the rebuke, but said she had
used Rizzio no otherwise than his predecessor in office; nor
would she be controlled in the management of her private
correspondence.

However imprudent Mary's conduct might be, there is no
reason to believe that her intercourse with her secretary
excited at this period of her life any further censure than
that she allowed too much influence in affairs of business
to a low-born foreigner raised from a mean condition. It
has been since used as affording a pretext for charges of a
grosser nature.

The influence of Signor David, as he was termed, was
accounted so powerful that Henry Darnley, in his suit to

Mary, conceived it prudent to secure the countenance of
Rizzio, whose vanity became more highly elevated by his
being supposed to possess influence on such an occasion.

Meantime Elizabeth, to her astonishment and mortification, learned that the queen of Scotland had formed an engagement with young Darnley, which was about to end
in marriage. That sovereign had, no doubt, hoped that, in
permitting Darnley to go down to Scotland, she was only
putting another puppet on the stage, whom she could withdraw at pleasure, since, having all the Earl of Lennox's
English property in her power, she might conceive that she
possessed the regulation of his motions and those of his son.
She was highly irritated at her disappointment. Her privy
council echoed back a list, which she herself had suggested,
of imaginary dangers attending Mary's match with Darnley,
and an ambassador extraordinary was sent to enforce at the
Scottish court the representations of Elizabeth and her council against the choice of an independent sovereign. Mary
would certainly have acted as a weak queen, and an unusually tame-spirited person, if she had submitted to this insult.
She avowed her intention of marrying Darnley, justified herself with dignity for so doing, affected at the same time a
great desire to reconcile her sister sovereign to the match,
and succeeded in adducing plausible arguments to prove that
her choice possessed those recommendations which Elizabeth
had in the commencement of their negotiation so pointedly
demanded. She even offered to delay the actual marriage,
if she could by that sacrifice obtain the approbation of her
good sister and ally.

From the firm tone of Mary's reply it was evident that
she had determined on the match; and Elizabeth saw it could
only be broken off by some domestic opposition among the
Scottish subjects, for exciting which the English queen possessed ample means. The most formidable of these was her
influence with the whole body of zealous Protestants, who,
since the wars with the French in 1560, looked upon Elizabeth as their especial friend, and the surest protectress of

their faith.   This influence was much increased at the crisis
we speak of, from the Earl of Murray having withdrawn
himself from the court, and placed himself in opposition to
the queen's intended marriage with Darnley.

The Earl of Murray had hitherto been the queen's principal minister, and had managed the affairs of the kingdom
with equal skill and good fortune.   But in this proposed
match he foresaw the loss of his power.   He was besides
especially offended that the Earl of Bothwell, his personal
enemy, was suffered to return to court, having been banished from thence for an alleged conspiracy against his life.
To remove this cause of complaint, Bothwell was again
driven into exile; yet no persuasion could make Murray
give consent to the proposed marriage.   Darnley, with the
rash folly and impetuosity of youth, had shown himself
unfriendly to his bride's brother, jealous of his power, and
envious of the large estates which that power had been the
means of accumulating.   On such topics he dwelt in the
hearing even of those who were sure to report what he said
to the jealous minister, whom it chiefly interested.   Foresee-
ing, therefore, an enemy to his own person and authority in
the queen's proposed husband, Murray's eyes at the same
time became rather suddenly opened to the great dangers
which this match was likely to bring upon the Protestant
religion.   Hitherto his zeal had not been alarmed at the
exercise of the Catholic superstition in the queen's household; we have even seen him in person, with his drawn
sword in his hand, defend the entrance of her private chapel
during the celebration of the mass.   But now that Mary was
about to take a husband of her own persuasion, though by
no means a bigoted papist, he joined the opinion of those
who held one mass to be more dangerous to the commonwealth than an invasion of ten thousand men.   A reconciliation was effected between the Earl of Murray and John Knox,
between whom a quarrel had previously arisen, on account
of the indulgence of the earl to Queen Mary; and as the
same difference of opinion no longer existed between them,

they once more thought with the same heart, and saw with the same eye, on the affairs of Church and State.

Murray, therefore, now countenanced the ministers of the reformed religion, who demanded, by a formal act of the national assembly of the Church, that the celebration of the mass should in all cases be restrained, as well before the queen's person as in view of the subject. This extravagant proposal was followed by the more reasonable request that some means of subsistence, out of the revenues and domains of the Catholic Church, should be assigned to the clergy. Then came a condition that the remainder of the church property, after deducting the stipends of the clergy, should be applied to the maintenance of the poor, and the support of schools and places of education. That this last stipulation should be granted, considering it must have greatly impoverished the nobles who had possessed themselves of these religious revenues, was very improbable; but it was followed by one which, in the present state of the world, was totally impossible, since it prayed for the entire suppression of vice and immorality. To these demands the queen mildly replied that she was not yet satisfied of the idolatry of the mass, and pleaded with much gentleness for the enjoyment of that liberty of conscience for herself which she was willing to allow to others. She promised relief to the complaints of the preachers, and regular payment of their salaries. The other demands she passed over in prudent silence.

The queen's proposals and exertions gained a considerable majority of the nobility to assent to her marriage; but Murray remained irreconcilable. The Duke of Chatelherault joined his party, in apprehension that the exaltation of the Lennox family would prove the destruction of his own, considering the deadly feud that existed between the House of Hamilton and that of Lennox, and not forgetful, probably, of his own claims to the throne, in case the queen died without issue.

The discord between the two parties, according to the

genius of the time, first broke out in secret conspiracies of the most deadly kind. Darnley engaged in a plot to assassinate Murray; and Murray laid an ambush for the purpose of making Darnley and the queen prisoners, with the intention of delivering up the proposed bridegroom to Elizabeth, and placing Mary in some place of secure confinement. Both plots were doomed to succeed, but not at the time or by the means now resorted to. They failed for the present on either side.

Matters being come to this crisis, the queen resolved to complete, without delay, the purpose which she meditated; and which, recommended first by considerations of policy, had now become an affair in which her heart was deeply though hastily interested. On the 29th of July, 1565, she married Darnley, a dispensation by the pope having been previously obtained, and the ceremonial being performed after the forms of the Catholic ritual. At their union he was declared king of Scotland.

Murray and the Duke of Chatelherault, together with Argyle, Glencairn, and Rothes, took arms, all, the duke excepted, zealous professors of the Protestant religion. But, ere they could assemble two thousand horse, they were attacked by the queen's army, the royal vassals having on Mary's summons appeared with good will and in great numbers. She herself, arrayed in light armor, and wearing pistols at the saddle-bow, rode at the head of her troops. The insurgents were obliged to retreat before the queen from one place to another, apparently without any aim or object save to escape her pursuit, from which circumstance their war was remembered by the name of the Roundabout Raid. The insurgent nobles were at length pressed so hard that they were compelled to disband their forces, and retreat into England, where, as they had taken arms in consequence of Elizabeth's instigation, they hoped for relief and protection. Murray and the abbot of Kilwinning, one on the part of the reformers, the other as representing his kinsmen the Hamiltons, were despatched by their associates to represent their necessities, and to crave the aid and support which they thought themselves entitled to expect from the English queen.

But their reception was very different from their expectations. Elizabeth now beheld in them persons who could render her no immediate services; and she was anxious to escape from the reproaches of the ambassadors of the principal European powers, who accused her of betraying the cause of sovereigns in general by the encouragement she had afforded to the rebels of Scotland.

Galled at finding herself exposed to reproaches to which her own notions of royal authority made her peculiarly sensitive, Elizabeth resolved so to deal with the envoys of the banished lords as should make them the means of clearing her from such a scandal at the expense of their own honor.

With this view she caused it to be secretly intimated to the Earl of Murray and his associate that they would lose Queen Elizabeth's favor and protection at once and forever, if they presumed to bring forward claims in virtue of any understanding between her and them previous to their insurrection. The envoys were forced to consent to this humiliating compromise, expecting, no doubt, that the queen would of herself recollect the promises which they, in obedience to her command, abstained from insisting upon.

Accordingly when Murray and the abbot of Kilwinning, in presence of the French and Spanish ambassadors, appeared before Elizabeth, she extorted from the fugitive Scots an avowal that she had not encouraged them in their rebellion, and, having thus secured her own exculpation, she turned short on them, saying, "You have now spoken truth, for neither I nor any in my name has instigated your revolt from your sovereign. Begone, like traitors as you are!" Notwithstanding this seemingly severe reception, the exiles were permitted to skulk about on the southern side of the border, and were secretly supplied with money by Elizabeth. The Hamiltons had co-operated but not coalesced with Murray and his associates. The insurrection of the former was on different principles from that of the latter.

The Duke of Chatelherault negotiated for himself and his party independently of Murray, and with much difficulty obtained on submission a separate pardon from the Scottish queen.

Mary was now at the summit of her wishes. She was wedded to the choice of her heart: all opposition to her will lay prostrate at her feet; and by pressing a prosecution against Murray and his associates, it was in her power to have their estates forfeited, and their persons banished from Scotland forever.

In a parliament which was convoked for this purpose, the queen entertained a hope that she might procure for those of her own communion at least some degree of toleration and some relief from the persecution of the other party. It was but a short time before that a Catholic priest had been seized in the act of saying mass at Easter. Invested in his garments, and with the chalice bound to his hand, he was tied to the market cross of Edinburgh, and there pelted with filth and mud, which the historian of the kirk calls serving him with his Easter eggs. Where such disgraceful violence could be permitted, the queen might be pardoned, when she desired that those who followed the same religion with herself might be sheltered at least from violence and indignity.

But we must record in far different terms Mary's accession to the League of Bayonne, the object of which, on the part of France, Spain, and the other contracting powers, was the utter destruction and deletion of the Protestant religion, by the means of fraud or force, as opportunity should most readily present itself. In becoming a member of this league, Mary assumed the right of lording it over the consciences of others, in the unjust and violent manner which she felt so oppressive when exercised toward herself and the Catholics. But, whatever the queen meant to do in behalf of those of her own religion, a course of events was now to take place which was doomed to end in depriving Mary of all power as a sovereign, whether for good or for evil.

CHAPTER XXVIII

Character of Henry Darnley—He quarrels with Mary—Conceives
Hatred against Rizzio, who is Murdered—The King forsakes
and disowns the Conspirators, who fly to England—Murray returns from Exile, and is reconciled to the Queen—Question as
to the Guilt or Innocence of Mary—Her continued Quarrel with
Darnley, who threatens to go abroad, and gives his Wife other
Subjects of Complaint—Bothwell rises in the Queen's Favor—
His History—He is restored upon his Enemy Murray's Exile,
and reconciled to him on his Return—Elizabeth exasperated
against Mary on her bearing a Son—Bothwell is made Keeper
of Liddisdale—Is wounded—Mary visits him at the Hermitage
Castle—Apparent Reconciliation between Mary and Darnley—
Darnley is Murdered—Consequences of that Atrocity—Acquittal of Bothwell—The Marriage of the Queen—Insurrection
—The Queen flies to Dunbar—Advances with an Army to Carberry Hill—Bothwell flies—The Queen surrenders—She is carried to Edinburgh—Insulted by the Populace—Sent Prisoner
to Lochleven—She resigns her Crown—The Earl of Murray is
declared Regent

THE feeble yet violent character of Darnley was the
primary cause of Mary's misfortunes; for, until
her marriage with that unhappy prince, her life
had flowed in a free and even channel, and her government for the last two years had been on the whole happy
and prosperous. From that unhappy era it was almost an
uninterrupted succession of misfortunes.

Yet in a superficial view the match had much to recommend it. It absorbed in that of the queen another claim of
succession to the English throne which might have been
preferred to hers. Her husband was handsome, lively, and
possessed of external accomplishments; while Mary, esti-
mating his intellectual qualities with the fondness which
is entertained toward a beloved object, gave him credit at
least for common sense and common gratitude

Unhappily the husband whom she had chosen was four years younger than herself, and, still more unluckily, he was an impatient and presumptuous fool, of violent passions and weak judgment, who could never have written himself man in the true sense of the word, had he lived to an antediluvian age. He was ungrateful to the queen, though she from attachment had shared her rank with him; and, without being thankful for the favors which her affection had heaped upon him, he was peevish and splenetic when anything was withheld. His father's authority he set at naught; so that the Earl of Lennox left the court in disgust, sick of beholding his son indulge himself not merely in youthful pleasures, but in youthful vices, with a disregard to decency which made Mary blush for her unhappy choice of a dissolute, disrespectful boy, of loose habits and ungovernable temper, to be her partner on such a throne as that of Scotland. Insolent and imperious in his temper, Darnley endured no check, however kindly given, and sought the crown matrimonial (implying an equal share with the queen in the sovereignty) with so much eagerness and impatience as greatly disgusted Mary. In fine, she became weary of the society of a man who could not govern himself, and would not be ruled by his benefactress or any one else. How can this be wonderful! since, while Mary did everything to please him, Darnley could not be prevailed on to yield to her in the smallest point, either to show his affection as a husband or his duty as a subject.

Darnley, finding that he lost ground in the queen's affections, was disposed, as is usually the case with persons of his temper, rather to impute this growing dislike to the suggestions of some private enemy than to his own demerits. The person who chiefly incurred his suspicion was Rizzio. This foreigner had been his friend before his marriage, and favored his suit to the utmost of his power, but since that event had taken the freedom to offer some remonstrances which were unacceptable. This increased the king's resentment; and when he began to impute to the Italian secretary the delay in bestowing on him the crown matrimonial, he hesitated not to seek revenge for the supposed offence by the most deadly means.

With this purpose the young king applied to the Earl of Morton and the rest of the Douglases, who, being related to his mother on the side of her father Angus, had seen his preferment with much interest. They had looked with pride upon their kinsman's advancement to a share of sovereign power, and in a country where human life was held cheap they were sufficiently ready to gratify him by ridding him of a wretched musician, who had intruded himself upon the affairs of state, and ventured to propose himself as a patron or an opposer of nobles. They were the more willing to render the young king this service, because they considered Rizzio as chief instigator of the severe measures menaced against the Earl of Murray and the exiled lords, and a great encourager of the Catholic religion.

When it was settled that Rizzio should die, the manner of his murder was next debated. Morton, Ruthven, and others of their party, proposed that the secretary should be seized as he crossed the court of the palace, or in his own lodgings, and then destined to the fate which Cochrane underwent, when the chief of the Douglas family acquired the title of Bell-the-Cat. But nothing would satisfy Darnley save that the victim should be seized in the presence of the queen herself, that she might share the alarm, and hear the taunts with which it was his purpose to upbraid her favorite. Considering that the queen was seven months advanced in her pregnancy when such a scene of violence and horror was to be acted in her presence, we recoil from the brutality alike of him who planned and of those who calmly undertook to execute an action so brutal and unmanly.

On the 9th of March, 1566, this bloody and extraordinary scene was acted. The queen was seated at supper in a small cabinet adjoining to her bedroom, with the Countess of Argyle, Rizzio, and one or two other persons. Darnley suddenly entered the apartment, and, without addressing or saluting the company, gazed on Rizzio with a sullen and vindictive look. After him followed Lord Ruthven, pale and ghastly, having risen from a bed of long sickness to be chief actor in this savage deed: other armed men appeared behind. Ruthven called upon Rizzio to come forth from a place which he was unworthy to hold. The miserable Italian, perceiving he was the destined victim of this violent intrusion, started up, and seizing the queen by the skirts of her gown, implored her protection. Mary was speedily forced by the king from his hold. George Douglas, a bastard of the Angus family, snatched the king's own dagger from his side, and struck Rizzio a blow; he was then dragged into the outer apartment, and slain with fifty-six wounds. The queen exhausted herself in prayers and entreaties for the wretched man's life; but when she was at length informed that her servant was slain, she said, "I will then dry my tears, and study revenge." During the perpetration of this murder, Morton, the chancellor of the kingdom, whose duty it was to enforce the laws of the realm, kept the doors of the palace with one hundred and sixty armed men, to insure the perpetration of the murder.

Darnley, as soon as this abominable crime was committed, was seized with the irresolution and fear which, in minds like his, often follow acts of extravagant violence. He would now have been well pleased to have been free from the guilt which had originated with him; and to atone in part for the violence which the queen had suffered, he aided and accompanied her in her flight from Edinburgh to the castle of Dunbar, where she was instantly joined by Huntley, Bothwell, and others, her most faithful nobles. She was soon at the head of an army of eight thousand men, a force against which the murderers of Rizzio could not hope to make a stand. Indeed, all the plans which were to have followed this atrocious action were disconcerted by the defection of Darnley and his unexpected reconciliation with the queen.

In the meanwhile the exiled Earls of Murray and Argyle,

having learned the success of the conspiracy against Rizzio, left England, hoping to find Morton and Ruthven at the head of affairs: instead of which, they met them reduced to extremity, and on the point of flying to that kingdom. Murray and his companions, however, reaped this advantage from the misfortune of their friends, that the queen, all resentment against their rebellion being lost in the sense of this later and deadlier insult, showed herself sufficiently willing to grant remission of their treasons provided they would detach themselves from Morton and his accomplices. To this Murray did not hesitate to agree; and thus was admitted to the queen's favor, while Morton and his associates went to occupy those quarters in Northumberland which had been lately tenanted by the lords concerned in the Roundabout Raid.

When Mary and Murray met together, the queen wept: she probably felt at the moment how much she had suffered by indulging a precipitate passion for Darnley contrary to her brother's advice. The earl was also moved; and could confidence have been restored between them even then, it is possible that neither might have filled a bloody grave. The fame of Mary was as yet untinged by scandal; for we may treat as a fiction of later date the gross impeachment of a criminal intrigue with Rizzio, which, indeed, must be regarded as totally impossible, unless by those who conceive her, contrary to the report of all who approached her person, to have been a monster of unlimited depravity.[1] The Earl

---

[1] Dr. Robertson, no partial judge of Mary's conduct, makes this clear. Rizzio's advancement to the post of secretary, which first gave him access to the queen's person, took place only two months before the arrival of Darnley at the court of Scotland. Darnley was early distinguished by the queen with regard, which terminated in strong affection. Rizzio was the confidant of the lover, and forwarded a suit which would have been fatal to his own influence if he had been the queen's paramour. For several months the queen's passion for Darnley continued unabated, and she proved with child soon after the marriage. "From these circumstances," says the historian, "it seems almost impossible that the queen, unless we suppose her a woman utterly abandoned, could carry on any criminal intrigue with Rizzio."—History of Scotland, book iv.

of Murray had as yet formed no connections so indissoluble as must have necessarily engaged him in a war against his sister's person and authority. But a deep jealousy had taken possession of both, and neither, it is probable, felt disposed to trust the other.

We have now arrived at a point of our history where we must either add another volume to a controversy which has produced so many, or by compressing into a concise form the events of the mournful tale, and expressing our own general opinion as it arises out of them, refer the readers who may doubt our conclusions, and desire means by which to form their own, to the works in which the charge has been urged and the defence maintained. Indeed, no inquiry or research has ever been able to bring us either to that clear opinion upon the guilt of Mary which is expressed by many authors, or guide us to that triumphant conclusion in favor of her innocence of all accession, direct or tacit, to the death of her husband, which others have maintained with the same obstinacy. Arguing from probabilities, where there are but few ascertained facts to guide us, we have been led to adopt the opinion expressed by Scottish juries, in a verdict of Not Proven, when they are disposed to say that there is an insufficiency of proof to ascertain the guilt of an accused person, while there yet exist such shades of suspicion as do not warrant his discharge without some formal expression of the doubts which the inquest entertain of his guilt or innocence. These things premised, we proceed in our narrative.

Henry Darnley was induced by the queen to publish a declaration, in which he boldly denied all accession to the act of violence which had been committed under his express instigation. But this mean step only brought upon him hatred and contempt. The queen prosecuted seven of the murderers of Rizzio; and it is certainly to the praise of her clemency that only two mean men were executed for a conspiracy of an odious character, in which so many persons of influence had been implicated. If Mary acted thus moderately in order to prevent the scandal which would have been caused by any of the superior conspirators alleging in defence the command of the king, she was ill requited by her husband for having sacrificed her own resentment to cover his honor. He resumed his vicious and offensive habits, indulged without restraint his propensity to low company and vulgar debauchery, and by his starts of arrogance and disrespect often, even in public, forced tears from the queen's eyes.

The birth of a son, afterward James VI., of whom Mary was delivered, June 19, 1566, created no reconciliation between his parents. Darnley's selfish and wayward temper was not capable of such restraint as to forbear repeated occasions of offence; and Mary, a queen and a woman, was receiving new insults, ere yet she had forgotten that the man whom she had raised up from comparative obscurity had so lately ushered a band of armed murderers into her bedroom to assassinate in her presence a favorite domestic. The consequence was a breach between them, which was every day more apparent.

Discountenanced by the queen, Darnley was equally disregarded by the nobility, and not only by such of them as were guided by her influence, but by others, who, allied to Morton and his associates, banished on account of Rizzio's murder, now resented Darnley's desertion of their cause. In one of those fits of impatience which he felt at the general neglect and insignificance to which he saw himself reduced, this silly and petulant boy thought of leaving the kingdom. His father, the Earl of Lennox, made the queen acquainted with this resolution, and in vain endeavored to bring him to renounce it. The queen had recourse to argument and even entreaty, to induce her wayward husband to explain the motive of his intended journey, which must be prejudicial to the honor of both. He was sullen, and finding that he had means of giving her pain, was proof even against her caresses, and no less against the arguments of the privy council.

During all this interval, the cause of the domestic quarrel, at least the scandal of its being made public, seems to rest on Darnley's side exclusively. He repined that he was not promoted to higher power or authority, although he was incapable of managing, and had most grossly abused, the portion which he already enjoyed. He complained he had not waiting and attendance suitable to his rank. Mary refuted the objection, by replying that her own servants were always ordered to attend on her husband, and that she could not compel the nobility to wait upon him, since it was only his own courtesy and urbanity which could bind them to his person. Historians have added to Darnley's complaints of ill usage one which he himself did not make, namely, that he was left unfurnished with money and necessaries. The books of the treasury state, in contradiction of this, that payments in money and furnishings had been made on Darnley's account, within three weeks, to a greater extent than the queen had drawn for six months. Le Crocq, the French ambassador, informs us, that at this period, when the queen has been certainly grossly misrepresented by those who labor to make her appear as culpable as possible, he never saw her majesty so much beloved, esteemed, and honored, nor had so great harmony ever prevailed at court; an effect to be entirely ascribed to Mary's own prudent conduct. This was also to be speedily changed by an unhappy alteration in those measures which produced it.

A favorite was now arising at court, to whose malign influence are to be imputed the principal errors of Mary's life and the greatest misfortunes of her reign. James, earl of Bothwell, was born of a powerful family, and was Lord High Admiral of Scotland. He professed the old religion; and was the only nobleman, except the Lord Seton, who had adhered to Mary of Guise during the war of 1559–60. In subsequent state commotions he had uniformly taken the part which was most in accordance with the queen's wishes. In other respects a bold ambitious man, of an impetuous temper, he was repeatedly engaged in feuds which he was often unable to support. The latest quarrel of this kind was with the powerful Earl of Murray, who accused him of an attempt to assassinate him. Bothwell, unable to defend himself, fled to France. He returned in 1564–5; but Murray still insisted on his being brought to trial; and as the accuser proposed to attend the justice-court with an army of five thousand men, the accused party, unable to face an opponent so powerful, withdrew a second time from the country. When Murray fell into disgrace for opposing the queen's marriage with Darnley, his enemies naturally regained Mary's favor. Thus Lord Gordon, whose father had fallen in battle with Murray at Corrichie, was restored to his honors and estates, and Bothwell was recalled from France. Their feud with Murray, then in his turn a banished man, was a recommendation to the queen; and Bothwell obtained the important charge of warden and lieutenant-general of all the marches. At the time of Rizzio's murder Bothwell attempted to resist the conspirators; and although he failed in that effort he afterward materially aided Mary's escape from Edinburgh to Dunbar; and furnished a part of the army with which she marched back to Edinburgh and drove Morton into exile. He was rewarded with the office of keeper of Dunbar Castle. As this strong fortress is situated in East Lothian, where the possessions of his clan lay, the office was of considerable importance to him. Lastly, when the queen was reconciled to Murray and Argyle, she made it a condition that these lords should become friends with Bothwell and Huntley.

All these instances of distinction conferred on Bothwell were thus far very natural, as the queen might be disposed to favor a subject of his high rank, who had remained uniformly steady to her cause, when others had been engaged in actions of outrage and violence against her authority. But, previous to the queen's confinement in June, 1566, Bothwell had not acquired any remarkable ascendency in the queen's counsels. For at that interesting period, when he and Huntley desired to be permitted to lodge in the castle of Edinburgh, they were denied admittance by **Murray,** without the queen's expressing any displeasure at the refusal of their request. There can be no doubt, however, that Bothwell soon after this date rose into eminent personal favor with his sovereign. As he was of an insolent and profligate character, he is said to have been generally hated. It seems probable that the reconciliation between Murray and this new favorite was deceitful on both sides, and that the former only gave way to the queen's pleasure, in hopes that the presumption of Bothwell would speedily engage him in some new trouble, and afford ground for a fresh charge against him. From July 19, 1566, when the queen's month of confinement ended, till the beginning of October in the same year, is the space allowed to be filled up by the accusers of Mary with the queen's growing passion for Bothwell, and its termination, as they allege, in a guilty intrigue. The time seems very short for the purpose, although, considering the situation of Mary and her husband, and the terms on which they stood, the space might be sufficient for Bothwell to climb to such a degree of favor as should encourage the daring ambition of a presumptuous man, and stir him to the boldest measures in order to its gratification. Meanwhile other and different actors were becoming daily more interested in hastening the fate of the unfortunate Mary.

Elizabeth, her powerful neighbor, had never looked on the queen of Scotland save with an evil eye; but the birth of the infant prince gave her rival such a decisive superiority, that on hearing of the event the queen of England could not conceal her mortification. She was in great mirth and engaged in dancing when the news reached her. But on hearing it the scene was changed. Elizabeth left the dance, and sat down, reclining her head upon her hand, and bursting out to her ladies with the melancholy exclamation, that the queen of Scots was mother of a fair son, while she herself remained but a barren stock. On the next morning she indeed recovered that command of herself which was habitual to her, and pretending the greatest joy at the news of her good sister's delivery, said that the pleasure she received from the intelligence had chased away a sickness which had before oppressed her. She accepted with apparent willingness the honor of being god-mother to the infant, and locking her discontent within her breast, strove to appear the kind kinswoman and friendly ally.

Elizabeth's private mortification at this event did not arise exclusively from female envy. The birth of an heir to the Scottish queen's pretensions gave them a popularity in England which they did not before possess; and Mary's ambassadors by their communication with persons of consequence in England, both Catholics and Protestants, successfully endeavored to form a faction in favor of their mistress who might combine to obtain from Elizabeth, what she was equally loth and fearful to grant, a recognition of her Scottish kinswoman as successor to her throne. A party began to appear even in the English parliament, who proposed to appease the general anxiety about the uncertainty of the succession after the demise of the reigning queen by such a declaration. And in these pressing circumstances Queen Elizabeth found additional reasons for disliking Mary, and for being heartily desirous to embroil her kinswoman's affairs at home, so as effectually to prevent her urging claims of succession in England. Fate and Mary's misfortunes or misconduct were not long in affording the English queen a more ample opportunity for this purpose than her most sanguine hopes could have augured.

Among other preferments which had been showered on the new favorite, Bothwell had received the important charge of keeper of the castle of Hermitage, and of the valley of Liddisdale. In the beginning of October, 1566, he set out for Liddisdale, to execute his charge as keeper of that disorderly country. On the 7th of the same month he was wounded by an outlawed borderer whom he attempted to make prisoner with his own hand. These tidings and the outlaw's head were instantly sent to Queen Mary, who was

then at no great distance from the disorderly district where
the accident happened, having arrived at Jedburgh about
the 8th of the month, with the purpose, according to a previous arrangement of the privy council, of residing there for
eight days, to superintend the proceedings of the circuit
courts held for the despatch of justice. On the 16th she
went from Jedburgh to Hermitage Castle, to visit Bothwell,
a distance of twenty statute miles, and returned, a circumstance to be specially noted, the same day. Her accusers
represent this as the visit of an anxious and fond woman to
a wounded lover; while those who favor Mary's cause attribute the step to a sense of consideration for a supposed well-
deserving subject, and to a desire personally to investigate
the cause of an outrage which was a high insult to her royal
authority. It is certainly a favorable circumstance, overlooked or misrepresented by the enemies of Mary's reputation, that her visit was not nearly so precipitate as has been
represented, but that eight days, at least, must have inter-
vened between her hearing of Bothwell's wound and her
visit to the castle of Hermitage. A journey undertaken
after such an interval has not the appearance of being performed at the impulse of passion, but seems rather to have
flowed from some political motive; and the queen's readiness to take arms in person both previously to the battle of
Corrichie and at the Roundabout Raid may account for her
dauntlessly approaching a disturbed district in her dominions, without supposing her to be acting upon the impulse
of a guilty passion, or even an inordinate favor for her
wounded officer. That the queen had much regard for
Bothwell cannot be doubted. The question is, whether she
carried it to a guilty extent; and in candor we cannot say
that this brief visit at Hermitage, undertaken eight days at
the least after she had heard that Bothwell was wounded
in the hand (for it is material to remark that the hurt was
not dangerous), carries to us the conviction which others
have derived from it. After her fatiguing journey, for she
rode to Hermitage and returned on the same day, a circum-

stance also material, Mary was seized with an illness which brought her to the point of death, and detained her for a month in the little town of Jedburgh, ere she was strong enough to prosecute her journey.

During all the period of the queen's illness Darnley came not near his wife; and it is little wonder that when he did appear at Jedburgh, on the 28th of October, he was so coldly received that, finding himself lightly regarded, he returned the next day. Everything argued a continuance of discord in the royal family; and the nobles around the queen were now engaged in intrigues which turned upon the dissolving of the ill-assorted marriage by some mode or other. Maitland of Lethington, Huntley, Argyle, Bothwell, and others, were accessory to these dark consultations, and we cannot suppose Murray wholly ignorant of them. It was resolved among them that a divorce between Darnley and the queen should be effected, and that the price paid by Mary for her emancipation from that yoke should be a free pardon to Morton and the exiles guilty of the conspiracy against Rizzio.

This, as the advice of a great part of her counsellors, was suggested to Mary, then resident at the castle of Craigmillar. She peremptorily refused her consent to the proposal of divorce, as a measure which could not be adopted without throwing discredit on her own reputation, and some doubt on the legitimacy of her child. But during the festivities of the christening of James, at Stirling, Mary lent an ear to the various intercessions urged in behalf of Morton and his accomplices, and granted them a free pardon excepting only George Douglas, the portulate, as he was termed, of Aberbrothock, who struck the first blow at Rizzio; and she purposed, according to Melville's account, to return to the mild and gracious kind of government which had distinguished her first arrival. "But, alas!" said that faithful servant, "she had too many evil counsellors about her." It was determined among them, that, instead of the proposed divorce, Darnley should be assassinated. With Morton, Bothwell united himself in apparent friendship; and we have the testimony of the former earl to prove that he was privy to the desperate deed which Bothwell meditated, although he alleges he yielded no consent to it.

Darnley attended the splendid christening of his son, but without meeting either notice or distinction. After lingering for about a week amid festivities of which he was no partaker, he went to join his father at Glasgow, where he took the smallpox. The queen despatched her physician to attend him, but went not to him herself; for which the health of her son was alleged as a reason. At length, about the 24th of January, Mary went from Edinburgh to Glasgow, and had a friendly interview with Darnley, with whom she afterward lived upon apparently good terms. If this was a constraint put on the queen, she had not long to endure it.

Mary and Darnley left Glasgow in company, and reached Edinburgh on the 31st of January. The king's illness was assigned as a reason for quartering him apart from the palace where his wife and child resided. A solitary house, called the Kirk of Field, in the suburbs of the city, where the college is now situated, was appointed for his reception. Mary regularly visited him, and sometimes slept in the same house. On the Monday before his murder, she passed the evening with him until it was time to attend a masque which was to be given in the palace, on the occasion of a wedding in the royal household. About two in the morning of Tuesday, Bothwell, with a selected party of desperate men, opened the under apartments of the Kirk of Field by means of false keys, and laid a lighted match to a quantity of powder which had been previously placed beneath the king's apartment. After a few anxious moments had passed, Bothwell became impatient, and despatched one of the ruffians who was present to see whether the match was still burning. The accomplice did not hesitate to obey the commission, and returned with information that the light was still burning and the fire would presently reach the powder. After this the party waited calmly till the house blew up, when Bothwell retired, satisfied that, as the price of this enormous crime, he had purchased a title to the hand of a queen. There is reason to believe that several of the principal nobles and statesmen were previously acquainted with the bloody purpose. The Earl of Morton confessed at his death that he knew of such an intention; and his cousin, the notorious Archibald Douglas, parson titular of Glasgow, was present at the execution. Whether Mary herself was conscious of this great crime is a question which has long been a controversial passage of Scottish history, to which we shall hereafter turn the reader's attention.

The energetic character of the queen, the activity with which she had hitherto suppressed all opposition to her will as soon as such was manifested, and the impulse which she had given to the machine of her government, prevented for a time the effect of the terrible shock communicated by this abominable murder, which made, nevertheless, a deep impression on the public mind. Compassion for the young king's fate gave Darnley, who enjoyed little love or respect while he lived, a degree of posthumous popularity; and the desire of seeing his murder revenged was soon a general sentiment. Placards appeared in the most public places in the city, and voices were heard in streets at dead of night, charging the murder on Bothwell, toward whom universal suspicion was directed, and insinuating that the queen had been privy to the conspiracy against her husband's life. The terms of discord on which she had lived with Darnley, and the high favor to which Bothwell had risen, combined to create such a rumor.

Lennox, the father of the deceased Darnley, had naturally shared his son's disgrace, though not his demerits. He now pressed the queen for vengeance, and declared his own suspicion of Bothwell. In answer to his importunity, a meeting of the privy council, held on the 28th day of March, named the 13th of April as the day of trying Bothwell for the murder of the king. Lennox the accuser complained of the precipitancy with which the trial was forced forward. He required that the person accused of such a crime should

be secured in prison, and, for decency's sake at least, excluded from the presence of the widowed queen.

The trial was nevertheless brought on at the appointed
period with most indecorous precipitation.   Bothwell appeared at the bar surrounded by armed friends and backed
by mercenary soldiers.   The Earl of Morton on the one
hand, and Lethington on the other, supported the prisoner
as he entered the court of justiciary.   Lennox, unable to
face such a confederacy, protested by one of his retainers
against any further procedure in the trial, as carried on
against law.   It was determined, however, that the trial
should proceed without respect to the remonstrance of Lennox; and as no prosecutor appeared, and no evidence was
adduced in support of the charge, Bothwell was of course
acquitted.   Lennox fled precipitately to England doubting
of his personal safety when a man of a character so violent
and profligate as Bothwell was possessed of the power of
triumphing over the laws.

The queen continued to treat Bothwell as if he had been
acquitted in the most ample and honorable manner.   In a
parliament which was held two days after the trial, he carried the sceptre before the queen's person, and received a full
confirmation from that assembly of all the gifts and honors
which Mary had lavished on him, not forgetting the keeping of Edinburgh Castle, the most important fortress in
the kingdom.   At the same time ratifications were made of
various grants to other nobles, so many in number that they
seem to be the division of the kingdom between her favorite
Bothwell and the great men who had thus far lent their
arms to aid him in his ascent, while, in fact, they watched
for the moment when his fall should be precipitate in proportion to the height to which he had risen.

Under the influence of this aspiring statesman the queen
was induced to take a step which she had hitherto delayed
and evaded, and which was totally inconsistent with her
accession to the Treaty of Bayonne, made for the express
support of the Catholic faith.   An act of parliament was

passed and received the royal assent confirming and ratifying in the most express terms the Protestant doctrines and church government. This important concession, which no representation of the Protestants had been able even in the most critical circumstances to extract from the queen, the influence of her ambitious lover had induced Mary at once to consent to. Bothwell, no doubt, expected that the legal security thus unexpectedly given to the reformed faith would silence the clamors of the churchmen, and give him, as the author of that security so long sought and vainly petitioned for, popularity with their hearers. Having paved the way, as he supposed, for his final advancement being received with general good will, this ambitious man ventured a more direct stride toward accomplishing his object.

For this purpose, immediately after the rising of parliament, Bothwell invited the principal members of that body to an entertainment in a tavern. There he plainly intimated to them his purpose of marrying the queen, and her consent to honor him with her hand; and proposed to all present to subscribe a bond, which he drew out of his pocket ready drawn up, in which, after Bothwell himself was recognized as totally free of the foul charge of having been accessory to the late king's murder, he, the same Bothwell, was warmly recommended to her majesty as a suitable match, in case she should humble herself so far as to think of sharing her bed with a subject, and the subscribers agreed to advance the said marriage at the risk of life and goods. It is probable that the principal persons present expected these proposals, and were prepared for them. Those of minor importance were compelled to follow their example, since neither the time nor place allowed much exercise of free choice. At a house usually called Ainslie's Supper, from the name of the publican by whom it was held, the bond was subscribed by eight bishops, nine earls, and seven lords: Morton and Maitland of Lethington are among the number. And thus fortified, as he imagined, by so strong a party, Bothwell proceeded to take the last step in his extraordinary advance to greatness.

Assembling about one thousand horse, under pretext of border service, Bothwell at the head of this company lay in wait for the queen as she came from Stirling, at a place called Fountain Bridge, near Edinburgh, and taking her horse by the bridle, appeared to render himself director of her motions and master of her person. His followers spared not to say, that this seeming violence was offered by the queen's own consent, and would be received as good service. The subjects appeared to suppose the same, for, ready upon former occasions to rise to protect their queen's person when in danger, they beheld her on the present occasion led pris-oner through the richest and most populous part of her dominions, while they looked on in silent astonishment. In this manner Bothwell conducted Mary to the castle of Dunbar, unopposed and unpursued, and made it his boast that gainsay who would, and even against her own consent, he would marry the queen.

To add another disgusting feature to this enormous con-duct, the reader must be informed that Bothwell was at this very moment the husband of Lady Jane Gordon, sister to the Earl of Huntley, and was pursuer of a process of divorce, on account of consanguinity, before the consistorial court. The countess, on her part, with every appearance of conni-vance and collusion, prosecuted a separate action of divorce, on the score of adultery, against her husband; and sentence of divorce was pronounced in both suits within a few days of each other.

In silence and amazement the nation waited the end of this extraordinary course of events; and if Mary had been in reality a queen subjected by an audacious subject to the utmost limits of personal insult and violence, she was singu-larly unhappy in finding none among her subjects who were induced to believe that the compulsion which she seemed to sustain was a restraint imposed on her against her own will. Her friends looked on with deep affliction: those who judged most favorably concluding she was led astray by such pas-sionate dotage as sometimes characterizes female affection:

while the powerful and numerous party who suspected Mary's morals because they doubted her religion carefully gathered up every levity of which she had been guilty since her return to Scotland, and cited them as instances of depravity, on which they alleged they were warranted, by the queen's present conduct, to put the worst interpretation.

At the end of twelve days Mary was liberated from Dunbar, conveyed to Edinburgh Castle, and apparently placed at liberty by the Earl of Bothwell; and the first use she made of her freedom was to utter a declaration that, though she had been displeased with the restraint lately put upon her by the Earl of Bothwell, yet, considering his former services, and what might be expected from him in future, she was not only disposed freely to forgive him, but also to exalt him to higher honors. And she kept her word: for after proclamation of bans, and after the earl had been elevated to the rank of Duke of Orkney, she conferred upon him her hand in marriage on the 15th of May, 1567:—a match which might be concluded every way ominous and unfortunate, without having recourse to the popular superstition derived by the Scots from the classic authors who attach bad luck to marriages in the month of May.

The only apology which the defenders of the unfortunate queen have made for this fatal and irretrievable error is, that her reputation having suffered from being for several days in the hands of a man so audacious and uncontrollable as Bothwell, she was placed in a position which rendered her marrying him an act of necessity rather than choice. On the other hand, those who assert the queen's guilt rest upon this unhappy, unseemly, and ill-chosen union as the most convincing proof of her being privy to the death of her husband, and all the consequences of the murder.[1]

---

[1] The acute David Hume being told of a new work which appeared, in which the author had made a well-argued defence of Queen Mary, "Has he shown," said the historian, "that the queen did *not* marry Bothwell?" he was answered of course in the negative: "then," replied Mr. Hume, "in admitting that fact, he resigns the whole question."

On the other hand, strong suspicions arose, out of their own conduct on the occasion, that Morton, Lethington, and others of Mary's counsellors, were treacherously and ungratefully concerned in the plot, which was at once to destroy their sovereign's fame and power. When pardoned by the queen for their share in the Rizzio conspiracy, which had been the fruitful parent of so many crimes, several of them had become privy to Bothwell's designs on the queen's hand, and formed a bond to favor his views as well in annulling the marriage with Darnley as in marrying the queen. These objects they had advanced by every argument in their power; and when death was substituted for the original intention of divorce, it does not seem to have alarmed these sturdy associates. They supported the murderer after the fact, and lent him their countenance upon his trial. They subscribed the bond at Ainslie's Supper. Not one of them joined in a spirited remonstrance which the gallant Lord Herries offered to the queen against her marriage with Bothwell. Not a spear was lifted, not a sword drawn, to rescue Mary from the power of that atrocious ruffian. She was suffered, without either warning or opposition, to unite herself with this worthless man; and it was not until her honor became inseparable from his that the same advisers changed their note, sounded an alarm to the nation, and called on all true subjects to rescue the queen from the control of Bothwell.

We cannot but suspect that these ambitious men, observing how readily the queen had been supported by the nation on former occasions, had determined not to interrupt her infatuated career till she had linked her fate to Bothwell so inseparably that she must needs share his ruin. Morton was aware that he should, by getting rid of Queen Mary, gratify his patroness Queen Elizabeth in the most sensible manner, and raise his own party, and eventually perhaps himself, to the prime management of Scottish affairs.

These considerations show why Morton and Lethington did not make the least effort to save the queen by preventing or at least remonstrating against her marriage. In the meantime Bothwell plainly showed both his grasping ambition and his gross ingratitude to the queen. His behavior in the palace, where he had so unworthily risen to so high a place, was like that of a debauched soldier unbounded in his dissolute discourse either by topics or terms, and totally neglectful of his duty and respect for the queen. He schemed and plotted to get into his hands the person of the young prince, with a view probably on his life or liberty; and because the queen, amid the dotage of her passion, opposed him in his purpose, he treated her with such reproachful language that she was heard in the height of her grief and indignation threatening to stab or drown herself.

The Earl of Mar, who had lodged the young prince in Edinburgh Castle, took care to keep both James's person and that important place out of the hands of Bothwell, though he had been constituted governor. Meantime the public indignation began to show itself more boldly. It was easy to find specious pretexts for raising in arms so warlike a nation as the Scots—the liberation of the queen from the control of Bothwell, and freeing the young prince from the restraint and danger attending his continuing under the guardianship of his father's murderer, were sufficient cause for calling the people to arms. Morton and most of the Protestant lords soon assembled a force and marched to Edinburgh. Bothwell and the queen were wellnigh surprised as they were banqueting at Borthwick Castle, in the vicinity of the metropolis, and escaped with difficulty to the strong fortress of Dunbar, where Mary summoned her subjects around her as on former occasions: they came, but it was with a total disinclination to the service.

The confederated lords marched eastward against Dunbar, but the queen, with her usual alacrity, assembled forces equal to theirs in number, and met them on Carberry Hill. When the two armies came in sight of each other, the French ambassador, called Le Crocq, endeavored to mediate between the parties, and succeeded in preventing hostilities. In the conferences which followed, Bothwell made a bravadoing offer to vindicate her innocence by single combat; but chicaned and retracted when several among the confederates offered to accept the challenge. In the meantime the queen's spirits failed her when she beheld the reluctance with which her own troops prepared for the combat, and heard Kirkcaldy of Grainge, on the part of the confederates, profess their willingness to respect and obey her as their sovereign, providing she would remove Bothwell from her presence and counsels. She dimissed Bothwell accordingly, who retreated to the Orkneys, and, driven from thence, committed some outrages on the trade of Denmark. He was finally taken, and immured in the castle of Malmoe, in Norway, where he died, after ten years' confinement.

Meantime the queen, who had surrendered herself upon terms to her insurgent subjects, was far from experiencing the reception of homage and respect on their part which Kirkcaldy had promised. The armed ranks closed around her with menacing gestures and expressions, which even the authority of their leaders could not restrain. When she reached Edinburgh the multitude became still more unruly; and the streets of her capital resounded with abusive exclamations against her. Some, to show their disrespectful feelings, did not hesitate to display before her eyes a banner, on which was represented the murdered Darnley with the person of the young prince kneeling beside it, and praying to Heaven for vengeance. While Mary sustained this degrading treatment from the commonalty, the confederated lords formed themselves into a committee of government, and ordered the queen to be conveyed under strong guard to the castle of Lochleven, situated on an islet, in the large lake so named, and placed under the custody of Sir William Douglas, a kinsman of Morton, lord of the castle, and his wife, the mother of the Earl of Murray, who pretended to have been lawfully wedded to James V., though, in fact, only his concubine, and was, therefore, hostile to the descendent of his actual marriage with Mary of Guise. This usage of the queen was contrary to the conditions which the associated lords had granted to her when she surrendered herself to Kirkcaldy of Grainge at Carberry Hill; and that gallant knight upbraided them severely with having broken their word to Mary, and made him the means of deceiving her. But to this they answered that the favorable terms alluded to had been granted to Mary on condition that she would break off all intercourse with Bothwell; notwithstanding which, they affirmed, she had afterward written to him in affectionate terms, agreeing to adhere to his fortunes, and had thereby forfeited the favorable terms which they had been willing to grant on condition of her positively renouncing him.

This state of things could not long endure. The Hamiltons, and many other nobles of great power, without challenging the propriety of the proceedings of the insurgents as far as the expulsion of Bothwell was concerned, were of opinion that, he being banished from the kingdom, Queen Mary should be restored to her sovereign authority. But the lords of the confederation, who had every reason to think that her talents, and the interest which she inspired in her kingdom, might soon enable her, if set at liberty, to revenge herself on those by whom she had been confined, determined that she should be dethroned on account of maladministration, and compelled to resign her crown to her son, while the government during his minority should be conducted by a regent.

This important office was reserved for James, earl of Murray. The reason of our late silence respecting this influential nobleman is his absence from the scene of action. Murray had remained in Scotland until he saw the termination of the conjugal disputes between Darnley and Mary, by the murder of the former. He then asked and obtained license to go to England, and from thence to France, where he remained during the insurrection, of which, however, he received the principal reward, being, as we have said, destined by the confederate lords to hold the place of supreme governor in the name of the infant prince. He was less objectionable to the queen than any other who could have been proposed, since his absence from the kingdom had separated him from the Carberry lords, at the time when their insurrection was most offensive to the queen. She might also hope something from affection, and much from gratitude for benefits received by her brother.

The Earl of Murray, summoned to Scotland to fulfil such high destinies, returned to his native country with all despatch, and took on him, though manifesting a decent reluctance, the office of regent. The queen had expected a good deal from the affection and gratitude of Murray; but at their very first interview he reproved her with so much severity for her errors that all ties of family affection or friendship between them were broken off forever. The unfortunate queen had been already compelled, not without circumstances of violence, to subscribe a resignation of her kingdom, and to sign a commission to her brother in the capacity of regent. Murray, by his skill and talent, speedily overturned the plans of the nobles who were favorable to the queen, obtained possession of the castle of Edinburgh, and placed himself as regent in full execution of the government throughout Scotland. Parliament sanctioned the change of rulers which had taken place, ratified the accession of the infant son, instead of the captive mother, and the authority of Murray as regent in the name of the king.

CHAPTER XXIX

Mary's Escape from Lochleven—The Battle of Langside—The
Queen's Flight into England—Mary offers to vindicate herself
to Elizabeth—Advantage taken of that Offer—Commission at
York—Question of Supremacy revived and abandoned—Proposal of a Marriage between Mary and the Duke of Norfolk—
Sittings of the Commission removed to Westminster—Murray
lodges his Accusation against Mary—Elizabeth declines pronouncing a decision, but detains Mary a Prisoner—Question of
her Guilt and Innocence—Morton's Confession—Proofs by the
Sonnets and Letters—Deemed inconclusive, and why—Confession of Paris—Elizabeth's Conduct toward Mary—A Party is
formed in Scotland for the Queen—It is joined by Kirkcaldy
of Grainge and Lethington—Murray betrays Norfolk to Elizabeth—The Duke is imprisoned—Murray assassinated by Bothwellhaugh—Inroads on the Borders

FATE had reserved to Queen Mary an additional chance
for repairing her broken fortunes. In Lochleven
Castle she was surrounded by those most deeply
interested for the Earls of Murray and of Morton; and
most inclined to support the power to which they had been
raised. But there was one person among them who beheld
her confinement and her distresses with an eye of compassion. This was a youth named George Douglas, brother of
the Lord of Lochleven, who, captivated by her beauty,
touched by her sorrow, and seduced by her promises, laid a
plan for her escape. This was discovered by his brother, Sir
James, who expelled the plotter from the castle.

Undismayed by this miscarriage, George Douglas lingered
on the shores of Lochleven, to assist the queen in any subsequent effort. Mary was not long in making such an attempt.
She entered a boat disguised in the attire of a laundress, but

was discovered, from her repelling the endeavors by the rude boatmen to pull off her veil with arms and hands far too white to belong to one of her assumed character.

Again the queen was replaced in her island prison, but about the same time a second ally in the garrison was won over to assist her escape. This was a lad of seventeen or eighteen, called William Douglas, otherwise the Little Douglas, a relative, probably, of the Lord of Lochleven.

This *little* Douglas, so named from his tender years or low stature, gave her his assistance to escape by night from the castle and island in which she was immured. He stole the keys for this purpose, set the royal prisoner at liberty in the middle of the night: to prevent pursuit, locked the iron gates of the town upon its inmates, and flung the keys into the lake as he rowed her to land. George Douglas, already mentioned, Lord Seton, and a party of the Hamiltons, received the queen on the shores of the lake, and conveyed her in triumph to Hamilton, where her friends hastened to assemble an army, and form an association for her defence. The engagement was subscribed by nine earls, as many lords, and a great many persons of consequence.

Placing the queen in the centre of their numerous battalions, they moved from Hamilton toward Dumbarton. It was their intention to deposit the person of the sovereign in that impregnable castle, and then to seek out the regent and give him battle. But his rapid movements anticipated their more tardy measures. Murray was at this time lying at Glasgow; and at the head of an army inferior in numbers marched to intercept the progress of the enemy toward the north. The vanguard of each army hastened forward, contending which should obtain possession of the village of Langside. They met with equal courage, and encountered with levelled lances, striving, like contending bulls, which should bear the other down. The spears of the front ranks were so fastened into each other's armor, that the staves crossed like a sort of grating, on which lay daggers, pistols, and other weapons used as missiles, which the contending

parties had thrown at each other. While they were thus
locked together, Morton led a detachment against the flank
of the Hamiltons, and decided the day. Mary's army was
broken and routed. The queen herself fled sixty miles without drawing bridle, when she arrived at Dundrennan Abbey,
in Galloway.

Here, against the opinion of her wisest counsellors, Mary
exercised her last act of free agency, by determining on the
perilous step of taking refuge in England, the realm of
Elizabeth, her sister and her foe.

That remarkable princess was not a woman to be de-
terred, by scruples respecting public faith or private honor,
from benefiting by the advantages which occasion had thus
thrown into her lap. Mary was received by the English
officers on the borders with the greatest appearance of respect; nor was Elizabeth sparing of kind expressions of
comfort and friendship toward her ill-fated sister.

But when the unfortunate queen of Scotland pressed for
an interview with Elizabeth, she was informed that an objection to this arose from the accusations which some of her
subjects had preferred against her. Mary naturally and
eagerly offered to justify herself against such charges,
whatever was their character; meaning no more than to
offer such explanations to the queen of England as friend
gives to friend, in justifying herself from any sinister report, but certainly not intending to constitute Elizabeth her
judge, or to descend from her state, and reply before the
queen of England to the accusations of her subjects at
the bar of her equal. Elizabeth, however, had obtained an
advantage which she determined to keep; and by means
of this she had an apology, such as it was, for assuming,
in her own person, the power of deciding upon Mary's guilt
or innocence. The point of justice was, indeed, untenable;
for the queen of England, on all occasions of rebellion against
her neighbor Queen Mary, had received the fugitive insurgents into her kingdom, supplied their wants, and lent them
countenance and succor, declining either to deliver them up,

or enter into cognizance of their offences. Whereas, when the queen of Scotland was compelled to take refuge in her kind sister's kingdom, the worst construction was put upon the cause of her retreat, and Elizabeth, the loving ally, instantly assumed the character of the strict and awful judge.

By command of Elizabeth a commission was appointed to sit at York, having the Duke of Norfolk at its head, designed to inquire into the guilt or innocence of Queen Mary. Before this board, composed of English commissioners, appeared the regent, with Morton, Lindsay, the bishop of Orkney, and above all, with Secretary Maitland, the Machiavel of Scotland. The bishop of Ross, Lord Herries, Lord Boyd, and others, the most distinguished of Mary's friends, attended on her behalf.

The first demand of Norfolk was, that the Regent Murray should do homage to the queen of England, as queen paramount of Scotland, seeing he had come voluntarily to plead as a suitor before Elizabeth's commissioners. This acknowledgment of the right of supremacy, resisted in so many centuries of bloody war, would have simplified the task of affording a foundation for Elizabeth's jurisdiction, since, if it had been admitted, she might have taken up the settlement of the disputes between the queen and subjects of Scotland, in the legitimate exercise of her power, as paramount superior, in which capacity Edward I. had decided the controversy between Bruce and Baliol. At the unexpected demand of homage, the blood rushed to Regent Murray's countenance, and he remained uncertain what to answer; but the ready wit of Lethington took up the debate. "Let England," he said, "restore to Scotland Cumberland, Northumberland, and the town of Berwick, and homage shall be done for these possessions as of old; but for the kingdom and crown of Scotland," he continued, "it is more free of dependence than England herself has been of late, while she paid Saint Peter's pence to Rome."

The sittings of the commissioners were resumed without more debate on the subject of supremacy, which the English tacitly abandoned. It might be observed, however, that there was a reluctance on the part of the regent and his associates to bring forward their defence to the accusation of rebellion against Mary, by retorting upon her the alleged offences of incontinence, and accession to the assassination of Henry Darnley. The fact was, that the fertile brain of Lethington had already devised a scheme by which the proceedings on both sides were to be guided, and which he proposed should put an end to the commission, in a manner which Elizabeth, under whose warrant it held its sittings, very little dreamed of. This project was to effect a match between Mary, her divorce from Bothwell being effected, and the Duke of Norfolk, wealthy, brave, accomplished, and at the head of a strong party among the English nobility, composed partly of Catholics and partly of Protestants, who were, for various reasons, hostile to the government and schemes of Cecil. Of this number the two great northern Earls of Westmoreland and Northumberland were particularly formidable.

The Regent Murray having in his eye the prospect of such a union must naturally have reflected that Mary, restored to her crown with increased security and strength, would be utterly implacable toward him, if he should render himself guilty in her eyes of having been her accuser before Elizabeth's commission at this peculiar crisis of her fate. He therefore temporized; and instead of pressing his charges against Mary, capitulated with Queen Elizabeth about the terms on which the accusation was to be brought forward; and that queen had the mortification to perceive that the regent, instead of persisting in the charge, showed some inclination to make peace with his sister, whom he had lately accused of such enormities.

Embarrassed at perceiving that Murray hesitated, Elizabeth resolved to change the scene of action, and appointed the conference of the commissioners to be removed to Westminster, that the business might be carried on under her own eye and that of Cecil. For the same purpose, without

regard to Mary's requests or entreaties, she removed her
from Bolton to Tutbury, that she might be more remote
from her own dominions and the frontiers of England, in
which districts she had many friends. She was hitherto
treated honorably, but with the most secure attention to
her safety.

The wily Cecil was not long in obtaining a perfect acquaintance with the negotiation between Norfolk and the
regent; and he gave Murray to understand that should he
continue to shrink from the task of accusation, or pursue
further a line of hopeless hesitation, he would totally alien-
ate his protectress Elizabeth, without having the effect of
conciliating Mary, whom he had offended beyond reach of
pardon. Intimidated by his threats, the regent at length
preferred his charge against the queen, in the broadest
terms. He accused Mary as an accessory to the murder
of her husband, and as plotting the destruction of the young
prince, her own son. The queen's commissioners expressed
the utmost surprise and resentment at these unqualified
charges. They demanded an interview of Elizabeth, and
they protested against all further proceedings of the conference. The regent, in reply, was called upon to produce
his proofs. This brought forward an incident famous in the
controversy. In corroboration of his accusation, the Earl
of Murray produced and deposited a silver box, or casket,
full of love-letters, sonnets, and contracts, alleged to have
passed between Mary and Bothwell during the life of her
murdered husband, Henry Darnley, and contended that, with
the decree of the Scottish parliament, these documents were
sufficient to establish Queen Mary's guilt, and to vindicate
the conduct of those who, having risen in arms against her
government, now opposed her restoration.

By forcing Murray to these decisive steps, Elizabeth attained the principal object of her wishes. She had, as far
as a foul charge could have such an effect, destroyed the
good fame of Queen Mary, and obtained the privilege of
dealing with her as one lying under the most odious sus-

picions, and unworthy the protection of the law of nations. This point gained, she resolved to avoid taking on herself the delicate task of declaring Mary guilty or innocent. She informed Murray, therefore, that, on the one hand, she acquitted him of all charges against his loyalty and honor; and that, on the other, she could not bring herself to be of opinion that he had produced any proofs of the charge against Mary sufficiently decisive to prejudice her sister in her good opinion; on which account she had determined to leave the affairs of Scotland as she had found them. It will be observed that this decision, while in words it placed neither party in the wrong, gave Mary the same disadvantages which would have followed from an express condemnation of the queen. She remained a prisoner, although found guilty of no crime; and Murray, the accuser, though unacquitted of the charge of rebellion and calumnious slander against his sovereign, left England, after having received a considerable sum of money, with an assurance that his party in Scotland should have the support of the English government.

But it may be asked what conclusion are readers of the present day to draw from these proceedings? and are we, with one class of writers, to conceive Queen Mary an injured saint, or with another the most profligate of women? We confess that, without more light than we at present possess, or ever hope to see thrown on a subject of so mysterious a character, we incline to think that on both sides this memorable case has been pleaded to extremity.

The beauty, the wit, and, in general, the amiable character of Mary, has raised up for her memory defenders of equal talents and zeal. But if we review the queen's conduct from the debate at Craigmillar, concerning the proposed divorce between her and Darnley, it is difficult to believe that she must not have entertained suspicions that many persons of an unscrupulous character were not indisposed, when that measure was rejected, to remove the unfortunate prince from his share of the throne by the readiest and most violent means, if legal and justifiable expedients would not serve the turn. The reconciliation between the husband and wife, after their long estrangement, which was patched up so suddenly and immediately before the murder, the violence offered to the queen's person by Bothwell, and so tamely acquiesced in by a female of such high rank and energetic character, are to us irresistible evidence that Mary, deeply injured by her ungrateful husband, and engaged by an unhappy attachment to one of the most wicked of men, suffered Darnley, without warning or succor, to fall into the conspirators' snares, if, indeed, she did not herself entice him into the toils. Revenge and love are great casuists; and supposing Mary so far concerned in Darnley's death as to foresee its approach without endeavoring to prevent it, she might endeavor to justify her conduct to herself, by considering that by his accession to the murder of her servant in her own presence her ungrateful husband deserved death, and that she at least was not obliged to give the alarm when a deserved punishment seemed about to overwhelm him. The evident favor shown to Bothwell on his sham trial, the too obvious farce of the seizure of the queen at Fountain Bridge, and her subsequent marriage with Bothwell, all lead to the same melancholy conclusion. And when we recollect that Mary had been educated in the profligate court of Catherine of Medicis, and was surrounded in her own by some of the worst and most wicked men who ever lived, he who can suppose that, tempted by love and revenge, she walked through the maze of iniquity occurring between Rizzio's death and her marriage with Bothwell without soiling the purity of her mind with the guilt which was so thick around her path, must have unusual confidence in human nature.

But though we are compelled to admit that a long train of coherent circumstances seems to evince that Mary was at least by tacit acquiescence an accomplice in Darnley's fate, we are not much moved by what has been termed the actual proof of her guilt and which was produced as such before the commission.

The documents contained in the silver box are the only direct testimony tending to involve Mary in Darnley's murder; and setting these aside for the present, there remains little which can directly implicate the queen.

At a later period, indeed, Morton, an unprincipled and fierce man, who, according to his own account on the scaffold, was privy to the whole bloody scene, says, that being invited to join Bothwell and Lethington in a scheme against Darnley's life, he refused to engage in the plot unless Bothwell would obtain an injunction upon him to that effect from the queen herself. But he proceeds to declare that Bothwell never was able to produce such a warrant. Here, therefore, the chain of direct evidence is broken, and the positive proof of Mary's guilt is not to be found. Laying Morton's direct oral testimony aside as being inconclusive, we come next to the celebrated casket and papers.

These letters and writings produced would indeed prove a great deal more than enough for conviction if they stood unimpeached as authentic documents. But great and serious suspicions attach to their authenticity. The internal evidence is unfavorable according to our ideas of the style of a sovereign expressing her attachment. They are described with suspicious variations, sometimes as being written by the queen's own hand, sometimes as being only subscribed by her. Above all, though their authenticity was challenged, and though the regent and his associates had in their power the persons through whose hands they were said to have passed, yet no care whatever was taken, by examination of any of these persons, to ascertain or corroborate the faith of documents so important to the cause of the accusers. The obvious and legal inference is, that where that is not proved which ought to have been verified, it must have been for want of the means of probation. It is notorious that these letters and papers had been long enough in the hands of the queen's enemies to have been tampered with to any extent; and the productions of copies and translations, instead of originals, is totally foreign to our ideas of judicial proceedings. Nay, there was so little attention to authenticate the casket or the documents contained, that although Dalgleish, the messenger from whose person they were alleged to be taken, was tried and executed for accession to Darnley's murder, not a single question was put to him either at his trial, or at his death, which could tend to prove he had e 'er seen them. His confession, also, which candidly admits his share in Darnley's murder, contains not a word respecting these papers. The only evidence of their having been taken on the person of this man was the declaration of Morton, who, if they were forged, was undoubtedly a person most deeply interested in the fabrication.

The queen, also, when she alleged that these manuscripts were forgeries, observed that there were many in her kingdom who could imitate her handwriting; and it was believed that Maitland possessed that accomplishment in a supreme degree.

Another document of direct evidence preferred against the queen was the confession of Paris, a Frenchman, and a servant of her household, who is represented as having given testimony respecting the circumstances of a conference with Bothwell, which, compared with the subsequent directions received by Paris from Mary regarding the delivery of the keys of the king's lodgings at the Kirk of Field, seems distinctly probative of the queen's knowledge of the murder before the fact. But to this also lies the same objection of a strong suspicion of forgery; and there arises the greater doubt on the subject, that certainly if Paris had been actually disposed to make such an important confession, his life ought to have been preserved, that he might deliver his evidence before parliament or in an unprejudiced court, allowing every chance to the royal person accused of so hideous a crime of disproving it by cross-examination or otherwise. The death of a miserable domestic, whose life was at all times in their hands, ought to have been deferred until his testimony had been publicly given, carefully investigated, and formally recorded. The fact of having put

Paris instantly to death, with every other person connected with the murder, resembles the art of the usurper in the play who stabs the warders of Duncan lest a public examination should produce other sentiments in the minds of the judges than those which he who really committed the crime desired should be inferred.

On the whole, the direct evidence produced in support of Mary's alleged guilt was liable to such important objections that it could not now be admitted to convict a felon for the most petty crime; and there is surely no equity in receiving it as absolutely conclusive against a queen. We have already stated our opinion of the moral proof of deep delusion, or perhaps actual guilt, arising from Mary's own conduct; but we own that our strong suspicions, arising from her favor to Bothwell, her union with that profligate man, and the time and circumstances of the marriage, are rather weakened than confirmed by the attempts to corroborate it by positive evidence of so very suspicious a description. When original documents are suppressed, and alleged copies only produced, when minutes of confessions privately obtained under threats of torture are urged as proofs, and the witnesses themselves, who might have given open testimony, removed by precipitate execution, the loose and improbable character of the evidence throws a suspicion over the whole proceeding, which goes far to neutralize the presumption of guilt arising out of the circumstances; and as it evinces foul practices used in order to convict the queen, it must necessarily induce us to lean to the side of acquittal. Queen Elizabeth was probably sensible of this when, by the result of the investigation, she saw herself obliged to acknowledge that the Scottish queen had come off guiltless from the charge brought by Murray and her rebel subjects; and the number and character of those who asserted Mary's cause in Scotland plainly intimates that a great part of her subjects were in no respect disposed to be considered as having faith in the evidence which later historians have received as conclusive against her.

The inquiry had terminated favorably for Mary, in so far that Elizabeth confessed by her own answer to both parties that she saw no grounds for the charges with which the Scottish queen had been loaded. It seemed to follow that a queen now pronounced to be guiltless, who had taken refuge in the dominions of a sister and ally in a moment of extreme necessity, should have been either received with honor or dismissed with safety. But, contrary to the laws of hospitality observed in the most barbarous nations, contrary to the tenor of a thousand declarations of friendship and even sisterly fondness, the queen of England determined not to enfranchise her prisoner, though she had dismissed the accusation under pretext of which she had at first refused to admit her to her presence. She was indeed so bold in availing herself of the advantage she had gained as to seem little anxious to justify the right to detain her captive, being fully possessed of the power.

Mary, therefore, was sent from Bolton Castle to Tutbury; and that no circumstance of meanness might be omitted, the royal captive had reason to complain even of the niggard temper of Elizabeth, which hardly allowed her prisoner fitting means of transport or adequate support, while she dragged her from one prison to another in inclement weather, and through the most rugged roads.

Leaving Mary to her melancholy fate, our narrative must follow Murray to Scotland. His presence there had become needful to the support of his own party; for the lords who were attached to Queen Mary having recovered from the terrors inspired by the battle of Langside were threatening again to take up arms. Murray averted the immediate danger by seizing on the Duke of Chatelherault and Lord Herries, and sending them prisoners to Edinburgh Castle. But the queen's party continued to assume a menacing appearance. Their leaders were much encouraged by the intrigues carried on by the Duke of Norfolk for the purpose of obtaining Mary's hand. Two men of eminence, who had been Murray's especial friends, were deeply engaged in this plot. The first was Maitland of Lethington, who was the original inventor of the scheme; the other, Sir William Kirkcaldy of Grainge, famed for his military talent, and not less so for a generosity of disposition which was by no means a characteristic of the period. He had been displeased at the severe conduct of the lords toward the queen, after she surrendered to him at Carberry Hill, and dismissed her army upon his warrant of respectful treatment and good usage. And although he afterward fought against her at the battle of Langside, yet, unconvinced of Mary's guilt, or supposing that it had been expiated by her sufferings, or yielding, perhaps, to the wonderful influence which the ingenuity of Lethington possessed over the minds of all to whom he found access, he was now disposed to join in any honorable expedient which might obtain Mary's liberty and forward her restoration. Grainge, being governor of Edinburgh Castle, wherein were detained the noblemen whom Murray had lately made prisoners of state, his friendship was, at such a crisis, of the last consequence to the party to which he should finally attach himself. He declared himself the protector of these captives as well as of Maitland of Lethington, whom he received into the castle, and who became, as usual, the soul of all the intrigues which were carried on between the parties.

The arrival of the regent in Scotland disconcerted these counsels. Murray had been made privy to the proposed marriage between Norfolk and Mary, and had given his assent to it while at York. But since that period he had openly stood forward as the accuser of his sister, and could no longer hope either safety for the future or indemnity for the past should she ever again ascend the throne. He therefore dishonorably betrayed to Elizabeth the whole treaty as it had been communicated to him by Norfolk, and thus furnished the English queen with proofs on which the duke was arrested and detained a prisoner. Immediately upon this arrest, which was regarded as inferring Elizabeth's perfect knowledge of the various plans which had been agitated among the malcontent lords, the Earls of **Westmoreland** and Northumberland, Catholics, and friends, of course, to the Scottish queen, arose in open rebellion, with the avowed purpose of liberating Mary and restoring the popish religion. But this insurrection, though in the outset extremely formidable, sunk and died away like a fire of straw before the active and vigorous measures of Queen Elizabeth. The two leaders fled to Scotland, where Northumberland fell into the power of the regent, by whom he was imprisoned in Lochlever Castle. The Earl of Westmoreland escaped abroad, and died beyond seas. This unsuccessful attempt at rebellion greatly broke the power of the Catholics in England, and confirmed the sway of Elizabeth, as the bursting of an imposthume often restores the vigor of the human constitution.

Murray, strengthened by Elizabeth's arms, and bold in her protection, was taking measures to complete the subjugation of the queen's party, and negotiating to have Mary's own person delivered into his hands by the queen of England, when he lost his life by the vengeance of an individual. Hamilton of Bothwellhaugh, a man distinguished for a vindictive disposition in an age when revenge was accounted a virtue and a duty, had with many of that name been made prisoner at the battle of Langside. With the other captives he had been doomed to death after the battle, and, like others, he had received pardon from the regent. But though Bothwellhaugh had been thus far favorably treated, a separate property belonging to him had been declared forfeited, and was conferred by Murray upon one of his favorites, who, brutally eager to obtain possession, drove the wife of Bothwellhaugh, then recently delivered of a child, half naked into the fields, where she became ere morning furiously mad. Her husband vowed vengeance on the regent as the original author of the injury; and the Hamiltons, his kinsmen, who had so much reason to hate and fear the present ruler of Scotland, encouraged him by applauding and abetting his design. Having taken singularly accurate measures for effecting his purpose and his escape, he lurked in an empty lodging in the street of Linlithgow, mortally wounded the Earl of Murray by a shot from a carabine as he rode through the town, and, though closely pursued, got in safety to France.

There is every reason to suppose that the crime of an individual had been countenanced and prompted by the spirit of a faction as well as of a powerful family. On the very night when the murder was committed, Buccleuch and Farniherst, chiefs of the names of Scott and Kerr, borderers, of the queen's party, invaded England with unusual fury, with the purpose, doubtless, of producing a breach between the two nations. One of the depredators showed that the party were conscious of the act which had taken place; for being asked by an Englishman how he would answer that night's work to the regent, who was wont to be a terror to the border plunderers, he replied, "Tush, man! your regent is cold as the iron bit in my horse's mouth."

Thus died the Earl of Murray, still remembered by the commons of Scotland as the good regent, and not undeserving of the epithet; for making allowance for the stormy times in which he lived, his general character will bear comparison with most statesmen of the period. He was wise, brave, and successful in his enterprises; but his uncertain and insecure state led him into intrigues from which he could not honorably extricate himself; and Elizabeth did not hesitate, both in the affair of the Roundabout Raid and in extorting a confession of his intrigues with Norfolk, to subject him to a just charge of meanness and treachery. Sir James Melville blames rather the avarice of Morton and others than that of the regent himself for the acts of severity and rapacity which hastened his death; and although it was he who chiefly profited by the murder of Darnley and the ill-concocted intrigues of Bothwell, there is no proof that he was conscious of or accessory to those dark and treacherous transactions, further than the suspicion which must attach to a man of his consequence, who could scarcely be ignorant of important events when they were passing around him. There is something like coldness and ingratitude in his harsh conduct to a sister who had favored and promoted him, and who is said to have shed tears over his death. But the steadiness with which he prosecuted and established the work of the Reformation seems to have arisen from sincere conviction, and constitutes Regent Murray's best title to a place among the benefactors of his country.

CHAPTER XXX

Commencement of the Civil War—English Invasion—The Borderers
chastised—The House of Hamilton almost ruined—Dumbarton
Castle taken—Scotland divided between King's Men and Queen's
Men—Cruel Character of the War—State of Parties—Raid of
Stirling—Death of the Regent Lennox—Mar succeeds, and la-
bors for Peace, but shortly after dies—Morton chosen Regent—
His Character—Mary corresponds with Spain—Duke of Norfolk
beheaded—Queen Elizabeth publicly owns the Right of James
—The Civil Wars still rage; but the Party of the Queen declines
everywhere save in the North, where it is supported by the
Gordons—The Queen's Adherents capitulate, excepting Grainge,
who holds out Edinburgh Castle—He is besieged by an English
Force, and compelled to surrender—He is executed—Death of
Maitland of Lethington

ON the death of the Earl of Murray, both parties in
Scotland prepared for war. The faction adhering
to the infant monarch chose for regent, instead of
Murray, the Earl of Lennox, father of the murdered Darnley, and grandfather of James himself. His authority was
strongly supported by Elizabeth, who despatched two flying
armies into Scotland to avenge the mischief done upon the
frontiers, and to co-operate with the forces of the regent.
One of these, under the Earl of Sussex, severely chastised
the border clans of Scott and Kerr by ravaging their lands
and burning their houses. The other army was commanded
by Lord Scroope of Bolton. A third body of English, led
by Sir William Drury, assisted Lennox in laying waste the
vale of Clyde, and desolating the mansions of Hamilton,
rendered obnoxious to the king's party by the murder of
the late regent, and to Lennox himself, whose father had
been slain by one of that clan, by the bitterness of feudal
hatred. Their vengeance was urged with such unrelenting

fury that the great family, whom it affected, was in all its branches brought to the verge of ruin.

In 1571 another advantage was obtained by the king's party by an extraordinary feat of courage and dexterity. Crawford of Jordanhall, an enterprising officer, undertook the venturous exploit of storming the almost impregnable castle of Dumbarton, which had hitherto, during the variation of the civil war, remained in possession of the queen's partisan, the Lord Fleming. A handful of soldiers advanced to the foot of the rock on a misty evening. By means of ladders they ascended to a ledge of rock where they were able to keep their footing till they could draw up and replace the ladders so as to attain the bottom of the wall. In the second ascent, a soldier, when half way up the ladder, was seized with a fit of epilepsy. Crawford caused the man to be bound to the steps; then commanding the ladder to be turned, they mounted over the indisposed person's belly. Surmounting the wall, the assailants surprised the ill-watched garrison, who were too confident in the strength of the castle to keep a due guard, and carried the place by an attempt, the boldness of which was unequalled by the siege of the Numidian fortress mentioned by Sallust, or the more modern surprise of Fecamp, on the coast of Normandy, by Bois-Rosé during the wars of the League.

The archbishop of St. Andrew's, natural brother of the Duke of Chatelherault, was taken in the castle of Dumbarton, to which he had retreated for safety as to an impregnable place of refuge. This prelate was highly obnoxious to the king's party from his profession, his talents, and his family; and being already attainted by parliament, lay open to their severity, which was carried to the uttermost. They conveyed the archbishop to Stirling, where he was publicly hanged without trial or ceremony. That he deserved this fate is highly probable. He was proprietor of the fatal mansion called the Kirk of Field, in which Darnley was blown up, and of the no less fatal lodging at Linlithgow, from which the Regent Murray received his death-wound; and there was little doubt of his being on both occasions aware of the purpose which the lodgings were to be put to. But his execution, without even a semblance of trial, in the heat of a civil war, was calculated to add fuel to its fury, and became the example and justification of numerous atrocities practiced by way of retaliation.

The civil war was now widely kindled, and raged in every province; and the fatal distinction into king's men and queen's men divided even private families. The king's adherents held a parliament at Stirling. The queen's lords assumed the same title at Edinburgh; and these assemblies fulminated decrees of forfeiture against each other. Skirmishes were fought in every part of the kingdom; and as the parties threw on each other the imputation of rebellion, those taken in battle were only spared by the sword to perish by the gibbet; for each party in these desolating hostilities relentlessly executed their captives as traitors.

The historian, Hume of Godscroft, has left us a species of parallel, showing how the great peers and families in the different parts of Scotland were divided between the two factions. By this it appears that the preponderance of the feudal nobility was on the side of Queen Mary, though the strength which the king's men obtained from the support of the reformed party decided the civil war in favor of her son. First, there were of the queen's side the Duke of Chatelherault, the Earls of Argyle, Athole, Huntley, almost all petty princes in their several countries and shires; also the Earls of Crawford, Rothes, Eglinton, Cassilis, the Lord Herries, with all the Maxwells, Lochinvar, Johnstone, the Lords Seton, Boyd, Gray, Ogilvy, Livingston, Fleming, Oliphant, the sheriff of Ayr and Linlithgow, Buccleuch, Farniherst, and Tulliebardine. "The Lord Hume did also countenance them, though few of his friends or name were with him, save one mean man, Ferdinando of Broomhouse; Maitland, the secretary, a great politician, and Grainge, an approved soldier, who was captain of the castle, and provost of the town of Edinburgh, embraced Mary's party. They

had the chief castles and places of strength in their hands—
Edinburgh, Dumbarton, and Lochmaben. France did assist
them; Spain did favor them, and so did the pope, together
with all the Roman Catholics everywhere. The same faction in England was great: all the Duke of Norfolk's party,
papists and malcontents, had their eye upon Queen Mary.
Neither was she, though in prison, altogether unuseful to
her side; for besides her countenance, and color of her authority, which prevailed with some, she had her rents in
France, and her jewels, wherewith she both supported the
common cause and rewarded her private servants and followers. Especially these resources served her to furnish
agents and ambassadors to plead her cause, and importune
her friends at the courts of France and England, who were
helped by the banished lords, Dacres and Westmoreland, to
stir up foreign princes all they could. Thus was that party
now grown great, so that it might seem both safe and most
advantageous to follow it. The other was almost abandoned.
There were but three earls that took part with Morton at first
—Lennox, Mar, and Glencairn; neither were these comparable to any of the foremost four. In Fife there was the Lord
Lindsay, and Glammis in Angus—no very powerful men, and
no ways equal to Crawford and Rothes. The Lord Semple
was but a simple one in respect of Cassilis, Maxwell, Lochinvar, and others; Methven in Strathern, a very mean lord;
Ochiltree among the meanest that bare the title of a lord;
and yet Cathcart was meaner than he, both in men and
means. Neither was Ruthven so great but that Tulliebardine and Oliphant were able to overmatch him. They had
no castles but Stirling and Tantallon, which belonged to
Morton. The commons, indeed, were very forwardly set that
way; but how uncertain and unsure a prop is the vulgar?
England did befriend them sometimes, but not so fully as
they needed, and even so far as did concern their own
safety." [1]

---

[1] Hume of Godscroft's History of Douglas, Edinburgh, 1743, vol. ii.,
p. 199.

In this view of parties, the historian, desirous to rate the strength of the king's faction as low as possible, in order the more to exalt the talents and worth of those who gained the superiority against such odds, considerably undervalues the assistance afforded to the king's lords by the burghs and commons. Nor does he give due weight to the countenance of England, which ministered to the assistance of the regent by effectual supplies of troops and money; whereas the courts of France and Spain and other Catholic powers supported Queen Mary by little more than splendid promises. Nevertheless, Godscroft justly says that the factions were so balanced as to make success dubious and the bloodshed and strife great and universal. The whole inland country was agitated through every province by the contests of king's men and queen's men; and, to use an expression of the period, in the wild borders and savage Highlands, the Clan Gregor and the Clan Chattan in the north, Buccleuch and Farniherst in the south, were bounded out to ravage the neighboring country with the full fury of predatory war.

Amid this scene of slaughter and confusion, a military movement, contrived by the talent of Grainge, had nearly brought the war to an unexpected termination. A body of five hundred men were privately assembled at Edinburgh, under the command of the Earl of Huntley, Lord Claud Hamilton, younger son of the Duke of Chatelherault, and Scott of Buccleuch. They made a night march to Stirling, occupied the town without opposition, and breaking into the lodgings of the principal lords of the king's faction, as well as the regent himself, made them prisoners, and were about to conduct them to Edinburgh. The obstinacy of Morton, who defended his house till it was set on fire, and the rapacity and want of discipline of the soldiers, who broke their ranks for the purpose of plunder, gave the king's party an opportunity of rallying. The garrison marched out of the castle, and fired upon the invaders from some half-built houses which still stand in the same unfinished state across the top of the main street: the inhabitants of Stirling imme-

diately joined in the attack, and the assailants, taken by
surprise in their turn, began to fly. In the scuffle, a man,
by command it is said of Lord Claud Hamilton, shot the
Regent Lennox with a carabine, in revenge of the death of
the archbishop of St. Andrew's. The queen's party fled,
nor could the others pursue them, the border men, followers
of Buccleuch, having carried off all the horses they could
find in Stirling. Morton, who had previously surrendered
to Buccleuch, now took his captor, who was related to him,
under his protection as his prisoner, and dismissed him uninjured. If Grainge himself had led the assailants on this occasion, the enterprise, so successful in the commencement,
might probably have terminated in the entire ruin of the
king's party.

As it was, the loss of the Regent Lennox was a disad-
vantage which the king's nobles hastened to repair, by placing in the vacant situation John, earl of Mar. Just, moderate, and patriotic, this estimable nobleman endeavored
to establish peace between the contending parties in the
State; and it is said the deep regret which he felt at being
impeded by Morton, and others of his own party, in the
work of reconciliation, brought on the disease of which he
died, 29th October, 1572.

The Earl of Mar's successor in the regency was the old
friend of the Regent Murray, James, earl of Morton; and
no election could have been made more dangerous to those
who followed the cause of Mary. Morton possessed all
Murray's faults in an exaggerated degree, many of his
talents, but few or none of his virtues. He was ambitious,
but his ambition was of that sordid kind that is sullied by
avarice; and he was willing to stoop yet lower to win the
favor of Elizabeth than Murray himself would have bowed.
As a judge, he was accessible to bribery; as a soldier, he
was a stranger to mercy; and it was from his name that
those skirmishes, in which prisoners were regularly executed
on both sides, were called the Douglas wars. If we compare
the two regents in other respects, the religion of Murray

seems to have been sincere, while Morton's pretension to it was that of a hypocritical profligate. As a partisan, Morton was so deeply implicated in the dark secrets of Queen Mary's reign that he must have regarded her return to the throne as an era to be followed by his own total ruin. It was his interest to prevent this, by a complete and abject dependence on Queen Elizabeth. In his personal deportment he displayed many of the qualities of the great House of Douglas, from which he was descended, being brave, proud, politic, and haughty; generally feared, and little loved, through a long and despotic administration.

While Morton held the ostensible government of Scotland, he steered his course almost entirely by the suggestions of the queen of England; and that princess was now more than ever desirous that the affairs of Scotland should either continue in an embroiled state, or remain under the management of a statesman who was sure to govern them in all respects according to her interests, and diametrically opposite to those of Queen Mary, to whom she was more hostile than ever.

The causes for Elizabeth's additional resentment against her unfortunate prisoner arose out of circumstances which were the natural consequences of the injustice which had made her captive. Anxious to obtain the liberty of which she was unjustly deprived, Mary naturally turned her eyes to the princes of her own faith for support. France, divided by civil and religious quarrels, no longer listened to her complaints with interest; but Philip II. of Spain willingly agreed to send troops and money to invade England, assist the distressed English Catholics, and avow the quarrel of Queen Mary. His agent Ridolphi found a vigorous second in the bishop of Ross, the able defender of Queen Mary, and was listened to, at least, by the Duke of Norfolk.

This last nobleman had been just released from prison, upon pledging his solemn word never to renew his project of marriage with Queen Mary. But on obtaining his freedom he immediately resumed the perilous intrigues which his imprisonment had interrupted: letters and love tokens passed between him and the captive queen of Scotland. The intercourse between Norfolk and Mary, thus renewed on the duke's part, seems fatal to an argument in proof of Queen Mary's guilt, much relied upon by Dr. Robertson and others. The letters and proofs produced before the commission must, they said, have been genuine, since Norfolk expressed his belief in them. That he expressed something approaching to such an opinion is unquestionable. But, first, he had an obvious motive for deceiving Queen Elizabeth on the nature of his sentiments toward Mary; secondly, if we are to decide anything on Norfolk's opinion, it must be upon that opinion which he finally entertained at the period when he sought her hand; an overture which he would hardly have resumed, if he had credited or continued to believe in the authenticity of documents which accused her of adultery and murder.[1] This intercourse did not long escape the eager eyes of Elizabeth and Cecil. Norfolk was again arrested, tried, condemned, and executed for high treason. That Mary was the motive and mainspring of this conspiracy was undeniable; and Elizabeth was not generous enough to see that it resulted entirely from her own conduct, and the situation to which she had reduced her kinswoman. The queen of England now threw off all mask and disguise; and announcing to the world that Mary had held criminal correspondence with her subjects, she declared she would never consent to her release, and that she would lend avowed and direct aid to maintain King James on the throne.

Possessing the regency of Scotland, Morton speedily showed how much he was the devoted servant of England, by delivering up to Elizabeth the banished Earl of Northumberland, a nobleman to whom he had been personally obliged

---

[1] After all, the question is less whether the commissioners of Queen Elizabeth believed, or pretended to believe, the authenticity of these documents, as whether the documents were themselves worthy of belief —a question which the present age is more competent to decide than one in which the law of evidence was so ill understood.

during his residence in England, and who was beheaded at York, in 1572, for his rebellion in 1569. What rendered the regent's treachery more infamous was his acceptance of a reward in money for this service, which was shared between him and his cousin, the Laird of Lochleven, in whose island fortress Northumberland had been imprisoned. The regent's base compliance in this respect was humiliating, as compared with his predecessor, Murray, who, although he consented to detain Northumberland a captive, had resisted all Queen Elizabeth's requests for having him delivered up to her revenge.

In the meantime Scotland bled at every vein. In the west, Lord Claud Hamilton with infinite courage and zeal continued to uphold the sinking cause of Queen Mary. In the south, Buccleuch and Farniherst maintained the same side. In the north, Sir Adam Gordon, a son of that earl of Huntley who was killed in the battle of Corrichie, made war in the queen's behalf with distinguished success. Grainge defended the castle of Edinburgh with his characteristic intrepidity. But notwithstanding the efforts of her adherents, the queen's cause declined in Scotland in every quarter, save Aberdeenshire. At length Huntley and the Duke of Chatelherault consented to a treaty of peace, concluded at Perth the 23d of February, 1573. By this treaty they agreed to acknowledge the authority of the king and the regent, and confessed the illegal character of all that they had done in the name of the queen. On the other hand, they and their followers were promised indemnity and remission of such dooms of forfeiture as had been launched against them. The adherents of the queen in other parts of Scotland acceded to this capitulation; and thus the banner of Mary sunk on all sides, save where it continued to float over Edinburgh Castle.

The dauntless intrepidity of Kirkcaldy of Grainge might have held out that strong fortress against all the force which the regent could muster within Scotland, ill supplied as it was with the means and skill necessary to carry on sieges.

But, in conformity with her proclamation, Elizabeth sent Sir William Drury with a formidable train of artillery to assist in reducing the castle.   Kirkcaldy held out with firmness worthy of his high military reputation, till his walls were breached and shattered, his provisions expended, the well choked with ruins and inaccessible, and the artillery silenced.   At the last extremity he surrendered the place to Sir William Drury, on a general promise of favorable terms.   In this the English general had undertaken for more than he could make good.   By Elizabeth's orders Sir William Drury saw himself obliged to surrender his prisoners to the vindictive regent.   Morton caused the gallant Kirkcaldy and his brother to be executed at the cross of Edinburgh; and Lethington, so long the sharer of his counsels, would have experienced as little mercy had not he taken poison and died, according to the expression of a contemporary, a Roman death.

With the melancholy fate of Kirkcaldy, one of the boldest and most generous warriors, and Maitland, perhaps the most subtle and accomplished politician in Europe, we may conclude the history of Queen Mary's reign, since from that period no subject acknowledged her as sovereign.

CHAPTER XXXI

Oppressive Regency of Morton—He sets the Example of the Tulchan
Bishops, and thereby offends the Church—Tyrannizes over the
Nobility—Disobliges the young King—Battle of Reedsquair—
The King desires to assume the Government—Morton offers no
Opposition, but resigns the Regency, receiving in return an Act
of Indemnity—He surrenders the Castle of Edinburgh—Retires
to Dalkeith, and builds a Castle at Droich-holes in Tweedale—
Meditates, however, the Resumption of his Power—Instigates
the Earl of Mar to take Stirling Castle from his Uncle, and thus
acquires Possession of the King's Person and the supreme Place
in the Privy Council—Argyle and Athole levy Forces against
Morton, but an Accommodation is agreed upon—Two Favorites
arise at Court—The Character of the Duke of Lennox—That of
Stewart, afterward Earl of Arran—Morton's invidious Persecution of the Hamiltons—Morton is impeached by Stewart—
Tried, condemned, and executed

THE kingdom of Scotland, exhausted both in property
and population, might have enjoyed a state of repose
similar to the stupefaction of an exhausted patient,
had it not been disturbed by the arbitrary and oppressive
actions of the regent. Though affecting zeal for the Protestant doctrines, he disobliged the Church of Scotland by a
device which he had invented to secure in the hands of the
secular nobility the lands and revenues of the Catholic
clergy. For this purpose he nominated to the archbishopric
of St. Andrew's a poor clergyman named Douglas, taking
his obligation to rest satisfied with a very small annuity out
of the revenues of the see, and to account for the residue
to his patron, the regent himself. This class of bishops, instituted for the purpose of cloaking some powerful lay lord
in the enjoyment of the emoluments of the see, was face-

tiously called Tulchan[1] prelates; and both the clergy and
their hearers execrated Morton's avarice, which had introduced the simoniacal practice.

The nobility were no less irritated against the regent and
his authority. The Earls of Argyle and Athole having quarrelled with each other, and arming on both sides, the regent,
by a very judicious exercise of the royal power, compelled
them to disband their forces. But while Morton meditated
how he might render their discord profitable to himself, by
bringing a charge of treason against two such powerful
potentates, they discovered his purpose, and, reconciled by
mutual danger, united their interest against the regent and
his power. In short, Morton, confident in the support of
Queen Elizabeth, became careless of maintaining favor with
the youthful king, or popularity with the Scottish nation;
and he had not held the regency for five years when a
scheme was laid to deprive him of it. A chance rendered
doubtful his receiving aid even from England.

The long slumbering spirit of hostility between the kingdoms broke out during his regency with an explosion so sudden that it had wellnigh cost Morton, the most devoted of
Elizabeth's partisans, the forfeiture of her protection. On
the 3d of May, 1575, a march meeting for the redress of
mutual grievances was held between Sir John Foster,
warden of the west marches of England, a particular favorite of Elizabeth, and Sir John Carmichael, an esteemed
follower of the Regent Morton, whom he had named keeper
of the middle marches of Scotland. The wardens, each supported by the most warlike clans of their districts, met at
a place called the Reedsquair, on the frontier between the
kingdoms, and near the source of the water of Reed. The
persons against whom the English had made complaints
had been delivered up according to custom; but when the

---

[1] When a cow had lost her calf it was customary to flay the calf
and stuff its skin with straw, that, being placed before the mother, it
might induce her to part freely with her milk. This was called a Tulchan, and its resemblance to the stipendiary bishops introduced by
Morton is sufficiently evident.

same justice was demanded on the Scottish part, there was an individual malefactor missing. Carmichael demanded delivery of the man with some warmth. Foster answered haughtily, and bid him match himself with his equals. This spark was enough to produce a blaze in an atmosphere so inflammable. The men of Tynedale, the fiercest of the English borderers, shot off a volley of arrows among the Scottish, who, surprised and greatly inferior in numbers, began to retreat. At this moment the array of the citizens of Jedburgh was discovered advancing to the place of conflict: the ranks of the Scots were restored; and the parties joined battle with the slogan, or war-cry, of "To it, Tynedale!" answered by that of "Jeddart's here!" The English arrows were requited by a volley of bullets, the Scots being superior in firearms. The fortune of the day was effectually turned: the English retired, rallied, and finally fled, leaving their leader, Sir John Foster, with Sir Cuthbert Collingwood, and other gentlemen of distinction, prisoners. Sir George Heron of Chipchase, with several other Englishmen, were slain.

The prisoners were sent to the regent at his castle of Dalkeith. Morton immediately set himself to anticipate the consequences of Elizabeth's resentment. He loaded the English captives with attention and kindness, and dismissed them with honor and without ransom. Gifts, too, were also bestowed, to assuage their angry feelings; but as Scottish falcons were among the presents bestowed on them, a facetious Scottish borderer could not help asking them the insulting question, whether they did hold themselves kindly treated since they got *live hawks* for *dead Herons?*

Elizabeth was incensed, but saw the right was with the Scottish; and was besides aware that it was not her interest to break terms with her friend and faithful vassal, the regent. Sir John Carmichael was despatched to England, to make his own defence, where he was honorably received and safely dismissed. This skirmish was the last of any note between the nations of England and Scotland.

Meantime the intrigues against Morton, at the Scottish

court, continued to proceed.   James VI., now twelve years
of age, March 4, 1578, was easily inspired with the idea
that he was fit to take the sceptre into his own custody;
and, encouraged by the suggestions of those around him,
resolved to summon a general council of his nobles to put
an end, by their sanction, to Morton's regency.   The nobility attended the king's summons with such readiness as to
show they were both numerous and powerful enough to second the wishes of the sovereign.   Morton, surprised at the
explosion of this confederacy, made far less resistance to it
than could have been expected either from a statesman of his
experience or from a warrior of his talents and resources.
It seems that he thought it most prudent to give way to the
first impulse of his enemies; and keeping upon his guard,
and attending to the safety of his person, was determined to
wait until opportunity should offer of recovering his power
by some revolution as secret and sudden as that which had
deprived him of it.

With this view, he retired into the castle of Lochleven,
choosing that strength for his safety which had lately been
the prison of Queen Mary: here he was visited by his own
allies of the Douglas family and others who had remained
attached to his government.   In the meantime the king
summoned a parliament, or rather a council of his nobles,
to which those who were opposed in politics to Morton, with
an equally great number who conceived they had reason to
complain of his personal severity or injustice to them, resorted, in hopes of redress or revenge.   On this assembly
many of Morton's friends also gave attendance, and, in
appearance at least, deserted the sinking cause of their old
leader.

The young king's government being thus apparently
strong, he caused it to be intimated to Morton that it was
his purpose to deprive him of his regency, and call him to
account for his conduct while he held the office.   Intimidated by these threatened measures of severity, Morton carried his submission to this new party in the State further

perhaps than he had himself originally intended. On March 12, 1578, he went to Dalkeith, and thence to Edinburgh, in company with the Lord Glammis, the new chancellor, and Lord Herries, the peers by whom the king had intimated his unfavorable intentions; and rendered himself a personal witness of the proclamation of the king's acceptance of the government into his own hands. Morton conducted himself, apparently, in the most dutiful manner: perceiving, as he said, "that wisdom and goodness which did perpetually increase in the king, and fully supplied the defect of years," he voluntarily resigned to him his full power and authority as regent. By this submissive conduct the earl obtained one advantage which he probably considered as of great consequence. An act of indemnity was passed in his favor, which, in the fullest and most ample form, pardoned the Earl of Morton whatever acts of illegal violence he had committed in the exercise of his authority, and ratified in the king's name his whole conduct as regent. No precaution was omitted which could render this act of indemnity so ample and explicit as hereafter to afford the late regent an effectual protection against any future accusation founded upon delicts committed during his government or in ascending to it. Nevertheless, we shall find that the intended security was not fully obtained.

The castle of Edinburgh was still in the hands of the regent, who was well inclined to have kept that fortress under his own power, and would willingly have had the king take up his lodgings within its ramparts. As this, however, would have been voluntarily to continue under the tutelage of the Earl of Morton, James would not give ear to the proposal unless the castle should be surrendered to such keeper as he should himself appoint; and Morton found it necessary, after some show of defence, to yield up that key of the metropolis to the lawful sovereign.

The late regent, thus reduced to the state of a private nobleman, took up his residence at his strong castle of Dalkeith, within about six miles of Edinburgh; where he apparently busied himself with his private affairs, and the management of his extensive estates. About this time, too, he constructed amid the mountains of Tweedale a house of strength or of retreat, called Droich-holes. It is a large and massive building, strongly situated, and so fortified that the regent might have defended it with safety, in case of emergency, until he should receive relief from his friends in England; he did not, however, live to complete this edifice, of which the frowning ruins still remain, the singular relics of a castle which was never completed or inhabited.

The general opinion of the mode in which the late regent passed his time was expressed by the name of *The Lion's Den*, which the common people bestowed upon the castle of Dalkeith. The lords who had succeeded to the management of the State entertained the same terror of Morton's secret intentions as was expressed by the common people in the name which they gave to his habitation: all expected the moment when the old lion should again burst from his retirement and make the kingdom tremble at his roar.

Accordingly it appears that Morton secretly engaged a part of the family of Mar and their dependents to resume forcible possession of the king's person. This was to be accomplished in an enterprise which Morton so conducted that it opened the way to the restoration of his own power, although at first it had the appearance only of a feud between the young earl and his uncle, Alexander Erskine. The Countess of Mar and the young earl had seen with impatience Alexander, called the Master of Mar, act as governor of the castle and guardian of the king's person, and they were easily instigated to an attempt to deprive their relative of the power of exercising those honorable offices which belonged to the nephew by hereditary right. Their suspicions were grossly unjust; for there is no reason to believe that Alexander Erskine was moved by other than the fairest motives in acting in behalf of his nephew, a youth who was not twenty. They found ready acceptance, however, with an ambitious woman and a petulant youth. But

Morton, it has been supposed, persuaded the Earl of Mar to seize upon Stirling, that he himself might find the opportunity once more to obtain possession of the king's person. He proposed to remove James, it was said, from Stirling to his own family stronghold of Lochleven Castle, the jail successively of the dethroned Mary and the betrayed Northumberland, where Morton might hope to detain the king's person in honorable captivity until he should attain to perfect age, or for as much longer a space as he himself should be disposed to rule in his name. In this plot Morton engaged the Earl of Mar and his mother; and so far as the seizure of Stirling Castle the enterprise succeeded with perfect ease. The uncle had no suspicion of his nephew or sister-in-law, who found, therefore, little difficulty in gaining possession of a fortress garrisoned by their own followers, who yielded ready obedience to their young lord and his mother. Thus the insurgents, or rather Morton, by whose counsel they acted, made themselves again masters of the king's person, expelling from the fortress the Earl of Argyle, Alexander Erskine, called the Master of Mar, and others who had been active in the measures against Morton. And thus this wily politician, having resumed his seat in the privy council, soon obtained the complete ascendency in that body, and was again placed at the head of affairs in Scotland.

But the Earl of Morton's power was too generally dreaded to enable him with ease to re-establish the fabric which had been already so sorely shaken. He felt that the parliament which had been summoned would not be satisfied without the king's presence, and that any attempt to remove James's person to the lake-surrounded tower of Lochleven must necessarily be regarded as an act of open rebellion. On the other hand, to trust James in the metropolis, where Morton was conscious of his own unpopularity, was to give the king an opportunity, supported as he was sure to be by the citizens, to throw off his yoke and destroy his authority forever.

The Earl of Morton endeavored to compromise these difficulties by a proclamation changing the place of convening

the parliament from Edinburgh to Stirling, where the possession of the castle gave him the means of detaining the
king within his power. Athole, Argyle, and the other enemies of Morton, arose in arms against this proposal. "The
king," they said, "was once more the prisoner of a Douglas,
who meant to seclude him from the rest of the nobility, and
detain him in captivity, while he ruled under his name."

They speedily raised about four thousand men, at the
head of whom they asserted that they meant to fight for
the liberty of the sovereign. The king, like his grandfather
James V. in the same circumstances, was obliged to lend his
name to proclamations, and troops marched, as if by his authority, against the noblemen to whom in his heart he wished
success, and whose insurrection he considered as good service.
The Earl of Angus, Morton's nephew, advanced against Argyle and Athole, at the head of forces equal to their own. A
bloody battle and the renewal of the civil wars seemed to be
impending.

Both parties were, however, unwilling to plunge once
more into the state of civil confusion, war, and bloodshed,
from which the country had so lately emerged. They made
an agreement upon the field of expected battle, by which the
enterprise of Argyle and Athole was acknowledged as good
service: the earls were themselves received into the king's
presence, and some alterations were made in the privy council, by which an accommodation of parties seemed for the
time to have taken place.

By this coalition, Morton's scheme of retaining the king
under his separate and sole guardianship was rendered altogether abortive. James was, it is true, still hampered and
limited by the influence of Morton in his councils; but after
this union of parties the earl was no longer possessed of his
former despotic authority.

The king himself had tasted the sweets of independence,
and longed to regain it. If he himself had been indifferent
upon so interesting a subject, there were two persons who
shared his secret thoughts, upon whom he had conferred a

species of unlimited confidence, and who, for the preservation of their own power and court interest, lost no opportunity to animate his displeasure against the veteran statesman
who had twice reduced his sovereign to a species of nullity.
These were men of very different talents and character, agreeing only in their apparent attachment to the person of the
sovereign and their enmity to the Earl of Morton.

The first of them in rank was Esme Stewart, termed the
Lord d'Aubigne. He was the son of a second brother of
Matthew, earl of Lennox, and consequently near cousin to
the king by his father, Lord Darnley. Lord Esme was a
graceful, well-accomplished gentleman, and had been educated in France, where he professed the Catholic religion,
which, however, when he came to Scotland, he exchanged
for the Protestant faith. Notwithstanding his conversion
he had never the good fortune to obtain the belief of the
Scottish churchmen in his sincerity. They considered him
as having professed himself a Protestant rather from temporal policy than religious motives, and they dreaded his
intimacy with, and influence over, the king, as likely to be
secretly employed in behalf of the court of France and the
Church of Rome. In temper the young favorite was candid,
liberal, generous and well-disposed, but he was entirely ignorant of Scottish affairs, and unable to decide as a statesman
in public business of any kind. This young nobleman the
king raised by hasty steps to the highest pinnacle of promotion, until he became Duke of Lennox, captain of the royal
guard, first lord of James's bedchamber, and lord high chamberlain; offices which required his constant attendance on
the king, and invested him in a great measure with the
protection of the royal person.

The Duke of Lennox's associate in the king's favor was
a man of meaner birth and pretensions, yet by no means,
as has been surmised, of ignoble lineage: he was James
Stewart, usually called Captain Stewart, the second son of
Lord Ochiltree, a family of some distinction among the numerous branches which claimed alliance with the royal house.

Stewart had those talents which are generally supposed to make way for their possessors at a court. He was ambitious to the highest degree, yet capable of stooping in order to catch an opportunity to rise: he was bold, daring, profligate, and unscrupulous, and possessed the art of making his own insinuations, however wicked and unprincipled, acceptable to men of better minds and morals than himself; and among such were to be reckoned the king and the Duke of Lennox. No religious feelings of any kind shackled the boldness of this adventurer's attempts; and he was equally devoid of that steady sagacity and respect for general opinion which often serves instead of a conscience to such politicians as are not fortunate enough to have any. It was he who animated both the king and Lennox to the violent proceedings against Morton, and promoted other steps which were less justifiable, either upon the score of justice or expediency.

It cannot be supposed that a statesman so sagacious as Morton was unaware of the peril to his own power attending the rise of these two young men, who must necessarily have felt the existence of his authority as tending to eclipse that of the monarch and their own. But he no longer possessed that unlimited ascendency by which he had the power of excluding from the king's company and intimacy any person whose favor might awaken his jealousy. He was obliged to keep measures with the monarch and with his favorites, the rather that he knew himself obnoxious to the courtiers in general, and especially to some of his own former friends. He was compelled, therefore, to witness the growth of a party who he was conscious looked upon him with jealous hatred, and loaded him with odious imputations.

A circumstance, probably casual, afforded ground in that suspicious age for much clamor against him—this was the death of the Earl of Athole, the chancellor, appointed to that high office upon the slaughter of Lord Glammis, who was slain in a fray between his domestics and those of the Earl of Crawford. Athole's decease took place shortly after a banquet given by Mar and Morton, chiefly to the statesmen of the opposite faction, and was, therefore, almost of course ascribed to poison. No inquiry was made; but the belief that Athole had died by Morton's crime was generally entertained.

It was not less unfavorable to the safety of the late regent that he was supposed to lend himself to the aid of Elizabeth in a species of policy of which she was believed very capable. The purpose of securing James, the heir of her kingdom, in her own strong possession, and of governing Scotland by Morton, or by some other satellite of the English interest, was regarded as a course of policy which she was inclined to follow, and in which Morton, it was supposed, would have been a ready instrument of her pleasure. Measures were hastily taken to secure the king against the danger of his person being seized and sent to England by the contrivance of his too powerful minister, alleged to be the willing tool of so dangerous an ally. The office of lord high chamberlain, as the immediate guardian of the king's person, was revived, as we have seen, in the person of the Duke of Lennox; that of deputy chamberlain was granted to Alexander Erskine, the Master of Mar, and the command of the king's guard, reinforced and carefully cleared of all suspicious persons, was intrusted to Captain James Stewart, all of them enemies to the Earl of Morton.

Fortified by these circumstances the cabal of Morton's foes, for public and private reasons, became so strong that little was wanting save a plausible point of accusation upon which the late regent might be brought to capital trial.

The veteran statesman's own avarice and overweening arrogance had excited new odium ever since his accommodation with Argyle and Athole. The cause was as follows: Morton's ancient hereditary enemies of the House of Hamilton had begun once again to raise their heads, notwithstanding the severity with which they had been treated by the Regent Lennox, assisted by the forces of Elizabeth in the year 1575. The Duke of Chatelherault had been several years dead; his eldest son, the Earl of Arran, had showed symptoms of derangement early in Queen Mary's time, and had never since recovered from his mental disease; but the duke had two younger sons, John, who was in possession of the family property, and Claud, titular abbot of Paisley. Both, but especially the latter, had made a distinguished figure in the support of Queen Mary's cause during the civil wars; and Morton, whose revenge as well as avarice were insatiable, directed the most vindictive measures. Specious pretexts were found in their accession, which was more than suspected, to the murder of Regent Murray, who was shot by Hamilton of Bothwellhaugh, one of their kinsmen, and to that of Lennox at the raid of Stirling, where Lord Claud himself had been present, and which was said to be done by his express command. The deeds were no doubt culpable in proportion to the dignity of the high persons that were slain. Yet if such facts, occurring in the heat of so bloody a civil war, were allowed as fair subjects of prosecution after arms had been laid down on mutual agreement, it was clear that the wounds of internal discord could never have been stanched. Morton, however, having determined to avenge himself upon the devoted Hamiltons, proceeded against them as outlawed traitors, ravaging their estates, which he afterward caused to be formally confiscated by parliament. The Lords John and Claud Hamilton escaped to England; and the alleged crime, of which they had neither been tried nor found guilty, was, with equal injustice and cruelty, visited upon their insane brother, the Earl of Arran, who had been all along in confinement, and had no accession to their guilt, even if in his disturbed state of mind he could have been made legally responsible for his actions. Doom of forfeiture was, nevertheless, pronounced against him; and this irregular and rapacious proceeding stirred up new enemies against Morton, who had already upon his hands a faction much stronger than he was able to contend with. All these lay waiting for a day of vindictive retaliation, which failed not at length to arrive.

We have said that Morton was covered, as if with a coat of mail, by the act of parliament which ratified the acts of his regency, and authenticated and pardoned all such breaches of law as he might have committed in the course of his government. But the ingenious hatred of Captain James Stewart discovered a flaw in this panoply. That Morton was in some degree associated with Bothwell in the murder of Henry Darnley had always been alleged; and it was positively given in evidence by those subaltern agents of Bothwell who died for the crime that Archibald Douglas, titular parson of Glasgow, the earl's relative and confidant, and a busy agent in many of the dark and bloody transactions of the time, was present at the guilty act. This was averred, with the addition of a precise circumstance, that Douglas, in his hurry to effect his escape, had left one of his slippers behind him. From this had been deduced as a consequence that Archibald's friend, relative, and patron, Morton, must have been a member of the conspiracy, the more especially as he continued to favor and protect his kinsman Douglas. Now the act of ratification and indemnity in favor of the Earl of Morton, while it contained the most copious remission of almost every other species of state crime, could not with decency have included a pardon, on the part of James, for the murder of his own father, and on this point, therefore, the late regent remained open to accusation and trial.

So very execrable were the politics of that time that even the process instituted by a son for obtaining the punishment of his father's murderer was conducted in a manner which allied it to the vulgar proverb—that it was a staff discovered for the express purpose of beating a dog, or in plain English, that the charge was insisted upon not out of regard for Darnley's memory, or the lawful and natural desire of punishing his violent and cruel murder, but for the purpose of depriving the hated Earl of Morton of his estate, honors, and life.

The ready agent in this tragedy was Captain James

Stewart, a man whom we have already described as being equally bold, profligate, and unconscientious. When the king was seated in full council he appeared before them, and, falling upon his knees, impeached the Earl of Morton as being art and part of (that is, accessory to) the murder of the late king, Henry Darnley, and offered to make good the charge, under the usual penalties if he should fail in his proof. Morton, with a disdainful smile, referred to the services which he had done the crown, and the severity with which he had prosecuted the murderers of Darnley, and offered to stand to his defence on that charge in any competent court. Stewart was about to reply, when the king imposed silence on both, and commanded Morton to be put into custody until an opportunity of trial should be given in due and lawful form. At the same time he directed a warrant to be issued for the apprehension of Archibald Douglas, who fled into England, and thus escaped prosecution.

The Earl of Angus, Morton's nephew, seeing the violent course which was pursued against his uncle, offered to raise the forces of his family, and make a desperate attempt for his rescue. Morton, however, proudly forbade all armed interference, saying, he would perish a thousand times rather than it should be supposed he was unwilling to face a fair trial.

Elizabeth, also, who foresaw the loss she must sustain in a Scottish minister so accommodating and deferential to her will as the Earl of Morton, sent a threatening message to the king, by an ambassador of the name of Randolph. She remonstrated against the favor conferred upon young Lennox, desiring that he might be expelled from Scotland as an enemy to both countries. She demanded that Morton, Angus, and their followers, should be restored to honor and favor, and adopted, on the whole, a menacing tone of language, which she supported by a display of troops at Berwick and Northumberland, under the command of the Earl of Huntingdon and Lord Hunsdon.

These menaces were ill qualified to serve their purpose:

they awakened the indignation of James, and roused the spirit of the Scottish nation. The king instantly assembled forces in his turn, and sent a messenger demanding to know explicitly whether the queen of England desired to have peace or war. Elizabeth, long accustomed to dictate in Scottish affairs, and to be obeyed without remonstrance, was not prepared for so spirited and independent an answer: she withdrew her troops from the frontiers, and left Morton to the fate which her interference had probably accelerated.

The earl was brought to trial, under circumstances indicating an unusual contempt of the established forms of justice. During the proceedings against him, his accuser, James Stewart, by an act of royal favor, which seemed to prejudge the question between them, was advanced to the honor and estates of the Earl of Arran. There was something very iniquitous in the manner by which he attained this dignity. The spoils in which the minion of James VI. thus dressed himself were the property and title of that unfortunate Earl of Arran, the custody of whom had been granted to the same James Stewart, with the burden of maintaining the insane earl out of his own estate; a burden which he had discharged in a manner scandalously parsimonious. By the oppressive proceedings of Morton himself against the whole family of Hamilton lately narrated, which extended as well against the lunatic earl as his brothers John and Claud, this earldom of Arran had become forfeited to the crown, although its possessor, even if he had been guilty of a crime, of which there was no proof attempted, could not in his state of mind have been a proper subject of punishment. And now, his title and fortune, of which he had been deprived by one rapacious minister, became the prey of another equally unjust and profligate.

It is remarked by historians that Morton, with the credulity of that age, had an anxious recollection of an ancient prophecy, which declared "that the bloody heart should fall by the mouth of Arran." This the regent interpreted to mean the downfall of the Douglases, designed, as was usual in such vaticinations, by their well-known cognizance, and that by means of an Earl of Arran. This, it is said, was the reason for his pressing the unfortunate family of Hamilton, who were the legitimate proprietors of that title, almost to their total destruction. When, therefore, he heard that the earldom of Arran was conferred upon his accuser, Stewart, he replied, with a surprised and desponding expression, "Is it even so? Then I know what I must expect."

When Morton was brought to his trial at Edinburgh, large bodies of men were drawn up in different parts of the city to overawe the friends of the accused. The records of the trial are lost, but there is evidence that the assize consisted in many instances of the earl's personal enemies; and that, although he challenged them on that score, his remonstrances were not attended to. His servants were also put to the torture in no common manner; for Arran thought it necessary, after the earl's execution, to sue out an immunity for the violence to which they had been subjected.

When Morton heard the indictment read he did not show surprise or emotion; but when the verdict of the jury brought him in guilty of concealing, or being art and part in the murder of Henry Darnley, he repeated, with considerable vehemence, "Art and part! art and part! God knows it is not so."

In his conferences with the clergy he more fully explained what he meant by this exclamation. He confessed to them that upon his (Morton's) return from England after his exile, for accession to Rizzio's death, the Earl of Bothwell had proposed to him, both personally and through the medium of his kinsman Archibald Douglas, to be concerned in the death of Darnley, assuring him it was a deed which had the queen's approbation. Morton stated that he had replied to this proposal, "that having so lately been released from a state of exile, he would not be implicated in such an important matter unless Bothwell would produce to him the queen's sign-manual in warrant of the deed."—"The Earl of Bothwell," he said, "promised to produce him such an assurance, but never did so, and therefore he remained a stranger to the conspiracy; excepting that he knew generally that such an action was meditated by Bothwell and others."

The condemned earl was naturally asked by his reverend visitors why, having become privy to so horrible a conspiracy, he did not take measures for unfolding the plot and preventing its execution. "To whom," replied the earl, "should I have made the discovery? If to the queen, she was herself at the bottom of the deadly plot; if to Lethington, or other statesmen of the time, they were accomplices to the execution; if to Darnley, he was a creature of so weak and fickle a temper that he would have communicated it to his wife, and in any case I should have been inevitably ruined." Thus far the apology seems reasonable, though it gives us a horrible idea of the court and councils of Scotland at the time.

But Morton had less to answer when his ghostly assistants demanded of him why he continued to show friendship and favor to Archibald Douglas, who had acted on this occasion as the confidant of Bothwell, and was generally averred to have been personally present at the murder, and whom, notwithstanding, he created a judge of the court of session? Nor was any satisfactory reply, which could be consistent with Morton's pretended abhorrence of the tragedy of the Kirk of Field, ever returned to this question.

Sentence of death immediately followed upon the Earl of Morton's being found guilty. He slept soundly on the night previous to his execution, and went through the services of religion with apparent devotion. On the morning, having received intimation that all things were ready for the execution, "I praise God," said he, "I am ready likewise."

As the fallen statesman who had once been so pre-eminent was conducted to the cross of Edinbugh, which was the place of execution, the mendicants craved alms of him; and he was compelled to borrow the sum of twenty shillings Scots to obtain the means of bestowing it, so low were reduced those hoards of wealth, the amassing of which had been one of the principal causes of this great noble's catastrophe. He met his death with the same determined courage that he had often displayed in battle; and it was remarked with interest by the common people that he suffered decapitation by a rude guillotine of the period which he himself during his administration had introduced into Scotland from Halifax: it was called *The Maiden.*

It was never known in what way Morton's treasure had been disposed of: some traditions report it to be still in existence concealed among the vaults of the castle of Dalkeith; but a more probable rumor states it to have been delivered over to his nephew Angus, and by him expended in the support of those who, after the Raid of Ruthven, shared his exile in England. To this the earl is supposed to have alluded, June 2, 1581, when, paying out a final sum of money for the behoof of those distressed persons, he observed, "It was all gone at last; and that, considering by what means it had been amassed, he had never expected to see it produce so much good."

The character of Morton shows dark even among the gloomy portraits of the period. When we have said that he was undauntedly brave and acutely sagacious, almost all his great qualities are set forth. His ambition could hardly be gratified with power, nor his avarice with money; and he united a degree of selfish profligacy with great pretensions to religious zeal. Yet his death was so conducted as to resemble a judicial murder; and the ministers who succeeded to James's favor made Morton's sway regretted, since, with all his looseness of principle, they wanted his good sense and political talent.

CHAPTER XXXII

THE death of the Earl of Morton restored the king in the full sense of the word to the management of his own affairs, in which it was his pleasure to use almost exclusively the advice and ministry of the Duke of Lennox and James Stewart, the new Earl of Arran. It is, therefore, now a proper time to make some observations upon the character of James VI., who, though in genius and disposition inferior to many of his long line of ancestors, was destined, by uniting in his person the crowns of England and Scotland, to attain a pitch of power which none of them before his mother's accession could have been entitled even to dream of.

It happens, in general, at least among civilized people, that accidents connected with the corporeal and outward frame alone seldom produce much influence upon the mind: nothing can be more common than to see a vigorous mind in a feeble frame, and a gallant resolution ill seconded by a puny person. In the case of James VI., however, this was extremely different; for a considerable part of that prince's habits and tone of thought and feeling may be traced to the consequences of the brutal assault upon Rizzio, committed in his mother's presence two months ere yet he beheld the light. A weakness in his limbs, which he never entirely recovered, gave him a singular, odd, ungainly, and circuitous mode of walking, diametrically opposite to that which we connect with the movements of majesty. The same shocking scene, probably, gave rise to a nervous timidity, by which James was affected to a ludicrous degree. It was remarked of him, that different not only from the disposition of his fathers, but from that of his mother Mary, who could look with an unshrinking eye upon all the array of war, James wanted the most ordinary personal courage, a virtue, and one is sometimes tempted to suppose the only one, of that age. The king could never behold a naked sword without shrinking, and he turned away his head even from that very pacific weapon which he was obliged to draw for the purpose of bestowing the *accolade* on a knight dubbed with unhacked rapier and from carpet-consideration. The same species of timidity ran through his whole mind and actions, like an extensive flaw in a rich piece of tapestry, defacing and rendering of little value that which would have otherwise been rare and precious. Thus, while nature had given him a sound and ready judgment, and a wit which was sometimes even brilliant, she withheld from him that accurate knowledge of propriety which is manifested in applying to its proper place, or using in its fit time, either what is serious or what is humorous, without which tact or sense of propriety wisdom sinks into a vender of proverbs, and wit into a mere buffoon. To remedy, if possible, these natural defects, James's education had been seduluously cared for; his tutor, George Buchanan, being not only one of the best scholars of the age, but capable of rivalling the purest classics in the composition of their own beautiful language. In this art he accomplished his pupil James, just up to that point where strength and vigor of thought is demanded to give animation to language, but unfortunately he could conduct the royal student no further. The ordinary subtleties of scholastic learning were easily comprehended by a mind which delighted in ingenious trifling; but a timorous disposition cannot form ideas of dignity and resolution, nor, of course, can a timorous mind frame, or a hesitating tongue give utterance to, a daring conclusion.

Yet it must be owned there were periods of James's life in which awakened pride and natural talent assumed the appearance of firmness and presence of mind, authorizing us, perhaps, to suppose that his want of courage arose from the defects of his nerves, which upon great occasions might be supplied by the energies of his mind, rather than from actual cowardice; which intellectual failing must always be most predominant when the danger is greatest.

In his ideas of government it naturally followed that James was influenced by his own situation; by his consciousness that his elevation to the crown had taken place neither from affection or respect to his person, but from the desire to obtain under the shadow of his authority an opportunity of dethroning his mother. This consciousness generated an apprehension, lest, through means of some conspiracy among his subjects, he should, in his turn, be overtaken by a fate similar to that which had banished his mother from Scotland, and occasioned her being confined as a prisoner in a foreign land. His fears on this score had been increased during the stern rule of Morton, who had, with singular imprudence, neglected the obvious means by which the pride and vanity of the youthful monarch might have been reconciled to his condition, through an ostensible show of respect and deference.

It may be added, that James, both from situation and taste, was very much disposed to study and to acquiesce in the numerous works at this time current in Europe, which argued in behalf of the despotic and unimpeachable authority of monarchs, as the direct delegates of Heaven, and as accountable for the use of their power to that divine authority alone by whom that power was conferred.

But though this species of reasoning in one point of view led James to a conclusion which was doubtless highly agreeable to him, yet in another, and that one of great importance, it might have been fatal to his right of immediate possession of the crown of Scotland. In the first place, his right had been, during his infancy, set up and maintained by a party who had assumed the government, issued laws, and even struck money in his name, expressing, as a fixed principle, that the control of the sovereign lay with the subjects; and that he might be resisted by them so soon as he ceased to use his authority for the public good. His own right resting on such a foundation, it could not escape so acute an observer as James that, in assuming and defending an opposite doctrine, he ran the risk of provoking that large and strong body of his subjects who had placed him on the throne, together with the whole clergy of Scotland, upon whose suffrages his right had been established, and by whose exertions it had been maintained.

But, secondly, if James had adopted in action, as he probably did in theory, the doctrines of arbitrary power and unchallengeable authority, however flattering in the abstract, he might incur not only the probability of alienating the affections and loyalty of the nobles and clergy by whom his government had been established, and by whose internal strength, as well as their close connection with England, it had been originally supported, but the certainty of losing the favor and support of those among his subjects who from interest or conviction might, like himself, rely upon hereditary right. It could not escape him that such right was not in himself, but that the doctrine which proclaimed it indefeasible must pronounce that it was still vested in the person of his unfortunate mother Mary.

Thus the theoretical pretensions of James to rule by divine right were at absolute variance with the mode in which he ascended, and the title by which he held the throne; and his natural indecision of temper was augmented by the difficulty of reconciling his own ideas of the right of a king *de jure* to his real condition of a monarch *de facto*. The consequence of such a collision happening in the person of a prince of an irresolute temper necessarily produced a vacillating and indefinite species of conduct, which led each faction in turn to suppose that the king was of their party. And although the indecision and inconsistency arising from this cause rendered James's conduct less respectable than that of a more daring and determined prince, yet it must be owned that this system of action, cloaked by bold words, and occasionally evincing some firmness, seemed rather the fruit of policy than timidity, and had the effect of excluding neither party from hope of his favor, and inducing all to abstain from violent measures against a prince whom none could regard as their declared enemy, though at the same time no one was entitled to consider him as their exclusive head and protector. The same uncertainty of conduct, the same good-natured pliability, rendered James, at a later part of his reign, disposed, as we shall see, to cultivate the good opinion of the various factions in England, in order to unite in his own behalf their different votes for the succession.

Thus the first monarch of Britain may be said to have reaped from his flexibility of temper the advantage claimed by the versatile Earl of Pembroke, when he accounted for his being a favorite through various mutations of Church

VOL. II.   5 ❧

and State during four reigns, from Henry VIII. downward, by confessing that he was born of the willow, not of the oak, or, in other words, that he had been a dexterous and unblushing time-server.

The same want of manly firmness in James VI. is to be discovered in his habits of favoritism. Wherever such attachment exists, it resembles some creeping plant striving to support itself by that firmness on the part of another which it does not find within itself; and like such parasite plants, also, James was not very nice in selecting the prop by help of which he proposed to raise and sustain his own resolution.

Another quality of James's mind was gratified by this tendency to rule by the means of favorites. Without apparently any strong sense of pleasure or disposition to unlimited indulgence in his own person, James was addicted to occupy his time in frivolous pursuits, or consume it in the languor of indolence. This last habit of inaction induced him to trust the execution of the necessary but troublesome parts of his kingly duty to favorites, who secured their master's good opinion by an affectation of extreme regard for his person, which the good-natured king appears never to have suspected of being counterfeit. Encouraged by such persons as had gained his ear, he readily adopted the belief in his own supreme wisdom, which was echoed and re-echoed by all around him; and he was unbounded in his reliance upon those who enjoyed his favor, because it never occurred to him that he could have been mistaken in choosing proper objects of affection and confidence, or that men so correct in admiring his wisdom might probably be themselves rather deficient in that attribute. With still more culpable negligence he was careless of the faults of those who had his favor: thus he often overlooked, if he did not actually encourage in their persons, a tone of vice and profligacy which did not apparently belong to his own character.

We have already shown reasons why as a king James was jealously attached to his privileges, yet cautious of exerting his power in such a manner as to provoke resistance.

In this case, perhaps, his constitutional timidity was of advantage to his subjects and himself, since it was the means of adjourning to another generation the contention between the prerogative of the king and those rights which began to be claimed on behalf of the people.

We must remark, in the last place, that James's attachments to his favorites, though inordinate while they continued, were in fact far from being deep-rooted; and there is reason to think that in many cases the usurpation over him, which his supine indolence permitted them to assume, was in the long run felt as a slavery, which, though he himself had not energy to throw off, he was not averse to see destroyed by any other means; at least it is certain that most of his favorites had become distasteful to him before their fall.

In a word, James VI. was an example that neither high rank, nor shrewd sense, nor ready wit, nor a deep acquaintance with the learning of the age, can acquire respectability for a man timid both by moral and physical causes, and incapable of acting, upon suiting occasion, with total carelessness to his own comforts, his own safety, or, if the case calls for it, his own life. With these remarks on the character of a monarch called to perform one of the most interesting parts in British history, and to close a long train of useless and unnatural wars between the divided portions of the island, we will close what we have to say on the subject, and return to the prosecution of Scottish history.

Such as he was, King James now threw the government of Scotland so exclusively into the hands of Lennox and Arran, that the nation at large were extremely disgusted with his conduct. Arran, in particular, had the rapacity of Morton, without either his wisdom or his experience; and in private life he set decency and morality alike at defiance. He had carried on a criminal intrigue with the wife of the Earl of March, a woman young and handsome, but in other respects infamously profligate. To make way for a union between her and her lover, the countess pleaded for divorce

from her husband upon the same scandalous reason which
was afterward alleged by the Countess of Essex; and having thus obtained her liberation from the band of matrimony, she conferred her hand in shameless triumph upon
her paramour Arran.   This gave the highest offence to a
nation which boasted of having reformed their moral system upon the pure lessons of the Gospel, and whose creed,
though sometimes strained to the toleration of acts of rapine
and violence in the ambitious and vindictive, was specially
adverse to the licentious excesses of a voluptuary.

For some time the two favorites who held an undivided
sway over James's affections pursued their course hand in
hand, or rather Stewart suffered the Duke of Lennox to appear the ostensible superior, and was contented to rank in
the capacity of his assistant and dependent.   When raised,
however, to the rank of nobility, and wedded to a woman
of ambition as irregular as his own, the new Earl of Arran
became impatient of the duke's precedence and superiority
in a degree which had never occurred to him when Captain
James Stewart.   He endeavored, by various means, to rival
his credit with the king, and inspired the people with jealousy of his favor.   Under pretence of friendship he found
little difficulty in instigating the inexperienced Duke of Lennox to quarrel with several of his soundest friends and best
advisers; and was thus the means of stirring up dissension
between the duke and the Master of Mar, Sir William Stewart, captain of Dumbarton, Alexander Clark, provost of
Edinburgh, and, above all, the Earl of Gowrie, treasurer
of Scotland, persons of considerable influence, and all well
inclined to the Duke of Lennox till estranged from him by
the intrigues of Arran and his lady.

This was not all, nor even the worst part of the evil rendered by Stewart to the young nobleman who had first raised
his influence at court.   He never failed, upon every possible
opportunity, to breathe into the minds of the clergy and
people that Lennox, whatever might be now his pretences,
was still at heart a devoted servant of the Duke of Guise,

a favorer of the Catholic religion, a tool of the court of France, and a dangerous person to retain any share in the king's affections. Now, although these insinuations, considering the quarter from which they came, might have been more than suspected, yet as they fell upon the ears of persons who were very much disposed to receive them as true, the circumstance of deriving their origin from the false and profligate Arran did not operate, as it would otherwise have done, to deprive them of credit. Strong jealousy, therefore, prevailed among the envoys and partisans of England, as also the clergy and reformed part of Scotland, all of which parties regarded the duke, being a stranger and a converted Catholic, as still retaining a dangerous partiality for the country and the religion in which he had been educated.

But these suspicions excited against Lennox did not at all raise in the public estimation the character of the Earl of Arran, by whom they had been infused into the mind of the people. On the contrary, whatever might be his success in representing his rival Lennox as the friend of France and Rome, he himself continued to be esteemed, by almost all except the deceived king and a few dependents who hoped to rise by his favors, a bold, bloody, and ambitious minister, regardless both of law and justice, and only intent upon amassing power and wealth by the wreck and ruin of others.

Scotland had been long accustomed to the use of violent remedies in state diseases, so that the apprehension of Lennox's partiality for France, and of Arran's general profligacy and oppression, soon excited a party among the nobles to remove these obnoxious favorites from the king's presence by force itself, if force should be found necessary. The members of this conspiracy were chiefly such nobles as had been attached to the king's party during the civil wars, most of whom considered the execution of Morton as a violent precedent, tending to place the lives and fortunes of other nobles at the discretion of the crown; since in the course of the late tempestuous times there were few or none who had not been at one period or another privy to, if not aiding in, matters which might be construed into high treason.

The principal conspirators were the Earl of Mar, the Master of Glammis, the Lords Oliphant, Boyd, and Lindsay, the abbot of Dunfermline, secretary of state, and others who had been formerly allied with Morton and the English faction. They were very desirous to draw to their party the Earl of Gowrie, a man so generally esteemed for courage and hardihood that he was known among his intimates by the name of Greysteel, being that of a champion in Scottish romance, bestowed at the time upon such as were held to excel in chivalry. But although the Earl of Gowrie was even by direct descent connected with those who drove matters on most severely against Queen Mary,[1] he does not appear to have been himself of a turbulent disposition, or much disposed to enter into the conspiracy, of which he afterward bore the chief blame, and for which he suffered the chief punishment. An agent, named Cunningham of Drumquhassel, was employed to persuade him that the Duke of Lennox had an intention to slay him at their first meeting. The belief of this false report induced the credulous earl to engage himself with the lords who were associated for displacing the king's favorite ministers, or, as they termed it, for reformation in the state. Their avowed purpose was to cause both Lennox and Arran to be removed from the king's presence by exiling the former to his native country of France, and imprisoning the more obnoxious minion, or putting him to death, should no less effectual mode of destroying his influence over the king be fallen upon.

The time selected for executing this scheme was that which the king had chosen to enjoy the amusement of hunting in the country of Athole, so well suited for that sport.

---

[1] He was son of that Lord Ruthven who played the principal part in Rizzio's murder, and who was so little affected with remorse for his share in that tragedy, that on his death-bed he spoke with great coolness of "the slaughter of David."

His favorite ministers did not attend him on this occasion. Lennox remained at Dalkeith, and the Earl of Arran at Kinneil, which had fallen to him as the principal mansion of the unfortunate earl whose title and property became his spoil. When, therefore, James returned from Athole toward the low country, with a small train of his household servants, it was natural that Gowrie should invite him to his castle of Ruthven, which lay in the king's road, and that the king should accept the invitation of a great officer of the court against whom he had no ground for apprehension. James had no sooner arrived at Ruthven than his reasonable suspicions were awakened by the concourse of armed men who surrounded the castle, and the arrival of guests augmenting the number of those formerly assembled, all known to belong to one faction in the state, and wearing not the thoughtless air of persons about to engage in sylvan sports, but the anxious and severe aspect of such as were bound on some perilous enterprise. He took care, however, not to let these suspicions transpire, and endeavored to act as if he apprehended nothing.

Next morning the king appeared early, dressed and ready to set out upon his journey; but the associated lords had no mind to lose an opportunity which might not have again returned. The principal persons concerned in the enterprise entered James's bedroom in a body, and delivered to him a petition or remonstrance, setting forth that they, the king's faithful subjects, had for the space of two years suffered such false accusations, calumnies, oppressions, and persecutions, by means of the Duke of Lennox and of the person who assumed the title of Earl of Arran, that like insolence and enormities had never been heard of in Scotland. Their manifesto further stated that their persecution was felt by the whole body of the commonwealth, but chiefly by the ministers of the Gospel, and the true professors thereof; and that while men who had been attached to his majesty's service during his youth were, though the king's best subjects, driven into banishment, and many of those who remained were subjected to partial prosecutions and oppressions, and while all of them were grossly calumniated, and violently excluded from the presence of the sovereign, they saw with indignation that papists and notable murderers were, on the other hand, daily called home from deserved exile, and either restored to such property as they had before enjoyed, or compensated by gifts out of the estates of the king's faithful subjects.

The same remonstrance charged Lennox and Arran with involving the king in plots and confederacies with the pope, the king of Spain, and the French papists, and with the bishops of Glasgow and Ross, the adherents of his mother, Queen Mary, by whom he was urged to effect her freedom from imprisonment, and associate her with himself in the royal authority.

However disagreeable this rough remonstrance might be to the king, the time and place rendered it dangerous to express his displeasure; so James received it, as prudence recommended, with complaisance. But upon his attempting to leave the chamber, with a general promise to give all due consideration to the petition of his beloved subjects, the Master of Glammis interposed between him and the door of the apartment, and gave him bluntly to understand he would not be permitted to leave the castle. After vain expostulation, the king burst into tears. "Let him weep," said Glammis fiercely: "better children weep than bearded men." These words sunk deep into the king's heart; and though generally of a placable disposition, the insult which they contained was never forgotten or forgiven.

For the present, however, James was compelled to submit to his fate, and to subscribe and issue a proclamation, declaring his purpose, by his own free consent, to remain for some time in the province of Stratherne, with such lords as were then around him.

When the news of this change of ministry, as it may be called, for such rude violence was in Scotland the frequent mode for transferring political power, reached the two favorites against whom it was chiefly levelled, each of them behaved in a manner indicative of his character. The Earl of Arran, as daringly rash as he was unprincipled and ambitious, rode headlong toward Ruthven Castle, at the head of a handful of armed followers, with whom he boasted "to drive the conspirators into mouse-holes." Had he encountered a considerable force under the Earl of Mar, which was lying in wait on purpose to intercept him, there is little doubt he would have been slain with his whole party; but the same rashness which endangered his life was, in fact, the means of saving it; for receiving some intimation of the ambush he separated himself from his own troop of horse, and fetching a circuit around the squadron of Mar, he rode to Ruthven Castle with two attendants only. What his purpose could have been in so rash a proceeding we are left to conjecture; but the result was more favorable to him than could have been anticipated. Arran was not permitted, of course, to approach the person of the king, but, on the contrary, made prisoner, and thrown into a dungeon. He was soon after transferred to Stirling Castle; and a strong inclination was exhibited on the part of the associated lords to have taken his life, for which specious pretexts could not have been wanting. But unwillingness, perhaps, to provoke James by an action so violent, and the protection of the Earl of Gowrie, who was destined, it would seem, to save the life of him who finally brought his head to the block, occasioned the favorite to be detained prisoner, and his life preserved, to be a principal author of future state commotions.

The Duke of Lennox, who seems to have rested his only hopes of power upon the favor of his sovereign, was no sooner given to understand that James was debarred of his liberty on account of the favor which he had shown to him than he generously resolved, by withdrawing himself from Scotland, to remove at least that pretext for continuing the captivity of his sovereign. Without making any attempt to restore the state of administration which had been altered by the enterprise now popularly called the Raid of Ruthven,[1] he capitulated with the lords who were concerned in the enterprise, and endeavored to obtain liberty to return to court. This license was sternly refused; and a proclamation was issued, by which he was commanded to leave Scotland. Lennox offered no resistance; but after some procrastination, in which he perhaps hoped that the ruling faction might relent, or the king regain some share of freedom and power, he at length retreated to Dumbarton Castle, and from thence returned to France by the way of London.

There is every reason to think that this young nobleman, who showed few bad inclinations and many gentle and generous qualities, returned the king's preference by a personal attachment to James more deep and sincere than that with which monarchs are usually repaid by their favorite minions. His melancholy at separating from Scotland was of so deep a kind that we can hardly assign disappointed ambition for its sole source, and willingly suppose that attachment to the sovereign who had so highly graced and favored him was a principal cause of Lennox's disease. Trouble of mind brought on a fever, which terminated his life at Paris. He died, declaring his sincere adherence to the Protestant faith, and refusing the succors of the Catholic Church, in contradiction to the calumnies which had such general circulation in Scotland.

James, who had been early imbued with the principle that the power of dissembling was essential to the art of reigning, now steered his course in conformity to the directions of the lords who had assumed the management of State affairs, and published a declaration, in which he acknowledged the Raid of Ruthven, with all its circumstances of violence toward his person and injury toward his feelings, to be laudable and good service, and prohibited any of his subjects to attempt a rising or assembling in arms under

---

[1] *Raid* signifies properly an inroad of a predatory character. But the Scottish applied it generally to any multitude assembled in arms for a violent purpose.

pretence of setting him free from the counsellors who had been then intruded upon him.

The conspirators themselves also published a long declaration, exaggerating the crimes and the presumption of the fallen favorites, and vindicating their violent removal as good service done to God, to the State, and to the king. The assembly of the Church, prejudiced against Lennox for his supposed attachment to the Catholic faith, and more justly abhorring the profligate life and tyrannic ministry of Stewart, earl of Arran, readily sanctioned the Raid of Ruthven, and required all sincere Protestants to combine with the lords by whom the enterprise was carried into effect. This act was appointed to be read by every minister to his congregation. The king also granted, what he had it not in his power safely to withhold, a remission, namely, to those concerned in the restraint of his person; and the convention of estates passed an act of ample indemnity on the same occasion.

Meanwhile James suffered in private all that could be endured by a young sovereign whose opinion of his prerogative was so lofty, and who felt that not his authority only but even his person had been grossly violated and insulted in the course of an action which he was now compelled to acknowledge to be good service, and not only to be pardoned, but to be rewarded as such. From some of those who immediately approached his person he did not attempt to conceal his internal feelings of being held under restraint by his present self-constituted counsellors.

To foreigners he was more reserved. Both the queen of England and the king of France had sent special ambassadors to inquire into the nature of the last revolution in Scotland, and, ostensibly at least, to offer the young king assistance, if he should complain of being placed under restraint by his subjects. To the French ambassador, Monsieur De la Mothe Fenelon, and to Bowes, one of those who were sent by Queen Elizabeth, the king made general replies, in the same tenor with his public declarations; namely, that he was well contented with the lords who were now about him, who conducted themselves as faithful subjects, although they had, perhaps, been rash in adopting some prejudices against Lennox and others by whom he had formerly been counselled. With De la Mothe the king did not think it safe to be more frank, because the clergy and the more severe disciples of the reformation regarded that nobleman as an ambassador of the bloody murderer, by which name they distinguished the Duke of Guise, and they somewhat indecently termed the white cross, which, as a knight of the Order of St. Esprit, De la Mothe wore upon his shoulder, the badge of antichrist. With a person so unpopular the king dared not exchange any confidence; and for reasons of a different kind he did not choose to communicate his real sentiments to Bowes, one of the English ambassadors.

But while he amused these individuals in terms expressing a general contentment with his condition, the king was more confidentially explicit to others. Hoping, perhaps, to interest Elizabeth in his favor, on account of her well-known general sentiments of respect to royal authority in the abstract, he privately declared to Sir George Carey, son of Lord Hunsdon, and kinsman to Queen Elizabeth, that he was in reality highly dissatisfied with the violence which had been put upon him, and displeased with the counsellors who had thrust themselves into the management of his affairs. Sir George Carey undertook to keep this communication secret from his colleague Bowes and all others save his mistress herself.

Whether he communicated James's private message to Queen Elizabeth or not is not known, and is of very little consequence, since that sovereign could hardly require express information to make her fully aware that James could not possibly look upon the Raid of Ruthven in a milder light than as an act of rebellion. Indeed, from her conduct she must be esteemed totally indifferent to the king's opinions and feelings on the subject, so long as the conspiracy had raised into power in Scotland a party disposed, like the lords in question, to act as the friends and partisans of England. She was, therefore, careful not to use any interference in her godson's behalf, if his complaints to Carey were actually transmitted to her, and left the affairs of Scotland to hold their own natural course.

The revolution in time began to take a turn in favor of James. By dint of the king's successful dissimulation, and confiding in the variety of pardons, remissions, and ratifications which they had accumulated for their protection, if necessary, the Earl of Gowrie and his party began to relax in the severity which they had at first exercised in watching the king's person, and permitted him to follow his hunting parties and journeys of pleasure without interruption. He failed not to take advantage of the freedom thus afforded him to draw gradually around him such other nobles and counsellors as were unconnected with or inimical to those who were presently in power; and opening his mind to them privately, he expressed his resolution either to free himself from his present restraint, or to die in the attempt to acquire his liberty. At the same time he promised, in secret to Melville and other wise and judicious statesmen, who shared his confidence, and recommended to him moderate counsel, that should he succeed in his attempt to regain his liberty, he would nevertheless abstain from pursuing any passionate or vindictive course against those concerned in the conspiracy of Ruthven. Nay, he even professed that he would not exclude them from his favor, so as to drive them to desperation. In a word, he affirmed it to be his intention to rule with an equal hand among his nobility of all factions, to discourage the party spirit, which, being the natural consequence of the long civil wars, had been so great an evil to the country, and, disowning all distinction of king's men and queen's men, he professed his purpose to use the talents indifferently of all whom he should find capable to render him service. These dispositions of the king, which were privately whispered abroad, not only awakened the hopes of such of the peers as were excluded from administration to look for a speedy change, but even inclined some of the statesmen then in power, and the Earl of Gowrie himself, to become fearful of the consequences of governing by a faction, and rendered them desirous that the king should be admitted to his liberty, and that the system of administration should be remodelled on a less exclusive footing, providing these points could be conceded to James without incurring the terrors of reaction and retaliation on the part of the faction readmitted to power.

While matters were in this state, James devised measures for his own escape from the lords who since the Raid of Ruthven had exercised the supreme power of the State, and retained possession of his person. In summer, 1583, while the king was residing at his hunting-seat of Falkland, a convention was appointed to be held at St. Andrew's for the purpose of settling some disputed affairs between England and Scotland. The king conceived that he saw in this appointment some means of acquiring his freedom. . His plan was to send letters to the Earl of March, the Earl of Montrose, Marischal, Argyle, and Rothes, all enemies of the faction of Ruthven, appointing them to come to St. Andrew's on a certain day; and as he did not send intimation of the time or purpose of meeting to the other noblemen connected with the Raid of Ruthven, he concluded it likely they would not appear. The faithful Melville endeavored to dissuade his majesty from the above, as a precarious and hazardous course: he represented that as the meeting of a convention was a matter which could not be well kept secret, the lords of the Ruthven Raid were likely to take the alarm from the very circumstance of their not having received the usual summons; and as their estates lay chiefly in Fife and Stratherne, they might assemble in force sufficient to outnumber those opposite peers, upon whose support the king relied, and who had to bring their followers from a greater distance.

Notwithstanding this representation, James, with more spirit than belonged to his character, resolved to proceed in the enterprise. For this purpose he determined to be at St. Andrew's two or three days before the time appointed for the convention, and consulted with Colonel William Stewart, the commander of the guard, how he might place his royal person in security, when he should take up his quarters in that town. Accordingly, unsuspected, as it appeared, by his ministers, whose want of intelligence or dulness of apprehension seems to have been rather surprising, he set out upon his journey for St. Andrew's, as if he had been riding a-hawking; having at that time no attendant of the Ruthven faction near his person excepting the Earl of Mar. The king came to St. Andrew's "as blythe," says Melville, "as a bird escaped from the cage." The archbishop, in the meantime, held the castle of that place in readiness for the service of his sovereign. A proposal of taking a view of the fine old fortress was acted upon by the king merely as if it had been an accidental suggestion of the moment, which had no deeper motive than curiosity. But he and his retinue had no sooner entered the castle gates than they were shut and barred by Colonel William Stewart, the drawbridges raised, and the gentlemen of the guard placed on duty in defence of the walls.

The next day the nobles of both parties entered the town: the discontented barons in greater number, better supplied with arms than the opposite party, and with the intention, it seemed, as well as the power, again to seize upon his majesty's person. A day of strife and battle seemed impending, in which the person of the king should be the prize of the victor, like that of his grandfather at the battles of Melrose and Kirkliston. But the exertions of James's friends, who brought a body of royalists into the castle from the town and neighborhood, made the malcontent lords unwilling to come to violence; while Gowrie, obtaining admittance to the king's presence, renounced as treasonable his share in the Raid of Ruthven, disclaimed all future proceeding of so unlawful a character, and after a grave admonition from James was once more admitted to the king's favor.

The principal accomplices in the late conspiracy, finding themselves too weak to dispute the matter in arms, and being thus deserted by the chief member of their party, took the course of peaceful submission, and coming one by one before the king, acknowledged their offence, and obtained his majesty's pardon, under condition, however, that they should submit to such temporary exile as James should please to inflict upon them. The language of the king, as well as his proclamations, was of a merciful and moderate character; and he appeared little elated at the victory which he had gained in a struggle that seemed at first so doubtful. He intimated, that although he had been for some time detained against his consent, in consequence of the Raid of Ruthven, yet it was not his intention to prosecute as a crime that or anything else done in his minority; but that he was, on the contrary, resolved to consider all offences which had occurred as arising rather out of the troublesome character of the times than owing to the criminal intention of the actors. He appointed two principal nobles of each faction —Angus and Mar on the one side, and Huntley and Crawford on the other—to withdraw from court for a season, as being in some sort the representatives of the contending parties, whose absence might prevent the renewal of factious debates. The king, in the interim, proposed to guide his affairs by the less violent partisans, selected indifferently from both sides, from those nobles whom he meant to retain about his person.

There can be little doubt that had King James pursued the wise and moderate course announced by these temperate proposals, in which he was sincere at the time, he could not have failed to have brought to good order the councils of his kingdom. But his propensity to favoritism, which so often interfered with his better thoughts, was destined on the present occasion to disturb his more deliberate, wise, and clement measures.

The Earl of Arran had, by favor of Gowrie, been lately freed from his prison in Stirling, having obtained permission

IACOBVS DEI GRATIA
MAGNÆ BRITANNIÆ FRANCIÆ ET
HIBERNIÆ REX, FIDEI DEFENSOR etc
1625

JAMES I.

to reside at his own house of Kinneil, upon his parole not to leave it, and particularly not to approach the court. Immediately upon hearing of the revolution which had taken place at St. Andrew's, he proposed to come to court and pay his duty to his majesty. By the advice of his present council, who were all aware of the favorite's deserved unpopularity, and apprehensive of his influence over the king's mind, James was induced flatly to refuse the permission requested. But some time afterward, under the specious pretence of paying his respects to the king upon one single occasion, he was admitted to James's presence, when, resuming that personal influence over his master which had been suspended by his absence, he became as great or a greater favorite than ever: the rather that Lennox, who had more than rivalled him in the king's favor, was now deceased.

The known want of faith of this wicked man prevented the persons who had been concerned in the last troubles, and particularly the agents in the Raid of Ruthven, from relying upon the word of the king, though repeatedly pledged, for their safety and indemnity. James, they thought, might in his person forgive the restraint inflicted on him, but his more vindictive favorite would be sure both to remember and revenge his own imprisonment at Ruthven and Stirling, his threatened estrangement from court, and the yet more hostile intentions, which had even menaced his life.

Accordingly, it was soon made evident that it was the avowed policy of this ambitious and rapacious counsellor to prosecute a violent course against those concerned in the Raid of Ruthven. A menacing proclamation was issued, in which the offenders on this occasion were treated as persons still lying under the lash of the law, and which summoned each of them to take out formal remissions or pardons for their several offences. This proclamation plainly intimated that conditions of a penal kind, but chiefly pecuniary mulcts, would be imposed on the persons who should apply for the offered pardons, and likewise implied that the criminal fact was considered as yet obnoxious to prosecutions, notwithstanding the several occasions on which the offenders had already obtained the royal pardon, both by express grant and by general proclamation.

This unwise and threatening manifesto struck terror into all those who had been accessory to this crime. Many of them withdrew from court, the more prudent actually left the country, and others prepared to follow the same example. Gowrie, himself, who had acknowledged his guilt, and received an explicit pardon, was driven from the court by the coldness of the king, and the insolence of Arran, whose evil nature was in this particularly apparent since Gowrie had not only been the means of preserving his life when made prisoner at Ruthven Castle, but also, by warmly urging his being again permitted to see the king after the revolution of St. Andrew's, had laid the foundation for his restoration to power. Forgetful of these causes for gratitude to Gowrie, Arran pressed the unfortunate earl so hard that, despairing, as it afterward appeared, of regaining the king's favor, he remained uncertain whether he should fly from the country, or renew his engagements with other lords in the same situation, who meditated some violent mode of defence and retaliation. The further consequences of this will appear hereafter.

Queen Elizabeth, seeing in the severity menaced against the lords of the Raid of Ruthven the probable extinction of the party in Scotland most attached to the English interest, seems to have resolved to try what impression could be made on James, a young, and, she might suppose, an ignorant person, by a letter of a character more magisterial and menacing than usually occurs in the correspondence of sovereigns while friendly relations exist between them. She reminded him of the noble lesson of Isocrates that a sovereign should hold his words to be of more account than the oaths of other men. She bemoaned him, she said, for permitting evil spirits to distract his mind, and lead him to think an honorable answer could be returned to her when all his actions gainsaid his former words. "You deal not with one," proceeded Elizabeth, "whose experience can take dross for good payment, nor with one that will be easily beguiled; no, I mean to set to school your craftiest counsellors." She was sorry, she continues, to see him bent to wrong himself in thinking to wrong others. She called upon him to remember what he had written to her with his own hand concerning the dangerous courses the Duke of Lennox was entered into; in contradiction of which, she alleges, that he now seemed to give the reproach of guilty folks to those who had preserved him from rushing upon that acknowledged hazard. "I hope you more esteem your honor," she adds, "than to give it such a stain, since you protested so often to have taken these lords" (meaning the lords concerned in the Raid of Ruthven) "for your most affectionate subjects, who had acted all for your best advantage." She concluded this magisterial expostulation, by beseeching him to pass no further on the course he was pursuing (that of severity, namely, against Gowrie and his friends) till he should consult with an ambassador extraordinary, whom she proposed to despatch toward him, and from whom he might receive better and more fruitful counsel than from all the dissemblers of his own court.

This singular epistle was written in Elizabeth's own hand, and that in which James replied is no less worthy of notice. James was at home when a dispute was to be maintained by classical quotation. He answered his godmother's quotation from Isocrates, by taking notice of another maxim of the same author, which directs us to esteem those less our friends who continually praise us than such as use timely reproof, in which kind view of her sharp admonition he is determined, he adds, to consider it as the fruit of sisterly love, although acting upon misinformation. It is true, he says, that he was compelled at the moment, when he was in the power of those noblemen, to publish such proclamations and subscribe such pardons as were presented to him in their favor. The circumstances of the times did not admit his disputing their pleasure. It was also true, he acknowledged, that while under the same restraint of a predominant faction he intimated in public to the French and English ambassadors that he was contented with his condition, and had none save friends about him; but he reminds Elizabeth that at the very time while he made this compulsory answer to De la Mothe Fenelon and Bowes, he communicated to Sir George Carey, her kinsman, his real feelings of his situation, and his determination rather to hazard dying honestly than to reign shamefully. He imputes the severe language used by Queen Elizabeth to the suggestions of partial counsellors, and declares that he will rather keep in memory her former effectual friendship than start at any wrong-placed syllable or sour sentence placed in her late paper at the instance of others. Respecting Elizabeth's desire that he will proceed no further against the Ruthven faction until a special ambassador should arrive on her part, he declares that, although Isocrates (whose maxims he has again at her service) advises princes to execute with speed that which is fitting to be done, yet he intends to abstain from doing anything which can justly offend Elizabeth until the arrival of her envoy, hoping and desiring that this person so trusted may be as willing to promote the effects of true love and friendship between them as he was assured was the desire and intention of Elizabeth as well as his own.

The ambassador whose wisdom was thus praised, and whose arrival at the court of James was so formally announced, was no less a person than the celebrated Walsingham, second to Burleigh alone as the favorite counsellor of Elizabeth, and one of the most accomplished statesmen in Europe. He was sent by Elizabeth, thinking, probably, that his gravity and learning might have some effect upon James, and obtain so much ascendency as might check his purpose of altogether destroying the Ruthven conspirators, and for the more general purpose of obtaining, by means of a statesman so well acquainted with mankind, an accurate idea of the character of the Scottish sovereign, with whom Elizabeth must necessarily have so many important affairs to transact, and of whom she was the more likely to receive different reports, as, in fact, James's character appeared very different to those who looked upon it in different points of view.

Walsingham, otherwise excellently qualified for his mistress's purpose, was aged and infirm, and the necessity of his using a wheel-carriage rendered his progress extremely slow; the rather as, being magnificently attended, the old statesman travelled with a train of eight-score of horse.   At his first audience of James, Walsingham required to know why his majesty had changed the counsels and company of the noblemen lately around him, they being the best and most religious of his peers, and those of whom the queen of England had the highest opinion, and with whom she most willingly held intercourse.   James made an immediate and well-turned answer, indicating, it may be supposed, his freedom as an independent prince to use what counsellors he pleased, and the reasonable expectation that those whom he trusted ought to receive the confidence of his allies.   This reply was so grave and pointed as struck wonder into the queen's old statesman, which he did not hesitate to express.

Walsingham had another audience with James, no other person being present; after which, the Englishman, taking Sir James Melville by the hand, declared his entire contentment with the Scottish sovereign.   "I have spoken," said he, "with an excellent young prince, ignorant of nothing; and of such happy expectation that I think my heavy travel in coming hither is well bestowed in having but seen him."

The Earl of Arran desired to enter into conversation with this celebrated statesman, who haughtily refused either to see him or to abide longer at the court, where it is probable, however well he was received himself, he found no token of his intercession being available in favor of the Ruthven party. This he imputed to the influence of Arran, whom he termed a scorner of religion, a sower of discord, and an enemy of true and honest men.

In revenge of the contempt with which he was treated by

Walsingham, Arran took a course of expressing his feelings more dishonorable to himself and to his master than to the English envoy. He intercepted a diamond ring, designed for Walsingham by James, valued at seven hundred crowns, and presented in its stead one which enclosed a piece of ordinary rock crystal. The knights and gentlemen of quality who attended in Walsingham's retinue were also discourteously treated in being excluded from permission to wait upon the king when receiving his court.

Walsingham passed over these petty expressions of spleen with the contempt which they deserved from a statesman of his wisdom and experience. On his return home, the report of this distinguished minister, concerning the wisdom and learning of James, was of high advantage to the king, especially among those of the English people who began to look forward to the days which should follow Queen Elizabeth's death, and were, therefore, disposed to inquire into the character of her presumptive successor. James's natural parts and acquired information qualified him to make a good figure in conversation, while his indecision of disposition, and his being so unhappily subject to the influence of unworthy counsellors, often prevented the maxims which he knew how to use in counsel from being seconded by actions conforming to them. Walsingham's high opinion of James was so boldly expressed as for a time to draw down on her ancient statesman some shadow of that jealousy with which Queen Elizabeth was apt to visit those who expressed a good opinion of any one near in her succession. On the whole, however, the queen was disposed to treat James in future with more respect than hitherto.

In November of this year Ludovic Stewart, eldest son to the late Duke of Lennox, arrived in Scotland, invited over by James, who took this mode of showing his kind recollection of his banished and deceased favorite. He was promoted to his uncle's dignity and dukedom, and in due time, for he was but very young at his arrival in Scotland, was promoted to considerable offices of dignity. By this kindness James evinced an amiable disposition, inclined to carry friendship beyond the grave.

In the meantime the troubles of Scotland daily increased. The conspirators of Ruthven sued out their pardons, which were not granted, but upon condition that they should depart the kingdom. Gowrie himself obtained license to go into France; but delaying his purpose, became involved in more dangerous counsels, which terminated in his violent death. The clergymen had also mingled in the troubles of the community; for having long since declared, by an act of general assembly, that the Raid of Ruthven was good service, individual preachers were from time to time induced to dilate upon the legality of the measure. When called to account for such political sermons, they pleaded the privilege of the pulpit as an ample apology for expressing their opinion upon State affairs; and contended that though they might from thence utter treason, or what was liable to be punished as such, they were not amenable to the king's privy council, or any secular judge, but must always be tried and judged by the church judicatories, at least in the first instance. Andrew Melvin, a preacher of talents and learning, set a bad example on this occasion to his brethren, accusing the king by the undutiful assertion that he perverted the laws of both God and man, and flying to England when he was commanded to enter into prison.

From all these subjects of complaint the disaffection grew so general that the Earls of Angus and Mar, conspirators in the exploit of Ruthven, united to seize the town and castle of Stirling, intending to render it the headquarters of their party, and expecting to be joined by the Earl of Gowrie, who had a part in their plot. This was on the 19th of April, 1584; but the king, who was at Edinburgh, was so well seconded by the zeal of his subjects, and particularly by the citizens of the metropolis, that on the 24th James was ready to advance toward Stirling with such a powerful army that the Earls of Angus and Mar did not choose to wait his arrival. They had learned that the Earl of Gowrie had suffered himself to be surprised and taken by Sir William Stewart, the captain of the king's guard, at Dundee; and despairing of success in their enterprise fled to England, leaving a few followers in the castle, by whom it was surrendered to the king, and placed under custody of the all-grasping Earl of Arran.

In the meantime the Earl of Gowrie was brought to his fate. He had hired a vessel to leave Scotland for France; but delayed his departure, as the commotions had begun to take place which appeared to promise a general insurrection. Some communication he appears himself to have had with Angus and Mar in their attempt to surprise Stirling; however, he declared at his death that he was engaged in no plot against the king's person, crown, or estate, but only moved by the hopes of saving his own family and fortune from ruin. He had remained for days and weeks uncertain what course he should adopt: want of decision, which was always his chief fault, and now proved his ruin, induced him to linger, until Colonel William Stewart, commander of the royal guard, arrived to apprehend him. The Earl of Gowrie defended his lodgings by force, and called upon the people of Dundee to join with him as a faithful Protestant pursued for his religion. The citizens, however, took part with the royal guard, and the earl was compelled to surrender himself. He was first taken to Kinneil, the abode of his enemy Arran, and afterward brought to Stirling, and tried with the usual irregularity of proceeding then used by the Scottish courts in cases of high treason. One point of the charge was singular: Gowrie had from his prison petitioned for an interview with James, for the purpose, he stated, of disclosing a secret which might have endangered the king's life and estate, if he himself had not stayed and impeded the same. The use made of this petition was to frame, out of the acknowledgments which it contained, a fourth article of indictment, which was added to three already charged in the earl's accusation. This additional charge bore that the accused earl, having intelligence of a weighty purpose concerning the life and estate of the king and of the queen, his mother, did treasonably conceal the same, and does as yet conceal the particulars thereof.

The inquest upon this unfortunate earl had no hesitation to find him guilty of high treason. He was executed with that declaration in his mouth, which has been ascribed to many great men in misfortune, that "if he had served God as faithfully as he had done his king, he had not come to an end so disastrous." Gowrie's death was the subject of general censure and regret. Whatever had been his accession to the Raid of Ruthven, he had been one of the first to desert the conspirators, implore the king's pardon, and lend his assistance to restore the liberty of his sovereign. It was not until he found that the pardon which had been so repeatedly and formally granted was not likely to protect him that he was induced to take measures for the safety of his life and fortune, by uniting himself with those who stood in the same peril. There was, therefore, injustice in imputing to the earl as voluntary guilt a line of conduct which was the natural consequence of a breach of public faith toward him; and the iniquity was more flagrant that the schemes of which he was accused seem rather to have been something which he thought of than what he had actually determined upon, so that they could be hardly termed even crimes of intention, far less offences actually perpetrated. At least, if Gowrie in strict law merited death, all men execrated the ungrateful rapacity of Arran, who drove matters to extremity against the very person without whose intervention he would have lost his life shortly after the Raid of Ruthven. Nor did the evil consequences of Gowrie's death expire with the earl himself, but will be found to furnish occasion to a future dark and bloody chapter in this history.

By this vindictive and cruel execution the king of Scotland, or rather his unpopular and profligate minister, was for the time placed beyond dread of attack by that party of nobles who, supported by England, and formidable in their own strength, had endeavored to establish a reformation, as

they termed it, in the administration of Scotland, by banishing Arran, and establishing a control over the person of the
king and government of the State.

But in gaining this victory Arran himself, daring as he
was, must have been sensible that he exposed himself to an
additional load of unpopularity. This event not only excited
the hostility of that class of persons, few, perhaps, in number, but respectable from their reputation for wisdom, who,
though sincere friends of the monarchy, were desirous of seeing its legal powers exerted with prudence and moderation,
but at the same time animated against him the deep and determined enmity of a large party, the friends, kinsmen, and
adherents of the nobles who had been driven into exile.   And
what was at least equally formidable, it exasperated against
the governing favorite the Church of Scotland in general,
and all those numerous congregations who, in zeal for their
religion, and love and reverence for their preachers, were
disposed to adopt the political sentiments which they heard
delivered from the pulpit, as authorized by the Holy
Scripture.

The measures which the minister adopted to· quell the
opposition which his severity had excited will be the proper
subject of the next chapter.

CHAPTER XXXIII

The Minister's Arrogance—The King disgusted with Business—
Arran pretends an Attachment to the Prerogative—The
banished Lords—Their Influence with their Vassals, Clans,
and Tenantry—Argaty and his Brother tried and executed for
holding Correspondence with the Exiles—Information against
Mains and Drumquhassel for a similar Crime—Suborned Evidence against the Accused—They are condemned and executed
—Arran's Attack on the Immunities claimed by the Church—
Privileges of the Kirk—Their extreme Apprehensions of Popery
—The Clergy usually in opposition to, and therefore become
unpopular with, the King—Arran, having courted them to no
Purpose, resolves to break their Power by a Series of new Reg-
ulations—Nature of the political Influence of the Clergy—A
Minister is imprisoned for petitioning to be heard on the Part
of the Church, and declared Rebel and Outlaw for protesting
against the obnoxious Laws—Arran's Ministry begin to desert
him and set up for themselves, particularly Maitland the Secretary and the Master of Gray—Arran becomes a Creature of
Elizabeth—His Meeting with Hunsdon—His Quarrels with the
Scottish Nobility, particularly with Lord Maxwell—He engages
Lord Maxwell in a Civil War with the Johnstones, in which the
former is victorious—Embassy of Wotton—Death of Sir Francis
Russell on the Borders—Disgrace of Kerr of Farniherst and of
Arran—The exiled Lords return to Scotland, march to Stirling,
and obtain Possession of the King's Person—The King aban-
dons Arran, who retires from Court in Disgrace—James re-
ceives the associated Nobles into his Favor, and establishes a
Government on a moderate and popular Model

THE youth and inexperience of James VI. may at this
period be admitted as a sufficient excuse for his giving way to the insidious counsels of a favorite who
as unworthy of the trust reposed in him. We learn from
e valuable memoirs of Sir James Melville that Arran, who
ad usurped in his own person, or distributed among his own
reatures, all the great offices in the government, used the

common arts of those in his situation to discourage the king
from attention to the business of the State and deliberations
of the council, and to engage him continually in those pursuits of sylvan sport to which he was naturally addicted.
The designing favorite also availed himself of his numerous
opportunities not only to exclude from the royal counsels
Melville and other courtiers whom he could not rely upon as
favorers of his schemes, but also to impose upon the young
monarch, as unanimous resolutions of his council of State,
violent measures which were framed and forwarded by himself alone. The affectation of extreme zeal in supporting the
royal authority, and the unbounded attachment which he
pretended to entertain for James's person, were, doubtless,
the further apologies by which Arran colored over a course
of despotic measures, designed to eradicate whatever influence the banished lords might retain in Scotland, and diminish or destroy the power which the Reformed Church had by
various means obtained in the political affairs of the State.
Of these sources of influence so obnoxious to the favorite we
are now to give the reader some account.

The banished lords formed a considerable part of the aristocracy of Scotland, which depended for its importance not
merely on the consequence and influence which its members
possessed, arising from their immediate power and wealth,
but also, and more especially, upon the attachment of vassals
and kinsfolk, a species of loyalty to their chief which these
followers displayed at every personal risk, even when those
who might claim it were expelled from their estates and remained banished men in a foreign country. The power of
the Scottish nobles became in this manner, in some respects,
indestructible. Thus the unusually severe measures by which
James V. had endeavored to destroy the House of Douglas
did not prevent that long exiled family from resuming a great
part of their feudal power as soon as the death of that monarch permitted them to return to Scotland, when they repos-
sessed themselves of their estates without even awaiting the
recall of their forfeiture. Numerous instances during the

reign of Queen Mary and the minority of James had fostered the same principle. By far the greater part, if not the whole, of the nobility of Scotland had, at one time or other, and for various causes, been banished from the kingdom, and yet had successively returned to it and reassumed their hereditary influence. While, therefore, their lords were absent on these unpleasant occasions, the vassals retained their faith and attachment unaltered, not only from love, affection, and gratitude, but from a reasonable expectation of the return of their chiefs as an event connected with their own interest. The friends and vassals of exiled nobles preserved the attachment to them in which they had been born and bred, and considered that their adherence during what they regarded as a temporary eclipse was likely to be remunerated when the cloud which obscured the fortunes of their masters should pass away.

From this it followed that the lords exiled on account of the Raid of Ruthven still possessed numerous friends and extensive correspondence in Scotland; and supported as they were by the power of Elizabeth, and residing within the English frontier, were at all times ready to re-enter Scotland with the certainty of being backed by a considerable force. It now became the business of Arran to destroy, if possible, the ramifications by which those exiles, against whom he had procured the doom of treason to be denounced, continued to maintain a correspondence and interest within the Scottish realm. For this purpose he procured denunciations to be made against all such as held correspondence, or, as it was called, traffic, with the exiles, and took all precaution to bring within the range of punishment such persons of inferior rank as should appear to be the correspondents or confidants of the banished lords. In 1584, in order to strike terror on this subject, David Home of Argaty, and Patrick Home, his brother, gentlemen of birth and fortune, were brought to trial for holding communication with the commendator of Dryburgh, who was banished on account of his accession to the Raid of Ruthven. The accused persons were

confessedly adherents of the same party, but covered by a
general pardon from being charged as accomplices to that
conspiracy. The correspondence for which they were tried
consisted of one or two short letters which had no reference
whatever to State affairs, but related entirely to some private
business left undischarged when the commendator was expelled from Scotland; yet both the gentlemen were condemned to death, and executed on the afternoon of the
same day on which they were tried—a severity universally
reprobated by common sense and common feeling.

To spread still further the terror inspired by this execution, a proclamation was made, that whoever should discover and make known any person corresponding on whatsoever subject with the exiled lords should, besides his own
pardon, receive an especial reward. In consequence of this
invitation and premium to traitors and informers, a man was
found base enough to avail himself of this offer, who was
generally believed to have added to the meanness of treachery the guilt of perjury. One Hamilton of Eglismachan
lodged an information against Malcolm Douglas of Mains,
and John Cunningham of Drumquhassel, stating them to
have conspired to seize the person of the king at a hunting-
match, for the purpose of detaining him in some stronghold
until the banished noblemen should enter Scotland with
forces and take possession of his person. The accusation
was generally considered as a forgery, yet willingly entertained by Arran, because both the accused gentlemen were
suspected by him; and Douglas of Mains, in particular, was
regarded as what was called in these times a man of valor
and action. To add probability to the accusation of Hamilton, which would otherwise have been supported by only one
evidence, being also that of an informer, held suspicious in
all countries, Sir James Edmonstone of Duntreath, a person
who had lived in great intimacy with the accused parties,
was included in the indictment, it being understood that he
was to plead guilty to the accusation, and to be remunerated
with a pardon on account of his candid confession. To this

arrangement the unhappy gentleman, to his great discredit, was, by Arran's threats, induced to consent.

The trial accordingly proceeded; and Sir James Edmonstone pleaded guilty to the indictment of having conspired, with Mains and Drumquhassel, to the plot as expressed in the charge. The scheme, he said, had been originally concocted by the Earl of Angus, and was communicated to him and the other two parties accused by John Home, commonly called *Black John*. Drumquhassel and Mains were next arraigned for the same criminal intercourse with Angus, and further with having been partakers of the Raid of Ruthven, an offence which must have been supposed to be incapable of pardon, since, after so many remissions, it was once more revived against the subordinate persons concerned. Drumquhassel's defence does not appear upon the record, but that of Mains was manly and firm: he placed the improbability, nay, impossibility, of such a conspiracy on the part of himself and his companion in misfortune so fully in view, that "all in court," says the historian Spottiswoode, though favorable, in general, to the measures of James, "in their hearts acquitted him." But the doom of the accused had been decided ere the accusation was brought. Cunningham and Douglas were both condemned; and, with a speed which argued terror in the government, were executed in the public street of Edinburgh, before the sun had set, on their day of trial. The informer Hamilton was generally execrated, and lived from that time in fear for his life, endeavoring to protect himself from the vengeance of the friends of the deceased, by keeping constantly near the person of Arran till the hour came, as the reader will hereafter be informed, in which the presence of him, at whose instigation he had committed the foul act, could no longer avail as his protection. These cruel and rigorous proceedings, says the historian we have just quoted, caused such general terror that all familiar society and intercourse of humanity was in a manner disused, no man knowing to whom with safety he could speak his thoughts, or open his mind. But the Scots, fierce by nature, were a people as unable to endure a despotic government, as to bear the foreign yoke, the imposition of which in the former part of their history they had opposed with such obstinacy.

Arran's attacks on the liberties and immunities claimed by the Church were not less violent, and were even more unpopular, than those with which he assailed the civil rights of his fellow-subjects.

The Church of Scotland, it must be remembered, had been founded and perfected in the midst of civil tumults. Its preachers had been accustomed, from the time of Knox downward, to regard themselves less as an ecclesiastic body, sequestered from lay business to teach the doctrines and duties of religion, than as a church militant, called upon to protect themselves and the Christian community over which they presided from the political attacks directed against them, not only by their direct and immediate enemies, the Roman Catholics, whom they regarded with that mixture of hatred, abhorrence, and fear with which the peasants, described by Spenser, looked upon the dead dragon,[1] but also by the king, ministers, and courtiers, whom they regarded, if not as absolute foes, yet as very cold friends to their spiritual establishment. This suspicion was sufficiently natural on the part of the ministers, when it is recollected that the Scottish aristocracy, though feeling or affecting the most vehement zeal for the doctrines of the

---

[1] The quotation, though long, is an animated picture of the jealous and sometimes fantastic apprehensions entertained of the outrages of the Church of Rome, which, in Scotland at least, had made no remarkable stand against the effects of sense and reason:

"Some fear'd, and fledd; some fear'd and well it fayn'd;
One, that would wiser seeme than all the rest,
Warn'd him not touch, for yet perhaps remayn'd
Some ling'ring life within his hollow brest,
Or in his wombe might lurke some hidden nest
Of many dragonettes, his fruitfull seede;
Another saide, that in his eyes did rest
Yet sparkling fyre, and badd thereof take heed;
Another said, he saw him move his eyes indeed."
                    —Spenser's "Faerie Queene," book i., canto xii.

reformation, had, in the first place, usurped the lion's share of the spoils of the popish hierarchy, and were now inclined, as the clergy supposed, to abridge the privileges of the Church, whose prerogative constituted all that was left to console an active, energetic, and influential body of men for the want, not only of opulence, but even of the means of decent subsistence. The preachers claimed for their order, as has been often hinted, the extensive privilege of canvassing public affairs in their sermons, acknowledging no responsibility, at least in the first instance, save to the judicatories of their own body, by whom they were not likely to be condemned for any exercise of their Christian privilege. During the whole of the actual reign of Queen Mary they had been repeatedly placed in direct opposition to the powers that wielded the State, and had even been at variance with the regents who severally succeeded that unfortunate queen, although men of their own persuasion. This constant opposition had become, in a certain degree, a habit; and spreading through so large a body of men, many of whom were doubtless desirous of distinguishing themselves, and attracting, by the boldness of their doctrine, the admiration of their congregations, there can be little doubt that the extensive privileges which they claimed were liable to frequent abuse. But this was an evil only to be cured by time, which modifies the violence of parties whether in politics or religion, added to much patience and much firmness on the part of the governors. Meanwhile these prerogatives, boldly claimed and acted zealously upon, gave great alarm to the sovereign. King James, although a Protestant in principle, had been bred in such dislike and terror of those more violent individuals among the churchmen, who were termed fanatics, that in his Basilicon Doron he has left it as a legacy to his son rather to trust a savage Highlander, or an outlawed borderer, than a hypocritical puritan.

To increase the monarch's early dislike to this party among his subjects, which was constantly kept up by the imprudent, indecent, and impertinent censures of individual

preachers, it so chanced that James almost always found the
opinions of the popular churchmen in diametrical opposition
to his own authority and the measures of his ministers.
There was, therefore, an almost continued dissension between the king and the most popular and authoritative part
of the clergy, which lasted, with little intermission, during
his whole reign, and in which one is sometimes called upon
to censure the unreasonable, irreverent, and irritating conduct of those who ought to have been the messengers of
peace, but oftener to admire the courage with which they
defended the liberties which had been handed down to them
by their predecessors, and the firmness with which they submitted voluntarily to poverty, banishment, and proscription,
rather than resign an iota of what they conceived to be their
lawful privileges as the servants of Heaven.

At the period which we treat of, the greater part of the
clergy were connected by opinion and principle with the
lords who were in exile on account of the Raid of Ruthven.
Arran had at different times made advances to gain the
favor of the Church; but even the occasional advantages
which the clergy obtained by means of the minister had been
received like the more important benefits which Bothwell
had procured for the Church from Queen Mary during the
brief time of his guilty prosperity. Both these worthless
and wicked men were total disbelievers in public principle
or private honor, and, conscious of the total absence of both
in their own persons, had hoped by what might be called
bribery to secure the attachment of a class of persons who,
by principle and profession, were votaries and teachers of
religion and morality almost to the verge of bigotry. Their
advances were, therefore, spurned in consequence of the
hatred inspired by their vices; and the ministers of the
Church of Scotland continued not the less their enemies
that they had endeavored to secure their goodwill by benefits to their order.

Convinced at last that the Church could not be conciliated by fair means, Arran, having the court at his disposal,

determined on carrying through such a series of restrictive laws as should debar the clergy in future from intermeddling with the affairs of State, under the penalty of answering to the temporal jurisdictions, which he hoped to retain under the management of the king, that is, under his own.

For this purpose, in the year 1584, the parliament was declared current, and convened on the 22d of May, in order to confirm the king's declaration respecting the Raid of Ruthven; pronouncing the doom of forfeiture against Angus and others, and the establishment of such a code of regulations as might in future intimidate the ministers of the Church of Scotland from exercising their wonted interference in civil affairs. Unusual pains were taken to prevent any rumors going abroad of the nature or extent of the intended measures. The lords of the articles, to whom was intrusted the concoction of all business to be brought before parliament, were sworn to secrecy concerning the subjects to be submitted to them. All access to the king's person was denied to persons suspected to be hostile to the administration; and under these precautions the following severe laws were passed for the purpose of restraining the privileges of the Church, real and assumed.

The king's authority over all persons, and in all cases whatsoever, was formally confirmed. "The declining his majesty's judgment and that of the council, in whatsoever matter, was," says Spottiswoode, "declared to be treason. The impugning the authority of the three estates, or procuring the innovation or diminution of the power of any of them, was inhibited under the same pain. All jurisdictions and judicatures, spiritual or temporal, not approved of by his highness and the three estates, were discharged, and an ordinance made, that none of whatsoever function, quality, or degree, should presume privately or publicly, in sermons, declamations, or familiar conferences, to utter any false, untrue, or slanderous speeches, to the reproach of his majesty, his council, and proceedings, or to the dishonor, hurt, or prejudice of his highness, his parents, and

progenitors, or to meddle with the affairs of his highness
and estate, under the pains contained in the acts of parliament made against the makers and reporters of lies.'' The
Church of Scotland was by these sweeping enactments totally altered in its constitution and privileges. A change
which we must regard in a very different light, if we consider the privileges which they claimed theoretically, or look
at their practical effects.

In the first point of view there appears no political wisdom in rendering a body like the clergy, set apart for duties
inconsistent with the bustle of active life, the depositaries of
a nation's liberty, otherwise than in matters of religious doctrine and conscience. But though such a charge was an
anomaly, it was still more essential to the liberties of the
nation that a power of reminding the subjects of their rights,
and the rulers of their duty, should exist somewhere, than
that it should be lodged in those hands which might be
theoretically preferred as the most expedient and best.

The Scottish parliament were, indeed, in theory, the natural and proper guardians of the people's freedom; but the
institution of the committee, called lords of the articles,
who had the previous privilege of arranging and garbing
the business which was to come before parliament, prevented
the efficacy of the national representatives in their proper
sphere. Besides, the warm and precipitate discord of Scottish factions was not of a nature which could abide the cold
decision of a parliamentary debate, or be decided by the orderly and peaceful vote of a deliberative assembly. When
a party was triumphant they held a parliament of their
own, at which those opposed to them took special care not
to give attendance; or if a statute was accounted injurious to the subject, they showed their sense of its injustice
not by opposing the bill in its progress through parliament,
but by disregarding and disobeying it after it had passed
into a law. It followed, therefore, that in most cases, as
during the administration of Arran, the parliament was
formed of persons chosen as being friendly to the prime

minister, and under control of a close committee of lords of the articles selected by himself, who were more likely to be the organs of the royal or ministerial pleasure than the means of controlling it.

The voice of the national representation being thus mute, it was highly essential that there should exist somewhere a privilege of reprehension and remonstrance against the inroads of power upon popular rights; and the Church of Scotland, from circumstances and habit, had obtained possession of a privilege, the existence of which was of vital importance to the welfare of the community. That this zealous and hardy class of men, little accustomed to carry moderation into their opinions or temper into their debates, should have exercised their right with uniform moderation and judgment, could hardly be expected of so large a body composed of persons so various in temper and talents; but that they uniformly exerted it with courage, and endured with patience and resolution the personal penalties which ensued, must be admitted as a compensation for much petulance and ill-timed interference on the part of the preachers. In a word, this peculiarity in the Scottish constitution resembled a case in architecture, easily conceived, and frequently occurring. An architect would be justly censured, who, in contriving a house, should make a window the ordinary vent for the smoke; but if by any accident the chimney is obstructed, an attempt to shut up some aperture, because anomalous, must have the effect to stifle the inhabitants. The destruction, therefore, of this privilege of the clergy, though rather of an inconsistent character, considering their sacred function, was a bold step toward the establishment of despotism in Scotland.

While the obnoxious measures were yet depending, the ministers of the Church sent one of their number to the king, with a petition that no act affecting the Church should be permitted to pass through parliament until the brethren should be heard upon its tenor. But mystery and precipitation are the usual attendants of arbitrary resolutions, while those of a different character are uniformly distinguished by calm deliberation and free discussion. Lindsay, the bearer of this moderate petition, was not permitted to approach the king's presence, but was arrested at the gate of the palace, and sent prisoner to the State fortress of Blackness. Another clergyman of Edinburgh, named Pont, who was also a senator of the college of justice, took a protest against the measures understood to be passing through parliament, on the ground that they had been adopted without consent or knowledge of the Church. In reward of what was termed his contumacy, Pont was declared a rebel, degraded from his condition as a judge, and forced to fly into England.

These violent measures raised universal terror. The most learned and conscientious of the clergy saw no remedy, save resigning their charges, or submitting tamely to be deprived of their privileges of freely expressing their sentiments. The ministers of Edinburgh set an example of the sacrifice. They adopted in a body the resolution of voluntary exile; and from the borders of England the devoted band wrote a letter to the provost and magistrates of Edinburgh, declaring that they left their charge, after a long wrestling, with the purpose of reserving themselves for better times, and of flying for the present from the death with which they were menaced, should they remain, for the purpose of bearing testimony against the iniquitous encroachments on the privileges of their order.

The pulpits in the metropolis being thus silenced, a gloomy discontent overwhelmed all ranks of men, but especially those who had most zealously professed the reformed doctrines; and James himself did not escape the suspicion of being inclined to bring Scotland back to the superstitious yoke of Rome. In many more instances than we have space to notice, the strife was maintained between the Church and the civil power by individual ministers, who plainly saw that by renouncing their claim to interfere in temporal politics they would deprive their doctrine of its savor, and render themselves as insignificant as they were already indigent.

Meantime Arran, the great mover of these perilous innovations in Church and State, neglected not to advance his own interest by means as unjustifiable as those which regulated his general government. The death of Argyle gave him opportunity to seize the office of chancellor. Thus he engrossed offices of rank and authority one after another, without considering that his power, like an ill-constructed building, rested on an imperfect foundation, and that every increase of height must only give it additional insecurity. His inordinate rapacity and vanity gave birth to a report that he meant to lay claim to the throne, which was founded on his having had the affectation to lodge in parliament a deed, on his part formally disclaiming the purpose of insisting on any right competent to him to claim the crown as a successor of Murdach, duke of Albany. The intimating the existence of such a right was considered as high presumption, and in secret could not but be deeply offensive to James himself.

The favorite's overgrown fortunes were thus evidently tottering to a fall; and it was a sure proof that the time was not far distant, when even the individuals who were raised into power by his own recommendations sought to advance themselves by separating their interests from his. He had raised to the office of secretary, John Maitland, the brother of the celebrated Lethington, and possessor of the family talents. This statesman, who afterward rose to great eminence, continued for a certain time to regard Arran as his patron, and therefore ruled his actions by that favorite's inclination; but perceiving that the headlong course which the earl pursued could not lead to permanent greatness or safety, he by degrees drew off from his party, and began to establish a separate interest of his own.

This was the case also with a young man of extraordinary talents, but unhappily of equal duplicity, who began at this time to be distinguished at first as a friend and afterward as a rival of Arran in the king's favor. This was the Master of Gray, personally handsome, witty, and accomplished in those exercises which gained James's eye and affection, but totally destitute of principle, whether moral or political. He concealed for a long time his private views of entering into competition with the ruling favorite, and seemed, on the contrary, to devote himself to the augmentation of Arran's greatness. This artful and rising young man, having considerable acquaintance with England, is supposed to have first impressed upon Arran the necessity of cultivating the friendship of Elizabeth.

This was, indeed, no easy matter; for the efforts of the English ambassadors had been hitherto systematically and uniformly directed to the destruction of Arran's power, either by secretly undermining it, or by openly accusing him of unfitness to be the minister. But Burleigh, deeply read in the politics of Machiavel, had disapproved of the open dislike avowed by Walsingham to the person of Arran, and held it better and more politic to dissemble with him while he remained in James's favor. Elizabeth, therefore, and her ministers, though entertaining no better opinion of Arran than before, yet were willing to adopt the policy of availing themselves of his present credit, by obtaining such advantages as could be derived from an intimate league with the prime minister of Scotland.

For cementing such an agreement, which, it is probable, neither party had the intention of keeping longer than served their own interest, Arran, with great splendor of attendance, and in capacity of royal lord lieutenant, held a confidential meeting upon the borders with Lord Hunsdon, the relation of Queen Elizabeth. Here Arran is said to have devoted himself to the interests of England, engaging, for the satisfaction of Queen Elizabeth's anxieties concerning the succession to the English crown, to keep the king unmarried for three years, by thwarting and disconcerting any match which might be proposed during that period. On the part of Hunsdon an elusory promise was said to have been made that, the three years being expired, James should be wedded to an unmarried princess of the blood of England,

who would then be marriageable, and invested by Elizabeth
with the title of second person in the English kingdom.
There is little doubt that this was one of those vague proposals by which Elizabeth hoped to stave off James's marriage to an indefinite period, as she had attempted in respect
to that of his mother. Upon the whole, the English counsellors deemed Arran far too flighty, vain, and unsettled,
to be much relied on; and although apparently engaging to
support Arran's interest with James, and avail herself in
return of that favorite's good offices, Queen Elizabeth was,
in fact, corresponding with those who had Arran's destruction at heart, and was privately determined to assist them
by every means in her power.

In the meantime, however, it was necessary to pay some
apparent attention to his remonstrances, made in the name
of his master, on account of the shelter afforded to the exiles
of Scotland. Angus and his companions were ordered to
London; and there was an affectation on the part of England of restraining their intercourse and their intrigues with
their own country.

Arran, confiding in his supposed friendship with England,
proceeded in the pursuit of his own interest with the direct
and disgusting rapacity which aims only at instant gratification without caring for consequences. The Earl of Athole,
the Lord Home, and the Master of Cassilis, great names,
and implying both rank and power, were severally imprisoned at his instance, for singular and very tyrannical reasons. The first, because he refused to divorce his wife, a
daughter of the deceased Earl of Gowrie, and entail his
estate upon Arran. The second, because he declined to convey to the tyrannical minister a portion of the lands of Dirle-
ton. The third, because he had refused to lend Arran money
when it was supposed he had some to spare—a species of
offence which can be comprehended in all stages of society,
though, happily for moneyed men, those disposed to be their
debtors have seldom the means of avenging themselves for
a repulse. Besides the enmity thus excited, Arran, in for-

warding certain partial views of his own, awakened a deadly
feud on the western borders of Scotland, so important as to
assume the character of a civil war.

The county of Dumfries had been long agitated by the
disagreement of the ancient and powerful clans of Johnstone
and Maxwell, who contended for the supreme influence. Of
these the family of Maxwell was by far the richer, the more
numerous, the more powerful, and possessed in the dale of
the Nith the more extensive and wealthy territory. The
Johnstones, on the contrary, were thorough-paced borderers,
living in the fastnesses of Annandale, a country nearly inaccessible, constantly engaged in war and depredation, and
possessed of equal readiness to take arms and skill to use
them. Their want of numbers or strength was made up by
an inveterate love of war and the most determined courage.
They were thus enabled to wage war with equal auspices
against a feudal enemy more powerful than themselves;
and it now suited the Earl of Arran to make them ministers of his vengeance upon the clan of Maxwell, against
whose chieftain he harbored a personal cause of complaint.
Arran had become desirous to exchange the barony of Kinneil, which he had succeeded to in the manner already mentioned, as a part of the insane Earl of Arran's most unjust
forfeiture, for the lands of Maxwellheugh, an ancient possession of the Lord Maxwell. The proposed exchange was
declined by Maxwell, who saw no reason to part with his
ancient patrimony, and had, perhaps, little confidence in
the security of the title by which he was to hold the new
acquisition offered to him in lieu of it. Indignant at this
opposition to his will and convenience, Arran resolved to
avenge himself by stirring up again the Lord Maxwell his
hereditary enemies the Johnstones. In order to attain this
point, by awakening the ancient rivalry between the houses,
he prevailed upon the chief of the Johnstones to accept of
the office of provost of Dumfries, now and for years past
held by the rival chief. Maxwell, understanding that the
citizens had received a letter from the king, directing them

to elect Johnstone for the provost, naturally interpreted this as done in scorn of his prior right, and resolved to occupy the town forcibly, and put Johnstone to death in case he attempted to stand the election. Changing his purpose, however, he contented himself with obstructing Johnstone's entrance into Dumfries, while he procured himself to be continued in the disputed office. To further his revenge, which had hitherto miscarried, Arran caused Maxwell to be denounced a rebel, for his obstruction of the king's pleasure in the matter of the provostry, and on account of certain border irregularities, of which pretexts were never wanting against the great men, who, like Maxwell, had rule in that disturbed country.

Commission was given to Johnstone to pursue and apprehend his rival; and two bands of mercenary soldiers were despatched to render him assistance in that enterprise. These hired soldiers, as they marched through Crawford Moor to join with their allies the Johnstones, were surrounded, defeated, and slain, or made prisoners by the Maxwells. Johnstone, smarting under this discomfiture, raised his banner, and invaded Nithsdale, burning and taking spoil with the usual border ferocity. Maxwell retaliated; and the clans, so long opposed to each other, having met in pitched battle, Johnstone was defeated and made prisoner—an affront which afflicted his proud spirit so severely that he died of grief shortly after he was liberated. The feud continued violent between the two great families: incursions, depredations, and skirmishes took place on either side, and all through the fault of the unscrupulous minister, who, in his desire to avenge a private grudge against Maxwell, had totally destroyed the peace of the country, where it was his duty as chancellor to see the laws equally administered, and tranquillity preserved among the subjects.

Nor had Arran's individual impolicy been less evident in fomenting this civil war than the neglect of his public duty. In Maxwell he had added to his own personal enemies a powerful and warlike chieftain, the head of a military clan, and situated so near the border that he might make common cause with the Scottish exiles, the incensed clergymen, and the minister's other enemies. Accordingly Arran was sensible of the danger too late. A convention of the estates was called, money was voted, and levies were set on foot for a royal expedition to suppress Maxwell; but the severe pestilence that broke out in Edinburgh occasioned the delay of the projected expedition.

In the meantime Elizabeth, relying little or nothing on the faith of Arran, who showed himself as devoid of wisdom as he was of popularity, was desirous, if possible, to rest her friendship with Scotland upon a more secure basis than that on which it had been placed by Arran's interview with Hunsdon.

For this purpose she chose to enter into a new negotiation, founded on the habits and character of James himself. The reports of Walsingham may be supposed to have produced some effect in favor of the Scottish monarch, at least so far as to make it appear politic to study his disposition more closely, and gain the personal favor less of his ministers than of the king himself. The queen selected for this purpose an envoy to reside at the Scottish court, singularly well adapted to further her views, whether he should find the Scottish prince of that character, at once solid and ingenious, which Walsingham ascribed to him, or whether James should be found, according to common repute, influenced by the silly habit of favoritism and overweening attachment to juvenile sports. This envoy was called Wotton. He was sent, according to the Master of Gray, not to tease his majesty with politics, or troublesome and thorny matters of business, but to partake with him in the honest pastimes of hunting, hawking, and riding, and entertain him with friendly and merry discourses; having been a great traveller, and seen various courts.

Above all, Wotton was recommended by Gray as a sincere friend and favorer of his majesty's title and succession to the throne of England.

Under this gay and gilded exterior, which was calculated
to advance him in the opinion of James, the English envoy
added the dangerous qualities of an experienced spy and
bold intriguer; and had from his mistress the delicate charge
of combining together and bringing to union all the discontented spirits whom he should find willing to engage in
opposition to Arran. The moment the experienced Melville
set his eyes upon the new envoy of England at the Scottish
court, he recognized the person of a young man whom he
had known at Paris acting the part of a spy in the disguise
of an Irish page, and forming the channel through which
some treacherous proposals were made to the constable of
France for the surprisal of Calais. This important discovery
he communicated to James; leaving it to the king to judge
how Wotton's former occupation agreed with the character
of a frank, jovial, light-hearted sportsman, assigned to him
by the Master of Gray. Although James was thus warned
of Wotton's real character, he could not resist being captivated with his accomplishments in hunting and hawking
and other sylvan pastimes, and admitted him far more into
his society than was either prudent or proper.

The matter of State on which Wotton was chiefly directed
to insist was one of the utmost importance to both parts of
Britain, being the formation of a league, offensive and defensive, among all Protestant sovereigns, to counterbalance
that which had been formed between the pope, the Spanish
king, the brethren of the House of Guise, and other Catholic
princes, having for its object the extirpation of the reformed
religion. Such a league was assented to with great formality
by the king in parliament, being offensive and defensive in
all matters which should affect the cause of religion. In
return for his brotherly zeal, Elizabeth settled on James the
solid benefit of a pension of four thousand pounds sterling,
which was highly acceptable to the Scottish sovereign, whose
revenue was in a most dilapidated condition. When this
ostensible purpose of his embassy was accomplished, it was
supposed that Sir Edward Wotton, the envoy extraordinary,

would have returned to the English court; but he had yet
a deeper and darker intrigue to conduct, in the destruction
of the power of the favorite Arran.

This had been considerably shaken: Gray and Maitland,
though they had risen under his favor, as we have seen,
were secretly his enemies: the king was in some late instances
known to express himself dissatisfied with his violence; and
a misfortune had of late happened on the border of a character which endangered the peace between the kingdoms,
which, if not directly imputable to his agency, was yet such
as he was considered liable to be made responsible for.

Sir John Foster, warden of the eastern marches of England, had held one of the usual meetings of truce with Sir
Thomas Kerr of Farniherst, warden of the middle marches
of Scotland, when a question of dispute arose concerning the
satisfaction claimed for certain cattle said to have been stolen
out of Scotland: the dispute waxed warm; and each warden
being surrounded by the usual number of armed borderers—
delinquents who found their own account in war and disturbance—they came very soon from words to blows. The
Scottish poured a volley of their firearms upon the English,
by which Sir Francis Russell, eldest son of the Earl of Bed-
ford, was mortally wounded, and died, bequeathing to the
fatal spot, which is on the farm of Auldton Burn, and exactly
on the march between England and Scotland, the name of
Russell's Cairn.

Queen Elizabeth was highly offended when she received
this information; and although such accidents were frequent, considering the inflammable temper of the clans who
usually attended on these occasions, it was her pleasure in
this case to impute the death of Russell to the special malice
of Farniherst, instigated by his patron Arran to take such
violent measures for breaking the peace with England. There
is no possibility of judging with certainty what might or
might not be true respecting a person of Arran's rash and
fickle temper. But considering that he had been so lately
courting the friendship of Elizabeth, as essential to his own

interest, it seems improbable that he should suddenly break it off in so violent a manner; and it is much more likely that Elizabeth, perceiving his credit at James's court beginning to fail, availed herself of this pretext of assisting to overthrow it entirely, with the hope of filling up his place in James's counsels by men upon whose principles she could better rely than on a favorite intoxicated with his undeserved advancement and devoid at once of faith and of sagacity. The remonstrance of his allies, skilfully enforced by the art of Wotton, had, no doubt, considerable effect upon James. He appointed Sir Thomas Kerr to enter into ward, that is, to remain a prisoner on parole in the town of Aberdeen, and commanded Arran to restrain himself to his mansion of Kinneil. Farniherst died in his imprisonment; for, being a man of a haughty spirit, and conscious of having rendered many services to Mary in her distresses, he resented the usage which he received from the son of his old mistress, and is said to have died of mortification.

Other agents were strangely intermingled in the dark intrigues.

About this time a judicial proceeding took place of a very peculiar character, which indicated the boldness with which the Scottish ministers pursued their criminal intrigues, their contempt of public opinion, and their reliance upon the extreme docility of King James.

It has been already mentioned that when Morton was accused of the murder of Darnley, on the last day of December, 1580, his cousin, Archibald Douglas, titular parson of Glasgow, was involved in the same charge; nay, a great part of the accusation against Morton rested upon his having favored and preferred this Archibald Douglas, although by the testimony of those persons who suffered for the murder Archibald had been himself present at the deed, and although by Morton's own confession the same person had proposed the crime to him on the part of Bothwell, and urged him to take part in the execution. Being thus involved in the alleged guilt of his patron Morton, even more deeply than the earl himself, Douglas was deprived of his office of a judge of the Court of Session, which he held by the favor of the late regent, and was obliged to fly to England. He was subjected to a doom of forfeiture in the month of November, 1581; and the king made repeated demands to Elizabeth that he should be delivered up to him for trial and execution.

Douglas was a man of that species of talents which suited the time; able, intriguing, bold, and audacious, unscrupulous enough to act with any party in any kingdom, and shrewd enough to take the full advantage of any circumstance which might occur in his favor. During his banishment in England he had intimately connected himself with Elizabeth's minister, Randolph, and others, whom she considered as most proper to maintain the oblique and indirect connections which her policy disposed her to entertain with the various malcontents in Scotland. The intrigues of the Master of Gray were closely connected with the same class of ministers; and it appears that he held, in consequence, an intimate intercourse with the banished Archibald Douglas. When Arran's influence at court began to fail, an act was passed under the great seal, releasing Douglas from the decree of forfeiture pronounced against him as both accessory and principal in Darnley's murder: it contained the extraordinary clause, that if, notwithstanding, Douglas on a fair trial should be found guilty of accession to the king's murder, the act of rehabilitation should lose its force. Under this species of assurance, limited as it was, Douglas had the audacity to return to his native country. For decency's sake he was subjected to a trial, which appears to have been in every respect collusive, and so managed as to insure the escape of the prisoner: it was so conducted as to place his fate in the hands of jurymen selected by the prisoner himself; others who were cited, having refused to attend, were supplied from a list summoned by an order of the king produced by the accused, and consisting, as far as can now be discovered, of jurors fully disposed for his acquittal; by jurymen thus packed, having the Master of Gray as their chancellor, in May, 1586, he was acquitted of the crime. It also occurred, as a singular feature on the trial, that the confession of Morton, who stated that Douglas, now accused, had been the person through whom Bothwell communicated with him upon the deed, was withdrawn from the record, and could not be produced against the accused. Thus collusively acquitted from an accession to the murder of the king's father, of which he was unquestionably guilty, Archibald Douglas continued to be a favorite channel of communication between the English intriguers in Scotland and Gray, and other favorers of their interest at James's court: and he appears shortly after this narrow escape from a trial for the crime of which he was certainly guilty, the murder, namely, of the king's father, to have been designed as ambassador for England. Unquestionably the object of this most indecent proceeding was to insure to the Master of Gray a safe, secret, and subtile agent, with whom he might communicate with his friends in England upon the measures to be adopted for accomplishing the downfall of Arran. A singular letter of Thomas Randolph, the most active agent in these dark and iniquitous transactions, is still preserved:[1] it is written in a strain of drollery not uncharacteristic of wicked men, who often concert and carry on their villanies in a tone of jest which renders them, perhaps, more indifferent in their own eyes than if they used the ordinary language of common life. He seems to consider Douglas as not quite restored in character, as we may infer from his tone of salutation, in which he addresses him as *domine non adhuc sacrosancte:* he talks of the Carrs as probably fled to the hills, in consequence of Elizabeth's resentment for the death of Russell, and alludes to tumults shortly to ensue in Scotland. "Look to your own person," he proceeds, "that you bring it shortly sacro-sanctified into England. Beware of the crafts of the Arranses, and hatred of the Carrs; for

---

[1] See State Papers of Murdin and Haynes, vol. ii., p. 558.

hereupon dependeth the state of your welfare, sarctifica-
tion, or reprobation." He proceeds, alluding possibly to
some libel or attack upon himself as well as Douglas: "As
notable a peece of knavery hath been of late wrote agaynst
my sanctitie *in esse*, and yours *in propinquo*, as any cun-
ninge knave in Scotland could ever have wrought." The
concluding paragraph of this remarkable letter not only
affords peculiar evidence of James's ruling taste, but serves
to show that the means by which Randolph studied to gratify
them were transmitted through hands so imperfectly cleansed
from his father's blood: "I have sent the kynge two hunting
men, verie good and skilfull, with one footman, that can
hoop, hollow, and crye, that all the trees in Fawkland will
quake for fear: pray the kynge's majestie to be mercifull
to poor bucks; but let him spare and look well to himself."
Within a few weeks Douglas, replaced in the secular possession of the benefice of Glasgow, which was, probably, great
part of the sacro-sanctification alluded to by Randolph, was
sent to England as the ordinary ambassador of King James;
and there can be little doubt that to him and to the Master
of Gray are to be imputed not only the fall of Arran, which
was in itself a deliverance to Scotland, but the death of
Queen Mary, which was accelerated by their nefarious
intrigues.

Arran was soon relieved from his confinement on account
of Russell's death; but cannot have been restored to the confidence of his sovereign, since intrigues were now carried
forward almost openly for the object of removing him from
power. With this view Sir Edward Wotton held secret communication with Maitland, Gray, and other counsellors in
Scotland hostile to Arran's interest, and no less with Angus
and the other exiles, on account of the Raid of Ruthven,
whom he encouraged to approach once more to the border
to unite with Lord Maxwell, the capital enemy of Arran;
and then advancing into the interior, to achieve by force of
arms a purpose which was scarcely now likely to be seriously
opposed, so numerous were the enemies of the favorite, and

so far had he declined in his master's opinion. For the same reason, the exiles of Ruthven, laying aside consideration of the ancient feud between the Hamiltons and Douglases, resolved to make one cause with Lords John and Claud Hamilton, disinherited by the oppression of Morton, and enter Scotland in the same company with them.

In autumn, 1585, Arran became aware of the intended invasion, and appointed a levy of the array of Scotland to join the king at the castle of Crawford on the 22d day of October, in order to meet and repel it. But the statesmen whom he himself had introduced into power now openly deserted his falling authority: Gray and Maitland, who were concerned in Wotton's intrigue, prevented the summonses from being circulated or attended to. The banished lords hastened to prevent the king's levies, and assembled a body of about a thousand men at the town of Linton, where they were joined by Maxwell with seven or eight hundred horse and three hundred infantry—a force almost equal to the united strength which his new associates could muster. They immediately set in motion toward Stirling, where the king and Arran lay, proclaiming the said earl and Colonel William Stewart abusers of the king's favor, for whose removal from the public councils and for the preserving of peace with England they declared themselves to be in arms.

The Earl of Bothwell and others hastened to join with them. Indeed, the avowal of such motives was so generally accepted that before they reached St. Ninian's their numbers were increased to nearly ten thousand men in arms. In the meantime the alarm at Stirling was great. Wotton, the English ambassador, who had been so busy in all these intrigues, thought it safe to withdraw from Scotland without taking farewell, when he perceived an explosion unavoidable. Some imputed this unusually precipitate departure to his having trafficked in some scheme for the delivery of the king's person into the hands of the discontented nobles; others supposed he was unwilling to be within the power of Arran when he should find himself overreached. He himself imputed his haste to his mistress's resentment of the delay in delivering up Farniherst, which is the least probable cause which could have been assigned, since a mortal malady had already arrested that unfortunate chief.

Arran, cooped up in Stirling, made some pretence of defending himself, although such had been his supineness or the treachery of those whom he had intrusted with the charge of affairs at this crisis, that neither arms, men, nor provisions were in readiness for the emergency. The night passed in fruitless debates. Ere the break of day a cry arose that the town was taken. The invaders, having obtained entrance by the connivance of some friends, were, in fact, in possession of the town. Arran fled; and having the key of Stirling Bridge about his person, was enabled to make his escape, locking the gates behind him to prevent pursuit. James remained in Stirling Castle with some courtiers about his person, but without garrison or provisions.

Deserted by his favorite, he opened a communication with the armed lords, and it appears they soon came to understand each other. The lords protested that their approach in that warlike manner was not meant to put any compulsion upon the king, but merely to obtain permission to reside on their estates, and to serve their country. James, on his part, manifested much moderation: he had never liked, he said, the violence of Arran; and was content to admit the noblemen to his presence and favor, provided he was assured of safety to those who had been his friends and active in his service.

Moderation being promised, on the part of the victorious insurgents, the king received the armed petitioners with a considerable degree of dignity. To Lord Hamilton, who, in precedence of blood, was the first to offer his homage, he replied, "My lord, I never before saw you; and I must confess, of all that are here, you have been most wronged, having been a faithful servant to the queen, my mother, during my minority, and subject to ill usage, when I understood not matters as I now do.—Others of you," he said, looking to the lords concerned in the Raid of Ruthven, "cannot but say that you have had your deserts, and suffered no more than your misdemeanors merited. For thee, Francis," he continued, addressing the Earl of Bothwell, who had joined the invaders since their entrance into Scotland, "what could move thee to come in arms against a sovereign who never offended thee? I wish thee a more quiet spirit and knowledge how to live as a subject, as otherwise thou wilt fall into much trouble." This Earl of Bothwell, whom James so apostrophized, was Francis Stewart, grandson of King James V., by his natural son, and, consequently, a cousin-german of the reigning monarch. The estates and honors of Bothwell and lordship of Liddisdale had been conferred upon him after the forfeiture of the infamous James Hepburn; but it seems as if the very title was doomed to infect those who bore it with a strain of inordinate and turbulent ambition. For this nobleman became a principal source of disorder during King James's reign, as he who had formerly borne the title was the pest and shame of Queen Mary's, so that the speech addressed to him by the king at the Raid of Stirling seemed, in some degree, prophetic.

The king's cordial reception of the lords seemed the preface to an amicable settlement. Some changes were made in order to give offices to the new-comers. Arran, deprived of his titles and offices, was suffered to reside in neglect and safety among his kinsmen, in the district of Kyle, where he lived obscurely, under his original name of Captain James Stewart. The contempt indicated by this neglect shows that there was no longer any reason to dread his influence over the king's mind, and that his hour of favor had passed away.

The blood of only one individual stained this remarkable revolution; and its effusion was lamented by no one. The slain man was Hamilton of Eglismachan, the person upon whose information Douglas of Mains and Cunningham of Drumquhassel were condemned and executed. Johnstone of Westerkirk, a brave and determined borderer, had made a vow to avenge the death of Mains, who had been his fellow-soldier. At his approach to Stirling in the van of the insurgent forces, as soon as he could set eyes upon Hamilton, he rushed to attack him. The informer, who had long lived in terror of such a fate, fled into the king's park, where he was followed and slain by the self-elected avenger of blood. Another incident, occasioned, it would seem, by remorse of conscience, threw light upon the undeserved fate of these two innocent gentlemen. Edmonstone of Duntreath, as the reader will remember, had been brought to trial along with them in the capacity of an associate, and had pleaded guilty, alleging that the plot for seizing the king's person had been concerted by himself and the gentlemen accused, on the instigation of Black John Home, a follower of the Earl of Angus. This confession, on the part of a supposed associate, was urged against Argaty and Drumquhassel. This same Edmonstone now came forward before the privy council, voluntarily and unsummoned, to acknowledge that his former confession was a tissue of falsehoods, which he had been compelled to utter by the menaces of James Stewart, the late earl of Arran. This contradiction of his former testimony was, probably, brought forward to obtain favor, or immunity, at least, from the Earl of Angus, whose name had been introduced as the original instigator of the conspiracy imputed to Mains and Drumquhassel.

Upon the whole, this revolution of affairs, as it was executed with moderation and without bloodshed, was of great advantage to the kingdom, by removing from the helm a steersman like Arran, at once shortsighted and reckless, interested and impetuous.

CHAPTER XXXIV

Queen Mary in Prison—Becomes the Object of Interest to all who
conspire against Queen Elizabeth—Elizabeth's Anxiety on her
Account—Her Removal from Carlisle to Bolton—From Bolton
to Tutbury, to Wingfield, to Coventry, to Chatsworth—Her
visit to Buxton—Account of her by Nicolas White—Her Amusements—Is more strictly guarded—And the Marks of Respect
shown to her diminished—Injustice of her Treatment—Causes
of Queen Elizabeth's Exasperation against her—The proposed
Match with Norfolk unpleasing to her—The English war
against the Queen's Party in Scotland—Attempt at a Treaty
with Mary broken off by the Scottish Commissioners—Norfolk
sent to the Tower—Mary desirous of an Interview with Elizabeth—Elizabeth incites the Feelings of her Subjects against
Mary, and endeavors to disgrace her in the Eyes of the Public
—Works against her circulated—Proceedings against her in
Parliament—Rigor of her Captivity increased

WHILE James VI. travelled through the slippery
and dangerous course of a Scottish minority, his
mother, though without any reason assigned other
than the will of Queen Elizabeth, remained an unpitied prisoner, sometimes in the house of one nobleman, sometimes in
that of another; all sensible that they offended the queen if
they treated the royal captive with anything approaching
to indulgence; and under the necessity, besides, of incurring
considerable personal expense, which their sovereign Elizabeth seldom dreamed of reimbursing in an adequate degree.
An active mind, and an early practice of feminine pursuits,
a turn toward religion, for which she was, perhaps, indebted
to adversity, with the power of studying and writing in various languages, enabled Mary to endure, with more than
female constancy, the long succeeding years of her weary

imprisonment. Hope, originally her frequent visitor, began to be less frequent in his attendance. As her places of residence were changed, her train was abated, the marks of honor rendered to her former rank were abridged, and her apartments, defended with bolts and filled with armed warders, bore more and more the undisguised air of a prison-house; and the question was not, as at first, how long her confinement should last, but merged in the darker inquiry, how or when she was to be relieved by death.

In the meantime, the fate of the Scottish queen, as it was sometimes the object of censure, and often of regret, among the most attached subjects of Elizabeth, stimulated to hopes and to enterprise the Roman Catholics of England, a numerous party, who could not be insensible to the sufferings of a princess of their own religion, even if she had not, in their opinion, possessed a title to their allegiance better than any which existed in the person of her oppressor. Repeated plots, discovered by the wisdom of Elizabeth's counsellors, had almost always for their object the liberation of Queen Mary, and were usually connected with some scheme for placing her on the British throne. The anxieties and perplexities in which Elizabeth was thus involved were not the more easily endured that they might be considered as the consequences of her own injustice.

In former days Mary, living in freedom and happiness in her own kingdom, might be to Elizabeth an object of inconvenient yet only occasional rivalry; but, captive and forlorn, she was now perpetually brought before her in every form which could render the contrast painful: to speak fancifully, the queen of England was somewhat in the situation of one who, having murdered his enemy, is ever after haunted by his spectre. The reflections upon her own injustice, and upon the effect which it was likely to produce, made her entertain the most fantastic apprehensions of the extent of Queen Mary's faculty of seducing, and the apprehensions of her rival's powers over her own most chosen favorites. She had seen Norfolk and other nobles of undoubted faith shoot madly from their spheres, as the poet expresses it, attracted by the charms of a suffering queen and a captive beauty. Shrewsbury, on whom she long imposed the unwelcome office of Mary's keeper, at his several castles of Tutbury, Chatsworth, Wingfield, and others, could not, though old and faithful, escape the suspicions of his royal mistress any more than those of his jealous countess: both suspected him of too much favor for the royal prisoner; and reproaches from court and domestic ill-humor was the consequence of the slightest indulgence extended to his captive.

Thus all that was dangerous, distasteful, and prejudicial to Elizabeth, came by degrees to be mixed up with her idea of her prisoner Mary, until dislike increased into hatred, and hatred joined with fear became fierce enough, like the Indian snake-god in Madoc, to demand a victim.

These considerations may account, though they cannot apologize, for the principles on which Elizabeth acted toward Mary, and in which the greatest queen that ever sat upon the throne of England, or, perhaps, upon that of any other country, seems to have been actuated at once by the jealousy of power incidental to the most ambitious mind, and by the peevish envy of disposition proper to the lowest female. It was not the least part of the distress and inconvenience inflicted upon Queen Mary that her place of confinement was repeatedly changed, upon the slightest suspicion that the neighborhood was friendly to her; and that some cause of alarm was always arising, and to such Elizabeth was sensibly accessible.

Mary had fled to Carlisle without either money or even a fitting change of clothes. Her attendants then consisted of about thirty, four or five of them being persons of consequence attached to her party, and as many ladies of rank, the rest menials of various degrees attendant upon the royal person. She was first removed from Carlisle, where her person was conceived to be in danger of rescue, especially when she followed, within sight of the hills of her own kingdom, the pastimes of hunting, and others from which it was not thought decent as yet to debar her. Her removal took place on the 16th of July, 1568, when her person was committed to the charge of Lord Scroope and Sir Francis Knollis, the former being the lord of the castle; and Mary remained at Bolton till the 26th of January, 1568-9. During the dead of winter, in a state of health which was always precarious, owing to an old hurt received in the bosom, through a cold country and during a rigorous season, she was transported to Tutbury. This journey was made with so little precaution that the captive queen suffered all the inconveniences of the most ordinary pauper in the present day. Tutbury was an ancient castle belonging to the Earl of Shrewsbury, who now became the guardian of the unfortunate queen. We have already said that this nobleman was married to a jealous and passionate woman, who mistook and misinterpreted the most ordinary marks of attention on the part of her husband to his royal prisoner. It is, perhaps, the strongest instance of despotism exercised by the imperious House of Tudor, that Elizabeth, by her royal authority, should for so many years compel a nobleman of the first rank to continue in a charge, the effect of which converted his house into a prison, his servants into jailers, involved him in a large expenditure, of which the queen hesitated to relieve him, and totally destroyed the peace of his domestic life by sowing discord between him and his lady, the most violent woman in England; and all this notwithstanding that the misery which Lord Shrewsbury suffered was so great as to affect his health and even his understanding. From Tutbury, Mary was sent for a season to Wingfield, another house of Shrewsbury; but the rebellion of the Earls of Westmoreland and Northumberland threw the north of England into such confusion that Elizabeth became doubly anxious for the security of her unhappy prisoner. Mary was, therefore, removed on short notice from Wingfield to Tutbury, and from Tutbury to Coventry, and back again, and dragged in bad weather through wretched roads from

one place of confinement to another, until, on the 4th
of August, 1570, she was suffered to repose in the manor
of Chatsworth.

From Chatsworth Mary was once more removed to Shef-
field, where there was then a strong castle, in which she continued to abide for a considerable time, with the variety of
one or two visits to Buxton for her health, leave for which
was reluctantly granted as an indulgence, all other patients
being excluded from the healing baths during the presence
of the suspected queen in their vicinity. In July, 1582, she
took leave of Buxton, to which she applied the following
Latin distich in bidding its baths adieu, perhaps, forever:

> "Buxtona quæ calidæ celebrabere nomine lymphæ,
>   Fortè mihi posthac non adeunda vale!"

In the course of these weary years of confinement, varied
by nothing save the change of prison, the reader may be
tempted to ask in what manner Mary, the queen of two
kingdoms, and accustomed to the exercise of her sovereign
will both in France and Scotland, contrived to support a
severe state of restraint, the more intolerable from the rank
and habits of her upon whom it was inflicted? We can
hardly give a more striking picture of the patience of the
unfortunate queen under her misfortunes than is contained
in a letter of Nicolas White, sent on purpose by Cecil as a
spy upon Mary's conduct and that of her keeper. The letter is dated 26th April, 1568.

White had asked whether she liked her change of air, in
allusion to her removal from Bolton to Tutbury "in the
depth of winter": to which she mildly replied, "that had it
consisted with her good sister's pleasure she would not have
removed for change of air at this season of the year; but
that she was so far contented with her removal from Bolton,
that she was so much the nearer her loving sister, into whose
presence she hoped soon to be admitted." To this White
answered, with the effrontery of an accomplished hypocrite,
"that although Queen Mary did not enjoy the actual pres-

ence of Elizabeth, yet it appeared to those who, like himself,
viewed the matter from a distance, that she had always the
virtual presence of the queen's majesty, who did in every
respect perform to her the office of a gracious prince, a natural kinswoman, a loving sister, and a most faithful friend."
This emissary of Cecil wound up his advice, by recommend-
ing to the unfortunate prisoner to "thank God that after so
many perils she had arrived in a realm where, through the
goodness of Queen Elizabeth's majesty, she had rather cause
to regard herself as receiving prince-like entertainment than
as suffering the slightest restraint." The poor queen answered meekly, "that indeed she had great cause to be
thankful to Heaven and to her sister for such ease as she
enjoyed; and that though she would not pretend to ask of
God contentment in a state of captivity, she made it her
daily petition that he would endow her with patience to
endure it." In reporting this singular interview, White
proceeds thus: "I asked her grace, since the weather did
cutt of all exercises abroad, howe she passed the time within.
She sayd, that all the day she wrought with hir needle, and
that the diversitie of the colors made the worke somewhat
lesse tedious, and that she contynued at it till very pain
made her to give over: and with that laid hir hand upon hir
left syde, and complayned of an old grief newely increased
there. Upon this occasion she (the Scottish queen), with the
agreeable and lively wit natural to her, entered into a prety
disputable comparison betweene carving, painting, and working with the needle, affirming painting, in hir own opinion,
for the moste commendable quality. I annswered hir
grace I coulde skill of neither of them; but that I have
redd pictura to be *veritas falsa:* with this she closed up
hir talk, and bydding me farewell, retyred into her privy-
chamber."

The fact that Queen Mary solaced the hours of imprisonment by the practice of those elegant arts of female work-
manship, in which she excelled, is ascertained by the preservation of a quantity of pieces of embroidery, tapestry, and

other labors of the needle and loom, still preserved and exhibited in different scenes of her captivity, where they had soothed the hours of imprisonment. The general effect of Queen Mary's manners and sentiments appear to have had an impression even upon the hypocritical agent of Cecil, at which he is himself surprised. He acknowledges the effect of her presence in the most striking manner, by desiring that if he might advise, few persons should be permitted to have access to the same seduction of which he had himself experienced the fascination. "But if," continues White, "I (whiche in the sight of God beare the queens majestie a naturall love, besyde my bounden dutie), might give advise, there should very few subjects in this land have access to, or conference with, this lady. For besid that she is a goodly personage (and yet, in truth, not comparable to our souverain), she hathe withall an alluring grace, a pretty Scottish speche, and a serching wit, clouded with myldnes. Fame might move some to releve her, and glory joyned to gain might stir others to adventure much for her sake. Sight, they say, is a lively infective sence, and cariethe many perswasions to the hart, which rulethe all the rest: myn own affection, by seeing the quenes majestie our souverain is dowbled, and thereby I gesse what the sight might worke in others. Hir hair of it self is black, and yett Mr. Knolls told me, that she weares heare of sundry colors."

While such were the queen's amusements during her melancholy imprisonment, and such the gentleness of deportment, which affected even the cold-blooded agent of Cecil, every other means allowed her for her greater convenience or more respectable accommodation was gradually restrained more and more.

At first, as we have just seen, her abode at Bolton and Tutbury was represented by this man White as being something almost voluntary, and for which she was told she ought to be thankful to Heaven. It is true that when she removed from place to place she was under guard of a stout band of soldiers. No consent of her own was asked when a journey was proposed, nor did her dissent when she desired to remain at Bolton prevent her being transported to Tutbury. It is no less true that she was not permitted to ride out for health or pleasure, although she was so much accustomed to the exercise that her health sunk under the confinement. It is true also that if, at any time, she was permitted to accompany her keepers upon the parties of hawking and hunting, which they practiced for their own amusement and not for hers, bands of armed men were in attendance, provided with swords and firearms, and having orders to put to death the captive princess, in case any attempt at escape or rescue should seem likely to prove successful. But these circumstances, while they convey to modern readers a strong idea of restraint, did not, in the opinion of Mr. White, partake of the character of imprisonment, or form an alloy to the sisterly reception on the part of Elizabeth.

In what, then, it may be said, was the queen of England's goodness manifested toward her prisoner? We can only answer that for a certain time the vain forms of royalty were practiced toward a sovereign who had less command over her own motions than the meanest peasant; and the empty form of a canopy of state was indulged to one whose life depended upon her abstaining from every attempt to assert the meanest and most ordinary privilege of a free person —that of going where she would. We shall see in the progress of her sad history that Mary was by degrees deprived even of the delusive tokens of respect, which were only at first conceded to her, to be gradually withdrawn, as she drew nearer to her fatal doom.

We have already mentioned the issue of the commission, the members of which, without any legal authority that can be imagined, took upon themselves the task of entering into and examining the accusations brought against the queen of Scotland by her insurgent subjects. Queen Elizabeth had declined to decide between the parties: "she had not seen ground enough," she said, "to declare the queen guilty of the horrid charges brought against her; nor, on the contrary, to find the regent and the rest of the Scottish lords of the king's party guilty of rebellion against the royal authority of Mary''—and such was the declaration of her sovereign pleasure. But while Elizabeth nominally abstained from judging in a cause which, indeed, she had no title to take under her consideration, her conduct was effectually the same as if she had found Queen Mary guilty and Murray and the king's lords totally innocent of the respective charges brought against them. The queen of Scotland was detained prisoner as a guilty person, while the regent was dismissed with a subsidy of five thousand pounds, enabling him to continue those military measures by which he had placed himself at the head of the Scottish government.

Queen Mary remonstrated strongly against a course of proceeding which, while it apparently acquitted her of all guilt, left her the inmate of a jail, and subjected her at the same time to the worst consequences of punishment. But the prejudices of Queen Elizabeth against her rival were so deeply rooted that no sense of justice could induce her to forego the advantages which she had received from Queen Mary's imprudent surrender of herself into her unfriendly hands.

It must be owned that circumstances occurred during the investigation at York which tended still further to increase her excessive jealousy of her sister-queen.

It was Mary's misfortune upon this occasion to give way to the suggestions of Maitland of Lethington, whose plots, though they indicated the extreme subtlety of his own genius, were often too much refined in their texture, and too complicated in their ramifications, for a period of violence, where the knot of every intrigue was liable to be severed by the sword of the soldier or by the axe of the executioner. The intrigue by which he involved Norfolk in a project of marriage with Mary was probably of the most fatal consequences to both. If he had, in fact, the welfare of his unhappy mistress in his view, Maitland ought to have seen that in her present condition she was entirely dependent upon Queen Elizabeth, and that any offensive course toward the latter sovereign must necessarily end in the ruin of the former. In this respect the proposed marriage of Mary with the Duke of Norfolk was sure to gall the English queen upon almost every point where she was most sensitive. Matrimony of any kind, where she was not herself the object, was never found a matter more agreeable to her than it usually is to the votaresses of celibacy; and that of Mary involved a prospect peculiarly disagreeable to her. The marriage of Mary promised to extend those claims of succession of which Elizabeth was sufficiently jealous even when they were now limited to a single youth; and she who could oppose by the most violent measures the union of Darnley and the Scottish queen was not likely to be scrupulous when this proposed alliance with one of the most powerful nobles of England seemed to renew all the fears which another marriage was sure to awaken. It was well known, also, that the duke in strengthening his party had cultivated the favor of the Catholic Earls of Northumberland and Westmoreland, who, from motives of religion as well as policy, were sufficiently disposed to prefer the title of Queen Mary to that of Elizabeth.

However prudent, therefore, a match between Norfolk and the Scottish queen might have been considered in the abstract, supposing Mary at liberty and in a capacity to make a free choice, the very surmise of such a connection was fraught with danger while she was in the power of Elizabeth; and that it should have been suggested by Maitland is only an additional instance how men of great parts can overreach themselves in matters of State policy, their very ingenuity and extreme subtlety becoming the means of blinding them to consequences which are obvious to those of duller capacity. It appears equally difficult to justify the conduct of Maitland, if we suppose that he believed it possible to carry on an intrigue of such importance without its coming to the knowledge of Elizabeth herself, a jealous and sagacious princess, and served by Cecil, Burleigh, and Wal-

singham, the most subtle ministers known in Europe
at the period. He might also have well foreseen the
inevitable defection of Murray from the project, whenever it should become known to Queen Elizabeth, upon
cultivating whose favor the regent's power absolutely depended.

The match with Norfolk naturally connected itself with
the dangerous insurrection of Westmoreland and Northumberland; and Elizabeth, not without good reason,
entertained suspicion of Mary as the hidden cause of
both, and of all the danger which they implied. Then
there is little doubt that they greatly prejudiced the queen
of Scots in her opinion, and furnished her with a specious
reason, founded upon State necessity, for detaining her a
prisoner. The English sovereign was indeed about to
have taken a more desperate step, by delivering up the
royal fugitive to the custody of the Regent Murray, had
not the sudden death of that nobleman prevented the
scheme from taking place.

After the death of Murray, the queen of England engaged
personally in the war, and, as we have seen, sent an English
army into Scotland. Out of this arose new arguments of
State for refusing the Scottish queen her liberty, however
unlawfully she had been deprived of it. It was not to be
supposed, said the English counsellors, that while Elizabeth
was making war against a faction in Scotland, she either
would or ought to set at liberty the captive who was at
the head of that faction. Yet it appears that the English
queen had some intention of freeing herself of the queen
of Scots, although she never took any effectual step to that
measure.

In the meantime, the alleged attempts of the northern
rebels to effect Mary's escape, together with that queen's
supposed interest with these insurgents, formed an excuse
for confining her more closely than formerly. Her minister, the bishop of Ross, complained that his mistress was
not permitted to take exercise on horseback, by which her

health was much prejudiced; and it was granted, obviously as a considerable boon, that the Scottish queen might ride forth to take the air, so that it were in company with the Earl of Shrewsbury. In the meantime, as if to realize the thoughts which the English queen entertained of parting with her Scottish hostage, two of her ministers, Cecil and Mildmay, were sent, November, 1570, to endeavor to settle some terms on which Mary might be liberated.

The principal proposals were that Mary should renounce any pretensions to the English crown; that she should adhere to the alliance between the kingdoms; grant pardon to the subjects who had been in arms against her during the civil war, and put into the queen of England's hands hostages of high rank, and some castles in Scotland, by way of guarantee.

It is plain that Elizabeth's only pretensions to obtain such articles arose from her having in possession the person of the queen of Scots, committed to her in a moment of unwary confidence; yet hard as these conditions were, Mary was in such a state as might have compelled her to subscribe to them or to worse. But no security could possibly have been granted adequate to soothe the real apprehensions of Elizabeth, and the affected scruples of her counsellors. The treaty was therefore disturbed, and finally broken off, by the introduction of commissioners in the name of the youthful king of Scotland, whose interests Elizabeth pretended she was bound to consult: these were the Earl of Morton and two other persons of his party, who interrupted the whole proceedings by maintaining the high Calvinistic principle of lawful resistance, on the part of the subject, even to sovereign authority. In such principles it was impossible that those acting for Elizabeth should dare to acquiesce; and though there can be no doubt that Elizabeth, upon this as well as upon former occasions, might have dictated to the Scottish commissioners how they were to limit their pleadings, yet she rather chose to consider the mode in which they had been entered as a total bar to further proceedings in the treaty, which was thus broken off.

In the meantime Norfolk, having been liberated after his first arrest, was again thrown into the Tower, and his intrigues and ambitious views finally closed by his public trial and execution. Mary appears to have taken the misfortunes of this nobleman severely to heart: she was confined to her chamber for ten days; and probably employed her leisure hours in deploring the fate of one who had adventured and lost rank, fortune, and life in her service. She expresses herself on the subject to her faithful counsellor, the bishop of Ross, then imprisoned in the Tower, as having had some accession to the intrigues of Norfolk; and her letter, expressing a singular mixture of despondency and firmness, has been published by Mr. Chalmers.

While her health was declining, and her comforts diminished, Mary still clung to one hope, which she nourished with uncommon tenacity, although it is difficult to conceive what she could have expected from it. From the moment she set foot on English ground the queen of Scots had reckoned a great deal upon the effect to be wrought on Elizabeth's mind in the personal interview which she never failed to demand. Yet what could it have availed the unfortunate queen to have had the means of convincing Elizabeth by ocular demonstration that she, so long hated as a rival, did in fact possess more beauty, equal sense, as much accomplishment, and wit and grace superior to her own? The suspicion that such was the case was what had originally excited Elizabeth's hatred to Mary; and everything which led to convince her of the truth of what she suspected could only enhance that evil feeling. It would also have been very difficult to have chosen and supported in such an interview a character which would have left her at liberty to act against Queen Mary the severe conduct correspondent to the part by which she might have already meditated closing the scene. Elizabeth might think there was less difficulty in executing a defamed and neglected prisoner than in taking the life of one whom she had admitted to her presence as a sister sovereign. She might hold with her father, Henry VIII., the truth of the popular adage, that

> A king's face
> Should give grace,

and therefore determine not to admit to her presence the victim whom she was resolved not to pardon. At any rate, she was determined in postponing and declining all Mary's pleadings for an interview, and at length hardly deigned to return any answer to her solicitations upon that subject. This period of their intercourse was strangely contrasted with that in which Sir James Melville, then the Scottish ambassador at the court of London, proposed, in a tone of jocose raillery, that Elizabeth should disguise herself as his page, and ride down to Scotland merely to see his mistress; to which, willingly accepting the compliment, she replied with a sigh, "Would to Heaven she might do so!" It is curious to compare the behavior of individuals to each other in sunshine and shower, in good fortune and adversity.

Meantime Queen Elizabeth called in to the aid of her policy the passions and feelings of those subjects who had so much reason to look up to her with gratitude as the mother of her people. Two points she, in particular, struggled to attain, if possible. The first was that of establishing to the public conviction the proposition that the safety of Queen Elizabeth was inconsistent with the life of Mary; of which, she herself being the judge, no doubt could be entertained. If we can believe a copy of doggerel verses, which we are surprised that Elizabeth's taste could permit her to be guilty of, the Scottish queen was the foundation of all the dissatisfaction and danger which threatened her government.[1] The editor of these verses has acquainted

---

[1] That doubt of future foes exiles my present joy;
And wit me warns to shun such snares as threaten mine annoy:
For falsehood now doth flow, and subjects' faith doth ebb,
Which would not be, if reason rul'd, or wisdom weav'd the web:

us that those *sweet* and *sententious* rhymes, those *sugared samples*, as he calls this trash, were written to express the queen's conviction of the extreme danger in which she was placed through the influence of a party among the nobility and Catholic gentry devoted to the interests of the queen of Scots; and Elizabeth seems to have deemed it necessary to impress the same terror, which she herself entertained toward Mary and her party, upon the people of England, to whose regard she had so many just claims that she might well call upon them to protect her against the alleged plots of a foreigner and papist.

This was not all, however: the queen of Scotland was not only to be represented as a person formidable to Queen Elizabeth, but also as one worthless and base in herself, and unworthy of claiming the ordinary compassion due to'strangers and exiles. Sir Francis Knollis, in a letter from Bolton, of January 1, 1568, seems very early desirous to warn Queen Elizabeth against her own gentleness of temper, which might withhold her from openly disgracing Queen Mary, and maintaining the insurgents in Scotland against her, even although the queen of Scotland should refuse to be conformable in the matters required of her by the English sovereign. This intimates an intention of permitting such accusations to be circulated against Queen Mary as might best counteract the prepossessions excited in her favor by her grace and beauty,

---

But clouds of toys untry'd do cloak aspiring minds,
Which turn to rain, of late repent, by course of changed winds.
The top of hope suppos'd the root of ruth will be,
And fruitless all their graffed guiles, as shortly ye shall see:
Those dazzel'd eyes with pride, which great ambition blinds,
Shall be unsealed, by worthy wights, whose foresight falsehood finds:
The daughter of debate, that eke discord doth sow,
Shall reap no gain, where former rule hath taught still peace to grow.
No foreign banish'd wight shall anchor in this port:
Our realm it brooks no stranger's force; let them elsewhere resort:
Our rusty sword with rest, shall first the edge employ,
To poll their topps, that seek such change, and gape for joy.
  —Chalmers' Life of Mary Queen of Scots, vol. i., p. 344.

as well as by the generous sympathy of the English nation
for the condition of a forlorn princess, who had thrown herself upon their compassion and that of their queen.

This design was prosecuted by suffering the works of
Buchanan and others, directed against Queen Mary's reputation, to be introduced and distributed through the realm,
while those composed in her defence were treated as contra-
band and prohibited publications. The accusations against
Queen Mary were thus left to make their way without answer or reply; and connected with the undeniable fact of
her having united herself with Bothwell so shortly after the
murder of Darnley, of which all recognized him as the
author, seemed to take from the unfortunate queen not
only the right to demand justice, but even that of request-
ing compassion. Her name was publicly soiled with the
foul charges of murder and adultery: the proofs which had
been rejected as informal and incomplete, even by Elizabeth
herself, were found far more than sufficient to gratify the
vulgar appetite for scandal accustomed to little nicety in
selecting its grounds of belief. Thus it remained no question with by far the greater part of the English people that
the safety of Elizabeth could only be insured by Mary's
death, or in what measure justice or injustice should be
dealt toward one whom they accounted so infamous as this
dethroned queen.

Acting under these impressions, the English house of
commons meditated a resolution, the effect of which must
have been to palsy the exertions of the queen of Scotland and
all who might be disposed to take her part. They sent a bill
to the house of lords, by which it was declared that the very
act of claiming any right to the crown was in itself high
treason; that it was equally so to affirm that the right of
any other was better than that of Elizabeth, or that the
parliament had not power to settle and limit the order
of succession. These enactments greatly abridged Queen
Mary's influence upon the public mind in England, and
afforded such an assurance of safety to the existing sover-

eign that Queen Elizabeth, deeming further procedure for the time unnecessary, ventured to adjourn the parliament.

After these proceedings, and, perhaps, as a natural consequence of them, the severities of Queen Mary's imprisonment were considerably increased: her most faithful agent, the bishop of Ross, as already hinted, was thrown into prison on account of his implication in the fatal intrigues of Norfolk; the queen's retinue was diminished; her means of taking exercise restrained; the expense of maintaining the necessary guards and attendants diminished; and Shrewsbury, after all his toil to accomplish his troublesome duty to Elizabeth's satisfaction, found he was the subject of her jealousy, and scarce less so of her proverbial economy, which left him even the honor, at his own expense, of providing the costly wine-baths which Queen Mary's infirmity compelled her to make use of.

CHAPTER XXXV

Interference of Foreign Princes in behalf of Mary—Her Intercourse
with her Son—Her Presents to him rejected—Nevertheless she
interferes with Elizabeth in his Behalf at the Period of the Raid
of Ruthven—He disclaims her Title and Cause—Her Sentiments
on that Occasion—The Catholics of England continue to make
her the chief Object of their Regard, and involve her Name in
their Conspiracies—The Plot of Throgmorton—Association of
English Subjects, chiefly directed against Mary—She is alarmed,
and willing to submit to severer Terms of Liberation—Elizabeth
cultivates an Interest with James and his Ministers; her Alarm
for Queen Mary in a public and national Point of View—Mary's
imprudent and offensive Letter—Sadler intrusted for a Time
with the Custody of the Scottish Queen—His Discontent with
the Duty imposed—Parry's Conspiracy—Severe Act of Parliament passed in consequence

WE have attended the changes of Queen Mary's
imprisonment, and pointed out some of its most
remarkable incidents. A more weary and dis-
tressing course of oppression, mingled, from time to time,
with deceitful glimmerings of delusive hope, is hardly to
be found in history.

But the reader may ask, with some surprise, since Mary
was queen-dowager of France, and an ally of the king of
Spain, whether no efforts were made in her favor by either
of these two powerful monarchs, who, for decency's sake
at least, were imperatively called upon to interfere in her
behalf? That such interference took place is undoubted, but
on the part of France it was of a cold and feeble character;
for the king was not of a temper to regard any one's interest
save his own, which at that period recommended friendship
with England. The Spanish ambassador, on the other side,
had in some respects lost his right to be listened to in the

affairs of Queen Mary, since he had mixed himself with the intrigues of Norfolk; and although his rank was too high to be arrested like the bishop of Ross, he at length received Elizabeth's commands to quit England.

With still more reason might it be demanded, what James VI., the only child of the unfortunate Mary, was doing in her behalf? He was not a twelvemonth old when he succeeded to her crown, and the years which had since passed, which had filled up to him a term of sovereignty, had been to his ill-fated mother, with the intermission of only a few days, a period of rigorous captivity.

Mary at least had not, in the meantime, forgotten the sole tie of affection which continued to bind her to this life. As soon as James had personally assumed the government, the imprisoned queen hastened to send him a present of a garment, embroidered by her own hands, with some jewels, such as her misfortunes had left in her possession. They were, however, addressed not to the king, but to the prince, of Scotland; as indeed it could hardly be supposed that Queen Mary was to acknowledge a title in her son, the existence of which was inconsistent with her reputation as well as her rights. On that account the gift was refused, under pretence of its being misdirected; nor was the bearer permitted to come into the royal presence.

We would gladly hope that James was no party to this undutiful proceeding; nor shall we attempt to estimate the distress of the unfortunate mother, when she received again the gift of maternal affection, ornamented by her hands, and probably stained by her tears, rejected as it was in this unfilial manner through a cold-blooded and insulting scruple of etiquette. Wherever she might cast the blame, maternal partiality prevented her from throwing it upon her son; for when he had soon after fallen into the power of the insurgent nobles at the Raid of Ruthven, her maternal anxiety broke forth in an epistle to Elizabeth, in which, throwing aside the humble tone in which she had pleaded her own sorrows, she remonstrated with warmth and dignity upon the injustice which had deprived her son of his liberty. She in that letter declares herself, with all her heart, willing to gratify her son, by resigning the throne. She desired only that the queen of England would protect him from practices at the hands of his rebellious subjects, such as she had been exposed to herself, and declared that she desired no kindness of her for herself beyond the company of two waiting gentlewomen, and the means of performing the duties of her religion. In reply to this intercession, Robert Beale, a rude and morose man, and clerk of Elizabeth's council, was sent to expostulate with the captive princess, for the freedom which she had thought proper to assume; nor was Queen Elizabeth affected otherwise than with anger by the tenor of the letter which she received.

It is probable that, while the unfortunate Mary indulged herself in all the tenderness of a mother toward the young king of Scotland, the feelings which he cultivated in return were of a cold and unresponsive character, for which, perhaps, his education is more to be blamed than his heart. He had doubtless been carefully trained in the opinion that his right to the throne depended upon the truth of those charges on account of which his mother had been precipitated from the royal dignity. He must have regarded her, therefore, with more aversion than affection, and was probably little anxious to obtain the freedom of one whose liberty might impair his own right to the kingdom of Scotland. To pursue, therefore, the course of James's rare and infrequent intercourse with his mother, we may observe that in 1585, under the direction and by the advice of the Master of Gray, of whom we have said something, and shall have occasion to say more in the sequel, James wrote to his unfortunate mother a harsh and highly undutiful letter; in the course of which he disowned her right to the throne, and expressed himself determined in no respect whatever to connect his own interest or title with hers. Mary felt the ingratitude of this insulting epistle, and expressed her indignation warmly in a letter to the French ambassador. "Am I thus," she said, "requited for all I have done, and all I have suffered, for this ungrateful boy? God knows I envied him not the kingdom which he possesses, nor did I ever wish to visit Scotland more, unless for the purpose of seeing him and blessing him. But let him beware how he prosecutes the ungenerous and ungrateful course upon which he has entered. Without my consent he cannot justly hold the regal dignity; and unless he amends his fault by repentance, I will bestow on him a parent's curse, and bequeath my kingdom to one who will know both how to occupy and how to defend it." This letter, no doubt, was dictated by a passing flash of irritation; but it shows a new instance in which it was Mary's misfortune to be afflicted through those channels of feeling which are usually, to others, the source of the purest happiness. The queen's greatest misfortunes had arisen out of her conjugal connections, and she was now doomed to see them augmented by the ungrateful scorn and negligence of her only child.

Other circumstances, which might in the general case be termed advantageous, were in like manner destined to prove fatal to this unhappy queen. She was, we have seen, the object of fear and suspicion, and even of the hatred naturally connected with these feelings, to the greatly more numerous body of the English, consisting of those who had embraced the Protestant faith, and were loyal subjects of Queen Elizabeth. It was the natural consequence that those of her own religion, who regarded the reign of the existing sovereign as the usurpation of an adulterous bastard, and cruel and heretical persecutor of the Catholic faith, should regard Mary as an innocent and holy sufferer, deprived of her native kingdom by heretical rebels, and most unjustly detained prisoner in that to which she had a better right than her persecuting relative who held the throne. As the English Catholics were zealous, as usual, in proportion to the disqualifications which they were subjected to and the persecution which they underwent, and as they were still numerous and powerful, they failed not to match the ruling

party in enthusiasm, and to form many schemes to bring
England once more within the limits of what, in their idea,
was lawful succession, and the pale of the only Catholic
faith. With all these plots the name and cause of Mary
was naturally connected. Nor was her name always used
without her consent. Some of the plots were undoubtedly
communicated to her; nor can we suppose it likely that she
should express resolute disapprobation of schemes which
tended to accomplish her own liberty, and the dethrone-
ment of her own rival, at whose hand she could expect
nothing but a continuance of the same malevolent severity
which had characterized Elizabeth's conduct toward her
since she took refuge in England. It is also plausibly reported that her name was used in intrigues of which she
never heard, but the managers of which conceived they
were calculated for her advantage, and therefore held themselves secure of her approbation, without her consent being
previously obtained. Thus there was an action and reaction
in the public mind; and the more the Protestants persisted
in regarding Mary as the enemy of their faith and government, the more the Catholics endeavored to fix the same
character upon her, by making use of her name and authority in their most violent conspiracies.

In 1584 a conspiracy of this nature was discovered of a
very extensive and dangerous character. One Francis Throgmorton, a Catholic gentleman of Cheshire, after undergoing
the torture, in consequence of some suspicious documents
found upon him, was unable to sustain a second interroga-
tion of the same nature, and confessed a private correspondence with the Queen of Scots, and a projected design to
invade England on the part of Spain, where most of the
English Catholics were alleged to be ready to join them in
arms. Arrangements to this effect, he stated, were made
with the approbation of the Spanish ambassador. The
House of Guise, the near relatives of Mary, were alleged
to be in preparation for the same purpose, and the Duke
of Guise was to be leader of the enterprise. The alarm

through England was extreme; and the discovery was of a nature which touched the main fear of all true Protestants. The immense power of Spain had been much increased by the late acquisition of Portugal; and the bigotry of Philip to the Catholic religion was well known to be sufficiently vehement to lead him to exertions in proportion to his immense means. The Duke of Guise was regarded justly as one of the chief defenders of the Catholic faith; and arguing upon Queen Mary's natural desire of freedom, and attachment to her relations, there was no reason to doubt the truth of Throgmorton's confession, when he accused her of being an accomplice in the conspiracy.

Queen Elizabeth, acting upon Throgmorton's confession, instantly, as already hinted, dismissed the Spanish ambassador from England. Throgmorton himself was tried and executed as a traitor. His behavior was such as to leave his guilt doubtful. He retracted his confession when placed upon trial, again confirmed it after sentence had been pronounced, and retracted it a second time when brought to the scaffold for execution, alleging that it was extorted at first by torture, and afterward adhered to from the fear of death.

A singular circumstance in Scotland augmented the general alarm excited by Throgmorton's plot.

One Crichton, a Jesuit, chanced to be on board of a vessel sailing from Flanders toward Scotland, of which last country he was a native: being chased by a corsair or pirate, Crichton tore to pieces and threw away certain papers, which an extraordinary eddy of wind brought back into the vessel. The fragments were picked up from the deck by some of the passengers; and being industriously pieced together, were found to contain the model of a plot for the invasion of England, upon the same footing with that which Throgmorton had confessed.

This reiterated alarm greatly affected the party in the kingdom of England who accounted that the peace and honor of the country depended upon the continuance of its present form of government in Church and in State. To

counteract by a public declaration any attempt to disturb
the present government, an association was formed, and a
document generally signed, by which the subscribers "bound
themselves to defend Queen Elizabeth against all her enemies, foreign or domestic; engaging, moreover, if violence
should be offered to the queen's life, in order to favor the
title of any one pretending a claim to the crown, they the
parties subscribing not only engaged, in such case, never to
acknowledge the title of the person in whose behalf so foul
a crime had been committed, but, moreover, to pursue such
person or persons to the death, and to her or their utter overthrow and extirpation." This association was obviously directed against the rights of Queen Mary, who was thus
unjustly rendered accountable not only for such connivance
at treasonable practices against Elizabeth as she might absolutely encourage, but for whatever schemes the fanatics of
her religion might form, without her consent, or which might
perhaps receive birth from the treacherous insinuations of the
spies of the English ministry.

This association had such an awful appearance that Mary
seems to have become intimidated by the danger to her person and right of succession which it inferred. She pressed
for permission to sign the association herself, and at the same
time offered more full concessions than Elizabeth had been
yet able to extort from her. She was, indeed, so humbled
in spirit that Walsingham gave it earnestly as his opinion
that her terms ought to be complied with, and she should be
admitted to her freedom.

But another effect of these discoveries was their recom-
mending to Queen Elizabeth the cultivation of a closer intercourse between King James than she had of late entertained.
The reader will recollect that the queen of England had of
late been disposed to support against the temper of the king
those nobles who had been engaged in the Raid of Ruthven,
and mixed reproof with requests in her application to James
on this subject. Under this interference the king of Scots
had repeatedly winced and shown signs of impatience, as

when he retorted upon Elizabeth the aphorisms of Isocrates. She became now apprehensive that this exertion of authority might prove a doubtful, and, perhaps, an ineffectual road to the influence which she desired to acquire in the affairs of Scotland. She resolved, therefore, to move by gentler methods; and instead of attempting to dictate to James the choice of his ministers, she resolved to rest satisfied with gaining over to the English interest those Scottish statesmen, who, being already the favorites of the king, were in possession of their master's ear, as well as possessing the direction of the government. For this purpose she spared no pains to bring over to her views the Master of Gray, in which she perfectly succeeded, and to form an alliance, even though it should prove merely temporary, with the usurping Earl of Arran.

These political considerations lead to another view of the question between Elizabeth and Mary. It would be injustice to the former to suppose that her personal interest and prejudices were the sole motives by which she was guided in her conduct toward her prisoner. It is no doubt true that from an early period the two queens had been rivals in the points in which women, from the princess to the peasant girl, desire to excel. They had been also rivals in power, for the premature usurpation of the title and armorial bearings of England was never forgotten by Elizabeth; yet that sovereign, patriotic as she certainly was, might justify her fear and hatred of Mary upon principles of a public and more generous nature, applicable to her country as well as to herself.

Elizabeth was well entitled to suppose herself able to maintain a contest with all her powerful antagonists abroad, though in the holy league which was adopted at Bayonne, and which united all the Catholic powers in Europe, they must necessarily have had the destruction of her power in view as their principal object. Even amid their wildest expressions of hatred and denunciations of vengeance, the queen of England had the noble confidence that with a united kingdom she might resist them with perfect security of the event. The state of Scotland was no doubt less secure than it had been during the regency of Murray and Morton. It was now under a separate prince, who, if he were hostile to English interests, must at all times be enabled, by a seacoast abounding in harbors, and an extensive southern frontier, to have opened an easy access to foreigners proposing to invade South Britain. But the character of James and the influence of Elizabeth in his court was such as might secure her on the part of that monarch. He was in no respect likely to prefer the sounding promises of France and Spain to the prospects of real and solid advantage presented to him by the friendship of Elizabeth; and the forfeiture of the succession of England would have been a sacrifice which could not possibly have been compensated by any indemnification which the monarchs of the holy league could bestow. James was also a Protestant prince, at the head of a people zealously Protestant, and therefore must be held upon principle to have viewed the prime object of the holy league with alarm and detestation.

Besides the security which James's circumstances and personal interests afforded to Queen Elizabeth, the measures by which she had insured a predominating influence in his court in almost any political change seemed to insure for her the zealous support of either party which might be predominant in the Scottish counsels. If Arran should remain the favorite of James, he had, since the meeting with Lord Hunsdon, become her instrument and pensioner; and though she must have contemned and despised his parts, he was not the less likely to be useful while his interest with the king remained unabated; nor was Elizabeth, however much she might wish his interest diminished or destroyed, the less willing to avail herself of it while it still existed. If, on the other hand, the restoration of the Scottish nobles engaged in the Raid of Ruthven should put the king once more into the hands of a party more zealously Protestant, they who had been lately the guests of Elizabeth must have been still more docile and attentive to her interests than the minion Arran, upon whom there could be no reliance, except through a direct appeal to his vanity or avarice.

Thus, in almost every supposable circumstance, Britain was invulnerable to Queen Elizabeth's enemies, excepting only through the charm which they possessed in the person and title of Queen Mary. To her the Catholic princes were most of them allied by birth or affinity, and all of them by similarity of religion, so that her name and title afforded the only plausible pretext under which they might urge even those Englishmen that were of their own persuasion to join the invaders of their native country.

From all this it follows that Mary was not only feared and hated by Elizabeth from the common motives of female rivalry, but that she was also dreaded by her as a patriotic princess, conscious of the baneful effects which the pretensions of the Scottish queen were qualified to produce upon the independence of England, and the institutions of the Protestant Church. So deceitful is the human heart, and so ingenious are mortals in imposing upon themselves a false view of the motives under which they act, that it may be doubted whether Elizabeth, conjured by high and low, exhorted by her prelates, her lords, and commons, to take measures for the protection of her own life, by suffering what they called the law to take place on her prisoner, might not have conceived that she was yielding to the voice of her people, and consulting their interest, rather than her own will, in conceding to their importunity what she might suppose she would have refused to her own irritated feelings. It is true that, justly considered, the danger arising from Mary Stuart lay not in her power but in her weakness. She had not the slightest show of a party left in her native kingdom. In England she was a close prisoner, attainted by parliament, and excluded from all intercourse with the world beyond her prison-house. The Catholics were more affected by knowing that she was suffering such grievous usage in their immediate vicinity than they could have been by learning that, liberated by Queen Elizabeth, she was living upon her dowry, at ease and at freedom, either in France or any other distant country. In their extreme jealousy for their own interest or for their sovereign's safety, the ministers of Elizabeth overacted their part, and were guilty of instigating conspiracies by the very mode which they took to discover them. Camden informs us "that there were at this time some subtle ways taken to try how men stood affected. Counterfeit letters were privately sent in the name of the queen of Scots and the persons concerned in Throgmorton's treason to the houses of Catholics. Spies were dispersed through the country to make remarks, and to report them to the government; and many individuals of rank were imprisoned and narrowly examined."

The Catholics, finding themselves thus in danger of being inveigled into imaginary plots, endeavored to obviate the danger by plunging into real ones; and thus the excessive precaution of Burleigh and Walsingham, and the unjustifiable mode in which it was manifested, increased the danger which it was intended to cure.

Neither was Mary herself, although, as we have seen, patient to a degree of unexpected self-possession, at all times able to forbear retaliation upon her good sister Elizabeth. Upon one occasion she took a female revenge, which, however much it might be justified by the ill-usage she had received, was, in point of prudence, the most impolitic course she could have pursued. Under pretence of writing to Queen Elizabeth the manner in which the Countess of Shrewsbury spoke of her, she transmitted (always professing to disbelieve them) a long train of charges equally dishonorable to Elizabeth as a queen, and highly offensive to female delicacy, and even disgraceful to her as a woman. Mary affirmed, in this imprudent letter, that the countess accused her sovereign of practicing the grossest indecencies, not only with the Duke of Anjou, who pretended to her hand, but with his favorite Simier; that she was so extravagantly attached to

Hatton that she hunted him as a hound pursues a stag; that having quarrelled with Hatton on account of some buttons of gold which he had upon his dress, and the latter having in disgust retired from the court, she had boxed the ears of Killigrew because he had not been able to prevail on Hatton to return; and that she gave three hundred pounds a year to a gentleman of her chamber who had been more successful on the same occasion; although she was so meanly narrow on other occasions that she had never made the fortune of more than one or two persons in her dominions. This cutting epistle, always under pretence of reporting Lady Shrewsbury's words, accused Elizabeth of entertaining as high an opinion of her beauty as if she had been a heavenly goddess, and that her maids of honor used the most extravagant praises to soothe her childish vanity, while they turned about and laughed behind her back at her excess of credulity. There were yet more degrading circumstances alleged by Mary to have been stated by the Countess of Shrewsbury concerning the person and habits of the queen of England; and, upon the whole, the letter contained an imputation of almost every vice which could affect the queen's reputation, and every foible which could wound her vanity. There is much reason to believe that this imprudent communication, while it gave Elizabeth great pain, and so far satisfied the purpose of the writer, was at the same time accounte an inexpiable offence, never to be pardoned or forgiven.

It was a natural consequence of the increasing discord between the queens that the imprisonment of Queen Mary should be rendered yet more rigorous than formerly. The Earl of Shrewsbury, who had been so long, to his great inconvenience, loss, and mortification, charged with the care of this unfortunate queen, was at length released and Sir Ralph Sadler was for a time intrusted in his place.

This ancient statesman, having been a servant of Henry VIII., was now advanced in life, and altogether unable to endure the restraints which Elizabeth's jealousy imposed upon those to whom Mary's custody was intrusted. His answer upon receiving an angry expostulation concerning his having carried out Queen Mary a-hawking, although he was attended by a strong guard, furnished with firearms, and having orders to put the queen to death should any danger, or suspicion of danger, have offered, is remarkable, and worthy of being quoted. In a letter to Walsingham he informed that statesman that having sent for his hawks and falconers, the better to pass the *miserable life* he led at Tutbury, he had been unable to resist the entreaties of his charge that she might be permitted the recreation of seeing his hawks fly, a sport in which she greatly delighted. In this he had three or four times indulged her, but under a sufficient guard, and never at more than three miles from the castle. "In this," Sir Ralph Sadler concludes, "he used his discretion, and he thought he did well; but," he adds, "since it is not well taken, I would to God some other had the charge, who would use it with more discretion than I can; for, I assure you, I am so weary of it, that if it were not more for that I would do nothing that should offend her majesty than for fear of any punishment, I would come home, and yield myself to be a prisoner in the Tower all the days of my life, rather than I would attend any longer here upon this charge. And if I had known, when I came from home, I should have tarried here so long, contrary to all the promises which were made to me, I would have refused, as others do, and have yielded to any punishment rather than I would have accepted of this charge; for a greater punishment cannot be ministered unto me than to force me to remain here in this sort; since, as it appears, *things well meant, by me, are not well taken.*" [1] One is here tempted to ask what must have been the feelings of the prisoner, when even her jailers felt their duty so intolerably irksome. While Mary was restrained with this severity, those changes took place in Scotland which removed Arran forever from the king's ear, and induced James to put the management

---

[1] Chalmers' Life of Mary Queen of Scots, vol. i., p. 418.

of his affairs under the guidance of statesmen of better morals and more judgment. It was by the advice of Maitland and others, that, taking his part between the great contending factions of Catholic and Protestant, which divided the civilized world, the king of Scots formed an alliance offensive and defensive with Elizabeth, in which there was no mention made of Mary's name and title. She might thus be considered as abandoned by her son, whom it would have well become to have mingled some stipulations for his mother's freedom, or her safety at least, with his laudable anxiety for the defence of his own rights. Meantime events rolled on, and the spirit of the times again gave rise to a conspiracy which was the more immediate pretence of Mary's fatal death.

While Elizabeth was fortifying herself by a more intimate alliance with Scotland, her life was again threatened by a Roman Catholic zealot. This was one Parry, a doctor of laws, who had a seat in parliament, and some reputation as a man of talents; but he had lately become a convert to popery, and, with the zeal of a new convert, had taken upon him the assassination of Elizabeth. Such a crime could only be committed by observing the most absolute silence upon his purpose, and exhibiting a total disregard for his own life while he attempted that of the queen. Upon such terms the life of the most powerful and best defended sovereign is at the mercy of one determined individual. Fortunately the mixture of desperate courage and resolved taciturnity is seldom met with. Parry possessed neither in the requisite degree. He was encouraged in his purpose by the pope's nuncio at Venice, the pope himself, and the Cardinal de Como. Yet, though he repeatedly obtained access to Elizabeth's person, his heart failed him when he should have struck the blow. In the dubious state of mind which his irresolution indicated, the secret grew too burdensome to be locked within his own bosom. He committed it to one Neville, by whom it was betrayed to the ministers of Elizabeth. The alarm was extreme, when the risk incurred from this desperate purpose was made public. Parry was arrested; confessed his nefarious purpose, and suffered the just punishment attached to it.

This meditated treason induced the English parliament, upon the 2d of March, 1585, to pass an act; the plain object of which was to make the queen of Scots, in her own person, responsible, with her rights and her life, for any attempt which might be made on the person or government of Elizabeth. It is thus abridged by Dr. Robertson, the elegant historian of this interesting period.

This remarkable statute confirmed, with the plenary power of parliament, the association already mentioned, which had been subscribed by so many of her subjects; and it was further enacted, "That if any rebellion shall be excited in the kingdom, or anything attempted, to the hurt of her majesty's person, by or for any person pretending a title to the crown, the queen shall empower twenty-four persons by a commission under the great seal to examine into and pass sentence upon such offences; and after judgment given, a proclamation shall be issued, declaring the persons whom they find guilty excluded from any right to the crown; and her majesty's subjects may lawfully pursue every one of them to the death, with all their aiders and abettors. And if any design against the life of the queen take effect, the persons by or for whom such a detestable act is executed, and their issues, being anywise assenting or privy to the same, shall be disabled forever from pretending to the crown, and be pursued to death in the like manner." [1]

---

[1] Robertson's History of Scotland, 4to ed., vol. ii., p. 108.

CHAPTER XXXVI

Enthusiasm of the Age— Projects of the Catholics against the Life
of Elizabeth—Plot of Ballard—He communicates with Babington—They have a Picture of their Associates—Contrive the Liberation of Mary—They are betrayed by the Spies of Walsingham—The English resent the Conspiracy as a Plot of Mary—
The Ministers of Elizabeth press the taking of her Life—She is
committed to the Charge of Sir Amias Paulet—Her Health becomes more feeble—Her Wants and Complaints—It is resolved
to bring her to Trial—Mary's Papers are seized; her Secretaries
made Prisoners; and her Cabinets broken open—She is transported to Fotheringay—A Commission appointed to try her—
She refuses to plead before it, but at length submits—Her Accusation and Defence—The Commissioners Remove to London—
Objections to the Evidence—The Commissioners, however, pronounce Sentence of Death—The Parliament press for the Publication and Execution of the Sentence—Elizabeth's hypocritical
Answer—Mary writes to Elizabeth; but receives no Answer—
James interferes, first by his Ambassador Keith, and after by
the Master of Gray and Sir James Melville—His Ambassador ill
received by Elizabeth—James sends more spirited Instructions
to his Envoys—The Master of Gray betrays the Cause of Queen
Mary, and the Purpose of his Embassy—James requires the
Scottish Church to pray for his Mother: they decline the
Office—Elizabeth's Uncertainty—She contrives to throw the is-
suing of the Death Warrant upon her Secretary and Council,
after some attempts to instigate Mary's Keepers to put her to
Death in Private—Mary resigns herself to her Fate—She is
executed

IT was the age of enthusiasm throughout Europe: those
of the ancient religion gloried in exerting themselves for
the creed of their fathers, at whatever risk of sharing
the fate of confessors or of martyrs; and those who adopted
the modern doctrines were equally proud of extending, at all
personal hazards, that liberty of conscience to others by
which they themselves had profited. In the present times

men do not inquire particularly into the religion of those
with whom they have to transact affairs, unless their general
business be otherwise connected with matters of the conscience.   In the less fortunate age of which we are treating,
the fact of belonging to a particular communion gave even
to the most liberal minds a general disposition favorable or
unfavorable to an individual, as his faith in religious matters
differed from or agreed with theirs.   These strong opinions,
which had an influence upon the dullest and most moderate
minds, excited the bold and enthusiastic to a species of frenzy,
which must account for men, otherwise humane and generous, giving way, in the supposed cause of religion, to acts
of deceit and violence which they would otherwise have abhorred and condemned, soothing themselves with the apology
that they might serve the cause of Heaven meritoriously and
conscientiously by engaging in enterprises which the spirit
of the Gospel as well as its precepts do most emphatically
condemn.   Upon this principle we are to account for the
many melancholy instances which occurred during the sixteenth century of men, otherwise wise, moderate, and virtu-
ous, engaging in plots and conspiracies inconsistent with
every idea of law, justice, and humanity.

The Catholic princes, by their engagement in that horrible conspiracy which gave rise to the massacre of St. Bar-
tholomew, had done much to set an execrable example to
those of their own profession; and it is not surprising that
so general and fearful an example of the grossest perfidy and
most unrelenting cruelty, practiced on a scale of such extent,
avowed by the Roman primate, and seconded by those potentates most attached to the See of Rome, should have been
received with enthusiasm among the Catholics of Protestant
countries, who felt themselves oppressed by governors inimical to their religion, and imagined that they served Heaven
by endeavoring to get rid of their Protestant rulers by the
most desperate and unjustifiable means.   On the other hand,
it must be admitted that the Protestants partook, to a certain degree, of the same spirit, and were disposed to retaliate

severely upon those in whom they thought they could place no faith, and whose religion they considered as hateful to the great Being whom both worshipped under different forms.

The extirpation of the great northern heresy was supposed to be chiefly dependent upon the destruction of the power of Queen Elizabeth in England. King James, from his quarrels with the Presbyterian clergy, and other circumstances of his conduct, was supposed to be not altogether unfavorable to the Roman faith; and the power of Scotland, even admitting him to be so, was not deemed such as could render his enmity very formidable, supposing England to be reconverted to the Catholic faith and placed under the dominion of his mother Mary, whom all of that persuasion held to be the legal heir of the crown.

Pope Pius V. had given the full authority of Rome to any enterprise by which the heretic Elizabeth could be deprived of her kingdom and life, by his famous bull of excommunication, which warranted all true Catholics to carry on the most violent proceedings against her as an enemy of God, and of the only religion by which, in Catholic estimation, her subjects could obtain salvation. This had been insisted upon and followed up by some enthusiastic Catholic priests, who had even called upon Elizabeth's attendants and the females of her train to put their sovereign to death with their own hands, and thus merit the praises bestowed on Judith, for her dauntless sacrifice of the Gentile commander who came to oppress her country.

When so much fire was scattered among matters peculiarly inflammable, there was little doubt that it would excite a conflagration.

Three priests, named Gifford, Gilbert Gifford, and Hodgson, feeling an extravagant impulse to act upon the principles we have stated, had associated themselves with Savage, an English Catholic and an officer in the Spanish service, daring and extravagant enough to propose the assassination of Elizabeth with his own hand.

Such a scheme was only feasible, if confined to very few; but another priest, named Ballard, was intrusted with it, for the sake of negotiating with the Spanish ambassador at Paris, that the conspirators might procure the assistance of an army of invaders, in order to take advantage of the confusion which must arise when the blow should be struck. Ballard was assured of strong support on the part of Spain, providing Elizabeth's death could be achieved; and was sent over to England to concert the means by which this main blow might be struck, which was considered as indispensable to the success of the conspiracy.

Returning to England on this commission, Ballard entered into communication on the subject of his treasonable purpose with a young gentleman, named Anthony Babington, of good parts, large fortune, and an amiable disposition, but addicted to romantic ideas on the subject of love and friendship, and an unhesitating zealot in the cause of the Catholic religion. It was agreed that it was rash to trust an action so important to the single arm of Savage, and that Babington himself, with a band of ten gentlemen, with whom he was connected by the closest bonds of community in studies and amusements, and by the ties of extravagant zeal for the Catholic religion, should be sharers in the glory and the merits as well as in the dangers of this desperate enterprise. The names of these gentlemen were, Windsor, Salisbury, Tilney, Tichbourne, Gage, Travers, Barnwell, Charnock, Dun, and Jones. The number was more than double that which had been judged requisite by Ballard and the friends of Queen Mary, with whom he had consulted both in France and England. But Babington reckoned himself assured of them all, from the close ties of familiarity in which they had long lived together, and even permitted a person of the name of Polly, a man of inferior rank, recommended only by a busy and bustling, and, as it proved, an affected zeal for the Catholic cause, to be admitted into the fatal conspiracy, and the conduct of the subsequent revolution.

The rash and romantic confidence of Babington made itself evident by another feature of his conduct, which indicated in an unusual manner an excited imagination. This was nothing less than the causing to be painted a picture containing the portraits of six of the principal associates, with Babington's own representation in the centre; the whole bearing a motto expressive of some hazardous purpose in which they were engaged. This childish, absurd, and unnecessary piece of vanity of itself indicated the total incapacity of the principal conspirators for the execution of the desperate task they were engaged in, which, to have a chance of success, ought to have been obscured in the deepest secrecy.

The conspirators continued, however, to prosecute their plot, arranging among themselves the special part which each was to perform. Babington, as might have been expected, assumed for his own share the most romantic and least guilty part of the enterprise, by undertaking the liberation of Mary from her place of confinement. What a man of such romantic character might hope from the gratitude of a queen released from prison, raised, as his extravagant plan inferred, to a crown far richer than that which she had lost, besides the great chance of recovering the government of her native kingdom, we can only guess at. Thus far is known, that Queen Mary, exhausted by imprisonment, disease, and suffering, no longer possessed those personal charms which might once have inflamed to feats of the most ardent and extravagant valor in her cause the sons of that chivalry which was not yet quite extinguished. When she was permitted to repair for the advantage of her health to the hot baths of Buxton, she is described as an elderly, lame, and bloated woman, altogether deprived, by long years of restraint and misery, mental and bodily, of those personal attractions which she once possessed in such an eminent degree. She was, however, sequestered from public view; and a warm imagination, like that of Babington, might figure her in his idea as still possessed of her unrivalled charms; or, perhaps, her high rank as a queen might, in his opinion, compensate for advanced age and personal deficiencies. Salisbury, with others, were to assemble forces in the neighboring counties, while Tichbourne, Savage, and four associates, undertook the assassination of Elizabeth. The portraits of the atrocious persons were there represented in the picture already mentioned, having that of Babington in the centre, who, though not to be the sharer of their deed, claimed the glory of being principal in the conspiracy.

While the heedless and presumptuous conspirators were thus pluming themselves upon the success of a yet unexecuted plot, Elizabeth and her counsellors were in full possession of all its details, and watched their machinations with earnest attention, yet without intimating the least alarm. Polly, already mentioned, as one who, by affectation of extraordinary zeal, had thrust himself into such intimacy with Babington that the whole circumstances of the conspiracy were intrusted to him, was in reality one of the spies of Walsingham, and one of the two Giffords had also become informer. The conspirators caught the first alarm from the arrest of Ballard, August 4, 1586; they took refuge in flight; but, with the exception of Salisbury, who escaped abroad, were severally arrested, and lodged in the Tower of London. Being separately examined, they confessed their guilt, were tried, condemned, and suffered the punishment which such a conspiracy had well deserved.

The people of England, with just gratitude to a sovereign who had conferred upon them so many benefits, and with general love to the religion professed by her and by themselves, which was aimed at through the person of the sovereign, were justly indignant at the atrocious plot by which a few romantic young men had undertaken to overthrow the government and religion of their country, murder a sovereign whom her people accounted the benefactress and mother of the State, and raise to the throne the native of a foreign country and the professor of a hated religion. In the tumult of their zeal, their ideas of vengeance, unsatisfied by the execution of the conspirators, went back to the imprisoned queen of Scots, with whom they conceived the plot must have originated, since its purport was directed for her benefit. There was a general clamor in England, that the queen of Scots, in whose favor the conspiracy was meditated, ought to be brought to trial, and on conviction should suffer death as its author and contriver, in the manner already provided for by parliament. In such bursts of popular feeling, the abstract dictates of justice are forgotten; and it did not occur to many who were clamorous for prosecution and punishment, that Mary, unjustly detained a prisoner, had a natural right to liberty, by whatever means she could acquire it, and that criminality could only attach to her in the event of her being legally proved accessory to the conspiracy against Queen Elizabeth's life.

The public clamor, however unjust, well suited the private views of Elizabeth and her ministers, disposed, for obvious reasons, to take any proffered opportunity to rid themselves of a prisoner personally detested, and whom it was supposed equally troublesome to keep and dangerous to dismiss.

Yet it appears to us, remote as we are from the scene of action, and unagitated by the passions which blinded the agents, that Elizabeth might even yet have rid herself of her dangerous prisoner without committing the great crime which has stained a life and reign otherwise so illustrious. Mary might, for example, have been safely surrendered to the custody of her son, who had shown no such warmth of filial affection as to make it likely that he would afford his mother the power of disturbing either his own title or that of Elizabeth, which he hoped to inherit. France, also, would have been willing to receive her as the dowager of a deceased sovereign; and with the Huguenots of that country Elizabeth possessed so strong an interest as to render it improbable that Mary, so surrendered, would have been suffered to gain any opportunity of disturbing her sister sover-

eign. Either of these courses was doubtless attended by
certain risks; but it was surely better that such should be
incurred, than that the sceptre of Elizabeth should be stained
with blood and her reign with injustice. Unhappily for
Mary, if that can be accounted unhappy which put a close
to a long train of captivity and sorrow, and most unhappily,
certainly, for Elizabeth herself, it was determined in the
councils of the latter that the present opportunity should
be taken to remove by a violent death one who had been
so long the secret object of fears and apprehensions.

It is probable that the female jealousies and rivalry,
which had gradually grown into hatred in the mind of
Elizabeth, would not have brought her to assent to so bloody
a purpose, had she not been urged on by statesmen, who
veiled their selfish hatred and fear under pretended apprehensions for the life of their sovereign. Burleigh and Walsingham, the principal counsellors of Elizabeth, were sensible that their own counsels had prompted all the former
rigorous proceedings against the queen of Scots, and that
if, by Elizabeth's death or any other contingency, Mary
might chance, as was at least possible, to be preferred as
next heir to the English throne, the account which, in such
a case, they would have to settle with her must have been
of an alarming description. It was therefore determined,
that, founded on the singular act of parliament which we
have detailed, passed in consequence of the machinations
of Parry, a commission should be appointed for the public
trial of Queen Mary, under the provisions of that extraordinary and severe statute, made unquestionably for the very
purpose to which it was now to be applied.

Sir Ralph Sadler, whose age entitled him to evince pee-
vishness even to the despotic Elizabeth, had been released
from his disgusting charge, which was now delivered up
to Sir Amias Paulet, a gentleman severe and harsh in his
temper, and attached to puritanical tenets, and, therefore,
although otherwise an honest and upright man, not unwilling to be the instrument of Elizabeth's strict orders for

the custody of this perilous captive, however far they might exceed the rules of courtesy and generosity, so long as they were within those of moral and religious duty. He viewed his task in so severe a light that he rejoiced when the infirmities of Mary rendered her a cripple incapable of moving from her bed; and the account which he gives of her state of confinement is thus quoted by Mr. Chalmers: "Throughout January, 1586, the queen enjoyed somewhat better health: she could use her limbs, but not without halting; and the defluxion had fallen into one of her hands."—June 3, 1586, he writes, "The Scottish queen is getting a little strength, and has been out in her coach; and is sometimes carried in a chair to one of the adjoining ponds to see the diversion of duck-hunting, but she is not able to walk without support on either side."

Even this state of convalescence did not last long. Soon afterward, Paulet represented the Scottish queen as being much worse, sleeping little, and eating less: the painful disease flying about her system, and showing itself in many places at once. She continued very ill, could not turn in her bed without help, and was in excessive pain. To this state of suffering and disease, we must add, that the economy of Elizabeth did not permit to her who had once been a queen the accommodations which are furnished in modern hospitals to invalids of the meanest order. We will use the words of her last and sternest warder, to show how far this miserable penury was carried. By quoting it more generally, we might well lay ourselves under the suspicion of exaggeration.

"Last year," said Paulet, writing to Walsingham, "when she came to Tutbury, she complained that her bed was stained, and ill flavored; and Mr. Somer, to accommodate her, gave her his own bed, which was only a plain ordinary feather-bed; and now, by her long lying in it, the feathers came through the tick, and its hardness caused her great pain: she begged to have a down bed; and Sir Amias said, 'he could not, in honesty and charity, refuse to mention her request to Walsingham, and desires it may be sent for her.'

The Scottish queen still continued very ill; and on the 17th of February was taken with a defluxion in the side, in so dangerous a manner that her recovery was despaired of." It is remarkable that some of the letters to Babington, pretended to be Mary's own composition, represent her as galloping through the park and shooting deer, when her utmost sport was to see a duck-hunt from her chair, and as taking active exercise, when she was in danger of her life. Mary was not, however, doomed to pass from the world in so easy or natural a manner.

After considerable debates in the council of Elizabeth, it had been resolved to proceed against the queen of Scots, under the terms of the act passed March 2, 1585, which ratified the association for the protection of Elizabeth's person, and directed, in certain events, the trial, under a commission, of any pretender to the crown, or the inheritance thereof, in whose behalf Elizabeth's person should be endangered by open rebellion or treasonable conspiracy.

The language of the statute places the life of such pretender to the crown in equal danger of attainder, whether the party shall or shall not be acquainted with and participant of the treasonable purpose. It was, nevertheless, extremely desirable to show that Mary was personally accessory to the schemes of Babington; and the most violent measures were resorted to in order to secure the necessary evidence to that effect.

Sir Thomas Gorges was despatched from the court with a special warrant for the purpose; and it was managed that he should arrive at Chartley, where Mary was then confined, at the moment when the royal prisoner was going out on horseback, for the purpose, it was alleged, of amusing her with the view of some gentlemen's seats in the neighborhood. During her absence, Naue and Curl, the French and Scottish secretaries of the queen, were separately arrested, and committed to different keepers: her money was seized upon, her cabinets forced open, her papers and correspondence, and all she could desire to keep most private, were made prize of and sent to Elizabeth. In her presence the whole writings were perused: among the mass of which, it is said, there were found sundry letters from English noblemen to Mary expressive of regard and attachment. On seeing these, Elizabeth, according to her favorite motto, Video et taceo—*i.e.*, "I hear and am silent"—laid them aside, without making any observation. The effect was that the writers of those letters, conscious of the degree of suspicion in which they were placed, took every opportunity, during the after proceedings, to escape from it, by showing themselves inimical to Mary, lest Elizabeth should have adopted an opinion that they had expressed themselves hitherto too much her friends.

The grief and mortification of Queen Mary, when she returned to Chartley, where the seizure of her papers had taken place, is, in some degree, intimated by the expressions which she made use of. "Alas!" she said to the poor persons who crowded round her, expecting an alms as usual, "I can no longer relieve your wants: I am a beggar as you are"; and when she found the extent to which she had been plundered, she indignantly remarked, "Of two things they cannot deprive me—my English blood, and my Catholic faith." After this outrage, Mary was divested of those poor insignia of royalty which she had been hitherto allowed to retain: the canopy of state was removed; the regal title was withdrawn; her keepers remained covered in her presence; and in speaking of her no longer designated her as the queen, but simply as the lady.

A final change of residence was now destined to her. The castle of Fotheringay, in Northamptonshire, was her last place of confinement. She was conveyed thither on the 25th of September, 1586. All was made ready for her trial. The judges, to whom the extraordinary act of jurisdiction was to be committed, were nominated by a commission under the great seal, according to the provisions of the statute. The list contained no less than forty persons, the most illustrious in the kingdom by birth or office, to whom were added

five of the principal judges. Before these men the independent queen of Scotland was to be tried upon the late-
made law as a person claiming the succession of the crown,
in whose behalf a conspiracy had been attempted against
the life of Queen Elizabeth, and who had become accessory
to their traitorous purpose. To such a jurisdiction Mary
refused to submit herself; and when called before a meeting of the commission held in the hall of Fotheringay, she
refused to acknowledge the right of those persons to proceed
in taking cognizance of the charge made against her. "I
am," she said, "no subject of the crown of England, and
sovereign princes alone can be the peers entitled to try me.
I am queen of Scotland, and queen-dowager of France. I
came into England seeking the queen's hospitality, but without the slightest purpose of subjecting myself to her sovereignty. I have been unjustly imprisoned during the space
of nineteen years: the laws of England have never protected
me; do not, therefore, let them be perverted into snares
against my life." Nevertheless, she owned she was not
unwilling to justify herself before a free and full English
parliament, but not before a commission deriving its power
from a law which seemed framed expressly to give a pretence of taking away her life.

In this resolution of declining the jurisdiction of the commission, Queen Mary remained for some time fixed, till it
was subtly urged by Hatton, the vice-chamberlain, that, by
avoiding an investigation, she might seem to shroud a guilty
cause; whereas, by entering upon her defence, she might
clear her innocence in the eyes of the commissioners, and
enable them to report to Elizabeth and to the English nation
that she was guiltless. This argument prevailed; but it was
only under a solemn protest against the validity of the commission that Mary condescended to plead before it. The
parties being thus come to an issue, the attorney and so-
licitor of Queen Elizabeth enforced the particulars of their
charge with the legal skill of their profession, and all their
personal ingenuity; and the queen's sergeant-at-law opened,

in a historical discourse, the conspiracy of Babington, and concluded that Mary, who stood accused before the commission, knew of it, approved of it, promised her assistance, and gave counsel for the means of effecting it.

Mary answered, with unabated courage, that she knew neither Babington nor Ballard; that she had, indeed, heard from various quarters that the English Roman Catholics were severely treated, and that she had written to Queen Elizabeth in their behalf. She added that divers persons utterly unknown to her had at different times written suggesting plans of escape; but that she had never returned answers to them, nor encouraged any man to attempts in her behalf which might incur punishment by the English law: other schemes might have existence without her knowledge, because, being closely shut up in prison, she had no means of knowing or preventing plots or conspiracies which might be entered into without her knowledge.

Copies of letters from Babington were then read, apparently addressed to Queen Mary, in which the whole conspiracy was detailed.

To this evidence she replied that it might be true that Babington wrote these letters; but it was false that she had received them. Various letters she had indeed received, but by whom sent she did not know.

To prove, on the part of the prosecution, that she had received the letters of Babington, notwithstanding her denial, there were read from his confession the contents of certain letters which he there stated himself to have received from her in answer to those which he wrote to her. Scrolls of letters, in her own cipher, were also produced, seeming to refer to the same correspondence. When in this part of the debate mention was made of the Earl of Arundel and his brothers, the queen burst into tears, and exclaimed, "Alas! what hath the noble House of Howard endured for my sake!" She then reassumed her composure; and pleaded with truth and firmness that the confessions of Babington could be no proof against her, and that such scrolls as seemed to be written in her cipher might easily have been forged. Finally, she protested that, although she had used her best endeavors to obtain her liberty, and to mitigate the persecution of those of her own communion, she would not have purchased the kingdom with the death of the least ordinary man, much less with that of Queen Elizabeth.

The testimonies of her secretaries, Naue and Curl, were then pressed against her; but this she refused to admit, contending that to make good witnesses they, being alive and within the kingdom, ought to have been produced face to face against her. Curl she described as an honest man, but completely under the influence of Naue, a wily politician, and whose integrity or superiority to the seduction of bribes she did not pretend to assert; neither was she able to say what effect the force of promises or fear of torture may have had upon him. She protested, once more, that she knew neither Babington nor Ballard.

"But you know Morgan well enough," answered the lord treasurer; "and this Morgan, to whom you have assigned a yearly pension, is the person who despatched Parry to England to murder Queen Elizabeth." To this charge, which was totally distinct from that relating to the conspiracy of Babington, Mary replied:

"I know not, save from what you tell me, whether Morgan is guilty of your charge or no; but I know well that he has served me to the loss of his whole fortune; and in that point of view I am bound to give him indemnification and support: if he be the enemy of Queen Elizabeth, let it be remembered that she has pensioned the Master of Gray and others, my bitter personal enemies, whose hatred to me has, perhaps, formed their best pretension to my sister's favor."

Thus through the whole sitting of the court, unaided by counsel or legal advice of any kind, she sustained and repelled the accusations brought against her by professional persons of eminence, with an ingenuity and address which could hardly have been expected from a person of her rank, sex and education. Her defences were naturally framed upon the general reasons of justice and good sense; but with legal advice to assist her, she would have known that in failing to bring in the witnesses on whose evidence she was to be convicted, Elizabeth's commission broke the express statute law of England, as well as the great rules of equity. The statute 1 & 2 Ph. & Mary, chap. x., sect. 11, declares, "That the two witnesses whose evidence is necessary to convict any one accused of high treason shall be confronted with the party accused, and shall in his presence make good their testimony; nor is this dispensed with unless in the case where the witnesses are dead or beyond seas, or the accused party shall confess the treason." But this most equitable and just statute, calculated to afford protection to the subject even against the grasp of the highest authority, was denied to a crowned head, whom chance only placed under the disposal of those who had no native superiority over her.

On the concluding day, Mary again insisted upon her former protestation, and lamented that the proposals she had made to Elizabeth had been rejected, when she promised to give her own son and the Duke of Guise's son as hostages, that England and its queen should not come through her to any harm or detriment: "Instead of which," continued she, "I am now most dishonorably dealt by and my regal honor and reputation called in question before ordinary lawyers, who by wresting conclusions can draw the most harmless circumstance into a criminal consequence." She added, once more, "that her making a voluntary appearance in such a court was only lest she should seem to neglect the justification of her own honor, which was dearer to her than any privilege of her dignity, or her life itself." After some further arguing, the sitting of the court, if it could be called so, was adjourned from Fotheringay, and the commissioners departed on their return to London.

On the 25th of October the commissioners held a meeting in the Star Chamber, where Naue and Curl, the two secretaries, examined upon oath, avowed, affirmed, and justified

the letters and copies of letters formerly produced at Fotheringay as true and real. It is scarcely necessary to observe
that on this occasion the most ordinary rules of evidence
were violated, and the witnesses, whose testimony alone
could give these documents the least weight in evidence,
were examined at a distance from the party against whom
they were produced, and without affording her the opportunity of cross-examination. The confessions of executed
traitors were not more effectual to support the truth of
what they affirmed: no one did or could know under what
circumstances Babington, Ballard, and the others, made their
final confessions, or whether they had made such or not. The
papers produced as such might either be altogether forged,
or they might be garbled and interpolated, or they might
have been extorted by torture, or granted under a promise
of life and favorable treatment. Some of the alleged letters
were made to show things altogether inconsistent with truth,
of which we have already shown an example.

Nor were the prosecutors entitled to complain, if they had
been deprived of the benefit of the evidence of Babington
and his companions, since it rested only with themselves to
have brought it forward in an unexceptionable form. The
lives of these unhappy persons being spared, nothing would
have been more easy than to have brought to Fotheringay
the persons of Ballard and Babington, while yet alive; and
the importance of doing justice to the cause of an independent sovereign must be certainly admitted as matter of more
weight than the instantly depriving of life a few youthful
enthusiasts.

Notwithstanding these considerations, the commissioners
subscribed, by unanimous assent, a sentence, declaring that
since the 1st day of June, in the twenty-seventh year of
Queen Elizabeth, and before the date of their commission,
"divers matters have been compassed and imagined, within
this realm of England, by Anthony Babington and others,
with the privity of the said Mary, pretending a title to the
crown of this realm of England, tending to the hurt, death,

and destruction of the royal person of our said lady, the queen. And also, that since the aforesaid 1st day of June, in the twenty-seventh year aforesaid, and before the date of the commission aforesaid, the aforesaid Mary, pretending a title to the crown of this realm of England, has compassed and imagined, within this realm of England, divers matters tending to the hurt, death, and destruction of the royal person of our sovereign lady, the queen, contrary to the form of the statute in the commission aforesaid specified."

A declaration was at the same time published by the commissioners and judges, declaring that nothing in the sentence should affect King James's title of accession to the crown, but that the same should remain as effectual as if the proceedings at Fotheringay had never taken place. The parliament was soon after convoked, in which they, with unanimous consent, petitioned the queen that, for the preservation of Christ's true religion, the quiet and security of the realm, the safety of themselves and their posterity, the sentence against Mary Queen of Scots might be published. They reminded her that the said queen was a member of the Catholic league made for the destruction of the Protestant religion. Moreover, that she had formerly assumed the royal title and royal arms of England; Elizabeth was affectionately conjured to remember the examples of Heaven's vengeance narrated in Scripture upon King Saul for failing to slay Agag, and upon King Ahab for sparing the life of Benhadad; and the chancellor and speaker added, finally, that they would not think themselves discharged of the engagements which they had come under by their loyal association without proceeding to the execution of this sentence.

The queen failed not to make a long and grateful speech, in which she expressed her thanks for the zeal of her subjects, lamented the extremities to which she was reduced by the machinations of one of her own sex, of the like quality and degree with herself, of the same race and stock, and so nearly related to her in blood. She had written, she said, privately, to her kinswoman, that if she would confess the treasonable practices in which she was involved, in a letter to be private between herself and Elizabeth, she would not permit the discovery to be further pressed against her.   Even yet, far as the matter had now gone, if she could be assured her kinswoman would forbear such practices, and that no one would make use of her name for stirring up treasonable attempts, she, for her part, could willingly pardon what had passed.   As to herself, she proceeded, if by her death could be obtained a more flourishing condition and a better prince, she would willingly lay down her life; for whether she looked to things past, to things present, or to futurity, she counted them happiest who went first from the stage.   After these rhetorical flourishes, she spoke more directly to the point, but still in an enigmatical manner, the sum of what she said pointing to the necessity of proceeding with severity, while the phrases she made use of insinuated a desire to act with lenity.   Their petition, she said, had reduced her to great straits and perplexities, as pressing upon her the punishment of a princess so near in blood to herself, yet, indeed, she must needs confess to them a further secret, though not as one who usually blabbed forth her knowledge of such matters; namely, that she had lately seen with her own eyes a bond subscribed by twelve persons, binding themselves to put her to death within a month.   Having thus introduced a topic well calculated to continue the general ferment on account of her personal safety, Elizabeth expressed herself confident that her good subjects would not press her to an immediate decision on an affair of such uncommon weight and interest, and promised to announce to them her resolution as soon as she should be able to form one.

Continuing the same train of deception and hypocrisy, Elizabeth sent the lord chancellor to the house of lords, and the speaker to the commons, praying these honorable assemblies to consider whether some alternative could not be found, by following which her own personal safety might be reconciled with pardon to Queen Mary.   A more unacceptable proposal, nevertheless, could hardly have been made to Queen Elizabeth than one which should seem to unite Mary's life with her own safety, and thereby impose upon her the necessity of sparing her kinswoman. Accordingly, neither lord nor member of the lower house presumed to vary from their former opinion, but were careful to adapt their reply to the hidden meaning, not the affected tenor of her majesty's letter. They could not, they said, reconcile the queen's safety with the life of the queen of Scots, unless, first, the latter should repent and acknowledge her offence, or, secondly, were kept under a closer guard, and sufficient security given for her good demeanor, or, finally, that she should be banished from the land. Of her repentance, they charitably declared they had no hope; a closer ward, stricter custody, or the security of oaths and hostages, they accounted as ineffectual, because Elizabeth's death, the mark at which Mary was esteemed constantly to aim, would, if achieved, cast all such obligations loose; and if they sent the queen of Scotland out of the realm, they declared they should expect nothing less than her return at the head of an army.

The lord chancellor and the speaker of the lower house added their exhortations to those of parliament, and reminded the queen that her high office obliged her to render justice to every individual who sued for it, and that she ought not to deny it when it was demanded by the general voice of the English nation. Thus these illustrious assemblies gave one instance of what has been sometimes remarked—that their votes are never so likely to be erroneous as when they are unanimous. Reasoning, however strong or irrefutable, seldom has the same effect of conviction on all minds; and unanimity, in many cases, infers that one common strain of passion or prejudice, as remote as possible from calm deliberation, has led or misled the general acquiescence. The queen continued to maintain an affectation of extreme embarrassment: she expressed herself surprised, yet not offended, at the unusual pertinacity with which her lords and commons pressed an execution which gave her mind so much pain. She gently chid them for their extreme anxiety on her account; and expressed her feelings that, since her security was desperate without the death of her relation, she found, nevertheless, in her own bosom, great reluctance to exercise that severity against a great princess which she had studiously forborne in the case of persons of inferior rank. She concluded a long harangue with this indecisive answer: "If I should say I will not do what you request, I might say, perhaps, more than I intend; and if I should say I will do it, I might plunge myself into as bad inconveniences as you endeavor to preserve me from; which I am confident your wisdoms and discretions would not desire that I should, if ye consider the circumstances of place, time, and the manners and conditions of men." Nevertheless, this train of hypocritical dissimulation, meant to express the exceeding grief of Elizabeth's mind at being in a manner compelled by authority of parliament to proclaim the sentence, did not escape the malign construction that the queen had acted in this instance like a true woman, who will seem to reject and disapprove of that which she most desires, in order that it may be forced upon her. The proclamation of the sentence contained similar expressions of the queen's reluctance, which met with the same degree of credulity.

When Mary heard that this final step toward her execution had been taken, she received the intelligence with a steady and composed countenance, and raising her eyes and hands to Heaven, thanked God she now saw the conclusion of her sufferings.

She wrote a remarkable letter to Elizabeth, dated on the 19th of December: in this she disavowed all hostile feelings, and thanked God for the sentence which promised a period to her lamentable captivity. The doomed princess then made, in gentle yet solicitous terms, one or two requests, which she entreated Elizabeth to take into her private and personal consideration, as she expected little favor, she said, from the zealous puritans with whom the English council was filled. First, she desired her body might be transported to France, where her mother's soul rested in peace. In Scotland, she said, the sepulchres of her ancestors were overthrown and violated: in England, she could not have the advantage of the ceremonies of her religion; and she desired to be laid where her spirit might be propitiated with Catholic rites, and her body might have that repose which, when living, it never enjoyed.

Secondly, she besought that she might not be put to death by any private means, or without Queen Elizabeth's knowledge; and that her servants might have an opportunity of observing her final departure. This fear of private murder she was observed to entertain, since all looked so black and menacing around her; and the mind shrinks from a fate which has so much uncertainty in time, place, and circumstance. It afterward appears that her fears were far from unreasonable.

Lastly, Mary desired her servants might be permitted to depart in peace and freedom, and with permission to enjoy those legacies which she should bequeath them by her latest will. These things she entreated of her kinswoman, in the name of their Redeemer, by their near kindred, by the soul and memory of Henry VII., their common progenitor, and in the name of those common decencies which even persons of the most ordinary rank generally observe toward each other. She complained that she had been despoiled of all her regal ornaments; alleged that, if her papers had been fairly produced, it would have appeared that her only cause of condemnation had been the overcarefulness and solicitude of some persons for Queen Elizabeth's safety. Lastly, she entreated a line or two of answer in the hand of Elizabeth herself. If Elizabeth received this affecting letter, she made no reply to it, even to assure her kinswoman that her life was safe, but from the meditated stroke of the law.

The news was soon general that the axe was suspended over the head of Queen Mary, and its fall only depended on the will of Queen Elizabeth. The king of Scots, whatever might be his feeling toward his mother, was called upon by every tie of nature, by respect for himself, and for his character in the world, and no doubt by a certain degree of natural affection, which we cannot, however, suppose to have been of a "singularly ardent quality," although so termed by Camden, could now no longer dispense with making such remonstrances as were most likely to shake the purpose of Elizabeth. He complained with spirit of the indignity and injustice attending a trial of the queen of Scotland, a princess also descended of the blood-royal of England, by a commission of English subjects.

James's ordinary minister at the court of Elizabeth was the notorious Archibald Douglas, already noticed, who after his collusive acquittal was, with much disregard to decency, sent to England as James's resident ambassador.

But James saw the scandal which must attend in trusting the necessary interference on behalf of his mother to the care of a dependent of Morton, Mary's most ruthless enemy, and chose an agent more like to be zealous in his mother's cause. His remonstrances in her behalf were at first uttered through the medium of William Keith, an envoy extraordinary, sent for the purpose of remonstrating against Mary's trial, with instructions to add that, however new such proceeding was, it would be still more extraordinary if his mother, an independent princess, should be put to death under a sentence so pronounced. As this remonstrance produced no effect, James wrote again to Keith, to state how unjust he held the prosecution against his mother, with a charge to remind Elizabeth, that if such a crime should be committed, it concerned him, both in respect of nature and honor, to be revenged; since remaining passive under such an injury without requiring the most ample amends, he must lose credit both at home and abroad. Keith therefore entreated at least for delay, till James should send an ambassador with proposals which might give satisfaction to Elizabeth, and at the same time save the life of his parent. When an application, couched in these terms of menace, was made to Eliza-

beth, she was at first so indignant that she had wellnigh
driven Keith from her presence: on taking time to consider,
however, she agreed to wait to hear any ambassador who
should come from King James *within a few days;* and
condescended to add, that she would suspend the execution of his mother's sentence until that period should have
elapsed.

The stern tone of irritation in which Queen Elizabeth
expressed herself seems to have daunted the spirit of King
James. In a subsequent letter to William Keith, he disowned any attempt to influence Queen Elizabeth by threats,
and intimated that he did not mean to plead his cause with
anything short of due respect to her individual feelings.
He declared himself satisfied that she was not a free agent
in the matter, nor at liberty to act upon her own clement
and generous disposition; but that, on the contrary, he knew
that she was pressed forward by those who urged to her the
peril of her own life. James declared, therefore, that he did
not impute to Elizabeth, personally or directly, the blame of
anything that had been done, and only required her to suspend any proceedings against his mother until the arrival
of the Master of Gray, through whom, as specially commissioned for that purpose, he meant to suggest such conditions as appeared to him sufficient for saving the life of
his mother.

The terms of this mitigated letter relieved Elizabeth from
what she might naturally have esteemed a very considerable
embarrassment; for an instant breach with Scotland, while
she was involved in so many dangers from the continent,
joined to the existence of a Catholic party in her own dominions, could not have been a subject of indifference to
her, upon reflection, how much soever she might be disposed
by nature and habit to answer threats with defiance. The
flexible tone, also, of James's last letter seemed to intimate
that he desired but to play the part of a dutiful son in the
eye of the world, and to the vindication of his honor in
the opinion of his subjects, without meditating any active

measures, if he could discharge what was due to decency. This point once gained by him, Elizabeth probably conjectured that the resentment of the king of Scotland, in case of his mother's execution, would be neither violent nor lasting; and she might consider the appointment of Gray, whose interest she had long secured, was no trifling assurance that in case of the sentence being executed against Mary, the resentment of her son would neither assume a very ardent or fatal character. Gray was accordingly despatched to England; but the suggestions of the council of Scotland, rather than any feeling of the king himself, laid James under the necessity of conjoining with the Master in his commission a colleague likely to be more active in the discharge of it. This was Sir Robert Melville, an old and faithful servant of the crown, whose exertions in the queen's favor might be relied upon much more than those of the venal Gray. The ambassadors extraordinary accordingly set out for England, charged with James's proposals for his mother's life; Melville filled with anxiety to discharge his duty so as might best advantage a mistress who had favored him formerly, and to whom he was sincerely grateful; the Master of Gray, as afterward appeared, with a very different purpose.

At their first audience with Queen Elizabeth, which they obtained with some difficulty, she expressed herself with her usual decision. She had been threatened, she said, by the king of Scots in his letter sent to William Keith, and demanded to know if they were charged with remonstrances of the like nature. Gray replied that an apology had been made for the terms of that letter, by one of a subsequent date couched in less offensive terms. The queen at once entered upon the business of the audience in a manner calculated to silence discussion, saying, briefly and fiercely, "I am unmeasurably sorry that there can be no means found to save the life of your king's mother with assurance of my own. I have labored to preserve the life of both, but it cannot be done." As she appeared to speak in passion, the ambassadors were silent, and withdrew for the time.

At a second audience the queen demanded of them what they had to propose on the part of James, adding, disdainfully, that a thing long looked for should be good when it comes. The Master of Gray then requested to know if Queen Mary was still alive, for a rumor of her death was even already current. "As yet," replied the queen, "I believe she lives; but I will not promise an hour." Gray replied, that his master's propositions were calculated to pledge his credit in behalf of his mother, to that effect interposing the chief of his nobility as hostages, that no plot or enterprise against Queen Elizabeth should be undertaken with the knowledge or countenance of Mary. Or, if it pleased Elizabeth to send Queen Mary into Scotland, King James would engage that the English realm should be safe from all interference on her part. Queen Elizabeth called to the Earl of Leicester, with other lords of her council who were in the chamber, and repeated to them the proposals of the king of Scots, in a tone of scorn, as totally inadequate to the occasion. Gray took the opportunity to ask why the queen of Scots should be esteemed so dangerous to her majesty? "Because," answered Elizabeth hastily, "she is a papist, and they say she shall succeed to my throne." Gray replied, that Mary would divest herself of such a right in favor of her son. The speaking of Queen Mary's claim of succession as real gave fresh offence. "She hath no such right," answered the queen hastily: "she is declared incapable of succession."—"Supposing that to be the case," replied the Scottish ambassador, "there is an end of danger from the papists, since they can trust nothing to a claim of succession which has been annulled, and therefore the reason fails which renders your kinswoman's life dangerous to your majesty."—Elizabeth replied, that "though Mary's right was indeed annulled, the papists would not allow that it had ceased to exist."—"If so," replied the Master of Gray, "the queen of Scots having demitted, with consent of her friends, all right of succession in favor of her son, could no longer pretend to exercise it in her own right, nor could she find support in so doing." The queen at first pretended not to understand the measure which was proposed: the Earl of Leicester explained it, by stating the proposal of Gray to be that the king of Scots should be placed in the rights of his mother. Elizabeth then burst into one of her characteristic passions. "Is that your meaning?" said she; "then I should put myself in worse case than before! By God's passion!" she exclaimed with much vehemence, "this were to cut mine own throat: he shall never come into that place or be party with me" (possess, that is, a share in her succession).—"Yet the king of Scots," answered Gray, "must become party with your majesty, when he succeeds, by his mother's death, to her claims of every kind. Thus the act which we now deprecate will only accelerate a position in respect to Queen Mary's son, of which your majesty is pleased to entertain an apprehension."

Sensible that in this logical discussion she was losing ground, Elizabeth waived further argument in a debate where reason obviously failed her, and took leave of the ambassadors with these words: "Let your king recollect what I have done for him, and how long I have maintained the crown upon his head, even since the hour of his birth. For my part, I am determined to keep the league between the kingdoms. If the king of Scots shall break it, he commits a double fault." With these words, as the last intimation of her pleasure, she was about to leave the apartment, when Sir Robert Melville followed her, beseeching for some delay of the execution; to which she replied, in the tone of authority which had distinguished her deportment during the whole conference, "No, NOT AN HOUR!"

It is scarcely necessary to point out to the reader the different manner in which Elizabeth received the addresses of the houses of peers and commons, pressing her for Mary's immediate execution, and the Scottish ambassadors entreating for delay of the same. To the first she replied with

SIR WALTER SCOTT

Scotland, vol. two

an affectation of feminine hesitation, and prayed her subjects would not press her too hard on a subject so painful. To the second she answered, in the tone of a lioness who has grasped her prey, "No, not an hour!"

It is probable that in this interview Gray expressed truly the proposals of his master James, and he certainly reasoned on the question logically and firmly; but by turning the point upon the claims of succession, which must descend to his master by the death of his mother, he obviously and probably designedly brought into the discussion the subject which was most disagreeable to Queen Elizabeth, and which was sure to incense her in the most sensible manner. So acute a diplomatist as Gray could not have fallen into so great an error by mere accident; and the necessary inference is, that he had no wish that his mission should be successful.

When the report of this angry conference had reached James he assumed a tone more becoming an independent prince pleading in behalf of a mother than he had hitherto ventured to use. In a letter written with his own hand he uses these strong and becoming expressions: "Be no longer reserved in dealing for my mother, for you have been so too long; and think not that anything will do good, if her life be lost, for then adieu to further dealing with that state. Therefore, as you look for my continued favor, spare no pains nor plainness in this case; but read my letter written to William Keith (alluding to that which Elizabeth had resented as containing threats), and conform yourself wholly to the contents thereof; and in this let me see the fruits of your great credit there (that is, at the English court), either now or never. Farewell."

But ere this mandate reached the Master of Gray he had adopted a very different course of proceeding: his interest at the English court alluded to by King James rested on a very different foundation than that of his fidelity to his master or his attachment to the honor and interests of his country. In order that a foreigner should have interest with

Queen Elizabeth and her counsellors, it was necessary that
they should conform themselves implicitly to the wishes and
dictates of that lofty princess. Gray was of that flexible
character which is very docile upon such occasions. He
listened complacently to the insinuations of Leicester and
other English counsellors, who suggested, that although the
king's interference in behalf of his mother was natural and
laudable, yet it should not be urged to such a point as might
endanger the favor of Elizabeth, nor, in short, carried further
than was necessary to secure for his master the character of
a dutiful and affectionate son; while it left him at liberty,
whatever should happen, to preserve the love and friendship
of Elizabeth, who, whether she put to death his mother or
not, was still the ally whose countenance or enmity might
most befriend, or in the highest degree injure his interest.
The Scottish envoy speedily learned the lesson thus taught
him; and conscious, perhaps, that his master wanted that
fiery spirit of resolution characteristic of most of his predecessors, he gave explicit hints to the English ministers that
by executing the sentence against Mary without delay they
would not incur any formidable intensity of enmity on the
part of his master. He repeated the Latin phrase, *Mortua
non mordet*, "A dead woman bites not," and made no
scruple to assure those with whom he had intercourse that,
were the deed once done, his master was likely speedily to
pardon what could neither be remedied nor revenged. He
even undertook to be himself a mediator, and take care
to disarm James's displeasure of all tendency to vengeance.
It is, of course, to be understood that in all this ambiguous
dealing, which went directly to defeat the main purpose of
his embassy, Gray concealed from his colleague Melville the
double-dealing intrigues which he held with the English
ministers.

Other measures were employed to deprecate the threatened hostilities of the king of Scots. Walsingham, famed
for his policy and his prudence, wrote to the king of Scots
to express his surprise at the stand which he had made in

behalf of his mother, seeing that the honest and religious Protestants in England were unanimously agreed that her life was inconsistent with the safety of the Protestant faith in both divisions of Britain, and conjuring him not to wreck the public peace, or disturb the prosperity of the reformed churches of England and Scotland, by taking to heart too anxiously the death of a parent whose life was forfeited to the laws and to an unavoidable necessity.

From all the preceding indications King James was made aware that the fate of his mother was decided; nor is it likely that any measure on his part, unless of a character far more energetic than was usual in his councils, could be of the slightest avail in saving her life. He preserved, however, the decencies of his situation; and, recalling his ambassadors from the court of England, commanded his clergy at home to remember his mother in the public prayers, under a form to which certainly there was nothing to which charity could object, since the tenor ran that it might please God to illuminate her with the light of his truth, and save her from the apparent danger wherein she was cast. The clergymen, however, remembering the Catholic tenets of Mary, and that aversion entertained to her by the original fathers of the Scottish Church, which had so large a share in her downfall, refused to comply even with this moderate request of their sovereign. In the capital, particularly, the refusal was wellnigh general, so that the king was obliged to appoint the archbishop of St. Andrew's to preach before him on a certain day, in order that he might hear the safety of his mother recommended in the prayers of his subjects. In this, however, he was disappointed. An enthusiastic young man named Cooper, who though not yet himself called to the ministry, intruded himself into the pulpit by the encouragement, it is said, of his brethren, and excluded the prelate.

The king arriving at the time appointed, and seeing the pulpit already occupied, addressed the intrusive preacher from his seat in these temperate words: "That seat, Mr. John, was destined for another; but if you mean to obey the charge which we have sent forth, and remember our mother in your prayers, you are at liberty to proceed." To this Cooper replied he would do as the Spirit of God directed him. Upon this, being commanded to come from that place, and refusing to obey, the captain of the guard was ordered to pull him from the pulpit. On hearing these orders issued, the hot-headed young man exclaimed that the violence which he sustained should be a witness against the king at the day of judgment.

If we can trust a current tradition, such contests between the pulpit and the throne occurred more than once in the face of the congregation. It is said a young preacher, dilating before James's face on some matter highly offensive to him, the monarch lost patience, and said aloud, "I tell thee, man, either to speak sense or come down." To which reasonable request, as it might be thought, the preacher stoutly replied, "And I tell thee, man, I will neither speak sense nor come down."

The archbishop of St. Andrew's then succeeded to the pulpit; and by the eloquence of a sermon, in which he insisted on the duty of praying for all men, pacified the tumult which so extraordinary a scene had excited among the congregation.

It is not improbable that, instead of entering into squabbles with his clergy on the mode of petitioning Heaven in his mother's behalf, had King James descended to look for earthly succors, and appealed to his subjects on so national an occasion, he might, on wonderfully short notice, have assembled upon the borders an army of forty thousand men, who would not willingly have seen the blood of their sovereign's mother shed upon a scaffold by command of a foreign power.

We have detailed at length the nature of James's intercession for his mother's life as an interesting part of Scottish history: the intervention of other powers for the same purpose may be briefly noticed. The king of France, though an enemy to the House of Guise, could not, were it only for decency's sake, avoid an application on the same occasion; but the arguments of his ambassador, Bellievre, were not so urged as to make much impression upon Elizabeth, who, aware, besides, of Henry III.'s dislike to the House of Guise, paid no attention to the arguments from that quarter.

Nevertheless Queen Elizabeth, though uninfluenced by the remonstrances of foreign courts, seemed, when the moment for decision was arrived, to hesitate upon striking the fatal blow. With whatever color she might cloak it to her own conscience, or represent it to the English nation, she could not be indifferent to the manner in which the death of Mary was likely to affect her fame through Europe at large. Neither was she entirely secure of Scotland; for although the Master of Gray pretended that the resentment which James might entertain for his mother's execution should be of no permanent duration, yet Melville, whose honor was known to her, had held different language; and the recall of the Scottish ambassadors seemed to announce a war, for which the queen of England, beset as she was by continental enemies, could not be supposed to be perfectly provided.

But although no such pressing cause for hesitation had exhibited itself, Elizabeth, like many others in a similar situation, seems to have found her courage fail when she approached close to the perpetration of the crime she had so long meditated. The sense that, though she might delude her own people by fantastic fears and jealousies, the rest of Europe would not be so easily gulled, must have made her reluctant to strike the final blow; and with her fears for her own reputation there doubtless was mingled some touch of womanhood, some feeling of female reluctance to shed the blood of her captive kinswoman. Although she could refuse Melville even the delay of an hour in the height of an angry debate, yet upon reflection she was unwilling to decide upon the execution, nor was she perhaps displeased to gain the credit of sustaining a struggle between her humanity and what she called her sense of justice. She exhibited every symptom of disquietude and abstraction, wandered through her palace with unequal steps, or was found alone musing, or heard uttering in a broken voice enigmatical expressions of doubt and irresolution. *Aut fer aut feri, ne feriare feri,* were words frequent in her mouth. They were taken from the quibbling mottoes and devices which were then favorite subjects of study, and served to express the uncertainty of Elizabeth's mind. Meantime various reports were dispersed to keep up the alarm, and persuade the people of England that the death of Mary was the life of Elizabeth, and the life of Mary was the death of her sister sovereign. Bravos were said to be hired by the French ambassador to assassinate the queen; the Spanish fleet was said, one day, to have arrived at Milford Haven; on another, the Duke of Guise was said to have landed in Sussex; a third rumor stated an invasion of the Scots; a fourth, an insurrection of the northern counties; a fifth proclaimed the city to be on fire; a sixth announced the death of Elizabeth. The people, distracted by these varying reports, grew almost frantic, and called loudly for the death of Mary, as the only remedy for the convulsions with which the nation was threatened.

It was therefore with the unanimous consent of her own subjects, or rather in compliance with their demands, that Elizabeth resolved to sign the fatal death-warrant against her sister.

The preparing of this deed fell officially to the charge of William Davidson, one of the principal secretaries of state, who was doomed, by a stroke of political management, to be the victim of Elizabeth's duplicity upon this occasion. Davidson received instructions from the lord admiral to prepare the death-warrant for the queen's signature. He did so, and laid it before her with other papers. She immediately entered upon the subject. After she had looked it over, she signed it, and laying it from her asked the secretary, jocularly, whether he was not heartily sorry that it was done. His answer was as might be expected, that "since

Mary's life was inconsistent with Elizabeth's safety, he preferred the death of the guilty to that of the innocent." She then commanded him to append the seal to the warrant, and to give it so ratified to the lord chancellor, with directions to use it as secretly as might be. "On the way," said she, jocularly, "you may show it to Walsingham, who will die of grief at the news.'" She expressed her desire that the execution should take place neither in the open court nor in the green of the castle, but in the great hall of Fotheringay; and being thus particular in her directions, left Davidson in no doubt that she was seriously determined on the bloody scene which she had thus contemplated, with every circumstance of time and place.

When Davidson was ready to depart with these instructions, the queen again called him, and entered into some complaint of Sir Amias Paulet, who, she alleged, might have eased her of this burden, commanding him and Walsingham to sound the dispositions of Queen Mary's keepers, and to hint to them the good service which they might do her by anticipating the execution of the warrant.

Such a letter as the queen desired, subscribed by Walsingham and Davidson, was written to Sir Amias Paulet and Sir Drew Drury, who were now conjoined in the custody of the unfortunate Mary.

It is of a tenor as extraordinary as any missive which can be pointed out in the ample portfolio of political profligacy. "The queen," says this choice epistle, "appears, by some speeches lately uttered, to note in you a lack of care and zeal of her service, in respect you have not all this time of yourselves, without other intimation, found out some way to shorten the life of that queen. In neglecting to do so, besides a kind of lack of love to Elizabeth, she observed that the keepers of Mary had not that care of the preservation of religion and the public good they would be thought to have, more especially having a ground of warrant for the satisfaction of their conscience, their oath of association, by which they had both solemnly pledged themselves, binding them to prosecute Mary to the death in event of the guilt being proved against her. The queen," continues the letter, "takes it most unkindly that men professing the love to their sovereign asserted by you should yet, for lack of discharge of their duty [that is, for not murdering by their private act their royal prisoner], suffer the burden of taking her life to fall upon Elizabeth herself, whose aversion to shed blood was so well known, and whom they might well suppose was still more reluctant to shed that of her relation and sister sovereign." This singular letter, in which two men of quality and honor are advised to commit an assassination out of mere loyalty and deference to the feelings of Queen Elizabeth, produced no effect upon those to whom it was addressed.

Paulet, in his own name, though the letter was also subscribed by Drury, laments that he should have lived to see the unhappy day in which he is required by his sovereign to do an act forbidden by the laws of God and man. His livings and life he declared to be at her majesty's disposition, nor did he wish to enjoy them but with her good favor; "but God forbid," he continues, "that I should make so foul a shipwreck of my conscience, or leave so great a blot to my posterity, or shed blood without law or warrant." Elizabeth was greatly disappointed at finding this scrupulous temper where she did not conceive any such was to be expected. Paulet used to be termed her "faithful Amias," "her most careful servant," whose double labors and faithful actions, whose wise orders and safe conduct in so dangerous and crafty a charge as that of the imprisoned Mary, her grateful heart accepted with an overflowing sense of kindness. When, however, he was found scrupulous in so slight a matter as making away with his prisoner, he became a "dainty and precise fellow, who would promise much but perform nothing." And she called it perjury in him and others, who, contrary to the oath of association, were desirous to throw upon their queen the whole odium of an unpleasant transaction. She still proposed, however, to have the business done by private violence, and spoke to Davidson of one Wingfield who was willing to undertake it. The secretary was at some pains to show that, by such a violent and secret course to rid herself of her prisoner, she could not hope to escape the general suspicion and obloquy which must attend upon such an action.

The by-ways of private assassination being thus interrupted, Elizabeth resolved to follow the broad and formal course which was already chalked out by the proceedings of the commission, taking care, at the same time, so to order the execution of the warrant that it should, as much as possible, appear to be the voluntary act of her ministers, with as little accession on her own part as could be avoided. At Davidson's next audience of Elizabeth she entered voluntarily into the subject of the danger in which she daily lived, and how it was more than time this matter was despatched, and, swearing a great oath, added, that it was a shame for them all that it was not done, directing Davidson to write a letter to Paulet, for the despatch of the execution. Davidson answered, that such a letter was unnecessary, the warrant being general and sufficient.

The secretary being thus, as he conceived, pretty well apprised of what would be accounted good service, laid the warrant before the privy council, who, instigated by zeal, as they pretended, for the queen's safety, or, more probably, by a desire to gratify her wishes, drew up a letter, under their hands as privy councillors, empowering the Earls of Shrewsbury and Kent, together with the high sheriff of the county of Northampton, to see the warrant for putting Queen Mary to death put in force, as the sentence warranted execution. This final authority was despatched by the hands of Beale, clerk of the privy council, a man always noted for harsh manners, puritanical zeal, and a bitter enmity to Queen Mary.

While Elizabeth thus fluctuated, not between remorse and desire of committing the crime, but concerning the mode in which it should be accomplished, Mary prepared herself for death with all the dignity of a queen and the firmness of a martyr. To her affecting letter to Elizabeth, already quoted, no answer had been returned, nor did the queen ever acknowledge having received it. The assistance of a confessor or priest of her own religion, though deemed essential by Catholics to salvation, was withheld from her by the stern puritanism of the times. The assistance of a Protestant bishop and a dean were indeed offered to her, but with these her communion forbade her to join in devotion.

With no aid, therefore, saving her own unbroken spirit, she prepared for death, as she had formerly done for trial. She received with the most dignified composure the Earls of Kent and Shrewsbury, who came to announce that she was to die on the next day. "I did not," answered Mary, "think that the queen, my sister, would have commanded my death by the hands of the executioner; but the soul is not worthy of Heaven which shrinks from the pang of death." The evening was employed in writing her testament, settling her worldly affairs, and comforting the outrageous sorrows of her female attendants.

The last night she slept soundly, and rising early in the morning, busied herself with her private devotions. At eight o'clock the high sheriff found her still kneeling before the crucifix. She came forth with her countenance and presence majestically composed, dressed in a mourning habit adorned with some few ornaments. As she descended to the fatal place of execution, her house-steward, named Melville, fell on his knees before her, and bewailed with loud lamentations that it should be his fortune to carry the tidings of her fate to Scotland. "Lament not, good Melville," said the queen, "but rather rejoice, since thou shalt see this day Mary Stuart released from her earthly miseries. Bear witness, I die constant in my religion, and faithful in my affection to Scotland and France." She then charged him to be loyal to her son, and to advise him to maintain friendship with the queen of England. She obtained the promise of the attendant earls that the distribution of her effects among her attendants should be attended to according to her wish. It was with greater difficulty that she obtained permission for one or two of her servants to attend at her execution; but the sad boon was at length granted, upon her undertaking that her maidens should not disturb the awful scene with their cries. The great hall of the castle of Fotheringay, hung with black for the occasion, was assigned as the fatal spot. A low scaffold placed in the centre of the hall exhibited the block and axe, together with the headsman and his assistant, the implements and agents of the bloody tragedy which was to follow.

Mary ascended the scaffold; and sitting down on a chair, placed for her accommodation, heard with indifference the death-warrant read over. Once more she refused the assistance of the clergymen, who with well-meaning officiousness pressed upon her the difference between the churches, and the preference due to the Protestant creed. She then prayed in Latin out of the Catholic manual of devotion, called the Office of the Virgin Mary, and then rose to prepare for death. One of the executioners having offered his service, she gently repulsed him, saying she was not accustomed to the service of such grooms, or to perform her toilet before so large a company. A low wailing took place among the female attendants: Mary quietly reminded them that she had promised that they should keep silence. Being divested of her cloak and upper garments, she knelt to the block, with devout expressions of resignation, and her head was struck from her body at two blows. A favorite lap-dog could not be separated from the corpse of his mistress. When the fatal blow was struck, the dean pronounced the usual form, "So perish Queen Elizabeth's enemies!" To which the Earl of Kent could alone muster voice to answer, "Amen"; all other persons present being drowned in sighs and lamentations.   Thus died Mary Queen of Scots—many parts of whose earlier life remain an unexplained riddle to posterity, which men have construed, and will construe, more according to their own feelings and passions than with the calm sentiments of impartial judges. The great error of marrying Bothwell, stained as he was by universal suspicion of Darnley's murder, is a spot upon her character for which we in vain seek an apology. Certainly the poor trick of the bond subscribed at Ainslie's Supper cannot greatly mitigate our censure, which is still less evaded by the pretended compulsion exercised toward the queen, when she was transported by Bothwell to Dunbar. What excuse she is to derive from the brutal ingratitude of Darnley; what from the perfidy and cruelty of the fiercest set of nobles who existed in any age; what from the manners of a time in which assassination was often esteemed a virtue, and revenge the discharge of a debt of honor, must be left to the charity of the reader. This may be truly said, that if a life of exile and misery, endured with almost saintly patience, from the 15th of June, 1567, until the day of her death, upon the 8th of February, 1586, could atone the crimes and errors of the class imputed to her, no such penalty was ever more fully discharged than by Mary Stuart.

CHAPTER XXXVII

ELIZABETH was no sooner made acquainted with the death of Mary than it seemed that the life or nonexistence of that unfortunate lady was alike to be the subject of distress and anxiety to her sister sovereign. The people of England, indeed, received the tidings with the acclamations usually attendant upon some event intimating great national prosperity. Bonfires and illuminations, and other demonstrations of joy, attended the news that Mary, nineteen years a prisoner, was now a corpse.

But the queen was aware that these appearances of joy were delusive; and that, besides, she had Europe to answer to as well as England. She had no sooner received the report of the execution than she evinced every symptom of the greatest surprise and indignation, pausing, faltering, and bursting into exclamations of regret and astonishment. Nor did she confine herself to these expressions of grief: she put herself into mourning; and denying all accession to or knowledge of the execution, rebuked her privy council, and dismissed them, in wrath, from her sight. She wrote to the king of Scots a letter with her own hand, in which, forgetting that she had refused, at the intercession of his envoy, to delay the execution even an hour, she affected the most inconsolable grief for the lamentable accident, as she termed it, which had happened contrary to her meaning and intention. This letter was despatched by Sir Robert Carey, a kinsman of Queen Elizabeth, who was understood to be personally acceptable to King James.

In this posture of affairs, Paulet and Drury had reason to rejoice that they had not been induced by the *sugared words* of Elizabeth to embark in the dark project of assassinating their prisoner, either for the purpose of sparing the queen's feelings, or displaying the fulness of zeal for her person; for the hard measure which the queen dealt toward Burleigh, and especially toward Davidson, who had authorized the execution in a legal manner, and by a formal warrant, plainly showed that had they fallen into the trap laid for them, or taken their prisoner's life by any secret practice, she would have disavowed the action to which she had herself instigated them, and left them to atone for their credulity with the loss of their heads.

James, incensed himself, and inflamed by the passions of all around him, breathed at first nothing save war and vengeance. Carey was not permitted to cross the boundary of the kingdoms, nor would the king of Scots admit him to his presence. This affront Queen Elizabeth was obliged to digest. By her order, Carey sent to the Scottish council the letters designed for the king, with a statement of what she was pleased to represent as the real circumstances of the

case. Carey protested in her name that it never once entered
into her thoughts to put the queen of Scots to death, notwithstanding the daily persuasions of her council, her houses
of parliament, and the almost hourly outcries of her whole
people. Nevertheless, as daily reports were abroad of the
landing of foreign armies, the escape of Mary from Fotheringay, and similar occurrences of an alarming nature, the
queen, merely by way of precaution, thought it best to deliver a signed warrant to her secretary Davidson, not intending that it should go out of his hands except in case of invasion from abroad or insurrection at home. Such being her
purpose, Davidson having, nevertheless, contrary to her intention, shown to one or two of her statesmen the warrant
for Mary's execution, the privy council thereupon held a
meeting, and sent a mandate for putting the warrant in
force, which "she protests to God," says Carey, "was done
before she knew of it. The secretary, however," he added,
"was committed to prison, and would not escape his sovereign's high displeasure. This is the tenor of my mistress's
message," concluded Carey, "which if I could express as it
was delivered to me, with a heavy heart and a sorrowful
countenance, I think the king of Scots would rather pity the
grief which she endures than in any respect blame her for a
fact in which she had no share."

To suit the queen of England's actions to her professions,
Davidson was brought to trial in the Star Chamber, where
it was agreed to lay upon him the fault of the whole proceeding. Burleigh, who was indispensable to her majesty's councils, had insinuated something as if what Davidson reported
of her majesty's wishes and intentions had induced him and
the rest of the council to despatch the warrant. The unfortunate secretary was therefore accounted guilty of a high mis-
demeanor, as having misrepresented the queen's intentions,
and misled the privy council in a matter of so much importance, and was therefore fined in ten thousand pounds, and
imprisoned during the queen's pleasure. Even Burleigh
himself became uncertain how far his own ruin might not

be determined by Elizabeth, in order to convince James of
the reality of his mistress's pretended innocence. He was,
however, restored to favor; and the total ruin of Davidson
was held a sufficient atonement for the death of Mary.

The king of Scots was for some time unwilling and probably ashamed to accept the patched and fabricated account
presented by Carey, irreconcilable as it was with truth and
with itself, as an apology for the death of his mother. He
held a parliament, the members of which unanimously professed their readiness to support him in revenging the death
of their late queen, an injury which they justly regarded as
affecting the people of Scotland as well as their king. But
time brought calmer counsels; and a number of prudential
motives reconciled James to remaining at peace, where war,
always a destructive, might actually prove a ruinous, expedient. The perilous state of the Protestant religion to which
he professed himself sincerely attached peremptorily forbade
a breach with Queen Elizabeth. The difference of force between the two countries was greatly in favor of England;
and such aid as he might procure from France or Spain was
neither of a certain nor of a safe description. The holy league
was directed against Scotland as well as against other heretical nations; and, however ready the Catholic princes might
be to avenge the death of the Catholic Mary, they could not
be supposed to entertain much zeal in the cause of the Protestant James. A high sense of filial affection and regal dignity would not indeed have stopped to weigh these circumstances with accuracy, and was likely to have impelled a
son and a sovereign prince, whose mother had been thus
cruelly murdered, into a conflict, in which, at every risk, he
might secure either vengeance or death. But such an affection James had never entertained toward Mary. He had
never known his mother: he had been placed upon her throne
while a child, and when grown up to *youth*, he had, with
cold prudence, declined to interfere in her behalf; his grief
and resentment for her death were not likely, therefore, to
be of an ardent character.

At any rate, the grand excuse for inactivity in such cases was open to James. The evil was done, and could not be repaired; and the question only remained whether it was wise to run the risk of ruin in endeavoring to avenge it. In the annual pension allowed him, which was almost the only fund he could dedicate to the necessary maintenance of his royal state, Queen Elizabeth had shown herself a generous godmother; and now, when he was deprived of a mother by her means, she might, probably, feel a disposition to supply, by even augmented liberality, the place of the parent of whom he had been deprived by her means. Above all, a war between Scotland and England was likely to become fatal to the hopes of the rich English succession, the right of which, by the death of his mother, had now devolved upon him, and no possible success in war could have made up to James so great a loss. These considerations acted powerfully upon cold feelings and a spirit naturally averse from warfare, and induced the king of Scots, after a decent time, to dissemble his resentment of his mother's death, to receive the exculpations of Elizabeth as if he gave credit to a story in itself so improbable, and to permit the amicable relations between the countries gradually to resume their ordinary course.

Some subjects of Scotland were impatient of their sovereign's inactivity and tameness, and declared fiercely for war. The Earl of Argyle, when the court were commanded to assume mourning for Queen Mary, intimated his sense of the ordinance by appearing in full armor, as the dress which best suited the occasion; but this and other hints to arms were suffered to pass unnoticed, and Mary occupied her grave in the cathedral of Peterborough forgotten and unrevenged.

One victim, however, besides the scapegoat Davidson, paid the debt due to his perfidy upon this occasion. The versatile Master of Gray, who, charged with the task of negotiating for Queen Mary's safety, had encouraged and hastened her execution, was now called to account for his

perfidy.   Gray was even at this time plotting a change of
court, to be effected by putting to death some of the persons
who then stood highest in the king's council; but his schemes
were interrupted by his own dependent, Sir William Stewart,
a brother of the upstart Earl of Arran, whom Gray had formerly deserted and betrayed.   By this gentleman the Master
was bluntly impeached of having betrayed and abused the
confidence reposed in him as a public ambassador, by writing, while on his embassy in England, a letter, in which he
encouraged the English ministry in the execution of the
king's mother: it was further added by the accuser that
he had privately corresponded with the king of France and
the Duke of Guise, for the purpose of obtaining toleration to
Catholics in Scotland; a species of machination accounted
by the age as being equally treasonable with his breach of
public faith and abuse of his power as an ambassador.
Lastly, he was charged with the purpose of assassinating
some of James's present ministers.

Gray made no defence, but submitted to the king's mercy;
confessing that he had trafficked for toleration of Catholics
further than he had license to do; and admitting that he entertained resentment against some of the persons in office,
but denying that he nourished any thoughts of violence
against them.   Lastly, he confessed that having, when ambassador in England, perceived Queen Elizabeth determined
to take Queen Mary's life, he had given his advice, with a
view to the prevention of war between the countries, that
she had better be put to death by private practice than by
public execution; and he admitted having used the phrase,
Mortui non mordent, though in a different sense from that
which the accuser put upon it.

For these misdemeanors the Master of Gray was banished
from Scotland, and resided in Italy for several years, though
he afterward returned to his native country.

Captain James Stewart, formerly the Earl of Arran, the
brother of Gray's accuser, Sir William, had expected that
upon these changes in the Scottish court he himself might

recover some favor: he was disappointed, however, for Maitland, now Lord Thirlstane, was declared chancellor, a title which the fallen statesman had hitherto retained, though without exercising the office.

The kingdom of Scotland about this period enjoyed some temporary repose; and a parliament was appointed to be held at Edinburgh upon the 29th of July, 1586, the king having now attained the years of majority. It is to the credit of James that he endeavored to solemnize his accession to manhood by what would have, indeed, proved the greatest boon which could be bestowed on the country over which he was called to reign. Not only the nobility of Scotland, but their gentry and barons, claimed and exercised, in the most frightful extent, the privilege of making war upon each other for the slightest causes, and with the most fatal and deadly effects. What greatly augmented this national evil was that whatever injury had been received by either party in those domestic quarrels, or in the skirmishes to which they gave rise, was handed down as a debt of vengeance, for which the family who sustained the loss were bound to exact vengeance to the latest period of time. It frequently happened that persons of consequence were reciprocally slain on the side of both contending parties, and it was then held indispensable to the honor of those tribes concerned that the retaliation on each side should be full and complete; for which purpose the feuds, as they were termed, were transmitted from father to son, and, in spite of the denunciations of religion and law, were, by the the obstinacy of popular prejudice, accounted inexpiable. Thus neighboring families and clans throughout the greater part of Scotland, but particularly in the highlands and borders, were engaged in endless and multiplied wars, of which the custom was so inveterate that it seemed as if no interposition of the civil authority, though repeatedly and anxiously attempted, had power to preserve the peace of the kingdom. This had been from all generations the prevailing evil in Scotland, even in the reign of firm and powerful princes, such as Robert I., James I.,

II., IV., and V. The practice had been somewhat checked by the severe exertion of royal authority, when cases of peculiar importance compelled its interference; nor was this done without such an effusion of blood as to leave a stigma of severity at least, if not of cruelty, upon monarchs who were otherwise accounted the benefactors of their country, and were, perhaps, chiefly so in the strictness with which they repressed breaches of the general peace.

But the civil wars in Queen Mary's time had given more ample scope to the currency of general violence than during the more severe administration of her father, James V.; the habits of war were become general through Scotland; the farmer left the cultivation of the ground to follow his landlord, sometimes to wars of a public, sometimes to those of a private, character; bondmen and cottagers were the only laborers who were expected to toil for raising the food by which the population was to be supported. By every man superior to a mere serf or bondager defensive armor was worn as a part of his ordinary attire, and offensive weapons as a protection, without which it was unsafe to stir abroad. Every province of Scotland, every neighborhood, was distracted by the quarrels of the nobles and gentry, which broke out from time to time when they were least expected, and frequently in retaliation of injuries which had been long ago sustained.

No time, place, or circumstance could limit the exercise of a deadly feud, or restrict the evils which its recollection excited. The streets of the metropolis resounded with quarrels fought out by armed men, which, though they sometimes lasted for hours together, the utmost exertions of the civil power were unequal either to put an end to or to punish. In the ante-chamber of the court, and even in the presence of the king himself, defiances were exchanged and insults given in the most brutal language; and the parties hardly gave themselves the trouble to go further than the palace-yard to bring the matter to deadly arbitrament.

To give one instance out of many, Sir William Stewart,

the brother of the Earl of Arran, whom we have just mentioned as the accuser of the Master of Gray, happened to
revive in the presence-chamber some ancient dispute with
Francis Stewart, earl of Bothwell, a man as choleric as
himself. In the process of their quarrel receiving a contradiction from the earl, he replied in such affronting language
as the lowest of the rabble in the present day might bestow
on his opponent in a drunken quarrel. Shortly after, Bothwell, a haughty and choleric man, encountered Stewart in
the public street, and repeating the words which had been
applied to him, killed him dead on the spot at a single
thrust. The earl left the town for a few days, but soon
returning, was never questioned for the action.

These bloody brawls took place without the delicacies of
formal challenges, equal arms, impartial witnesses, or the
other requisites with which the modern code of honor limits, or endeavors to limit, the indulgence of private revenge.
On the contrary, if the barons of the sixteenth century did
not, as was frequently the case, absolutely lie in wait for
their enemies, and assail them with every advantage of
numbers, their factions at least fought where they met,
without regarding which was best armed, or backed by
most friends or retainers; and the stronger party thought
no more of laying aside any part of his superiority than a
modern general would dream of equalizing his army with
the weaker battalions of an adversary. They accounted
feud to be equivalent to a state of open war, which each
party endeavors to prosecute by every advantage in his
power.

The legislature had done their part to restrain an evil so
intolerable, in which public peace gave little breathing space
to the country, since violence and slaughter continued yet to
ravage Scotland under the pretence of private war. The
temper and habits of James, naturally averse to blood and
violence, and disposed to the extension of lawful rule and
royal supremacy, was peculiarly dissatisfied with this growing and continued national evil; but though his tempera-

ment inclined the sovereign to be sensible of the mischief,
both that and his circumstances deprived him of the power
of curing it.   A just and strict administration of the laws,
begun at first with a certain degree of lenity, but maintained
more severely when the nation had become accustomed to
such wholesome restraint, would have been the natural and
evident course of remedy for this wasting pest.   However,
the king had not strength to enforce a remedy, far more obvious to be discovered than easy to be pursued.   The royal
domains, wasted and dilapidated during the civil wars, were
so little able to maintain a force sufficient to assert the royal
authority, even in the comparatively civilized parts of Scotland, that, with the help of James's pension of five thousand
pounds from Elizabeth, he had hardly the funds necessary
for maintaining his household; and in his disposition possessed neither the turn for economy nor the audacity of enterprise, which render small means adequate to achieving
great purposes.   On the other hand, the same good-natured
indolence which rendered James improvident in money con-
cerns, and unwilling to lead troops, made him also incapable
of the power of refusing the petitions for pardon and remission which thronged upon him when crimes of slighter or
deadlier dye were committed, so that a perpetual impunity
encouraged the repetition of these constant offences.

Yet James had the sincere desire to put an end to this
general rage for war and slaughter, and attempted it by a
species of reconciliation to be accomplished under his own
eye, and to be sanctioned by his own authority, which was
meant to close at once and forever the deadly feuds which
existed among the Scottish nobles.

For this purpose the king invited to a public banquet the
Scottish nobility, and, in particular, all those who were
known to nourish deadly feud against each other.   Previous to this banquet he read them a lecture upon the dis-
loyalty to himself, and public danger to the country, incurred by their taking into their own hands the decision of
their controversies, and persuaded them to consent to remit

their differences to his decision. This could not, in words, or appearance at least, be decently refused. They consented, accordingly; and James, having made them take hands, each with his mortal enemy, led them himself in procession from the palace of Holyrood House to the Cross of Edinburgh, where they were regaled with a splendid collation at the expense of the city, the magistrates and citizens looking on with great joy, while the lords, who had lately been in discord, drank pledges to each other, and his majesty quaffed peace and happiness to them all. It is remarkable that the Lord Yester, the ancestor of the family of Tweedale, more vindictive or less complaisant than the rest, refused to be reconciled with the Earl of Traquair, and was sent prisoner to the castle of Edinburgh. It was obvious, indeed, that this apparent reconciliation was only the closing by emolients an unhealed abscess, which required the severer treatment of steel and cautery; yet it evinced the king's goodwill to his subjects, and might perhaps have the effect of furnishing an honorable opportunity of dropping feuds among such of the nobles as had maintained them solely because a point of honor prevented their suffering them to fall asleep. If to the arguments with which he had recommended peace to his nobles he had or could have added a strict and severe execution of justice toward those who infringed the laws and disturbed the peace of the country, James would have conferred a real benefit on his subjects. As it was, the reconciliation feast passed off as a piece of theatrical effect; and most of the nobles who had joined hands at the king's command drew their swords upon each other shortly afterward, as if it had never taken place.

Of this we shall quote an individual instance, which happened a few years after this supposed reconciliation, and which may give the reader some idea of the extent of this complicated pest, by which the nobility were not only obliged to engage in wars with each other, but were involved in every dispute and affray among their vassals, whose quarrels they were obliged to maintain upon all occasions, however unreasonable or however trifling; thus it frequently happened that an idle brawl between two persons of no distinction or consequence involved a considerable province in all the horrors of a civil war.

Thus, in the month of July, 1595, a person named Forrester, and another called Bruce, both families residing in the Carse of Stirling, and what were then called *clanned* men, paid their addresses to the same lady, and quarrelling together, Bruce received a hurt—a sufficient injury to provoke that spirit of revenge which was then the most active passion in the bosom of the natives of Scotland. The Bruces could not, it seems, obtain an opportunity of discharging their rage on the person who had wronged their kinsman; but as they understood that another person of the same name, a magistrate in Stirling, was to travel from thence to Edinburgh on a particular day, they waylaid and slew him, although he was no way connected with the original quarrel. The slain man being a retainer of the Earl of Mar, that nobleman next took up the quarrel: he caused the corpse of Forrester to be brought from Linlithgow to Stirling in solemn procession: he himself attended with his banner displayed, and a great body of horse; a flag was also borne in the procession, on which was represented the picture of the deceased mangled and bloody, with the wounds which he had received. In this guise the body of the murdered man was conveyed through the territory of the Bruces and the Livingstons, and so to Stirling, where he was finally buried. The contemporary historian adds, that he inserts this form of defiance for the rarity thereof, and because he expects that some signal revenge is likely to ensue.

The parliament of 1587 passed some acts against missionary Jesuits and seminary priests, who at this time visited Scotland in numbers, with the view of making proselytes.

Two other remarkable laws were passed: the first annexed to the crown such lands of the Church as had not been inalienably bestowed upon the nobles or landed gentry;

these were still considerable, and were held either by the titular bishops who possessed the benefices, or were granted to laymen by rights merely temporary. The only fund reserved for the clergy who were to serve the cure was the principal mansion-house, with a few acres of glebe land. The fund from which their stipends were to be paid was limited to the tithes. By this sweeping enactment all the former alienations of Church benefices acquired by the laity received a parliamentary ratification, and the king was put in possession of what, prudently managed, would have been the source of an adequate royal income. But James, though, like misers of a particular temper, he was unwilling to part with money which was actually realized and in his power, was improvidently lavish of such funds as were only expected to become valuable in course of time. It cost his greedy courtiers scarce more than the trouble of asking to obtain from the thoughtless king the reversion of property, which, although, for the present life, rented by annuitants, was sure upon their death to have added largely to the royal income. The crown, therefore, was little benefited by an enactment which, detaching the Church lands from all connection with ecclesiastical persons, totally ruined the order of bishops, for the restoration of whom, with some dignity and authority, King James, and his successor afterward, expressed considerable anxiety.

Another institution of the parliament, 1587, respected the representation of the people in parliament. James VI. perceived the superiority which the nobles had obtained in the national councils by the non-attendance of the lesser barons or freeholders. He endeavored, with considerable ingenuity, to balance this, by reviving the ancient statute of 1427, by which the lesser freeholders, or minor barons, as they were called, had a dispensation from giving personal attendance on parliament, where, properly, they were all entitled, or rather obliged, to give attendance, on condition of sending two freeholders from each county to represent them in parliament. The policy of King James's addition was to ren-

der the attendance of such representatives compulsory, and
thereby to secure their presence in parliament, which had
hitherto been precarious and uncertain, thus establishing a
regular and constant barrier against the power of the nobility.   This was a great step to diminish the authority of the
aristocracy.   It could not, however, be opposed by the nobles,
because, by the constitution of the nation, the king had the
right to call to the great council of the people the whole or
any number of the lesser barons whom he might choose to
summon; and, in limiting this power to a representation of
two from each county, he seemed to lessen the importance
of these smaller freeholders, while he was in fact enlarging
it.   Left to their own choice, and considering their duty in
parliament as a burden rather than a privilege, they had
seldom chosen to give attendance; whereas, by this edict
of the king, a considerable number were positively required
to be present.   This in some degree replaced an equipon-
derance between the king and his peers when convened in
parliament, which had been much destroyed since the fall
of the spiritual estate, by which the Scottish crown had
been usually supported before the reformation.

A great national crisis now approached.   The Catholic
sovereigns, who had united in the holy league, had obtained
eminent success in France, and driven Henry III. from his
own capital.   The utmost exertions were made by Philip II.,
a prince equally ambitious and bigoted, to assemble the most
powerful fleet and army which the world had yet seen, for
the purpose of accomplishing the conquest of England.   To
the throne of that kingdom he raised a claim upon two pretences, of which it is impossible to tell which was the more
frivolous—the first being his descent from the House of Lancaster, and the second, a liberal donation from Pope Pius V.
With this view the celebrated armada, called the Invincible,
was assembled at Lisbon.   The object of this tremendous
expedition was not made public, but no one doubted its
destination.   The soldiers of England had supported the
quarrel of the insurgents in the Netherlands; the navy of

England had insulted the coasts of Spanish South America; above all, Elizabeth was the principal support of the Protestant religion in Europe, and the object at whose life and power the purposes of the holy league induced them to aim their most formidable blows. No one questioned that the present was intended for a mortal one.

The accession of James was, in case it could be gained, of the utmost consequence to the Spanish enterprise; and Philip sought it with more anxiety than consisted with the haughty superiority which the House of Austria usually assumed over less powerful sovereigns. He applied for James's friendship with the most flattering assiduity; he reminded him of his mother's wrongs, and urged him to seize an opportunity so favorable for vengeance; and he offered him, in token of intimate alliance, the hand of his daughter Isabella in marriage. Queen Elizabeth was no less anxious than Philip to secure the friendship of James, who, by his power to open or close the ports of Scotland, might so greatly facilitate or impede the invasion of England. She could not feel at ease when reflecting upon the execution of Mary, nor did she know what spirit of vengeance, suppressed by a sense of inferiority, might be yet slumbering in the bosom of the Scottish monarch. She sent an ambassador, named Ashby, to labor by every means in his power to attach King James to her interests at the present crisis. He appears to have been a plausible man, insinuating in his manners, and in no degree sparing of the most liberal promises. He undertook that James's succession to the English crown should be formally acknowledged in parliament; that an English dukedom, with a competent revenue, should be conferred upon him, and that he should even be admitted into some share of the English government.

On such promises made in Elizabeth's name, at such a period, James did not probably greatly rely. He himself described an ambassador as an honorable person sent abroad to tell lies for the benefit of his country; but sounder views led him to the conclusions which Ashby's flattering proposals were qualified to recommend. He consulted his statesmen and the parliament of his kingdom; and fortunate it was for Britain and for the Protestant religion that James's mind was not then under the dominion of any of those extravagant partialities which formerly, in the case of Arran and Gray, and afterward in that of similar rash, giddy, and profligate young men, subjected his counsels to their wild and often interested pilotage. Maitland the chancellor, with ..hom he chiefly consulted, was a man of mature sense and steady character, who, with a mind as acute as that of his brother, the celebrated secretary, possessed more practical judgment and more sound moral principle. He was, according to Spottiswoode, a man of rare parts, deep wit, learned, full of courage, and most faithful to the king. In the present crisis, the most important, perhaps, which the world had for a long time seen, James acquainted his parliament with his sentiments. "The intention of Spain," he said, "is for the present against England alone. To England I am lawful heir; and should I now suffer the Spaniard to possess himself of that kingdom, what likelihood is there that he would afterward give place to my right, when he is settled in possession of a conquered province? The pretext of religion which the Spaniard uses to justify his invasion would turn him as naturally against Scotland as against England; nor do I desire to enjoy either regal right or life itself separated from the cause of the Protestant faith. I am not ignorant that many persons are of opinion that this would be a proper opportunity to revenge myself for the unkind and unfriendly treatment which I received in my mother's death. But whatever resentment I may feel upon that account, or whatever I may think of the excuses which have been made upon the subject, I do not incline for such personal cause of resentment to put in peril the fate of my kingdom, my country, and my religion."

The wise and patriotic views of the king were almost unanimously felt, applauded, and adopted by his parliament; and universal preparations were made for resistance, in case the Spaniards should attempt to land in Scotland. There was a general muster through the realm. Watches were placed at all the seaports; beacons erected; and every means taken to prepare the most effectual defence against the apprehended invasion. In the meantime, love of the old religion, or desire for new changes by which they might profit, had associated a few of the Scottish lords into a faction favorable to Spain, and formidable from the rank and power of those whom it included. The Earls of Huntley, Errol, and Crawford, were all Catholics; the first by hereditary descent, the two last by recent conversion from the faith of their fathers. Lord Maxwell, also, whom we have already seen make an important figure at the Raid of Stirling, held the same faith. He had been subsequently discontented on account of his losing the title of Morton, to which, on the attainder and execution of the regent, he made pretence in right of his mother.

Maxwell had retreated to Spain in discontent; and at this crisis returned with the purpose of assisting the Spanish king's enterprise, by making an insurrection in Scotland. He went suddenly, therefore, to the west border, and began to assemble his forces; but James, placing himself at the head of a body of troops, made a rapid movement into Nithsdale, where he dispersed the forces of Maxwell, took him prisoner, and seized upon his castles.

With the exception of these popish nobles, Scotland in general showed the firmest determination to support the king. A bond of association was entered into for the maintenance of true religion and defence of their lawful sovereign. This association was signed with emulous alacrity by subjects of every rank, and was the model upon which the celebrated League and Covenant in the reign of Charles I. was afterward founded, though for very different purposes.

The fate of the Invincible Armada, in 1588, as it was proudly termed, is generally known. Persecuted by the fury of the elements, and annoyed by the adventurous gallantry of the English seamen, it was driven around the island of Britain, meeting great loss upon every quarter, and strewing the wild shores of the Scottish highlands and isles with wreck and spoil. James, though in arms to resist the Spaniards, had such resistance been necessary, behaved generously to considerable numbers whom their misfortunes threw upon his shores. Their wants were relieved, and they were safely restored to their own country. The fate of one body of these unfortunate men is strikingly told by the Rev. James Melville, whose diary has been lately published. (He was a clergyman, and must be carefully distinguished from Sir James Melville, the statesman often quoted. His diary has been published by the Bannatyne Club of Edinburgh.) He describes at some length the alarm caused by the threatened invasion, and its effects. "Terrible," he says, "was the fear, piercing were the preachings, earnest, zealous, and fervent were the prayers, sounding were the sighs and sobs, and abounding were the tears at the fast and general assembly at Edinburgh, where we were credibly told sometimes of their landing at Dunbar, sometimes at St. Andrew's, and again at Aberdeen and Cromarty." On a sudden these rumors were dispelled by the account that a shipful of Spaniards were arrived in Melville's own harbor of Anstruther. The minister hastened to meet them, and found himself in presence of Don Juan de Medina, a commodore of twenty vessels. He was a reverend man of tall stature, a grave and silent countenance, great beard, and so humbled by his condition, that in bowing to the clergyman he swept his shoe with his sleeve. His tale was most melancholy. They had been shipwrecked upon the Fair Isle between Orkney and Zetland, had experienced the utmost extremity of hunger and cold, had, after some weeks of misery, hired a bark from Orkney, and were now come to entreat protection from the king of Scotland. Melville replied that, though there could exist but small friendship between them, considering their being at war with their friends and neighbors of England, yet he and the townsmen were determined to show that they were men moved with compassion for the distress of men, and were Christians of a better persuasion than their own. Juan Gomez de Medina and his men were accordingly treated with honorable kindness by the people of Anstruther. Melville procured for the Spaniard's information a printed account of the dispersion of the armada, and their numerous losses in the North Seas. He burst into tears and wept bitterly. Having set forth on his return to his own country, the noble Castilian found a ship belonging to the town of Anstruther under arrest at Cadiz. He instantly undertook a journey to court to labor for her discharge, and reported to his monarch his high sense of the Scottish hospitality. The vessel being liberated, he showed great kindness to the crew, and dismissed them with many commendations to the good people of Anstruther. "But," concludes Melville, very naturally, "we thanked God with our hearts that we had seen them among us in that form."

Thus passed over in Britain that dreadful period of 1588, which the astrologers, whom chance had for once guided to a veracious prediction, had distinguished as the "marvellous year."

When the danger was over, Elizabeth no longer evinced any thought of making good the liberal promises made to the king of Scots by her envoy while matters were yet doubtful. Ashby, conscious of having exceeded his commission in the hopes which he had excited, or commanded to act as if he were so, left Scotland privately, and without taking leave. Sir Robert Sidney, an ambassador of higher rank and greater responsibility, was sent instead, to congratulate King James on the issue of the great naval struggle, and on his firm and steadfast good offices in behalf of England, and to get clear of Ashby's engagements as well as he could.

Sidney was well received by the king, who frankly assured him that he regarded the fair language and profuse offers of Philip in the light of the promise of the Cyclops, that Outis should be the last devoured. At the same time, he mentioned the liberal promises of Ashby. Sidney replied generally that nothing could be so dear to the queen as the welfare and honor of her beloved James, whom she regarded as her own son.   Nevertheless, he disclaimed the explicit offers made by Ashby as relating to matters exceeding that person's commission, who by secretly leaving Scotland had shown a consciousness that he stood engaged for more than was likely to be made good.   Sidney also pressed King James, on the part of his ally, to seize the present favorable opportunity to subdue and punish those Catholic nobles who were well known to have held themselves in readiness to have abetted the attempt of Philip had his forces come to a landing in Scotland.

James permitted the proposals of Ashby to pass out of memory without further notice, persuaded, doubtless, that there would be more loss than gain in putting Elizabeth in remembrance of that which she desired to forget.   The Catholic lords themselves, though much disconcerted by the failure of the armada, continued to negotiate with the Prince of Parma, soliciting him for a body of six thousand auxiliaries, by means of whom, added to their own followers, they proposed to make him master of Scotland, and enable him to enter England with a triumphant army.   Huntley, Crawford, and Errol were the chief persons in this conspiracy; but they were joined by Francis, earl of Bothwell, a turbulent and ambitious man, who alone of the Scotch Protestant nobility had advised a war with England, and even engaged soldiers to follow him in it at his own expense. Their correspondence with the Prince of Parma being discovered to Elizabeth, she commanded Sidney to lay the letters before the king of Scotland.   The guilty noblemen were condemned to imprisonment; but King James, who was not willing to encounter the odium of the Catholic party lest it should interfere with his claim of succession to the throne of England, and who might in his heart desire to reserve some power in Scotland itself to balance the violent Protestant party acting under the instigation of preachers always unfavorable to him and his family, released the rebellious earls after a short confinement.

They testified their thankfulness for his clemency, first, by an attempt to seize his person, which was disconcerted by the precautions of the chancellor; secondly, by an open rebellion in the north of Scotland. The king marched against them with an army hastily collected; and the rebels, unable to withstand the royal forces, dispersed their troops, and submitted to James's clemency. Once more they were committed to prison, once more to experience the lenity of their sovereign, who took an opportunity again to release them, in consequence of a joyful event which shortly after took place at the court, and which we are next to narrate.

James was now of full age, the last of his race; and his subjects, who had more frequently than any other nation in Europe suffered from disputed claims to the kingdom, and from long minorities, were naturally desirous to see the royal family free from the uncertainty which attended its dependence upon the life of one man. Yet the choice of a royal bride was attended with much embarrassment.

A Catholic princess would have increased the dread which, not without reason, was entertained for the predominance of that communion. A Protestant bride might have been found in England; but this would have thrown into the management of Queen Elizabeth the power of completing or disconcerting a match which she of all persons in the world least desired to see accomplished. It remained only to seek in the northern courts a princess of the Protestant religion, fit, by birth and manners, to wed with the young king of Scotland.

So early as 1584 ambassadors came from the king of Denmark for the avowed purpose of treating for the redemption of the Orkney Islands, which, as formerly mentioned, were pledged to Scotland in security of a sum of money which Christian of Denmark was bound to pay as the dowry of his daughter, espoused to James III. of Scotland. The ambassadors had, however, a more private commission, the union, namely, of the young king of Scots to the eldest daughter

of Frederick II. of Denmark, being esteemed a fitting mode
of accommodating the question between the kingdoms.
Stewart, earl of Arran, was at this time in full favor; and
he had recently pledged himself to Queen Elizabeth that
King James should not be married for the space of three
years. To break, therefore, the purpose of the Danish
match, in all other respects fit and desirable, the ambassadors, through the influence of the insolent favorite, had been
treated with every species of neglect and insult, until they
were obliged to leave the court, in high indignation at the
treatment they had met with. As a parting insult, they
were informed that the king was to send them horses to
convey them from Dunfermline to St. Andrew's, at which
last place they were appointed to receive their despatches.
The ambassadors accordingly booted themselves for the
occasion, and waited long for the palfreys which were never
to arrive. Concluding themselves laughed at and insulted,
they took their departure on foot, with such feelings, respecting the hospitality of James, as this treatment was like to
occasion. James, informed by Sir James Melville, immediately despatched horses for their use, which only overtook
them after they had made a considerable part of their journey, high booted as they were, and in mortal indignation at
such usage.

But Arran continued his intrigues to disgust them further.
In St. Andrew's they were treated with the like insolence;
and the populace, always uncivil to strangers, were encouraged to offer them every species of mockery and ridicule.
The wisdom of Sir James Melville found a partial remedy
for these evils. He was able to make the angry ambassadors sensible that the insults of which they complained were
not to be imputed to the king himself, but to the insolence
of his arrogant favorite. It was time there should be some
interposition or explanation. The gravest of the embassy
already threatened war; and Dr. Theophilus, a dignitary,
declared that their king was insulted, and would be revenged. They were, at length, with difficulty persuaded

to make such a report as should not breed debate between the two countries, who had many reasons for remaining friends, and none which should make them enemies to each other. Negotiations were accordingly entered into for a marriage between James and one of the Danish princesses. But powerful efforts continued to be made to thwart, disconcert, and interrupt the treaty.

Queen Elizabeth was earnest in disconcerting a match which was likely to prolong for another generation the claim of succession to the English crown, which she had hoped, perhaps, to bury in Mary's bloody grave, so that by the influence she used with Arran, Gray, and the other Scottish ministers with whom she had interest, so many delays and obstacles were thrown in the way of the match, that Frederick, conceiving himself trifled with, gave his eldest daughter, who had been the object of James's suit, in marriage to the Duke of Brunswick.

James's pride and his passions were now seriously roused. He plainly saw that unless he made some decisive advances on his own part, Queen Elizabeth, directly or indirectly, would be able to baffle every attempt he might make toward marriage, and condemn him for life to a state of barren celibacy.

No sooner, therefore, was the match proposed with the eldest daughter of Denmark rendered impossible by her espousals, than King James, now freed from the baleful influence of Arran and Gray, and guided by the wise and sound counsels of his chancellor, Maitland, paid his addresses to Anne, the second daughter of the king of Denmark. Here again the malign influence of Elizabeth interfered: she recommended to James, in preference, a match with Catherine, sister of the king of Navarre; and she prevailed, by the secret agency which she still retained among the Scottish statesmen, upon the privy council of Scotland to enter into a resolution disapproving of the Danish match. But the populace of Edinburgh had caught an opinion, which seemed warranted by what had happened, that Elizabeth, through whose practices Queen Mary had lost her life, was now laboring to prevent all succession in the royal family of Scotland, and was like to be again successful in her views. They became furious, as is usual with a multitude under the influence of such feelings; and their violence was adopted by the king as an excuse for hastening the match, which some of his counsellors would have still delayed.

The earl mareschal, with a splendid retinue and full powers, was sent over to Denmark to conclude the marriage definitively; and the terms being accepted by her father Frederick, the princess embarked, with the purpose of repairing to Scotland. The weather being stormy, and the winds adverse, the royal bride was encountered by a storm which drove her back to Norway, and so much damaged the vessels which conveyed her with her suite, that there remained no hopes of their being repaired and made once more fit for the voyage before the next spring.

King James must have felt deep disappointment upon this occasion, since it led him to a feat of chivalrous adventure rather inconsistent with his pedantic habits and cold passions. He determined, suddenly, that, since his bride could not come to Scotland, he would, in person, repair to the northern regions to seek her. The winds which were contrary to her voyage must necessarily be favorable to his; and he no doubt possessed an inward fear that any interval which might be interposed between the contract and the nuptials would give Elizabeth an opportunity to abrogate the former, and to prevent the latter. He vindicated his resolutions in a proclamation addressed to his subjects, which is too characteristic to be suppressed, although it is difficult to forbear smiling at some parts of it.

It sets forth, on James's part, that, being king of Scotland and heir-apparent of England, he was blamed by all men for the delay of his marriage, because a single man was as no man, and that the want of succession bred contempt, "as if he were a barren stock": these and other important causes moved him, he said, to hasten the treaty of his marriage: for without urgent reasons of state, he assured his subjects that his personal temperance could have delayed the union for any length of time that the welfare of the country permitted. When he had heard of the impossibility of the princess's pursuing her voyage, although neither rash, passionate, nor unreasonable in the decision of weighty affairs, he became strongly, he says, impressed with the idea of going to Denmark, since the princess of Denmark could not come to Scotland. This resolution, he solemnly protests, was formed upon his own meditation, and without the suggestion of others, by the same token that Craigmillar Castle was the place in which he first adopted the resolution. He appears very jealous that his people would scarcely give him credit for exerting so much will of his own; and reiterates, at considerable length, "I took this resolution only of myself, as I am a true prince; and with myself only I consulted which way to follow forth the same." He intended at first to have gone privately in a squadron of ships, commanded by the Earl of Bothwell, lord high admiral; but the expense which Bothwell had already bestowed in preparation for James's approaching marriage had been so great as to render it impossible for him to rig out a royal navy for the proposed expedition. The difficulty of finding funds for this equipment obliged the king on this proclamation to admit the whole council into his secret; and in order to make them earnest in aiding his purpose he was compelled to threaten them, with great vehemency, that if no man of rank could be found to accompany him he would himself, nevertheless, go, were it but in a single ship. On this the chancellor offered his person to attend him, and that, says the king, upon three respects, first, to remove the general suspicion which upbraided him with a desire to postpone the royal nuptials; secondly, out of zeal to the royal service; and, lastly, from his extreme fear that the king might make good his threat of going alone. "These things," says King James, "I had hitherto concealed from the chancellor, until they were laid before the whole council, lest he should undergo the odium of putting such a hazardous enterprise into my head, which had not been his duty, since it becomes not subjects to give princes advice in such high matters. Therefore, remembering what envious and unjust burden he daily bears for leading me by the nose, as it were, to all his humors, as if I were a creature without reason, or a helpless infant, that could do nothing for myself, I was unwilling to be the occasion at this time of heaping further unjust scandal on his head. These truths," continues his majesty, "I speak in behalf of the chancellor, as also for my own honor's sake, that I may not be unjustly slandered as an irresolute ass, who can do nothing of his own motion."

Having thus afforded to the nation an admirable example of a man who knew his own frailty, and was afraid of being upbraided with it, James, by another proclamation, recommended to all authorities the regular discharge of their duties during his absence, with special appointments of guardians or governors for particular provinces. He required the ministers to remember him and his estate in their prayers, and to exhort the people to peace and loyalty during his absence.

Having made these arrangements, James sailed northward in person, attended by the chancellor, some nobles, and a retinue of three hundred men. The king was received in Denmark with all the hospitality which the frank confidence of his visit merited: the severity of the northern winter rendered his immediate return a matter of some danger; therefore, when his marriage was solemnized at Upsal, in Norway, where he found his bride residing, James accepted an invitation from his father-in-law to Copenhagen; and repairing to the Danish court with his new married wife, spent the remainder of the winter season in mirth and festivity with the royal family, and then returned to his native kingdom.

The time spent in this expedition, which lasted from the 22d of October, 1589, till the 1st of May, 1590, was a period of unusual tranquillity in Scotland. The people appeared to have felt as if the absence of James was, in fact, a committing of the royal authority to the loyalty of the subject, which they should dishonor themselves in misusing. Each order of men in their rank strove to show themselves worthy of trust. The great abstained from their factions, the populace from their tumults, the clergy desisted from the habit, which some had contracted, of hatching jealousies of the king's motives, and infusing them into the minds of their hearers; and answered the king's hopes so well in aiding the preservation of peace and good order as to merit, on his return, his peculiar thanks and gratitude. In a word, there was no era of Scottish history more orderly and peaceful than this short period.

CHAPTER XXXVIII

THE wife with whom King James allied himself appears to have been one of those females whose
character is not very strongly marked. Anne of
Denmark was fair in complexion, comely, of good aspect,
and pleasing manners. She loved festivity and gayety, and
was rather an encouragement than a restraint to the king's
extravagance. The coldness of his temper prevented his
regarding her with uxorious fondness; but he was good-
natured and civil, and the queen was satisfied with the
external show of attention. In her younger days she mixed

in the stormy politics of the Scottish court, and her name was to be found in the intrigues of that period. Little credit is due to the scandalous authors who have assailed her character as a private individual; nor has she left such traces in history as call either for much censure or high praise. She was the mother of a fair family, and excited the hopes of James, as well as of his party in England, by speedily making him the father of two sons, Henry and Charles.

The first died early, and was lamented accordingly, though, perhaps, upon no better grounds than was inspired by the disappointment of those hopes usually fixed upon the opening virtues of most princes who have died without enjoying the power to which they were born. Charles, the younger of the princes, was doomed to carry into England that same train of misfortunes which had persecuted the Stuarts since their first accession to the throne of Scotland, and to perish like his grandmother Mary by the blow of a public executioner. A princess Elizabeth was married to the prince palatine, and had her share of misfortunes.

King James and his new spouse were received with all the splendor which the means of the country could achieve. The queen was inaugurated with solemnity; but so low was the order of bishops now held, that the ministry of a Presbyterian clergyman was used upon this ceremony. Nor was the zeal of the clergy altogether satisfied with some points of the ceremonial. Scruples were entertained at the anointing of the queen, as a Jewish ceremonial abrogated by the Christian dispensation. Mr. Robert Bruce, however, a man of great repute among the Scottish clergy, performed the ceremony at the queen's coronation after the ancient form. James and the Presbyterian clergy had never been upon such good terms as they were at present. He was sensible that the order and regularity which prevailed during his absence was in a great measure owing to the anxious care of the clergy to restrain the people within the bounds of law and authority. This inclined James to express himself very favorably on the discipline and doctrine of the Church, and to clear the way, as speedily as could be conveniently done, for recalling those restraints upon the Presbyterian Church which had been imposed by the Earl of Arran in 1584, and of which, though little acted upon, the clergy still highly complained. Accordingly, in the year 1592, a parliament was held, in which the acts of 1584 were explained or recalled, and the discipline of the Presbyterian government, in its general assemblies, synods, presbyteries, and kirk sessions, was fully and amply established. The king and Church of Scotland appeared now to have lived together on a footing of mutual confidence and regard; but the storms of hatred and jealousy, by which this unhappy country was harassed, did not suffer its atmosphere to remain long in serenity.

The Earl of Bothwell, already often mentioned, was the king's near relation, and an example of his lenity, not only on account of James having pardoned the slaughter of Sir William Stewart, and other violences of the like nature; not only on account of his having forgiven the earl for having urged and endeavored to precipitate a war with England; but also from his forgiving Bothwell's participation in the rebellion of the Catholic lords, without having to plead even the excuse of religion.

A matter now occurred in which it was the pleasure of the king to see more guilt than in any of Bothwell's former offences.

The occult arts, as they were called, were then in the highest credit. The mummery of astrologers was mingled with the political counsels of princes; and the belief was universal alike in soothsayers, who could foretell the future, and witches and wizards who could operate strange cures, and inflict as wonderful diseases, by their intelligence with the infernal powers. The king, who was passionately addicted to the searching out and punishing these imaginary crimes, soon discovered that some political intrigues were connected with them, and became much alarmed in consequence. Two soothsayers, or wizards rather, above the miserable caste who usually bore that character, had confessed having been the cause, by magical rites, of raising the storm by which the queen's fleet had been driven back to Norway; and that they had also consulted about doing harm to the fleet or person of the king.   To which their infernal master had replied, hiding, we may suppose, in the obscurity of a foreign language, a want of power which he was ashamed to acknowledge, *Il est homme de Dieu.* Thus far the king was flattered; and Agnes Simpson and Richard Graham might have been quietly burned alive without much stir about the matter.   Unhappily, they had also to confess that Francis Stewart, earl of Bothwell, had submitted for their consideration certain very suspicious questions concerning the duration of the king's life. Considering that these persons usually practiced the art of poisoning as well as bewitching, King James might be excused for entertaining apprehension from such interrogatories being put to such personages by a daring, turbulent, and ambitious man, possessed of the power to do much mischief, and not likely to want the will to exert it.   Bothwell was committed to prison, or as the phrase then went, was put in ward in the castle of Edinburgh.   Impatient of restraint, he made his escape by bribing his jailers, and fled to the borders, where he had personal friends and followers of great influence, and where there were always enough of desperate and disorderly men to follow any banner which should lead to bloodshed and to spoil.

The king took measures of severity against his unquiet relation; and as Bothwell still lay under the forfeiture of treason pronounced against him for his association with Huntley, he caused the doom which hitherto only hung over his head in the way of intimidation to be proclaimed, in consideration of these new offences.   Upon publication of his sentence of forfeiture, several of Bothwell's friends upon the border forsook him.   Buccleuch, who was his son-in-law, had submitted to an order of the king which had sent him abroad for some time, and was thus out of the road of temptation. The Earl of Home, who, as a Catholic, had been Bothwell's friend on former occasions, withdrew from him when he engaged in open rebellion.

Nevertheless, some persons in court, from dislike to the chancellor, upon whom Bothwell threw the blame of his forfeiture, invited the insurgent earl and his followers to attend at a back passage to the palace of Holyrood, which gave entrance through the Duke of Lennox's stables, and thus obtain the means of seizing upon his majesty's person and the gates of the palace. James Douglas of Spot was engaged in this conspiracy, by the following concurrence of circumstances: His father-in-law, George Home of Spot, had been recently slain by certain borderers of the name of Home and Craw. Sir George Home, nephew to the slain gentleman, conceived that Douglas was at the bottom of this murder, instigated by a jealousy that the deceased intended to transfer to his nephew some of the estate which Douglas claimed as husband of his only daughter. On this suspicion three of Douglas's servants were seized upon, imprisoned in Holyrood, and appointed to be examined by torture. Douglas made every exertion to obtain his servants' freedom, either out of regard for them or fear of what they might confess; and finding it impossible to procure their deliverance by entreaty, he thrust himself into this conspiracy that he might liberate them by main force. Bothwell appeared at the appointed time, and was admitted; but James Douglas made the plot public prematurely by an attempt to break open the prison in which his servants lay. The noise occasioned the discovery that strangers had broken into the palace: the uproar became general; the king betook himself to the defence of a strong tower; and the chancellor, whose life was aimed at, defended himself in his chamber. The citizens of Edinburgh, hearing the tumult, rushed to the palace in arms and drove out the assailants. Bothwell and his party fled, eight of their number being either taken or slain.

It was subsequently learned that Bothwell had betaken

himself to the west part of Scotland, where he was nearly apprehended. Letters were directed to several nobles for pursuing the refractory earl and his followers with fire and sword. But this led unhappily to a new catastrophe.

A report had been spread that the Earl of Murray was seen with Bothwell's party in the night of the tumult, and it was deemed the more probable as Bothwell and he were cousins-german. The king placed in the hands of the Earl of Huntley a commission to bring Murray presently before him. To the tenor of the order there could be no objection; but there was the highest reason for having lodged the commission in other hands.

The houses of Huntley and Murray were mortal enemies. The fatal battle of Corrichie was an event not to be forgotten nor forgiven; and even very lately a Gordon of some consequence in the family had been killed by a shot from one of the houses of the Earl of Murray. Their rivalry for obtaining a predominance in the north was constant and unremitting; and there, probably, was not a more fatal or decided feud through the whole disunited kingdom of Scotland than existed between these two families.

In the present circumstances, Murray, with the most peaceable intentions, so far as can be known, was residing at his house of Dunnibirsel, having with him only Dunbar, the sheriff of Murray, and a small retinue. Huntley, who had crossed the firth with a body of a hundred horse and upward, surrounded the castle, which was not very defensible, with the purpose of executing the arrest enjoined by the king. Murray refused to surrender to his feudal enemy; a shot was fired from the house of Dunnibirsel, by which a Gordon was killed. The Earl of Huntley then forced the castle by using fire. The situation of the besieged became desperate. "Let me sally forth," said the sheriff, with the devotion of a friend of these days, when friendship was as devoted and disinterested as their hatred was relentless and enduring; "I will be taken for you and slain, and thus you may escape." The gates were thrown open; Dunbar

rushed forth and was slain, as he anticipated.   But the Earl
of Murray did not profit by the sacrifice: the attention of the
assailants, now in their most savage mood, was arrested by
his superior stature; and the sparkles which had set fire
to his streaming locks, and the silk tassels upon his head-
piece, enabled the Gordons to trace him in his flight to a
cavern on the sea-shore, where Gordon of Buckie inflicted
upon the earl a mortal wound.   Partly alarmed at what
he had done, partly, perhaps, out of native ferocity, Buckie
insisted that Huntley should also become a participant of
the deed; and the chief with an ill-assured hand struck the
dying earl in the face with his dagger.   Even in the agony
of death, Murray had not forgotten the symmetry of countenance and person which procured him the popular surname
of the "*bonny*" (or handsome) Earl of Murray.   With his
latest breath he said to Huntley, "You have spoiled a better
face than your own."

When this tragedy had been acted, Huntley felt no
inclination to return to the king, conscious of the degree
in which he had exceeded his commission.   He hastened
to the castle of Ravensheuch, belonging to Lord Sinclair,
who gave him admission with an expression of doubtful
welcome.   "You are welcome here, my lord," he said; "but
should have been more welcome to have ridden past my
gates."   Huntley proceeded northward in the morning to
his own dominions, plainly showing his sense of danger from
the act he had committed.   In his haste he left upon the
field Innes of Invermarkie, one of his followers, a man of
some distinction, who was wounded, and unable to accompany his chief in his retreat.   Being sent to Edinburgh,
where the story had excited general horror, the wounded
gentleman was tried and executed.

Nothing could have happened more likely to trouble the
king's affairs than this unhappy act of violence.   Huntley
was a Catholic, who had been lately in rebellion for his
league with the king of Spain.   Murray was a Protestant,
a favorite of the common people, on account of his youth,

beauty, and personal accomplishments, and dear to the Church as the representative of the Regent Murray, who had done so much toward the foundation of the Protestant faith and the Presbyterian system. The outcry against Huntley was universal, and the desire of revenge general. In the north the Lord Forbes, a hereditary enemy of Huntley, hung the bloody shirt of Murray upon a spear, and under this banner levied a band of men to avenge the earl's death. In imitation of a practice before noticed, the picture of the earl's body, having the hair on fire, and mangled with many wounds, was also publicly shown to excite general resentment. Popular scandal, which is always willing to adopt the grossest calumnies, accused the king of being conscious of the slaughter, and alleged as the cause an ideal jealousy, on James's part, of the bonny earl's supposed favor with the queen.

The bodies of the deceased Murray and Dunbar were brought to Leith; but their friends refused to commit them to the earth until the slaughter should be avenged. The clamor of the metropolis was universal, so that the king, not esteeming it safe to remain in Edinburgh, betook himself to Glasgow, where he held his court; until Huntley, in obedience to the royal charge, surrendered himself a prisoner in the fortress of Blackness. The resentment of this slaughter, which had so strong an effect upon the common people, gave the greatest encouragement to Bothwell in his desperate attempts; especially when the people found that Huntley, instead of being brought to trial, was dismissed, upon giving security for his appearance to answer for the crime.

The numbers who now joined Bothwell encouraged him to a new attempt upon the king's person, which took place upon the 28th of June, 1592, while James was residing at his hunting palace of Falkland. Early in the morning Bothwell appeared at the head of three hundred horse, chiefly, as usual, borderers and broken men; but relying, it was supposed, upon some friends within the palace. The king, however, had enough of faithful followers to make good the donjon, or great tower of the palace. From this, as from a citadel, they maintained a fire which rendered it impossible for the assailants to approach the palace gate; and Bothwell, finding no assistance from within, and that the people of the neighborhood were assembling in great force, was obliged once more to retreat. The king, fortified by the assistance of the men of Fife, gave chase to the assailants in their retreat, and took some of them in the moors, so overcome with sleep as to be unable to prosecute their flight on horseback. Bothwell, therefore, fled once more to the borders, and found harbor either in Scotland or England at his pleasure; for Queen Elizabeth, although she had complimented King James upon his marriage, pursued her ancient policy of maintaining such disorders in Scotland as might keep the king as much as possible under her tutelage. Several persons were prosecuted in consequence of this last attempt of Bothwell, especially one gentleman named Wemyss of Logie, a gentleman of the king's bed-chamber; the means of whose escape rendered his imprisonment remarkable. He had paid his addresses to one of the queen's Danish maids of honor, Margaret Twinlace by name, who, considering her lover's extremity, and his life in danger, pretended a commission from the queen. Obtaining admittance to the prisoner under this pretext, she gave him a ladder of ropes, which afforded him the means of escaping from the window. Logie was pardoned on account of the lady's generosity, who hazarded her reputation for his safety, and they were married.

Shortly afterward an affair broke out which placed in its issue new dissensions between the king and the Church, and bred at the same time much alarm in the country, on account of the machinations of Spain with the Scottish papists which it manifestly implied. The affair had also that mysterious cast which is sure to awaken and excite the feelings of the public. Those of the Catholic persuasion were now of the suffering, and, considering the severity of the penal laws, we may say, the oppressed religion; and the persecution which they underwent had its usual effect in riveting their attachment to their own faith, and kindling the enthusiasm of the missionary priests and Jesuits, who had dedicated themselves to the cause of extending the doctrines of Rome. These zealots, instigated by Spain, and supplied with money from the same source, haunted various parts of Scotland, and were frequently successful in making converts to their religion even among the great and powerful; while, uniting politics with theology, they pressed their converts into a union with Spain, for the purpose of a new invasion of Britain; the principal object of which was to be the relief of the Catholic community. There was one George Ker, brother of the Lord Newbattle, who being called upon to make declaration concerning his faith before the Church, and conscious of having relapsed to the Catholic faith, fled to the small islands in the mouth of the Clyde, called the Cumrays, and took a passage on board a vessel bound for Spain.

The minister of Paisley, learning this circumstance, came suddenly with a body of twenty-four armed men, boarded the vessel, took Ker prisoner, and with him seized on a large parcel of letters from seminary priests and Jesuits, together with a number of blanks in the form of missives or letters, containing no writing, but subscribed by the Earl of Huntley, the Earl of Errol, and Patrick Gordon of Auchindoun, Huntley's uncle. These blanks were, in some instances, addressed to the Spanish monarch, and others were drawn up in the form of contracts, signed and sealed. Ker was sent prisoner to Edinburgh. It was Sunday when the mysterious circumstances of the discovery reached the capital. A great tumult arose. The clergy, contrary to their wont, made a short sermon, and the king being then absent at Alloway, the preachers held meetings with the lords of the privy council, and spread the alarm through the country at large, inviting the different presbyteries in the kingdom to send representatives to Edinburgh, to consider what should be done in a case so dangerous to the

Church. The engagement of Angus in such a treason was
the more strange, as he came of an old Protestant stock,
and had been very lately employed in settling some dis-
cords between Huntley and the Mackintoshes; and, having
succeeded in his errand, was expected immediately in Edinburgh, to report his services to the king. His father was
the nephew of the famous Earl of Morton, and a man of
sense and talent. His death, according to the apprehension
of the vulgar, and even the more learned, was caused by
witchcraft; and when he was advised to use some counter
spells, to destroy the effect of the sorcery under which he
was supposed to labor, he protested he would rather die than
do aught to obtain life contrary to the dictates of religion.
The relapse of the present earl, the son of a Protestant
father, was the more unexpected. He no sooner reached
Edinburgh than he was arrested, at the instigation of the
ministers, by the provost and bailies of the city.

The king, alarmed at this discovery, hastened to his metropolis, of which the churchmen appeared disposed to take
the command. Ker being examined, confessed that Crichton,
Gordon, and Abercrombie, three Jesuits, had devised this
contrivance of the blanks, as the safest mode for opening a
communication between the king of Spain and the Scottish
Catholics. They were to be filled up in Spain, with the stipulations of the subscribers; of which the principal was, that
the king of Spain should send an army of thirty thousand
men to Scotland, half of which were to remain in the kingdom, for the purpose of establishing the ancient faith, or, at
least, securing an absolute toleration, while the other fifteen
thousand men should invade England.

Angus, being examined upon these matters, denied all
knowledge of the blanks, and affirmed his subscription to be
a forgery; but he presently afterward showed a sense of his
guilt, by making his escape out of the castle of Edinburgh.
David Graham of Fintry, who was apprehended on suspicion, corroborated the declaration of Ker, and being found
guilty, in terms of his own confession, was presently exe-

cuted. The king once more marched with an army into the territories of the Catholic lords, who withdrew themselves to the mountains, and lay concealed, while their vassals were obliged to avow their loyalty to the king and firm adhesion to the Protestant faith.

Notwithstanding all which James could do in the way of prudent precaution, his subjects retained a provoking degree of incredulity on the subject of his real desire to subdue the insurgent Catholics. Nothing less than the most extreme degree of rigor could have satisfied the Church; and Queen Elizabeth adopted the same tone, insisting, by her ambassadors, that the utmost severity should be used against persons whose designs were equally dangerous to both kingdoms. In the meantime the queen of England, negligent of no means by which her neighbor could be harassed, and his councils distracted, was pleased, as we have before stated, to take Bothwell under her protection, and receive him and his followers in her kingdom, when obliged to retreat to the borders. This was, in the particular instance, inconsistent with the general policy of Elizabeth, since Bothwell, in the year 1588, had been decidedly averse to the continuance of peace with England, and had then leagued himself with the Catholic lords who were disposed to encourage the Spanish invasion. Being, however, a man of no religious principle of any kind, and finding that the general temper of the people was moved by the ministers against the king, on account of his supposed favor to Catholics, the earl now adopted the popular tone, and alleged the danger of the Protestant cause as a principal reason for pursuing his tumultuary attacks upon the king's person. He had, probably, the most total indifference as to the further consequences of his attempt, providing only it succeeded in raising him to the authority he desired. Neither is it likely he had any enmity against King James's person, which he only wished to be possessed of, as he would have desired to hold a seal, or other symbol of authority, which should give him the pre-eminent command in the government. The annals of Scotland afforded many instances of the same ambitious purpose being successfully pursued by means equally violent. Angus, during the minority of James V., had long exercised the principal authority, by such means as Bothwell now meditated; and the Earl of Morton, and, subsequently, the Earl of Gowrie, had for a time succeeded in similar attempts in the present reign.

The time began to seem auspicious to Bothwell's purpose. The young queen had taken some distaste at the chancellor, which had been fostered by the king's relations, Lennox, Athole, Ochiltree, and others, who were of opinion that the chancellor's influence intercepted the favor which the king would otherwise have shown to his own friends of the name of Stuart. By their connivance Bothwell, with Douglas of Spot and others, the boldest of his followers, forced their way into the royal presence, well provided with pistols and drawn swords. Archbishop Spottiswoode says, that when Bothwell saw the king, he threw himself on his knees and asked forgiveness, and that the king with dignity replied, "Strike, traitor, for you have dishonored me"; and placing himself in his chair of state, repeated the expression, "Strike, and end thy work, for I desire to live no longer." A worthy citizen of Edinburgh, a faithful journalist of the times, reports James's demeanor in less royal fashion. "The king's majesty," he says, "coming from the back stair with his breeches in his hand, in a fear; howbeit it needed not." By the entreaties of the queen's faction, and the intervention of the English ambassador, the king was persuaded to sign articles of agreement with the insurgents. The first stipulated the pardon of Bothwell for his past offences, and likewise for his recent violence. The second provided that Lord Home, who, from being the ally of Bothwell, had of late become his bitter foe, should with his friends and kinsmen be banished from the court. The third article stipulated that a parliament should be called in November next. And it was lastly concerted that Earl Bothwell and his followers should be considered as good subjects.

It cannot be denied that in such an emergency the king must have conducted himself both with prudence and spirit to obtain such favorable resolutions, which, though they imposed upon him for the time the necessity of receiving Bothwell with apparent favor, yet left him a prospect of getting free of his turbulent kinsman.

For this purpose James appointed a convention at Stirling, in the beginning of September, which was well attended. Bothwell, on his part, had little sagacity to guide his ambition: he appears to have been unequal to the task of securing a superiority in the convention, though it was generally easy for such as were in possession of the king's person to carry that material point. His enemies were predominant there, as appeared from their very first proceedings. The king laid before the convention his agreement with Bothwell; and having narrated the indignities and offences repeatedly practiced against him by that nobleman, he required the opinion of his parliament, that they would take into consideration the conditions which he had been compelled to subscribe, and decide how far he was bound by them in honor or conscience. The reply of the convention was, that the attempt of Bothwell to intrude himself upon the king's presence was in itself treasonable, and that the king was in no respect bound by the articles which had been imposed on him in consequence of that armed intrusion. In respect to Bothwell's pardon, they declared it a matter at his majesty's discretion.

The king cannot be said to have abused this victory, when, after having thus obtained liberation from the articles which had been extorted from him, he tendered to the Earl of Bothwell a free pardon, on condition that he should depart from court, and not presume to approach the royal person unless summoned by the king. It was added that the king expected he should retire abroad for some time. Bothwell appeared at first satisfied with the conditions imposed on him; but presently returning to his old practices, he made an appointment with Athole, one of his courtier allies, to meet him at Stirling with all his forces, and disperse the convention. Their meeting was disconcerted by the alacrity of the king's party; and Bothwell, cited to the privy council, and not appearing, was of new denounced a rebel.

In the meantime the affair of the Spanish blanks, and the impunity of the Catholic lords concerned, continued to agitate the minds of the clergy: there was, they thought, an obvious intention on the part of the king to pass slightly over a matter which, when first heard of by Mr. Ker's confession, he had declared beyond the reach of his power to pardon. Since that time Ker had escaped, or, as the ministers supposed, had been permitted to leave prison, and the Catholic nobles were no longer afraid that his testimony would be brought against them. Confident in this hope, and in the lenity which King James was disposed to extend to them, the Catholic Earls of Huntley, Errol, and Angus, appeared suddenly before the king, during a journey to the south, and offered to submit themselves to a fair trial; and James, without causing them to be arrested on the spot, appointed a day for their appearance, and suffered them to depart in freedom. This interview between James and the accused nobles augmented the worst suspicions of the clergy respecting the king's motives, and the utmost anxiety was expressed for the event.

The nobles had accepted a day of trial, and were preparing themselves to appear at the bar, with large bands of their friends and followers, whom they accounted strong enough to protect them.

The ministers expressed the greatest alarm at this conjuncture, and proposed, by their own authority, to levy such bodies of Protestants as might enable the prosecution to proceed. That they might not spare their own exertions on the occasion, they directed the curse of excommunication to be fulminated against the Catholic lords.

A single synod took upon themselves to pronounce this sentence, which carried with it the civil pains of treason against Errol, Huntley, and Angus, and also against the

Earl of Home, who was a Catholic, though not involved in the Spanish negotiations. The body of the Church seemed determined to take the conduct of this important case into their own management. They demanded of the king that the Church of Scotland should be permitted to appear by her representatives in the character of prosecutor, while they offered that their hearers should supply the place of guards and lictors. The king, by this warm proceeding, was placed in a delicate situation. He had determined to avoid extreme procedure against the Catholic lords, as he was willing to hope that, by toleration and gentle usage, they might be restrained from their dangerous intercourse with foreign powers. On the other hand, while he adopted such policy, it was imputed to him, not without an appearance of reality, that he was indifferent concerning the form of religion which should predominate in Scotland, and was only desirous of the security and augmentation of his own regal power. The misunderstanding between the king and the Church was inflamed by Lord Zouche, the English ambassador, who, having been sent to Scotland for that purpose, privately instigated the ministers to persist in their claims, and more openly importune James to show the utmost severity against the Catholic conspirators.

On November 26, 1593, the king, with sound policy, referred matters to the convention of estates, who came to this formal agreement: That the three earls of Huntley, Angus and Errol should be exempted from all further inquiry on account of their correspondence with Spain; that the first day of February should be fixed as a day before which they should either renounce the errors of popery, or remove out of the kingdom; that they should signify their choice against the first of January. But by the moderate measures which he pursued the king made no impression upon any party. The Catholic earls continued their communication with Spain, and their measures to support each other; the Church and anxious Protestants remained as jealous as ever of the king's sincerity; Zouche, the English ambassador, continued to worry James with remonstrances on the part of Elizabeth; and Bothwell, under the almost avowed protection of the queen of England, prepared new aggressions upon his sovereign.

On the second of April, 1594, this restless earl, at the head of about four hundred horsemen, arrived at Leith, at three in the morning, in the expectation of forming a junction with Athole and others, who favored him, and who were levying forces in the north, with the intention of moving upon the same point. The king, hearing of this alarming incident, went in person to the church, the day being Sunday; and having but few nobility and gentry in attendance upon him he reminded his lieges of the congregation of their duty to protect their sovereign, and requested them to consider whether the superiority of Bothwell and his borderers, men given to theft and robbery, was consistent with the safety of their families and property. The preacher did not fail to throw in a word of advice on so tempting an occasion. "God," he said, "would raise up against the king more Bothwells than one, and each a worse enemy than he, if James did not show the same zeal in the cause of Heaven (meaning against the popish lords), which he now exhibited in his own private quarrel." He gave, however, his sanction to the congregation arming and following their sovereign. The sermon was no sooner over than Bothwell learned that the king with a strong body of infantry, consisting of the citizens of Edinburgh, and a party of cavalry, composed of such noblemen and gentlemen as were at present attending the court, was moving against him. He drew up his cavalry upon an eminence called the Hawkhill, near Restal Rig; and from thence, on the king's approach, he held southeastward around the hill called Arthur's Seat, as if about to return to Dalkeith. He made this retreat slowly and in good order, followed and observed by the Lord Home, who commanded the king's cavalry. James himself, apprehensive that it was the purpose of Bothwell to make a circuit around Arthur's Seat, and attack Edinburgh upon the southern side, returned from Leith, and, marching through Edinburgh, drew up his forces on the Borough Moor, to be ready to receive the enemy, should he approach in that direction.

Home, in the meantime, pressed upon Bothwell's retreat with such incautious vehemence that Bothwell, indulging his antipathy to him as a personal enemy, charged him so suddenly with a superior body of horse as compelled Home to fly. The skirmish took place near Woolmet; and Home's discomfited cavalry ran back in confusion upon the body of infantry commanded by the king. Here again occurs a difference between the courtly Archbishop Spottiswoode and the journalist Birrel. The former says, that on beholding the rout of the royal cavalry, those around the king conjured him to return into the town, which he refused, saying, "He would never quit the field to a traitor." Birrel plainly says, "The king's majesty fled himself upon beholding the chase." His infantry stood firm, however; nor was Bothwell in a condition to attack them. His own horse had fallen in the chase, and he was severely bruised. A retreat to Dalkeith, and from thence to the borders, was the necessary consequence of his inability to obtain a complete victory. After escaping this danger, which was sufficiently imminent, the king sent ambassadors to Elizabeth, to complain of the conduct of her envoy Zouche, and of the reception and shelter which Bothwell met with on the English border, where he had not only occupied fortresses belonging to the queen, but had also received a considerable sum of money, with which he had hired soldiers, both English and Scottish, for his last treasonable attempt. The ambassadors had commission to promise a severe prosecution of the popish lords, in case they should not embrace the terms of submission which had been offered to them.

The queen promised fairly, and henceforth seems to have discontinued the encouragement which she had previously given to Bothwell.

Meantime, in 1593, the violence of feudal quarrels, which so nearly approached the presence of the king, spread blood and devastation through every part of the country. The deadly feud already noticed between the Johnstones and the Maxwells broke forth again in this year, with the violence of the most savage times. When we last mentioned this dispute, Maxwell, then in arms against the king, had obtained a superiority over Johnstone, James's lieutenant, who was made prisoner, and died of grief. Maxwell, after several changes of fortune, had been in his turn received into court favor, and enjoyed the office of warden of the western marches. The Laird of Johnstone, on the contrary, had given King James much offence, by uniting with Bothwell in some of his unlawful attempts, and affording him the assistance of individuals of his clan. For this he had been declared a rebel; and being imprisoned in the castle of Edinburgh had broken out of it on the 4th of last June. Such was the situation of the two chiefs with respect to the government; in relation to each other they had, by as formal a league of pacification as could be devised, put an end to the feudal quarrel which had so long subsisted between their houses. In consequence of this recent alliance, the Johnstones, therefore, according to their way of thinking, esteemed that Lord Maxwell's promotion to the wardenry inferred a mutual compact, that while they on their part should do nothing to injure or harm one of their new ally's clan, Maxwell, on the other hand, should overlook what loss other families might sustain through the depredations of the Johnstones. Thus fortified, as they conceived themselves, by their alliance with Maxwell, the Johnstones made their inroads upon the low country of Nithsdale with more fury than ever, and drove large preys of cattle from the estates of the Crichtons, the Douglases, the Griersons, Kirkpatricks, and other families of distinction in that neighborhood.

Those who had sustained injury by their incursions to a very considerable amount repaired to Maxwell to request his interference as warden. They found that he entertained their complaints coldly, and that his disinclination again to awaken the old feud with the Johnstones rendered him remiss in executing his duty to the country. The Lords Sanquhar, Drumlanrigg, and others interested, finding him thus indifferent, proposed to him that they would agree to grant him bonds of man-rent, and engage to follow him in his quarrels, provided he would effectually protect them by discharging his duty as warden, and thereby suppressing the power of the Johnstones. This temptation, which promised to place him at the head of many warlike and powerful families, and thus greatly increase what the Scots nobles called "his following," was irresistible; and Lord Maxwell, with the gentlemen of Nithsdale, entered into a bond in the terms proposed. Johnstone, obtaining information of this league, which seemed to be formed for his destruction and that of his clan, demanded an explanation from his ancient foe and recent ally. Maxwell at first denied the existence of the bond in question, and then explained it by the plausible apology of the public service, and the necessity of doing his duty as warden without respect of persons. Johnstone was not to be satisfied by these reasons, and the chieftains stood once more on terms of defiance.

Both clans upon this prepared for war with the solemnity of separate nations. The Johnstones, far inferior in numbers, summoned to their aid the Scots of Eskdale and Teviotdale. Five hundred of this clan came, not led by the chieftain, who was then abroad by the king's command, but by Sir Gideon Murray of Elibank, to whom he had intrusted the management of his affairs, and who bore upon this occasion Buccleuch's banner. The Elliots of Liddisdale, the Grahams of the debatable land, and other western borderers, came also to Johnstone's assistance; sharing general habits of depredation, and unwilling to give free passage to the warden's jurisdiction.

Maxwell, on the other hand, levied a powerful army, consisting not only of his own numerous followers, but of all the families and clans which we have mentioned as having engaged in the bond. They entered Annandale with displayed banner and the avowed intention of destroying the

houses of Lochwood and Lockerbie, strong castles belonging
to the Laird of Johnstone.   Maxwell had besieged the latter
fortress when the Johnstones came upon him, and, profiting
by some advantage obtained by their prickers or skirmishers,
charged Maxwell's main body suddenly, and totally defeated
them.   Maxwell, it is said, had his hand cut off, and was
struck from his horse before he was slain; and tradition
avers that he received the last deadly blow from the hand
of a female, daughter of the late Lord Johnstone, who had
died his prisoner.

The king was much affected by this fatal violence; but
the state of his affairs did not permit him to avenge it in
person, nor were there any who had power enough to accomplish such an object by royal commission.   Johnstone,
therefore, remained unpunished; and was shortly after himself appointed warden of the west marches: this was in 1596.
The unhappy tale may be concluded by saying, that on the
6th of April, 1608, he was treacherously murdered at a meeting with Lord Maxwell, the son of him who was slain at the
battle of Dryffe Sands, who took this dishonorable but not
infrequent mode of revenging his father's death.   Polity
was now grown more strong; and the murderer, being apprehended, was beheaded at the cross of Edinburgh; and
thus terminated the long feud between the Johnstones and
Maxwells, having cost each house the lives of two chieftains.
The battle of Dryffe Sands has a claim to be noticed, as the
terminating action of that long series which had been fought
upon the border during so many centuries.   The fate of the
Lord Maxwell was much lamented: "he was a nobleman,"
says Spottiswoode, "of great spirit, courteous, humane, and
more learned than men of his rank usually are; but aspiring
and ambitious of rule.   His fall was lamented by many; he
being considered as one who did little wrong to any one
excepting to himself."

In the year 1594, the momentous affair of the Catholic
lords was brought to a head.   Huntley, Angus, and Errol,
confident in the numbers of their followers, and the inac-

cessible nature of their country, had rejected with scorn the alternative of the king to change their religion or retire into exile. They renewed their correspondence with Spain; from which court they received a considerable sum of money to enable them to take the field.

The king, now for his own sake, as well as to redeem the pledges which he had repeatedly given to the Protestant party, saw the necessity of acting with vigor: this was the more difficult, as he was in great distress for money, the expenses of a royal baptism (though the cause may appear inadequate) having recently exhausted the coffers of the king. He held a convention on the 8th of June, 1594, to obtain their counsel in so important a case. The accusation of the Catholic lords being read, the authenticity of the Spanish blanks was proved, and a sentence of high treason, in its most rigorous form, pronounced against the Earls of Huntley, of Angus, and of Errol. Thus, at length, the Protestants were gratified, and the Catholic lords subjected to a doom of forfeiture: but the manner of enforcing it was a consideration of more difficulty. Queen Elizabeth, though she had remonstrated so much against the indulgence shown to these popish lords, and although their design was as much directed against her as against James, refused to contribute anything to the expense of suppressing three powerful peers, in the remote provinces, the only place in which they possessed extensive interest, and where it was equally difficult to introduce troops or subsist them when in the field. It was evident that the king could not creditably go himself upon an expedition unprovided with the most ordinary means of expense. It remained only possible to induce some nobleman to act as his representative upon the occasion. No one was thought more suitable for the office than the young Earl of Argyle, both from the situation of his estates and the number of Highlanders whom, by his authority and their natural love of spoil, he was sure to draw to his standard. He was propitiated with a promise of Huntley's rights and possessions in Lochaber, which stood forfeited to the crown, and lay peculiarly convenient for augmentation of the Earl of Argyle's family possessions and feudal power. The young earl had spirit and ambition, and did not decline the trust reposed in him. Lord Forbes, the hereditary enemy of Huntley, was united in the same commission.

Meantime the Catholic lords used their utmost influence to provide the means of defence. They sought out connections with such disaffected courtiers as they hoped might assist their cause; and under this hope formed a conspiracy to seize the person of the king, who was to be confined in the fortress of Blackness, the commander of which they had corrupted. The ministry of the Earl of Bothwell was to be used upon this occasion. This versatile and turbulent man had been already an accomplice of the Catholic lords in the year 1588; but in his later incursions had stated the immunities and impunity afforded them as a principal cause of his being in arms. In his last proclamation, distributed at the Raid of Leith, the Catholic lords were designed as enemies "to the true religion, and friendship of both crowns, and the practicers for inbringing of strangers; a company of lewd, pernicious persons crept into the state, to the high contempt of God and dishonor of the king, who authorized mass in several of the countries, permitted seminary priests to travel with impunity, and labored for bringing in the cruel Spaniard." Yet now he felt himself at liberty to throw off all regard to the true religion, as he formerly styled it, and engaged with those whose object it was to subvert it, undertaking to assist them in their plot against the king's person and liberty.

The activity of James's measures, however, prevented the plot being carried into effect. Argyle, by means of his own extensive jurisdictions and clanship, and by the prospect of plunder which his enterprise afforded, drew together six or seven thousand Highlanders, including the Clan of Maclean and others from the western islands. Of this army of mountaineers, fifteen hundred men carried firearms, and the rest were armed, after the Highland fashion, with bows and arrows, two-handed swords, Lochaber axes, and partisans. The purpose of Argyle, their commander, was to descend from the hills upon Huntley's principal castle, then called Strathbogie, with the purpose of occupying that fortress, and also of joining his force to those which the Lord Forbes was raising in Aberdeenshire.

The suddenness of the attack permitted Huntley no time to receive aid from the Earl of Angus, whose forces lay at a considerable distance. The Earl of Errol, who was his nearer neighbor, joined him upon the alarm of the danger with two or three hundred of the clan of Hay, of which he was chief. The smallness of their number was made up by their character, which was that of gentlemen, with their personal followers, men of high birth and ready courage; all serving on horseback, and well mounted and armed. Huntley himself assembled about a thousand men, who were chiefly gentlemen of the name of Gordon, and provided and armed like those of Hay. He had, however, a train of six field-pieces, to the use of which the Highlanders were unaccustomed. These were under the management of an expert soldier named Captain Ker, by birth a borderer, but for many years a follower of Huntley, in whose service, during the civil wars of Queen Mary's reign, he had been distinguished by his military skill as well as by his cruelty. The expected encounter came thus to resemble that of Harlaw, where the force of the ancient Gael had been tried in mortal contest with that of the low-country Saxons.

Each party was confident of success. The Lowland men were of opinion that the multitude of Argyle's tumultuary forces would be ill matched with their own completely equipped and high-spirited cavaliers; and the Highlanders entertained no idea that an army could be embodied in the low countries before whom their own fiery courage would give way.

Huntley used the politic precaution to lay the country waste, to render the support of Argyle and his army a matter of difficulty; but as the want of provisions equally affected the subsistence of his own levies, he found himself compelled to risk an action, which perhaps he would have otherwise willingly avoided.   Argyle, having now arrived at the head of Strathdon, sent a herald to Huntley and Errol to announce that he came as the king's lieutenant, and to charge them to withdraw their forces and give him open passage to the castle of Strathbogie.   Huntley replied that, since such was his purpose, he would himself be porter, and welcome him upon the road to his castle, as courtesy required.   He then convened his own people, and exhorted them to defend themselves for the glory of God and the liberty of their consciences.   He protested, that although the king was animated against him by the instigation of his enemies, he loved and reverenced him with such true devotion that even in the best cause he would never lift a weapon against him. But now, since they were exposed to a barbarous enemy, who had neither fear of God nor obedience to the king, nor the most ordinary habits of civilization, he exhorted his followers to act valiantly, as men who, if vanquished, must be subject to the pleasure of the most savage conquerors.

The armies met in a district called Glenlivet, at a place named Belrinnes.   Argyle's numerous army were stationed on the side of a mountain, which, far from being easily accessible by horsemen, had so steep an ascent in front that even footmen could hardly keep their feet upon it.   Nevertheless, Captain Ker, who was appointed to survey the ground, reported to the earls that a brisk attack upon their barbarous enemy would quickly disperse men, who, like the Highlanders, had no knowledge of war as practiced by civilized people.   Huntley then arranged his men in this manner: Errol was appointed to lead the van, accompanied by Sir Partick Gordon of Auchindoun.   Huntley himself commanded the rearguard, designed for their support, with a strong body of cavalry.

Errol, with his vanguard, began to ascend the hill in the very front of the Highland line of battle; and between the roughness of the heather and steepness of the ascent his horsemen were compelled to advance at a very slow pace. But, masked for a time under cover of the movement of the vanguard, four pieces of artillery had been brought into a position to annoy Argyle's line of battle, without the possibility of the Highlanders observing it. The sudden discharge of this battery spread dismay through the Highlanders, who were unaccustomed either to the noise of the cannon or to the operation of shot so far beyond the range of the missiles with which they were acquainted. Some fled, all were confused, and Errol, with the Hays, continued to advance uninterrupted. The ascent, however, became so steep, that to make their way directly upward was almost impossible: the horsemen were compelled to wheel to the right and form a column, which, in order to gain the hill by an oblique movement, obliged them to expose their flank to the enemy. The Highlanders perceived this advantage, and showered on them a tremendous volley of bullets and arrows, hurting many horse and men. The Hays were, however, valiantly seconded by Huntley, who, coming up to their aid, made so fierce an attack upon the centre of Argyle's army, where his standard was displayed, that the banner was borne down, and Campbell of Lochinzell and his brother slain in its defence. When the horsemen attained the more even ground, where their horses could gallop, the resistance of the Highlanders, who had no lances to defend them from the shock, became impossible. They were hurried down the opposite side of the hill on which they had been drawn up, and their pursuers mingled with them, doing much execution. The chief of Maclean alone, a man of uncommon strength and courage, dressed in a shirt of mail, and armed with a double-edged battle-axe, defied the efforts of the assailants for some time, but was at length compelled to flight. The battle lasted for about two hours. Argyle himself was forced off the field, weeping with anger and shame, and imploring his men to return to the charge. The loss of the vanquished was not great; for the roughness of the ground, which rendered the victory difficult, made the pursuit impossible. Little quarter, however, was given to the Highlanders, which is chiefly imputed to the difference of language between the victors and vanquished. The battle of Glenlivet, chiefly remarkable as being fought between the two races which divided Scotland, took place upon the third day of October, 1594. Sir Patrick Gordon of Auchindoun, an uncle of Huntley, was slain, with only twelve others, on the side of the victors. Huntley had his own horse killed under him, and many of his followers were wounded and dismounted. Argyle lost some chiefs and men of note, and about seven hundred common soldiers. The issue of the battle was fortunate for the country, which would have been pitifully plundered had the victory remained with the barbarous Highlanders.

The Lord Forbes, with an army hastily assembled of such clans as were hostile to the Gordons, put himself in motion to form a junction with Argyle, and persuade him to resume his enterprise. But a gentleman of the name of Irvine being, in the darkness of the night, slain by the shot of a pistol, the accident spread such general distrust in an army composed of various clans, among whom there lurked reasons of feud, that the host dispersed itself, and could not be again assembled.

James VI. was disturbed, in the hour of midnight, at Dundee, to which he had then advanced, by news of the defeat of Argyle, and the victory of Huntley and Errol. He showed that he felt the force of the emergency, by the energy with which he prepared to meet it. Animated with an unusual spirit of promptitude, he hastened, by pawning the crown jewels, to raise a sum of money sufficient to support a small army, with which he marched into Aberdeen-shire against the Catholic lords. The king was there joined by various clans, the feudal enemies of Huntley and Errol. But either weakened by the effects of their own victory, or faithful to the principles of loyalty expressed by Huntley on the eve of the battle of Glenlivet, the Catholic earls offered no opposition. The king marched through the country, casting down and dismantling the fortresses of Strathbogie and Glaimis, and returned home with the honor of having suppressed, by his personal exertions, a threatening and triumphant rebellion. He left behind him the Duke of Lennox, who, under the title of lieutenant, hanged many of the poorer sort, and inflicted heavy fines upon the wealthier persons who had borne arms under Huntley and Errol.

The time was now come when Bothwell's ferocity, cunning, and versatility, could avail him no longer. His last change to the popish and Spanish faction had offended Queen Elizabeth beyond forgiveness, nor was there any mercy to be looked for at the hand of his natural sovereign, whom he had so often and grievously offended. Unable to obtain shelter in Scotland, where the king caused him to be diligently sought after, and obtaining no harbor, as formerly, upon the English borders, he fled to France. Here also James's resentment followed him, and demanded of Henry IV. that he should be delivered up to punishment, or at least banished from France. The generous Henry answered that he would give no encouragement to a person so obnoxious to his ally, but that he could not refuse a miserable exile the free air of his kingdom. Even this retreat Bothwell forfeited by his turbulent temper, which induced him to transgress that wise monarch's edict against sending challenges. Banished from France, Bothwell went successively to Spain and Naples, and purchased his bread meanly and miserably by abjuring the Protestant religion. His principal possessions were bestowed upon Scott of Buccleuch and Ker of Cessford, in return, as may be supposed, for their having given up his friendship and alliance at a time when their adhesion might have been dangerous to the state.

King James, placable and easy to be entreated in favor of other offenders, would never listen to any petition in favor of this arch-traitor; he died at Naples, in poverty and infamy. Such was the end of unprincipled ambition, which, supported only by reckless courage, had disturbed the state by so many conspiracies.   About this time also fate finished the career of another guilty votary of unscrupulous ambition.

Captain James Stewart, for some time prime minister and chosen favorite of the king, expelled from court, as we have already stated, at the Raid of Stirling, in 1585, had never since made his appearance there; but at this time the death of the wise and excellent Chancellor Maitland took place.   This great statesman had been for some time in a species of disgrace with King James, from the dislike which Queen Anne had expressed toward him, for no better reason, probably, than that he was the favorite of her husband. James, however, retained his affection for him, and honored his memory with an epitaph couched in tolerable poetry. Captain James Stewart, although, indeed, he was neither beloved nor befriended by any who were not as profligate as himself, had always conceived this statesman, who was his successor as chancellor, to be his greatest enemy.   He appeared at court accordingly, in hopes that the king's favor might again prefer him to the same eminent situation, now vacant by the demise of Maitland.   The king received him so well as to induce him to lend belief to a soothsayer, who had told him that his head should presently stand higher than ever.   But the general alarm and disgust was so great at the reappearance of this ill-omened and wicked man, that he was counselled in all haste to withdraw himself from court and return to his place of residence in Ayrshire, where he had been permitted to remain unnoticed and in obscurity. As he rode back to his dwelling, by the way of Symington, with only one or two attendants, he was cautioned not to travel openly through the country, for fear of the vengeance of the Douglases, to whom he had given mortal offence, as the author of Morton's impeachment and death.   Stewart answered, with his usual rash courage, that the Douglas lived not for fear of whom he would screen himself or quit his road.   One of those tale-bearers, who are always at hand where mischief is to be disseminated, carried this expression to Douglas of Torthorwold, a near relation of the Regent

Morton, who conceiving himself defied, presently got upon horseback, with three or four followers, and pursuing Stewart, overtook him in a pass of the mountains called the Gateslack, ran him through with his lance, and cut off his head, which he set upon his castle of Torthorwald, and thus in one sense realized the prophecy of the soothsayer, by placing it higher than it had yet been raised. The body of this man, once so proud and powerful, is said to have been neglected in the waste road until it was mangled by swine.

Neither did Torthorwald, who had been, unlawfully on his part, the means of executing deserved vengeance on this wicked man, escape without his reward. It was not very long after this bloody exploit, when he was accidentally met in the street of Edinburgh by Sir William Stewart, the nephew of the deceased, who, in revenge of his uncle's death, drew his sword without speaking a word, and passed it through Torthorwald's body, who fell dead on the spot, thus making good the expression of Scripture, that "mischief shall hunt the violent man."

The death of Lord Chancellor Maitland threw the king's affairs in a great measure into his own hands. As is usual in a disturbed state, the principal difficulty lay in the finances, which were reduced to a very low ebb. The aid of Elizabeth was applied for in vain. She had promised her assistance when the king should seriously set himself to destroy the force of the Catholic lords. But, economical even in her youthful years, the queen had reached that period of life when the love of money becomes a passion, nor was it possible for James to extract any assistance from her. This induced him to apply to a better resource than all the treasures of England could have afforded him. He resolved manfully, by practicing strict economy, to render his own revenue equal to his own wants; and for that purpose determined it should be collected with more accuracy, and expended with more frugality. For this purpose, he made a remarkable change in his administration, equivalent to what in a private case is called executing a deed of trust, transferring to others the management of the grantor's own estate.

James committed the care of his finances to eight persons belonging to the profession of the law, upon whom the whole duty of receipt and expenditure, settling accounts, and expediting grants, in a word, every article of national expense, should be devolved; so that the whole duties of the exchequer were destined to be performed through the means of these eight persons, or at least of a quorum of five of them. The king, conscious of his own facility of temper, bound himself upon the word of a prince that he would not subscribe any letter or deed of gift unless it was previously approved by this board, who were, from their number, termed the Octavians: he agreed, also, not to add to the number of these eight comptrollers; and that in case of a vacancy in their number by death that it should not be filled up without the consent of the survivors. The eight commissioners, on their side, made oath that, next to God and a good conscience, they should in all things respect his majesty's weal and honor, and the advancement of his revenue; and neither for tenderness of blood, advantage to themselves, nor awe or fear of any one, agree to the disposition of any part of the patrimony of the crown: also, that they would not give their consent to any proposed measure separately, but would deliberate and act together as a body, holding their meetings in exchequer, and five being a quorum.

This singular devolution of these general powers was such an unusual trust that it was generally said that the king had resigned his royal authority to commissioners of no high rank, and had not left himself the means either of cherishing the attachment of his subjects, or of rewarding their services by the slightest boon from government. This clamor was especially raised by the greedy courtiers, to whom the king's facility of disposition had afforded undue opportunities of enriching themselves under the ordinary system. The Octavians used the trust reposed in them with as much moderation, perhaps, as could possibly have been expected;

and by their knowledge of business, and the exercise of a rigid economy, they brought the affairs into much better order than they had ever been during James's reign.

It would have been too much, however, to have expected that men intrusted with so much power were altogether to abstain from using it to their personal advantage. The authority of the Octavians over all the officers of state entitled them to call them to the closest accounting; and as few of them were prepared for rendering such a strict reckoning, several chose to resign lucrative situations, which were filled up by the Octavians out of their own number. In this manner a great popular clamor was excited against the new managers, much increased by the clergy, who were not satisfied with the soundness of doctrine entertained by some of the Octavians. The king himself also became tired of the restraint under which he lay; and after enduring public odium, and, finally, the displeasure of their sovereign, from the 12th of January, 1595, the Octavians resigned their commission into his majesty's hands in the parliament, in 1596.

CHAPTER XXXIX

Kinmont Willie made Prisoner by the English—The Scottish
Warden attacks Carlisle Castle, and liberates him—Elizabeth
demands that Buccleuch should be delivered up, which is refused by the Scottish Parliament—He visits England of his own
Accord, and is honorably received—The Catholic Lords give
new Trouble—James proposes that they shall be reconciled to
the Church—The Scottish Clergy take Alarm, and establish a
Standing Committee of the Church at Edinburgh—Black
preaches a Sermon highly disrespectful to the King—He is
called before the Privy Council—The Clergy encourage him to
disown the Jurisdiction of the Judges—He is found guilty, and
banished to the North—Misunderstanding between the King
and Church—Great Tumult in Edinburgh—The King leaves the
City, and removes the Courts of Justice—The Clergy apply to
the Lord Hamilton to support them, but in vain—He returns
to Edinburgh, attended by the Border Clans and others—The
Citizens are alarmed for fear of being Plundered—James makes
a Composition and pardons them—He becomes desirous to new
model the Church of Scotland, by introducing Episcopacy; but
is obliged to proceed with great Caution—The Order of Bishops
is established under strict Limitations

AN incident took place in the beginning of the year 1596,
which had almost renewed the long discontinued wars
upon the border. Excepting by the rash enterprises
of Bothwell, these disorderly districts had remained undisturbed by any violence worthy of note since the battle of
the Reedsquair. Upon the fall of Bothwell, his son-in-law,
Sir Walter Scott of Buccleuch, had obtained the important
office of keeper of Liddisdale, and warden of the Scottish
borders upon that unsettled frontier. According to the custom of the marches, Buccleuch's deputy held a day of truce
for meeting with the deputy of the Lord Scroope, governor

of Carlisle Castle, and keeper of the west marches on the English side. The meeting was, as usual, attended on both sides by the most warlike of the borderers upon faith of the usual truce, which allowed twenty-four hours to come and go from such meetings, without any individual being, during that short space, liable to challenge on account of offences given to either kingdom. Among others who attended Buccleuch's deputy was one Armstrong, commonly called Kinmont Willie, remarkable for his exploits as a depredator upon England. After the business of the meeting had been peaceably transacted the parties separated. But the English, being on their return homeward, at the south side of the River Liddle, which is in that place the boundary of the kingdoms, beheld this Kinmont Willie riding upon the Scottish bank of the river alone and in absolute security. They were unable to resist the tempting opportunity of seizing a man who had done them much injury; and, without regarding the sanctity of the truce, a strong party crossed the river into Scotland, chased Kinmont Willie for more than a mile, and by dint of numbers made him at length their prisoner. He was carried to the castle of Carlisle and brought before Lord Scroope, where he boasted proudly of the breach of the immunities of the day of truce in his person, and demanded his liberty, as unlawfully taken from him. The English warden paid little attention to his threats, as indeed the ascendency of Elizabeth in James's councils made her officers infringe the rights of Scottish subjects with little ceremony; and on the score of his liberty, he assured Kinmont Willie, scornfully, that he should take a formal farewell of him before he left Carlisle Castle.

The Lord of Buccleuch was by no means of a humor to submit to an infraction of the national rights, and a personal insult to himself. On this occasion he acted with equal prudence and spirit. The Scottish warden first made a regular application to Lord Scroope for delivery of the prisoner, and redress of the wrong sustained in his capture. To this no satisfactory answer was returned. Buccleuch next applied to Bowes, the English ambassador, who interfered so far as to advise Lord Scroope to surrender the prisoner without bringing the matter to further question.   Time was given to advertise Elizabeth; but she, being in this as in other cases disposed to bear the matter out by her great superiority of power, returned no satisfactory answer.   The intercourse between the wardens became then of a more personal character; and Buccleuch sent a challenge to Lord Scroope, as having offered him a personal affront in the discharge of his office.   Scroope returned for answer that the commands of the queen engaged him in more important matters than the chastisement of the Scottish warden, and left him not at liberty to accept his challenge. Being thus refused alike public and private satisfaction, Buccleuch resolved to resort to measures of extremity, and obtain by means of his own force that redress which was otherwise denied him. Being the chief of a numerous clan, he had no difficulty in assembling three hundred chosen horsemen at Woodhouselee upon the Esk, the nearest point to the castle of Carlisle upon the Scottish marches, and not above ten or twelve miles' distance from that fortress.   The hour of rendezvous was after sunset; and the night, dark and misty, concealed their march through the English frontier. They arrived without being perceived under the castle of Carlisle, where the Scottish warden, taking post opposite to the northern gate of the town, ordered a party of fifty of his followers to dismount and attempt to scale the walls of the castle with ladders which had been provided for the purpose.   The ladders being found too short, the assailants attacked a small postern-gate with iron instruments and mining tools, which they had also in readiness: the door giving way, the Scots forced their way into the castle, repulsing and bearing down such of the English guards as pressed forward to the defence of the place.   The alarm was now given.   The beacon on the castle was lighted, the drums beat, and the bell of the cathedral church and watch-bell of the mote-hall were rung, as in cases of utmost alarm.

To this din the Scots without the castle added their wild shouts; and the sound of their trumpets increased the confusion, of which none of the sleepers so unseasonably awakened could conceive the cause. In the meanwhile the assailants of the castle had delivered their countryman, Will of Kinmont. In passing through the courtyard he failed not to call out a lusty good-night at Lord Scroope's window, and another under that of Salkeld, the constable of the castle. The assailants then made their retreat, abstaining strictly, for such was their charge, from taking any booty, or doing any violence which was not absolutely necessary for executing the purpose for which they came. Some prisoners were taken and brought before Buccleuch, who dismissed them courteously, charging the most considerable among them with a message to the constable of the castle, whom, he said, he accounted a more honorable man than Lord Scroope, who had declined his challenge; telling him what had been done was acted by the command of him the Lord of Liddisdale; and that if, as a man of honor, he sought a gallant revenge, he had only to come forth and encounter with those who were willing to maintain what they had dared to do. He then retreated into Scotland with his banner displayed and his trumpets sounding, and reached his domains with the delivered man in perfect safety.

The general spirit of the people of Scotland received the account of this stratagem of war with the highest applause. It seemed a revival of the ancient spirit which had so long enabled Scotland to protect her independence against a superior enemy; and the common saying among the people was that such an act of vassalage had not been performed in Scotland since the time of Sir William Wallace. Elizabeth, on the contrary, was highly offended; and either could not perceive, or would not acknowledge, that the fault of her own officer had given occasion to a retaliation which, everything considered, had been conducted with extreme moderation. By the queen's directions her ambassador lodged a violent complaint before the Scottish parliament, setting forth that the Lord of Liddisdale had invaded the queen of England's castle, wounded her subjects, done violence, and offered dishonor to her country, and to her warden; and as these insults had been offered during the time of profound peace, she required that the person of Buccleuch should be surrendered to England, to be treated according to his demerits. The matter was conducted with great solemnity; the king himself urging to the parliament the necessity of giving satisfaction to Elizabeth, and the secretary arguing the question in behalf of Buccleuch. The parliament came to a decision that the recovery of a prisoner unlawfully taken, achieved with such circumstances of moderation, was in itself lawful; and that to deliver Buccleuch to be punished for such an action would be totally unreasonable, and tend to the degradation of the king and whole realm of Scotland. The matter was summed up by the secretary, who said with a loud voice that Sir Walter Scott of Buccleuch should pass into England when it should please the king himself to go thither, and not sooner. To escape the risk of displeasing Elizabeth, James, notwithstanding this spirited decision, personally requested of Buccleuch that he would present himself of his own free will before the queen of England, under the assurance that he should be permitted to return in honor and safety. Buccleuch readily agreed to a compromise which was to satisfy Elizabeth's point of honor, and relieve James from a serious difficulty. It is said, by tradition, that when he presented himself before Elizabeth, the queen asked him, with the air of imposing dignity, which she knew so well how to assume, how he had dared to commit so great an outrage in her dominions? —"May it please you, madam," answered the border chief, "I know not the thing that a man dares not do." Elizabeth was pleased with his spirit; and having detained him for some time at her court, dismissed him with tokens of honor and regard, thus extinguishing the last spark of that conflagration of hostility which had raged between England and Scotland for perhaps twenty centuries.

It would have been an ill time for Elizabeth and James to have harbored any discord which might be forborne, since Philip of Spain was again agitating the most gigantic schemes for the conquest of Britain. This occasioned the deepest anxiety on the part of King James, embarrassed as he was by the difficulty of dealing between the Catholic lords so lately in rebellion and the ministers of the Church. Huntley, Angus, and Errol had wandered in foreign parts since the king's march into the north and the end of their rebellion. Finding their reception and entertainment colder than they expected, they began to cast their eye back to their own country, aware that they would find little opposition on the part of the king if they could only evade or satisfy the suspicions of the churchmen. The banished earls returned secretly into Scotland, and soon after sent a petition to the king and convention, praying for permission to reside in their own country, under security for their good behavior. The king laid this petition before a convention which met at Falkland upon August 12, together with these sensible observations: only one of two courses, he said, could be pursued toward these unfortunate noblemen; either they must be utterly destroyed and exterminated with their whole race and family, a task of some difficulty, and of a most vindictive and unchristian character, or else they must be admitted to pardon upon expressing a humble acknowledgment of their offence, and finding security for the safety of the Church. It was therefore agreed by the convention that the petition of the earls should be granted upon such conditions as the king in council should attach to the boon so conferred.

When this news transpired, the jealousy of the Church was excited to the most violent and unreasonable degree. The ministers held meetings, wrote circular letters, commanded the churchmen to read from every pulpit the excommunication of the Catholic lords, and enjoined them to impose the same sentence on all those who should show the least attachment to the popish religion, or disposition

to favor the Catholic earls.   They summoned a committee
of the most eminent clergymen, and enjoined them to come
to Edinburgh, where, with the ministers of that city, they
were to form a permanent committee, called the Standing
Council of the Church, with power to exert the supreme
authority of the whole body in case of any apparent danger
to the ecclesiastical establishment.   These violent measures
greatly offended the king, who was desirous that his subjects, both Catholics and Presbyterians, should live peaceably together, attach themselves to his government, and abstain from domestic quarrels.   For this purpose, he pleaded
for some terms of reconciliation with Mr. Robert Bruce, a
minister of talents and respectability, with whom he had
hitherto been on good terms.   With difficulty Bruce was
brought to allow that Angus and Errol might be admitted
to remission on the part of the Church; but sternly insisted
that Huntley, the most able as well as most powerful of
the three, should be declared incapable of pardon.   "Your
grace," said the preacher, with an unusual degree of insolence, "may make your choice between Huntley and me;
but you cannot have the friendship of both."

While the king and the Church were on these evil terms
with each other, slight causes, arising from the want of
sense and temperance of individuals, occurred every moment
to add fuel to the flame.   One Black, a clergyman of warm
passions and contemptible understanding, had, in a sermon
at St. Andrew's, cast forth the most bitter and despiteful
reproaches against the king and queen, the judges, and servants of the crown, and Elizabeth herself.   The king took
this opportunity to act upon the resolution formed to check
the insolence of the ministers, and he caused Mr. Black to
be cited to appear before the privy council.   The charges
contained in the summons against this turbulent clergyman
accused him, first, of having affirmed in the pulpit that the
popish lords had returned into the country with his majesty's
knowledge, and upon his assurance; and of having said that,
in so doing, James had discovered the treachery of his heart.

Secondly, he was charged with having called all kings the devil's bairns; adding that the devil was in the court, and in the guiders of it. Thirdly, in his prayer for the queen he was charged with having used these words: "We must pray for her, for the fashion; but we have no cause; she will never do us good." Fourthly, that he had called the queen of England an atheist. Fifthly, that he had discussed a suspension, granted by the lords of session, in the pulpit, and called them miscreants and bribers. Sixthly, that, speaking of the nobility, he said they were degenerated, godless dissemblers, and enemies to the Church; likewise, speaking of the council, that he had called them holliglasses, cormorants, and men of no religion. Lastly, that he had convocated divers noblemen, barons, and others, within St. Andrew's, in the month of June, 1594, caused them to take arms, and divide themselves in troops of horse and foot, and had thereby usurped the power of the king and civil magistrate.

It would have been more than could have been expected, at this unenlightened and fanatical period, that the Church of Scotland, though containing many learned and wise men, should have viewed the polemical disputes between the two religions with the liberality that did not belong to the time: they would, in that case, have seen that pressing the king to the destruction and extermination of three great and powerful barons was involving him in a task neither easily accomplished nor suitable to his means, since James had neither a standing army nor revenues capable of keeping one on foot. They would also have seen that the earls themselves could have no interest to assist the oppressive and ambitious designs of Philip II., unless they were driven to these extremities by exile from their country, plunder of their estates, and oppression of their consciences. This was not, however, the reasoning of the times; and the Roman Church was in fact scarcely more intolerant than the Kirk of Scotland, except that the latter was content to limit the rigor of their opinions to this world, and to allow that, in the next, a Catholic might be capable of salvation. **During** their stay in this world, the Protestants alike invoked against those who dissented from them the censures of the Church and the sword of the temporal power. There was no room, they contended, for toleration to papists, either on the part of the king or on the part of the Church.

But although this severe doctrine was so deeply entwined with their notions of church government, it might have been expected that the wise and discreet among the ministers would have discerned the danger of useless and unnecessary quarrels with James, by such scandalous imputations as those for which Black was called before the council. It was the business and interest of the Church to have instantly disavowed this rash man; and by imposing upon him the censure and punishment of his own order, his spiritual superiors would have taken away from the king all the jealousy which he might otherwise have retained of the irresponsibility of the clergymen to the temporal power. They ought to have recollected, with some feeling of gratitude, that King James had abolished those acts of parliament passed in the year 1584, by which the clergy had been declared liable to censure and punishment in lay courts for offences committed in the pulpit. Besides this, the position of James rendered it every year more politic to secure his power and favor. The prospects of King James's succession to the English throne became yearly nearer; and as he must be then invested with the power of a large and wealthy kingdom, it would have been of importance to have preserved his affection and good opinion while he was in the less powerful condition of a mere king of Scotland.

But these reflections had no weight: the clergy made the cause of Black that of the order at large: they again revived the dispute concerning the ecclesiastical immunities, pretending that the clergymen in the exercise of their office were only subject to the general assembly, and their other spiritual superiors. For such doctrine as he had promulgated from the pulpit the council of the Church, therefore, enjoined

Black to refuse to plead before the privy council, or answer any questions which might be there put to him; and they ordered their resolutions on this head to be circulated through every presbytery in the kingdom, and subscribed by every minister. It was now impossible for the king to give way; and he must have either persevered in his purpose of punishing Black, or lost all estimation as a king who could not avenge the most flagrant and injurious insults of the clergy. He published a proclamation for dissolving the committee of ministers called the Council of the Church: it set forth that certain ministers residing in Edinburgh, and assuming authority over their brethren, had presumed to publish a paper declining the regal jurisdiction, and calling on others to subscribe the same. The king, therefore, charged them by name to depart from the town, and return to their charges within twenty-four hours, under pain of treason. The commission, thus in danger of being dissolved, applied first to the Octavians, who returned them a short answer, saying that as these controversies were begun without their advice they should end without their interference. The commissioners next applied to the king himself, who seemed very willing to accommodate the affair. If they would pass, he said, from the objections to the jurisdiction of the privy council, or would declare that they only used them in a particular case, he would on his part desist from the prosecution of Black, notwithstanding the high indecency of his behavior. As this accommodation did not suit the clergy, although a considerable portion voted for accepting it, they resolved to stand by their proposed immunity.

The king, highly displeased, caused the proclamation to be issued, dissolving the commission of the Church; and though some attempts were made to accommodate the matter with Mr. Black, it ended in the privy council proceeding against him, notwithstanding his claim of privilege. Having adduced proof of the offensive expressions which he had used, they declared him guilty of the scandalous charges brought against him, and referred his punishment to the king. James, though sufficiently jealous of his own authority, was not unreasonably severe in the punishment. He appointed Black to be sent to the north for some time; and at the same time he required from the ministers that a bond of obedience to the king should be subscribed by each of them, under pain of their stipends and means of living being sequestrated; at the same time, Black was ordered to depart upon his banishment. The clergy and their congregations were alarmed at these proceedings. Other reports, as is usual in such cases, augmented the fears and anxieties of men's minds. The king was, on his part, informed that a nightly watch was kept in Edinburgh around the ministers' houses, as if to defend them from some apprehended danger. James was so far moved by this intelligence that he was induced to command about twenty-four of the burgesses, most zealous in the cause of the clergy, to absent themselves from the town.

This increased the general suspicion of the Church, which was brought to a crisis by a letter received by Robert Bruce, and by him communicated to Mr. Walter Balcanqual, who was to preach at the hour of sermon. The paper stated (falsely) that the ministers ought to look to themselves; for Huntley had been with the king last night, and was the author of the proclamation against the ministers and citizens. The preacher, inflamed by this report, pronounced a fiery discourse, in which he cast gross reflections upon such statesmen as he concluded had given the king their advice in the late disputes with the Church. Turning then to the nobles and barons who were present, he reminded them of the zeal shown by their forefathers in establishing the reformed religion, called upon them to follow the example of their predecessors, and for that purpose conjured them to assemble after the sermon should be ended in a neighboring place of worship, called the Little Kirk. While the clergy and the congregation, already much irritated, were heating themselves and exasperating their mutual passions, the king came to attend the sitting of the court of session,

which was then held in the Tolbooth, close to St. Giles's
Church, in which these tumultuary scenes were exhibited.
This vicinity made it an easy matter for the meeting which
had been held in the Little Kirk to send a committee of their
number to wait upon the king. They were admitted to his
presence, and declared that they were sent by the meeting
convened in the Little Kirk, to bemoan the danger which
was threatened to religion. "What danger does your wisdom apprehend?" said the king, angrily. The committee
replied, that the ministers and best affected people were
banished from town; that the Lady Huntley was received
at court; and that it was shrewdly suspected her husband
himself was not far distant. "And who are you," said the
king, "who dare assemble contrary to my proclamation?"
"We are such as dare do more," said the Lord Lindsay,
who was one of the deputies from the Little Kirk; "we are
those who will not see religion pulled down." At this time
numbers of people thronged boldly into the room; observing
which, the king arose, and leaving the apartment in which
he was sitting, retreated to a lower one, and commanded the
doors to be shut. The committee gave to the crowd who
were waiting in the Little Kirk an alarming account of their
want of success. "There is but one course to be taken,"
said Lindsay, fiercely: "let us stay together, such as are
here, and stand by each other; let us send for our friends
and those who favor religion, and let the day be either theirs
or ours." This extravagant proposition was received by
minds in a highly excited state; for during the absence of
the committee, a clergyman named Cranstoun had been
reading to the multitude the story of Haman, as a lesson
appropriate to the subject. A great alarm then arose, some
crying, "God and the king!" others, "God and the kirk!"
until the whole people of Edinburgh rose in arms, and none
knew for what purpose. Some also called out, "The sword
of the Lord and of Gideon!" others shouted, "Bring forth
the wicked Haman!" Mischief of some kind would certainly have been done had it not been for the sense and

courage of a stout citizen named John Watt, smith, who
was principal deacon of the craftsmen of Edinburgh. He
caused the artisans of the several incorporations to take
arms, and coming at their head, demanded to see his majesty. The king showed himself from the window, and received the loyal proffer of the citizens to live or die with
him. The tumult being in some degree composed, John
Watt, with the trades as they are called, escorted the king
safely to the abbey of Holyrood, and the night ended peaceably. In the meantime the clergy, and such barons, gentry
and citizens as adhered to them, drew up a petition to the
following purpose: They prayed that professed papists
should be sent from court; that the president, the lord
advocate, and Mr. Elphinstone should be discharged from
the council, as enemies to religion; that all the acts of council, proclamations and others unfavorable to religion, passed
within the last five weeks, should be repealed; that the commissioners of the Church, and the burgesses who were banished, should be recalled by proclamation; that the order
for subscribing the bond of obedience should be discharged
as prejudicial to the Gospel; lastly, that an act of council
should be made, recognizing as lawful whatever had been
done by the actors in that day's disturbance. By the proposal of such high terms, which, indeed, comprehended
everything which was in question between the crown and
the Church, and decided all in favor of the latter, it is evident that the ministers entertained a mistaken belief that
the victory was their own, if they could only maintain firmness enough to take advantage of the tumult, which, it was
supposed, must have made a deep impression upon the king's
mind. The petition was committed to the charge of a select
party of the assembled clergy and gentry; and though the
hour was late and the night dark they were required to proceed to the palace without loss of time, to deliver it to James
in person. As they left the town of Edinburgh, however,
and entered the more courtly suburb of the Canongate, the
news which they received was unfavorable to their mission.

The Laird of Bargany, the principal person among them, was taken aside by a friend, who informed him that the king was irritated to the highest degree at the proceedings of the day, and that whoever should apply to him with such proposals as he and his companions were intrusted with must necessarily be in danger of incurring his severe displeasure. On receiving this intimation, Bargany excused himself from proceeding further upon the embassy; and those who were conjoined with him in the commission declined interfering in a business from which the principal commissioner withdrew himself. So the purpose of the petition was no further insisted on that night.

On the next morning a new scene opened. The king and council had left Holyrood early in the morning; and a proclamation was published at the cross of Edinburgh, stating that the seditious and armed tumult of the preceding day, the irreverence used toward his majesty's person, and the audacity of the clergymen, by whom the citizens had been encouraged to put themselves in arms, had rendered the capital an unfit place for the administration of justice. Therefore the courts of session, the sheriffs, and other judicial persons of every sort, connected with the courts of justice, were commanded to withdraw themselves from the said town of Edinburgh, and hold themselves in readiness to repair to such place as his majesty should assign; and a strict prohibition was laid on all nobles, barons, and others, discharging them from assembling either in Edinburgh or elsewhere without his majesty's license, under pain of his severe displeasure.

The trade in the metropolis at that time greatly depended upon the residence of the nobility, gentry, and others who attended the court, and that of the great number of residents brought thither to attend the courts of law. On such serious intimation of the king's displeasure, the citizens began to consider the necessary consequences to themselves and to the city, and looking sadly upon each other, seemed generally to desire that some accommodation might be resorted to. The ministers evinced greater courage, and used their utmost endeavors to induce the laity to join them, and to subscribe a bond, which they drew up, binding themselves to abide by the defence of the Protestant religion in those points in which it was now assailed. They applied, especially, to the Lord Hamilton and to the Lord of Buccleuch, inviting them to repair to Edinburgh and countenance the cause of religion. They resolved to excommunicate the lord president and the advocate, and only postponed doing so that the ceremony might be perfected with more solemnity at the next general assembly. Meanwhile they appointed fasts and sermons, in order to maintain and encourage the spirit of the people. The tenor of these discourses might be conceived from one preached by John Welsh in the High Church, in which he said the king was possessed with a devil, and that one devil being driven out of him, seven worse were entered in the room thereof; so that the subjects were legally entitled to arise and take the sword out of his hand, as in the case of the father of a family seized with a frenzy, whose children and servants are in these circumstances entitled to disarm and to bind him. They also spread reports that the Earl of Errol had come as far as the Queen's Ferry with five hundred horse, and had only returned on hearing of the tumult at Edinburgh. By thus taking upon themselves the odium of being the causers of the sedition, the ministers evidently showed that they remembered how Knox, in the days of Queen Mary, had, by the energy of his preaching, animated the multitude, given courage to the nobility, kept alive hope when it was well-nigh extinct, and remained victorious in the end. But they forgot that John Knox advocated the general cause of reformation of the Church and liberty of conscience, while they only wished to interest the feelings of others in defence of immunities claimed by the clergy, the propriety of which was extremely dubious: they had also forgotten that the nobles and barons who stood so firmly by the first Scottish reformers had in their view the private advantages which might arise to them from the occupation of the property belonging to the Catholic Church. The ministers on the present occasion had no such bribe to offer; and they might have remembered the proverb then current, that "Men cannot lure hawks with empty hands."

It proved as might have been expected: Lord Hamilton carried to the king the letter which invited him to put himself at the head of the godly barons, who by the word and motion of the blessed Spirit had gone to arms, and invited him to Edinburgh for that purpose. King James was extremely offended by this epistle, addressed to one so near to him in blood. It does not appear what answer was made by Buccleuch, to whom a similar invitation was made; but he was certainly no way disposed to avail himself of it.

The first vindictive movement of the king was a letter commanding the magistrates of Edinburgh to imprison the ministers. They received timely information, however; and finding their hopes of obtaining the support which they had expected altogether vain, they fled to England, to escape the displeasure of the king. Deputations were in vain sent by the town of Edinburgh; for although the sturdy John Watt was of the number, to whom, probably, James owed his life, by his firmness during the tumult, they could not obtain an audience of James. He said that "fair and humble words could not excuse so gross a fault; and that ere long he should come to Edinburgh in person, and let them know that he was their king." The tumult was by the council declared to have been treason; and all who were accomplices or maintainers in the same were declared liable to the doom of traitors. Language was even held at court which authorized more terrible suspicions; for it had been said that the destruction of the city was the only punishment which could atone for their sacrilegious insurrection.

It was, however, James's secret intention not to injure, but only to intimidate and humble his capital. For this purpose he summoned the attendants of Highland nobles and the chiefs of border clans with their followers, wild in speech, aspect, habit, and manners, formidable from their renown as lawless depredators, and most likely to strike terror into the inhabitants of a peaceful metropolis, possessed of a comparative degree of wealth. Attended by such an ominous retinue, James prepared to return to his capital, in all the terrors of offended majesty surrounded by the means of vengeance.

The alarm in the capital was great; and is best described by the burgher journalist Birrel, who witnessed the scene and shared in the alarm: "On the last day of December, 1596, the king came to Holyrood House; and command was given, by open proclamation, that on the morrow the Earl of Mar should keep the West Port, while Lord Livingstone, Buccleuch, Cessford, and sundry others, should guard the High Street. At this time, and before, there was a great rumor among the townsmen that the king designed to send in Will of Kinmont, the common thief, with as many Southland men as should plunder the town of Edinburgh. Upon this rumor the merchants took their merchandise out of their booths or shops, and transported the same to the strongest houses that were in the town, where they remained with their servants, looking for nothing but a general scene of plunder. In like manner the craftsmen and ordinary citizens removed themselves with their best goods, as it were ten or twelve households, into one which was the strongest house, and might be best defended from being spoiled or burned, and there watched, armed with hackbut, pistol, and such other weapons as might best defend them. Judge, gentle reader," says the honest annalist, "if this were play!" On the morning the streets and points of strength of the city were occupied by the lords and clans appointed for that purpose, and the capital was thus placed at the absolute disposal of the sovereign. The king, attended by a great retinue of his nobility, entered the city, and rode up the High Street, through the ranks of these unwonted guards. The provost and magistrates made the submission on their knees, and underwent a long harangue upon the character of their offence. A large sum of money, the best mediator upon the occasion, was disbursed by the city to propitiate their sovereign; and Edinburgh was deprived for a time of several of its most honorable privileges. Notwithstanding there was among the citizens general congratulation and rejoicing at their escape, even on these hard terms, from Will Kinmont, the Southland men, and the fear of universal plunder. The effect of suppressed insurrection, especially if the explosion has been in no degree formidable, and if the extinction has been decisive, is always that of strengthening the party against whom it has been raised. This proved eminently the case with the tumults of Edinburgh. The king availed himself of them to control the power of the Church, as well in the violence used in their sermons as in several of their rights of jurisdiction and discipline. But the dispute between James and the Church of Scotland upon this occasion was productive of more lasting effects, nor were the mortal offence and aversion which James entertained upon this occasion forgotten or forgiven during his whole reign. It was a sense of the violence displayed by the churchmen, not so much in inciting a meditated insurrection, for the tumult appears to have been entirely accidental, as the desire they showed to avail themselves of the popular discontent to raise a civil war, which rendered James from that period desirous once more to introduce into the Scottish discipline the institution of bishops, by which, in the English and most Lutheran churches, the republican system of Calvin was tempered with a hierarchy of priesthood; which united the whole order, to a certain degree, with the crown.

It is easy to see how, at an earlier period, the Scottish clergy, by using their privileges moderately, might have insured a longer possession of them. For at the period of the king's return from Denmark he was favorably disposed to their measures, system, and authority; and, naturally inclined to peace, would have been little disposed to seek a quarrel with so powerful a party, if they had shown the least disposition to abstain from an actual collision with his

authority.   As it was, the gauntlet was thrown down; nor
was the contest desisted from until dissension and blood of
a whole century had at length brought the dispute to a
termination.

James had, indeed, reinstated the lay jurisdiction in all
the powers of controlling the Church judicatories, or the
clergy at large, in the full force in which the restraint had
existed by the act of 1584.   But he was shrewd enough to
perceive that this could only lead to a perpetual contest of
dubious issue, arising from collisions between the civil and
ecclesiastical jurisdiction, which the former might not be
always willing to enforce, and which the clergy, in every
instance, would be certain to resist.   By introducing into
the Church a superior body of clergy, having a higher rank
in the State and a place in the legislature, he hoped he might
be able to give the crown, with whom the promotion must
necessarily rest, an influence among the clergy in general,
and the power of securing a party of supporters in church
assemblies and church judicatories.   But in this he was
compelled to act with extreme caution.

We have already mentioned that the ancient order of
bishops had fallen into general contempt with the clergy
and people, their funds being seized on by the crown and
their persons held in contempt by the people at large.   The
king of Scots prevailed upon a commission of assembly to
petition the parliament, that, as the clergy had during
former ages been entitled to representation in that body,
which had lately been entirely discontinued, a certain number of the most qualified of the clergy should again be entitled to a seat there.   The parliament, in compliance with
this request, enacted, that those ministers upon whom the
king might confer vacant bishoprics or abbacies, should have
the right of sitting in parliament; but it was remitted to the
general assembly of the Church to declare what degree of
authority the members possessing this privilege should hold
over their brethren in the Church.   This scheme was most
fiercely opposed by the severe Calvinists, with whom the

general quality of churchmen and its pure republican form
was a principal recommendation of the Presbyterian system.
They were not deceived by the fair pretexts held out by the
present scheme, in which they saw at bottom the provision
for an order of clergy privileged above their brethren by the
enjoyment of political power and superior right. "Cover it
as you list," said an old Calvinist leader, "busk it as bonnily
as you will, I see the horns of the mitre." But notwithstanding a determined opposition, the general assembly at
length, by the exertion of much influence over individuals,
and the hopes of preferment held out to many, was prevailed
upon to declare the lawfulness of ministers sitting in parliament, and the expediency of the Church having a representation there. These representatives, however, were to be
chosen in the following manner: A general assembly of the
Church was to present a list of six persons to any benefice
having title to a seat in parliament, out of which list the
king should choose one for holding the same. All jurisdiction and authority over their brethren was strictly renounced
and prohibited by the persons so chosen; and although they
were to be considered as the representatives of the ecclesiastical body in parliament, strict precautions were taken that,
except in that body, the person promoted to a privileged
benefice should be merely an ordinary pastor, bound to do
his duty like others in his cure, and asserting no superiority
over his brethren. This was only a step, in the purpose of
James VI., to introduce the hierarchy of bishops into the
Scottish Church. But he was content with what he had
gained, reckoning upon the power of making further advances by degrees; and the Calvinists, on their part, thought
this innovation dangerous less for its present extent than the
probability of its leading to further alterations.

CHAPTER XL

SINCE the king had attained a decisive victory over the discontented churchmen, Scotland had enjoyed, for so disorderly a country, an unusual degree of serenity. But an event was now to take place, most singular in all its circumstances, which, in the first place, placed James's life in extreme hazard, and has since, even down to the present day, entailed upon his memory, though most unjustly, a degree of doubt, as if some point of policy or purpose of revenge had induced him to hazard a very desperate crime for the purpose of destroying two persons of noble birth. In fact, the celebrated Gowrie conspiracy, which we are now approaching, is one of those mysterious transactions of which we can never expect a complete explanation; since those who calmly investigate or peruse history can never conceive the power of false views and erroneous motives acting on the minds of men who, from strong and peculiar excitement, engage in dangerous, secret, and criminal adventures. They are generally undertaken by persons whose minds are so much warped at the moment from the natural and moral bias, that the actors cannot be properly termed sane, nor are the principles upon which they act such as can be estimated by men who, undisturbed by passion or prejudice, are in the ordinary possession of their reasoning powers.

The reader must turn his recollection back to the Raid of Ruthven, a treasonable violence committed upon the king's person while he was yet a boy. The Earl of Gowrie, who lent his house for the purposes of the conspiracy, was considered as its principal conductor, and in the end became its victim, being executed at Dundee in the manner already related. He left a large family of sons and daughters, who, by their father's death and confiscation, were reduced to considerable necessity. The eldest son was, by the king's humanity, restored to the family estate and honors, in the year 1586, and died two years afterward, in 1588: he was succeeded by his second brother, John, the third earl of Gowrie, who went abroad in August, 1594. This nobleman was a youth of quick parts and fine accomplishments, and made great proficiency in all the graceful and manly exercises, which were supposed to be best taught in France and Italy. Neither did the young earl neglect the pursuits of learning and science, though, it may be observed, those which he most eagerly followed were such as promised to extend the knowledge of man beyond its natural sphere, and to engage those who persevere in them in difficult and mysterious undertakings of precarious success. This may be gathered from some indications which appear in the proof concerning the earl's character. It was said, that a party with which he was hunting having found and slain an adder in the moors, the Earl of Gowrie told his companions that, had they not killed the reptile, he would have shown them the power of the cabala of the Jews, by pronouncing such a charm as should have arrested the adder and made it incapable of leaving the spot. He was known, besides, to carry upon him papers inscribed with spells and characters, containing, perhaps, the horoscope of his nativity, and was angry when they were meddled with, or questions asked concerning them. His conversation, at times, turned upon the subject of conspiracies against princes; upon which he was known to observe, that all such plots as were upon record were foolishly devised, too many people being admitted into a secret which can only be safe and successful while concealed within the breast of the deviser. The clergyman to whom he used this language advised him to lay aside such speculations, and betake himself to safer studies; but the discourse was not of a kind to attract much attention at the time. These things were considered as indicative of a turn to secrecy, and to machinations of a dangerous character. In the present age they can only be considered as traits of character.

The Earl of Gowrie's younger brother, Alexander Ruthven, was a young man of great hopes, and both were considered as possessing a share of the king's favor. Learned, handsome, young, and active, they belonged to the class of men which most readily attracted the king's notice; and generous, brave, and religious to a degree not common with men so young, they were the darlings of the people. Alexander Ruthven was made a gentleman of the bed-chamber; one of his sisters advanced to be a chief attendant upon the queen; a considerable post in the government was designed for Gowrie himself; and no house in the kingdom appeared more flourishing, at the very time when a number of violent and mysterious circumstances brought on its total ruin.

On the 5th of August, 1600, as the king, then residing at Falkland, had taken horse at daybreak to follow his favorite exercise of stag-hunting, he was joined by Alexander Ruthven, who requested a private audience, and communicated to James, as they rode together, apart from the other huntsmen, a story of a most extraordinary kind. He had been, he said, walking near his brother's house at Perth, when, in a retired spot, he encountered a fellow of a down-looking aspect, and altogether suspicious in his appearance, who was wrapped in a cloak, and seemed desirous to escape observation. Ruthven continued that, conceiving it his duty to lay hands on this man, he had, in so doing, discovered on his person a large pot full of gold pieces of foreign coinage. He then deemed it his duty, he said, to carry the stranger to his brother's castle, and privately imprison him, in a remote apartment, in order that his majesty might have the earliest information upon a subject so extraordinary; he urged the king, therefore, to ride with him instantly to his brother, the Earl of Gowrie's castle, in the town of Perth, examine the captive himself, and secure the treasure for his own royal use. The king replied that he saw no reason why the man should not be regularly examined by the magistrates of Perth, of whom the Earl of Gowrie was provost. This proceeding young Ruthven eagerly opposed; alleging the necessity that a matter so mysterious should be subjected to the king's own scrutiny, so much deeper than that of any subject, and stating eagerly the risk of the treasure being embezzled, if any inferior person was to be trusted with the examination. He, therefore, repeatedly urged James instantly to ride with him to Perth; and this in a manner so hurried and vehement that the king was induced to ask some of his attendants whether Ruthven had ever been known to be affected with fits of insanity: they replied that they had never known him, save as a sober and sensible young man. Reassured by this information, feeling, it may be supposed, the compliment paid to his superior wisdom, and desirous to secure a windfall which did not often come in his way, James agreed that as soon as he had seen the buck killed he would accompany Alexander Ruthven to Perth, and examine the prisoner.

During the whole chase, which was a short one, Ruthven hung upon the king, and at every opportunity which it afforded plied him with earnest importunity to set out upon his journey. It must be observed that a person named Andrew Henderson, a dependent upon the Earl of Gowrie, and whose part in this affair is not the least extraordinary in the whole mystery, was then at a distance in attendance upon Alexander Ruthven, who, after his conferences with the king, ordered Henderson to ride back with the utmost speed to Perth, and announce to the Earl of Gowrie that the king was coming immediately to Gowrie House with a small company. Henderson reached Perth about ten o'clock in the morning. So soon as ever the earl saw him, he came apart from the persons with whom he was speaking, and inquired secretly what tidings he had brought him from his brother Alexander. Henderson delivered the message which he had received from Mr. Ruthven; adding, he had no letter to his brother, which the Earl of Gowrie seemed to have expected. Henderson then asked what service his lordship had for him to do, who, within an hour afterward, bid him put on his armor, as he had a Highlander to take prisoner in the town of Perth. It does not appear that the Earl of Gowrie at this time made any preparation to receive the king, although apprised of his approach, nor did he even put off the service of his own dinner until that of his majesty should be provided. On the contrary, he proceeded to his own meal, with one or two chance guests who happened to be in the castle, at the usual hour of half-past twelve o'clock. Their dinner was scarcely finished when notice was given of the king's near approach.

Upon the death of the stag, the king fulfilled his promise of riding to Perth with Mr. Ruthven; but before this, which is material, by the by, to the evidence of the case, he communicated to the Duke of Lennox the story of the treasure which had been found. The duke replied he did not think the tale a likely one. In consequence, perhaps, of this communication, the duke, the Earl of Mar, and a small train of gentlemen followed the king to Perth. They were met by the Earl of Gowrie, who, although he appeared surprised at the visit, conducted him to his mansion, a large Gothic building, walled in and defended by towers, and having a garden or pleasure-ground which extended straight down to the river Tay. The king, according to etiquette, dined by

CHARLES EDWARD, THE PRETENDER

Scotland, vol. two

himself. Lord Lennox, the Earl of Mar, and his train, had their repast served in another apartment. The dinner was cold and ill-arranged; and everything had the air of haste and precipitation, which need not have existed had the Earl of Gowrie been disposed to avail himself of the timely information which he had received from Henderson. The conduct of the entertainer himself was cold, abstracted, and unequal, unlike to that expected from a subject who is honored with the presence of his sovereign as a guest. When the king had dined, he good-humoredly reminded the Earl of Gowrie that he ought to go into the next room and drink a cup of welcome to the lords and gentlemen of his train. Gowrie did so; and upon his leaving the room, his brother Alexander whispered to the king that this was the fitting time to inquire into the business of the prisoner and the money pot. The king was, apparently, not altogether void of suspicion, though probably it extended no further than a floating idea that Ruthven, whose tale and conduct were so extraordinary, might possibly, after all, be distracted. He had, therefore, in the course of their journey to Perth, privately desired the Duke of Lennox to take notice where he should pass with Alexander Ruthven, and to follow him. But as they were in separate chambers, the duke had no opportunity to observe the charge given to him.

Alexander Ruthven conducted the king from chamber to chamber, until he introduced him into a large gallery, at the angles of which were two rounds or turrets, which gave room, as is usual in such buildings, the one to a small closet or cabinet, the other to a private passage called a turnpike stair. On Ruthven's opening that which constituted a cabinet, the king discovered, to his surprise, a man not bound or captive, but armed and at liberty.

This was Henderson, already mentioned, whom the brothers had employed in their plan, though they had not deemed it safe to trust him with its purpose. His deposition bore, that after his return from Falkland, and his assuming his armor by the earl's orders, Gowrie had asked him for the key of the gallery chamber. It was not at first to be found, so little were things prepared for an attempt so dangerous. Being at length found, the earl commanded Henderson to go there, and to act as he should be directed by his brother Alexander. Henderson obeyed with the unresisting and ready submission of a vassal of the time; and Ruthven planted him in the little cabinet in which he was found, and locked him in. These preparations made, the man became afraid where all this might end. Left alone in the cabinet, he prayed to God to guard him from approaching evil; and after waiting about half an hour, Ruthven and the king appeared. The account of the extraordinary scene which followed rests upon the evidence of the king and Henderson. They agree in the main, but differ in several minute particulars. This is in no way surprising. Upon scarce any occasion do the witnesses of a perturbed, violent, and agitating scene agree minutely in narrating what has passed before their eyes; and there often exist circumstances of discrepancy much more remarkable than any that occur in the present case, which, nevertheless, are not considered as affecting the general truth and consistency of the evidence. The truth is, that the surprise or shock which the mind receives when an individual witnesses anything very extraordinary has an operation in preventing exact circumstantial recollection of what has passed, and the witness, insensibly on his own part, is, in the detail of minute particulars, extremely apt to substitute the suggestions of imagination for those of recollection. There may be also seen, in the varieties of the king's declaration and the evidence of Henderson, a desire on the part of each to set his own conduct in the best point of view; Henderson taking the merit of assisting the king in one or two instances, where James ascribes his safety to his own personal exertions.

The outline of the fact is this: So soon as Ruthven and the king entered the cabinet, the former exchanged the deference of a subject for the demeanor of an assassin: he threw his hat upon his head, snatched a dagger from the side of

Andrew Henderson, and placing the point to the king's breast, said, "Sir, you must be my prisoner. Think on my father's death." Henderson pushed the weapon aside. As the king attempted to speak, Ruthven replied, "Hold your tongue, or, by Heaven, you shall die!"—"Alexander," replied the king, "think upon our intimacy, and remember that at the time of your father's death I was but a minor, and the council might have done anything they pleased. Even should you slay me you cannot possess the crown; for I have both sons and daughters, and friends, and faithful subjects, who will not leave my death unavenged."—Ruthven replied by swearing that he neither sought the king's life nor blood.—"What, then, is it you demand?" said the king.—"It is but a promise," answered the conspirator, who seems to have been irresolute, or intimidated.—"What promise?" demanded James; and added, with becoming spirit, "What though you were to take off your hat."—"My brother will tell you," replied Ruthven, uncovering, in obedience to the king's command.—"Fetch him hither," said the king. And Ruthven, having first taken James's word that he would not open the window or raise any alarm, left him, in order, as he pretended, to seek his brother, although, as Henderson says, he thinks that Ruthven never stirred from the gallery. He retired, most probably, only with the purpose of fortifying his own failing resolution, or preparing the means of binding the king. During his absence, the king demanded of Henderson how he came there. "As I live," answered the poor man, much alarmed by all that had passed in his presence, "I was shut up here like a dog." The king then asked if the Ruthvens would do him any injury. "As I live," answered Henderson, "I will die ere I witness it." The king, finding this person at his command, desired him to open the window of the turret. It had two, one of which looked down toward the castle garden and the river side, the other to the courtyard in front of the castle. The king, with the presence of mind which he seems to have maintained during the whole transaction, see-

ing that Henderson opened the former of those windows,
from which no alarm could be given, called out that he undid the wrong window.   Henderson was going to the other,
when Ruthven again entered, with a garter in his hand, and
laid violent hands upon his majesty, declaring there was no
remedy.   James, replying with indignation that he was a
free prince, and would not be bound, resisted Ruthven manfully, and, though much inferior to him in strength and
stature, had rather the better of the struggle.   Henderson,
who appears to have been confounded with terror, and divided between his respect for the king and for his feudal
lord, took no part in the struggle, otherwise than by snatch-
ing the garter from Ruthven's hand, and, as he says, Alexander's hand from the king's mouth.   Ruthven had expected
his co-operation; for he exclaimed, "Woe worth thee! is there
no help in thee?"   Meantime the king, by violent exertion,
dragged the conspirator as far as the second window, which
Henderson opened.   The king then, still struggling with
Ruthven, called out "Treason!" and "Help!" and was
heard by his followers in the courtyard below.

   We must here give some account how the royal train
came to be so opportunely within hearing of their master's
cries.   After drinking the pledge which had been recommended by the king, the Duke of Lennox and the rest of
the royal retinue arose from table; the former recollecting
the charge which he had to follow his majesty, when he
should see him go out with Ruthven.   The Earl of Gowrie,
however, alleged that the king desired to be private for a
few minutes; and calling for the key of his garden, carried
his visitors to walk there until James should descend.   They
had stayed there but a few minutes when John Cranstoun,
a retainer or friend of the earl, came into the garden, and
said that the king was on horseback, and already past the
middle of the South Inch, upon his return to Falkland.   The
Duke of Lennox and the other attendants of James, conceiving them failing in their duty, instantly hastened out of the
garden toward the courtyard, and called to horse.   The

porter at the gate informed them the king had not passed. As they stood in surprise, the Earl of Gowrie entreated them to stay till he should obtain sure information concerning the king's motions. He entered the house, and returning almost immediately, declared that the king was actually set forth.

The porter still contradicted the report of his master, replying to the royal attendants that the king must be still in the mansion, since he could not have gone out without his having seen him. "Thou liest, knave!" exclaimed the earl; and to reconcile his own account with that of his servant, Gowrie alleged that the king was gone forth at a postern-gate. "It is impossible, my lord," answered the porter, "for I am in possession of the key of that postern." During this dispute cries of treason and help were heard from the turret. "That is the king's voice," said the Duke of Lennox, "be he where he will." James's attendants looked up to the window from whence the noise was heard, and perceived the head of the king partly thrust out at the window, inflamed by struggling, and a hand grasping him by the throat.

The greater part of the king's attendants reentered the mansion by the principal gate to hasten to their master's assistance, while Sir Thomas Erskine and others threw themselves upon the Earl of Gowrie, accusing him of treason. Gowrie, with the assistance of Thomas Cranstoun and others his retainers and servants, extricated himself from their grasp, and at first fled a little way up the street; then halted, and drew two swords, which, according to a fashion of the time practiced in Italy, he carried in the same scabbard. "What will you do, my lord?" said Cranstoun, who attended with the purpose of seconding him. "I will either make my way to my own house," said the earl, adopting, it would seem, a desperate resolution, "or I will die for it." He rushed on, followed by Cranstoun and other friends and domestics, who also drew their swords. A lackey, named Crooshanks, threw a steel head-piece upon

the earl's head as he passed. Cranstoun, for the least circumstance is of importance in a case of minute evidence,
called to one Craigengelt to keep the back yett, meaning
a postern giving exit to a secret staircase which descended
from the gallery into the court. Craigengelt, accordingly,
seconded by others, defended that door, which had already,
however, given access to some of the king's retinue.

A dreadful scene in the meanwhile was taking place in
Gowrie House. Lennox, Mar, and by far the greater part
of the king's attendants, endeavored to find their way to the
place of the king's confinement by the public staircase of
the castle; but this only conducted them to the outer door
of the gallery, within which, and from one of its extremities,
opened the fatal cabinet in which the king and Alexander
Ruthven were still grappling with each other.

It must be remembered that a scene, the details of which
take some time in narrating, passed in the course of two
or three minutes. Sir John Ramsay, a page of James, who
had in keeping his majesty's hawk, had heard James's cry
of distress; and while the other attendants of the king ran
up the main staircase, he lighted by accident upon a small
turnpike or winding stair which led to the cabinet in which
the struggle was still taking place. Alarmed by the noise
and shuffling of feet, he exerted his whole strength in such
a manner as to force open the door at the head of that turnpike, which introduced him into the fatal cabinet. The king
and Ruthven were still wrestling together; and although
James had forced his antagonist almost upon his knees,
Ruthven had still his hand upon James's face and mouth.
He also saw another form, that of the passive Andrew Henderson, who left the closet almost the instant he saw Ramsay
enter.

The page, at the sight of his master's danger, cast the
king's hawk from his hand, and drew his whinger, or hunting sword. The king, at that moment of emergency, called
out, "Fie! strike him low, for he has a pine doublet"—meaning a secret shirt of mail under his garments. Ramsay

stabbed Ruthven accordingly; and James lending his assistance, they thrust the wounded man down the turnpike by
which Ramsay had ascended. Voices and steps were now
heard advancing upward; and Ramsay knowing the accents
called out to Sir Thomas Erskine to come up the turnpike
stair, even to the head. Sir Thomas Erskine was accompanied by Sir Hugh Harris, the king's physician, a lame
man, and unfit for fighting. Near the bottom of the turnpike Sir Thomas Erskine in his ascent met Ruthven, bleed-
ing in the face and neck, and called out, "Fie! strike! this
is the traitor"; on which Alexander Ruthven was run
through the body, having only breath remaining to say,
"Alas! I had no blame of it."

Sir Thomas Erskine pressed to the head of the staircase,
where he found the king and Ramsay alone. "I thought,"
said Erskine, "your majesty would have trusted me so much
as at least to have commanded me to await at the door for
your protection, if you had not thought it meet to take me
with you." James replied, and the words first spoken in
such a moment of agitation are always worthy of notice,
"Alas! the traitor deceived me in that as he did in the rest;
for I commanded him to bring you to me, but he only went
out and locked the door."

At this point of the extraordinary transaction the Earl
of Gowrie entered with a drawn sword in each hand, a steel
bonnet on his head, and six servants following him in arms.
In the chamber there were only three of the king's retinue,
Sir Hugh Harris, Sir John Ramsay, and Sir Thomas Erskine, with one Wilson, a servant. Of these, Sir Hugh Harris
might be considered as unfit for combat. They thrust the
king back into the turret closet, and turned to encounter
Gowrie and his servants, exasperated as they were by the
death of Alexander Ruthven, whose body they had found
at the bottom of the turnpike stair. The battle was for a
short time fierce and unequal on the part of the king's retinue; but Erskine having exclaimed to the Earl of Gowrie,
"Traitor, you have slain our master, and now you would

murder us!" the earl, as if astonished, dropped the point of his sword, and Erskine in the same moment ran him through the body. The thrust was fatal, and the earl fell dead, without a single word. His servants and assistants fled.

The king's composure during this dangerous tumult was marked by a singular circumstance. The hawk which Ramsay had, in the first moment of alarm, flung from his hand, was flying at large through the apartment; and the king, either from instinctive habit, which will sometimes govern men's motions in moments of great danger, or else from a presence of mind little consistent with his general character, put his foot upon the leash, and so kept the bird safe during the mortal scuffle.

The uproar was not yet over: a dreadful noise was heard at the door of the gallery. This proved to be the Duke of Lennox, the Earl of Mar, and the greater part of the king's attendants, who had come up the main stair of the castle, found the door of the gallery locked, and, hearing the clashing of swords and tumult within, were endeavoring to force their entrance by violence. Those within having learned who they were undid the door to admit them, and thus the king's retinue was assembled around him in the gallery.

But the adventures of the day were not yet closed, nor its dangers ended. The deceased Earl of Gowrie had been exceedingly beloved in the town of Perth, of which he was provost. His retainers, who had seen him fall, and probably knew nothing more than that he had been slain by the king's attendants, spread a wild alarm through the town, calling out, Murder and revenge! A furious multitude was speedily assembled, who ran headlong to Gowrie House; some carrying a large beam to be used as a battering-ram, others calling for powder to blow up the mansion; and all declaring that if their provost was not delivered to them in safety the king and his green-coats should smoke for it. The domestics of Gowrie were among the populace, calling loudly that they were all unworthy of such a provost who would not fight in revenge of his death. The moment seemed extremely critical; for the king's retinue had no weapons but hunting-knives, and especially had no firearms. The magistrates of the town, however, threw themselves among the rioters, and by their remonstrances assuaged their fury. The king himself spoke to them from the window—gave some information of the circumstances in which he was placed, and succeeded in pacifying the tumult and dispersing the rioters. After all was quiet he returned to Falkland, having passed through a day of great peril and violent excitation.

The scene which had passed was of a most unintelligible description, and for a length of time nothing seemed to render it explicable. Henderson, who had played so strange and passive a part, surrendered on promise of pardon, but his evidence threw very little light upon the extraordinary transaction. According to his own account, he knew nothing earthly about the traitorous transaction to which he had so strangely been a witness. Three friends and servants of the Earl of Gowrie who had assisted him in his battles with the king's retinue, and were afterward officious and active in the tumult, were tried, condemned, and executed, protesting with their last breath they knew nothing about the transactions of the day further than that they took part with their master.

Viewed in every light, the conspiracy seemed to the public one of the darkest and most extraordinary which ever agitated the general mind; and it cannot be wondered that very different conclusions were formed concerning it. The king was particularly touched in point of honor in making good his own story; but experienced no small difficulty from the mystery which hung over the bloody incident. Faction and religious prejudice lent their aid to disturb men's comprehension of what was in itself so mystical. Many doubted the king's report altogether, and conceived it more likely that the brothers should have fallen by some deceit on the part of the king and court, than that they

should have attempted treason against the life or liberty of
the sovereign in circumstances so very improbable. Many
of the clergymen, particularly, continued to retain most
absolute incredulity upon the subject; and he was thought
no bad politician who found an evasion by saying that
he believed the story because the king told it; but that
he would not have given credit to his own eyes had he
seen it.

The ministers of Edinburgh were peculiarly resolute in
refusing to give avowed credit to the king's account of the
conspiracy, and took the most public measures to show their
incredulity. The council having required them to return
solemn thanks from their pulpits for the deliverance of
James, they excused themselves, saying that they had no
acquaintance with the particulars of the danger which the
king was said to have escaped. It was replied to them that
their minute acquaintance with the affair was not necessary;
it was enough for them to know that the king had been
delivered from a great danger. They answered, with imper-
turbable pertinacity, that the pulpit being the chair of truth,
nothing ought to be said from thence of which the speaker
was not himself perfectly convinced. This mode of appeal-
ing to his subjects being intercepted, the king caused the
privy council to appear in public at the market-cross, where
the bishop of Ross, after a narrative of the king's danger
and deliverance, expressed a public thanksgiving, in which
the populace seemed frankly to join. On the Monday following, the king attended in person at the market-cross,
where a sermon was preached by his own minister, Mr.
Patrick Galloway, in which he dilated on all the particulars
of the conspiracy. An order for a solemn and public thanksgiving on a day fixed was then sent forth, and the divines
who should scruple to perform the duty of the day were
threatened with banishment. Most of the recusants submitted, after some altercation. "You have heard me, you
have heard my minister; what assurance can you desire
more?" said the king.

"Your majesty," said one of these reverend men, "ought not to have been so hasty as to have slain the master of Ruthven upon the spot: you should have had the fear of Heaven before your eyes."

The king, irritated beyond patience, replied, "I tell thee, man, I had neither heaven nor hell before my eyes: I was in mortal fear of my life."

All the clergy at length submitted to the king's pleasure, except the Reverend Robert Bruce, who could be brought no further than to say he would reverence his majesty's reports of the accident; but could not say he was persuaded of the truth of it. He was banished for his incredulity, and repaired to France.

The parliament, by giving the fullest credit to the king's account of the accident, may be supposed to have designed to console him for the incredulity of the clergy. They heard the witnesses upon the trial, and not only pronounced sentence of forfeiture against the deceased brothers, but disinherited their whole posterity, and proscribed the very name of Ruthven. Honorable rewards and titles were bestowed on Sir Thomas Erskine, Sir John Ramsay, and Sir Hugh Harris, who had been the instruments of James's preservation. Alms were dispersed, and every other means adopted which could impress upon the people the reality of the king's danger and the sincerity of his gratitude to Heaven for a providential deliverance. But it is an observation of Tacitus that one of the misfortunes of princes is that conspiracies against them are not believed until they are carried into fatal effect.

A considerable party in James's kingdom, thinking, perhaps, better of his audacity and worse of his morals than either the one or the other deserved, still refused to believe that the king's danger had been real, or the death of Gowrie and his brother on the memorable 5th of August excusable. Their arguments rested upon the string of improbabilities of which it is impossible to divest the story, and which, indeed, can only be refuted by opposing to them the greater difficulties which attend the embracing a different solution. It was said to be grossly improbable that, meditating so violent an action, a principal part should have been intrusted to a man like Henderson, totally unacquainted with the deep purpose in which he was engaged, and, as it appeared, of too vacillating and hesitating a character to give the support required and expected; it was noticed that his evidence, though in general it agreed with the narrative of James himself, differed, as we have already observed, in some more minute particulars.

It was also remarked that, supposing the conspiracy to be real, every circumstance necessary to carry it into effect was left unprovided till the very last moment. The key of the gallery chamber, the designed place of the attack on the king's person, had to be sought for only an hour or two before James's arrival at Perth; and so little preparation seemed to be made for any deed of violence that, when Ruthven wanted to intimidate James into submission, he was obliged to snatch out Henderson's dagger, having no weapon of his own but a walking rapier. Their train were no less unprovided. Craigengelt, Lord Gowrie's steward, sought his own room and his master's ere he could light on the two-handed sword which he used in the fray. In short, all was so ill prepared that huntsmen might be said to take more precaution and make greater preparation for destroying a stag than these men thought necessary to the murder of a king.

Others have been disposed to allow a hypothesis, inferring that Alexander Ruthven, actuated by some wild passion of his own, was actually guilty of the attack upon the king's person, but that his brother was not conscious of it, nor accessory to it. They who hold this opinion insist that the earl's own conduct is to be very naturally explained by the circumstances as they arose. When Sir Thomas Erskine, say they, assailed the Earl of Gowrie before the gate of his house, nothing was so natural as that he should shake him off, or that, having freed himself from Erskine's gripe, he should attempt to regain his own castle; or, finally, that, finding his brother's dead body lying across the threshold, the earl should have attempted to revenge it upon those of the king's retinue whom he found with hands and swords bloody from the recent slaughter. They found, too, on these the minute circumstance of Gowrie's death; and remark, that when he was charged with the king's murder he sunk his sword's point in astonishment, and omitted to parry the fatal thrust which was in that moment dealt to him.

We shall mention what occurs in confutation of this last hypothesis, before noticing the opinion of those who deem both brothers alike innocent.

The conduct of Alexander Ruthven, mysterious enough under any circumstances, approaches the verge of madness, if we suppose him acting without instructions and the cooperation of Gowrie. What end could his conspiracy in such a case have aimed at? If merely to the king's death, many modes of effecting it would have been preferable to doing the deed in a house not his own, and where the only servant whom he could get to assist him in the execution was of such a complexion as Henderson, alike ignorant of the conspiracy and without the will to assist him in it.

If it was Alexander Ruthven's only object to deprive the king of his liberty, what benefit could he have derived, or by what force have executed such a purpose? If we suppose him to have acted alone in the affair, we can only suppose his motive to have been some sudden fit of insanity; a supposition not to be resorted to when any less violent mode of solution remains.

But ceasing to argue upon presumptions, there is positive evidence enough in the case to show that the Earl of Gowrie was acquainted with, and consequently the principal conductor of, the whole of the enterprise. This appears from the following circumstances of real evidence: First, when Henderson brought word to the Earl of Gowrie that the king was coming with a small train to dine with him, he told him nothing but what Gowrie seemed to expect. He questioned Henderson how the king received Alexander, and seemed well acquainted with his brother's morning expedition to Falkland. Yet, instead of making provision to receive the intended honor, he commanded his own dinner to be served up, and made no preparations for that of the king; evidently to impress upon all who should witness this event the idea that the king arrived at Gowrie House totally unexpected by the owner. Secondly, it was Gowrie himself who commanded the key of the gallery chamber to be produced; and it was he, no less, by whose orders Henderson put on his armor, and attended upon the commands of Alexander Ruthven, by whom he was placed in the fatal closet; he was, therefore, active in preparing the scene, and disposing the actors in the drama which followed. Lastly, the conduct of the Earl of Gowrie, at the moment when Lennox and the other lords arose from table, was decisive, as to his acquaintance with and accession to the conspiracy. He imposed upon them a story that the king had withdrawn for an interval, and led them into the garden, where presently afterward a cry arose that the king was already on horseback, and half way through the Inch on his return to Falkland.

It is remarkable that Mr. Thomas Cranstoun was the most active in propagating this false report. On his examination he stated that he caught it up from some persons who were buzzing such a rumor around him; but it is more probable he received it from the earl himself. At least it is certain that when Gowrie's porter contradicted the report of the king having gone off, the earl was very angry with his servant, and continued to assert that the king was gone, having passed through a small postern-gate. Contradicted in this circumstantial falsehood, also, the Earl of Gowrie undertook to procure the lords genuine information of the king's motions, and ran, under that pretext, into the castle; and although he neither did nor could have seen the king, who was at that moment grappling with his brother, he returned to his guests, who were becoming anxious, with the positive assurance that James had actually left the castle. This chain of real evidence plainly evinces that the Earl of Gowrie was apprised of his brother's conspiracy, and took measures, in turn, for disguising its commencement, and for carrying through the perpetration. If he had succeeded in his last attempt, to get rid, namely, of the king's retinue, the coast would have been clear, for an hour at least; and that space would have been time enough to dispose of his majesty's person in the manner which it is most probable the conspirators had in view.

More generally, if we incline to disbelieve King James's account of the Gowrie conspiracy, we shall find ourselves obliged to adopt a system beset by more and greater improbabilities, and far less supported by anything like evidence. Some scraps of tradition are indeed quoted as contradictory of the king's report, and there are two or three incoherences in the evidence, as we have endeavored to show is often the case where various eye-witnesses give an account of the same agitating scene; but what species of suppositions are we to receive if we are to adopt the idea that the king was laying a snare for Gowrie and Alexander Ruthven, instead of his being exposed to one at their hands? We must suppose that a monarch remarkable for timidity, and by no means thirsty of blood, had devised a scheme for murdering two noble individuals to whose whole family, and especially to themselves personally, he had shown great marks of favor. For the execution of this purpose, we must hold James to have repaired suddenly to Gowrie House, a strong building, filled with the servants of the earl, and situated in a town where he was provost, and greatly beloved by the citizens. Far from selecting any part of his train, a few attendants follow him at random, with their hunting equipage and armed only with hangers for hunting. Was this a retinue with which James, or a much more valiant man, would have thought of attempting the slaughter of two noblemen? Such an idea cannot be entertained without reversing every notion which we have, not only of James's constitutional timidity and the natural lenity and humanity of his disposition, but of his common sense and share in the instinct of self-preservation.

The argument founded on the absurdity of the accusation might be carried still further; for how is it possible to account for the king's going apart, without an attendant, into the recesses of an unknown house, himself the sole companion of one of the men whom he meant to murder, who, as it is proved, was supported by a retainer in complete armor, the king himself not having even a sword at his side? These are suppositions too gross to be admitted. Again, if we admit the conspiracy to have been the king's stratagem, we must suppose the Earl of Gowrie to have been the object of the royal hatred in the principal degree, and his death chiefly intended. Yet the earl's death happened only incidentally, in the course of a general brawl, which might either never have happened or have terminated in a very different manner; and he must resign the Gowrie conspiracy as totally inexplicable who shall decline to receive the account given by the king himself.

Nine years after the death of the two brethren, a discovery was made which seemed tolerably to prove the general scope and tendency of the plot, though it leaves in uncertainty the nature of those machinations by which it was to be accomplished.

One Sprot, a notary, who appears to have been a busy, intermeddling man, suffered it to be understood through some oblique hints, by which persons of his character love to indicate that they are wiser than their neighbors, that he was acquainted with matters relating to the Gowrie conspiracy. Being seized and examined before the privy council, he made the following deposition, which was partly voluntary, partly extorted by torture. Logan of Restal Rig, a person of a wild, fierce, turbulent disposition and dissolute morals, had, according to Sprot, been in correspondence and intimacy with Gowrie during the whole concoction of the conspiracy, and had been privy to it in every stage.

The fortress called Fastcastle is a strength which then belonged to Logan, and overhangs the German Ocean, occupying almost the whole projecting cliff on which it stands; connected with the land by a very narrow path, and of such security that, manned with a score of desperate men, it must in those days have been impregnable, save by famine. Logan, who had squandered away a large estate, designed, by means of this fortress, to recover his wealth, or obtain an ample indemnification; he was, therefore, according to Sprot's account, deeply engaged in desperate schemes. He wrote five letters, three of them without any direction, one to Gowrie, and one to an old man called Laird Bour, who was trusted with this dangerous secret. Being ignorant himself of the art of writing and reading, this Bour was in the custom of carrying to Sprot such letters and papers as he was charged with, for the sake of learning the contents; and the busy notary was unable to resist the temptation of stealing from the laird the five letters which concerned the conspiracy. They are written half in an earnest and passionate, half in a species of satirical or drolling style. Mention is made of revenge to be had for the death of Graysteel, a name given to the Earl of Gowrie's father, beheaded at Stirling in 1584: the strength of Fastcastle is commended; "in which," says Logan, whose principles we may estimate by his friendships, "I have sheltered the Earl of Bothwell in his greatest necessities, let the king and council say what they would." Allusion is made to an important captive; to a signal to be made by a vessel and answered from the castle, with several other hints, which were, doubtless, distinctly understood between the parties. Above all, secrecy was recommended, and the burning of such letters as should pass on the subject. It is singular to remark that, in spite of Logan's repeated cautions on this subject, and no less in spite of the closeness and reserve of the Earl of Gowrie, who thought most conspiracies failed by being intrusted to confidants, the impertinent curiosity of a newsmonger like Sprot, and the stupid carelessness of an old fool like

Bour, were the means of preserving these letters of such deadly import.

According to the tenor of the correspondence, and the explanations of Sprot, the king, being secured in Gowrie Castle, was to be embarked upon the Tay, and the vessel which bore him, standing out of that estuary, was to make Fastcastle, on the coast of Berwickshire, and there to land the king as in a place of safe custody. The eventual intention, no doubt, must have been to have delivered him into the hands of Elizabeth, who had always been desirous of exercising sovereignty in Scotland. Perhaps she desired little more than that the brothers, attached by principles and family descent to the English interest, should renew the attempt to secure the king's person, and conduct his administration thereafter according to their own pleasure, always subservient to her interest. This was the part which their father endeavored to act, encouraged also by the queen of England; and although he had failed in it, Elizabeth still continued to regard his memory with respect, to protect his accomplices, and to be generous to his family. If we look at the attempt of the brethren as connected with some such issue as we have stated, it removes a great part of the difficulty and obscurity attending the conspiracy. If the king was only to be secured, not slain, the brothers might have the better reason to rely upon the assistance of Henderson. He does not appear to have been, in ordinary circumstances, a man of irresolution, having been in the habit of being employed by Gowrie in arrests and other·dangerous services. Little more seems to have been expected of him than that he should have looked bold, and by the terrors of his armed presence should have intimidated the king into silence. We can easily conceive that the brothers, judging from James's ordinary character, might have expected that the king would have been browbeaten into submission more easily than they found to be the case; and that the courage with which James behaved himself was as unexpected as the extremity of Henderson's consternation and hesitation. Alexander Ruthven seems, from the ex-

pressions he used, to have reckoned on this man's assistance
in the moment of the struggle. If James had come, as Ruthven desired, altogether without followers, or if Gowrie had
succeeded in dismissing the royal retinue, there could have
been little difficulty in executing the rest of the plot: the
condemned turnpike, or secret stair, so often mentioned,
would have given access to the gardens of the castle stretch-
ing down to the river Tay; the king might have been conveyed to the water's edge without difficulty, and placed in
a well-manned boat. With wind and tide to favor her voyage, the vessel in which he was embarked might have soon
left the Tay and reached the fortress of Fastcastle, engrafted,
as it were, upon the precipitous rocks which stretch northward from St. Abb's Head. The issue of the enterprise
must have been under the management of Elizabeth.

But ere this explanation of their mysterious schemes had
been afforded, the two brethren had been slain, and Logan,
and Bour, his messenger, had been long dead. The discovery of these letters, however, occasioned some singular law
proceedings; nor did the memory of Logan escape prosecution for treason, as if even the grave could not protect those
who were liable to be charged with this state crime. A peculiar process, borrowed from the civil code, was used on
such occasions. In order to satisfy the letter of the law,
ordaining that each party accused of high treason should be
present upon his trial and conviction, a legal fiction introduced the production in open court of the dead body, or the
bones of the accused person, in order to obtain conviction
against him. Under these ghastly circumstances, the memory of Logan was attainted of treason. His estate was forfeited; and as some property near Edinburgh, which formerly
had belonged to him, was afterward found in possession of
the Earl of Murray, a cry has been raised, as if Logan's letters, found in Sprot's possession, must have been forged, in
order to procure the means of enriching a favorite courtier.
Later researches have proved this to be wellnigh impossible;
for the operations of the law, enforcing the demands of credit-

ors, had stripped Logan of his large possessions before his death, and left none to tempt the cupidity of the crown; there is little room, therefore, to challenge the authenticity of these letters, though the circumstances of their preservation are so singular and extraordinary.

Sprot's idle curiosity proved fatal to himself: he was brought to trial upon a charge of having concealed the treasonable enterprise, the knowledge of which he had so strangely become possessed of. He was condemned to die for this misprision of treason, and was executed. He adhered to his confession to the last; and to give the people a sign that it was true, he even in his mortal agony clapped his hands three times, after he was thrown off, on the gibbet. This last circumstance is attested by the historian Spottiswoode, who, nevertheless, seems very sceptical upon the subject of Sprot and his discoveries. However, as the reverend historian chiefly rests his incredulity on the improbability that a youth of Gowrie's character would unite with such a man as Logan was known to be, his argument would carry him further than he intended. Having admitted that Gowrie was actually engaged in a conspiracy, the inference must be that he was necessarily obliged to stoop to communicate with the desperate or depraved characters whose agency was necessary to carry it on. Treason, like misery, makes a man acquainted with strange companions. Leaving this dark matter to time and the further researches of antiquaries, we return to what remains to be said of the history of Scotland.

King James, about the commencement of the seventeenth century, undertook an object of considerable policy, which would have rendered great honor to his memory had he been able to achieve it. The Highlands, torn to pieces during the civil war by domestic feuds, were become as lawless as they had been for many ages; and to add to the confusion which their wildness occasioned, the state of the Hebrides was still more savage than that of the mainland. James VI., as a wise prince, was desirous of finding a remedy for this increasing evil; but a better did not occur to the king and his counsellors than to commit the task of civilizing the islands to associations of gentlemen, chiefly proprietors in Fife, with their friends and kinsfolk, who undertook to settle in the Lewis, Uist, and other isles convenient for the fisheries, where these gentlemen, called the Undertakers, proposed to expel or subdue the natives, to build towns, to cultivate manufactories, and to do all that could have the effect of introducing civilization into these wild regions. Amid all this, it was never asked who were the patriarchal chiefs to whom the country belonged, or by what authority the king gave away, or the Fife undertakers accepted, the settlements of the Hebrides? Most of them, no doubt, might be liable to a doom of forfeiture; but it was for transgressing laws of which they had never known the tenor or experienced the benefit, and of which, therefore, they ought not to have experienced the rigor. But the rights of the natives were as little thought of as if the settlement intended had been in India or America, and the persons who were to be dispossessed had been savage heathens. The undertakers, therefore, proceeded on their adventure, without troubling themselves with any doubt upon the subject of the real right of property.

They commenced with the Isle of Lewis, where Murdoch M'Leod, a natural son of the old chieftain, at that time commanded. After some struggle he was driven by the undertakers out of the island. The colonists sent home Learmouth of Balcomie to intimate their success; but ere he had left the shores of Lewis, the ship, being becalmed, was assaulted by Murdoch M'Leod, with a number of boats: he killed many of the mariners, and took Balcomie prisoner, who, having been ransomed by his friends, died afterward in the Orkney Isles. In revenge of this injury, the undertakers caused Murdoch M'Leod to be betrayed by one of his brothers, and delivered into their hands. They finally sent him to St. Andrew's, and he was there executed. The undertakers continued their proceedings, being now secure, as they thought, of their possessions; but, when they least expected it, their settlement was invaded by Norman M'Leod, another son of the old chief.   He stormed their village, set fire to the houses, and compelled the colonists to surrender on the following conditions: first, that they should procure for Norman a full pardon of all irregularities which he might have committed; secondly, that they should surrender their right to the isle to their aforesaid conqueror, Norman M'Leod; and, thirdly, that they should deliver hostages for obtaining the pardon, and resigning the right, in terms of the two first stipulations.   An attempt was made about three years after this period to renew the settlement, but without better success.

CHAPTER XLI

King James's Claim of Succession to the English Crown—Is agreeable to both Countries—And why the Prospect of a masculine
Reign was acceptable—James's personal Character favorably
estimated—More extensive national Views arise out of the
Union of the Crowns—The Catholics of England are favorable
to James—Mysterious Intercourse between James's Secretary,
Balmerino, and the Pope—Claims of Spain, of France, and Lady
Arabella Stewart, are postponed to those of the King of Scotland, even by the Catholics—He maintains a Scottish Faction
at the Court of Elizabeth—The Queen's Failings become more
visible in age—Chivalrous Character of Essex, her Favorite—He
is at the Head of the Swordsmen in her Court—Robert Cecil at
the Head of an opposite Faction, consisting chiefly of Civilians
—He shuns connecting himself with James, but refuses to enter
into any other Interest—The Quarrel with Essex—Essex's Miscarriage in Ireland—He is disgraced—Enters into a rash Insurrection—Fails—Is made Prisoner, tried, condemned, and
executed—Anecdote of Lady Nottingham—The Earl of Mar and
Bruce of Kinloss sent by James to London with private Instructions to advance his Interest—The Earl of Northumberland
and the Catholics propose violent Measures, which James declines—Cecil joins his Party, but with much Precaution—His
Intercourse with Scotland is nearly detected—Opponents of
James's Claim few and disunited—Scotland exhibits a tranquil
Appearance—The Queen discovers the Fraud of the Countess
of Nottingham, and falls into a mortal Malady—Dies—Carey
bears the News to Scotland, which is confirmed by authentic
Intelligence—James takes Leave of his ancient Subjects, and
sets out for England—Meets the Funeral of Lord Seton—One
Gentleman attends the King's Progress—His Reason—James
is received in Berwick triumphantly; and the History of Scotland concludes

A MOST critical period for Britain was now approaching,
not only on account of James's personal interest but
in a much more extended view. Both parts of the
island, which, after so long a separation, if indeed they
could ever be said to have formed the same country, were

now advancing to that happy state which was destined to put the whole island under the government of a single monarch. Providence had by a singular course of events removed the objections upon either side, which, at an earlier period, bade fair to impede forever this happy consummation.

The national pride of each country found in the prospect of the union of the crowns something to soothe its vanity. The English people had now for many years preserved a degree of political ascendency in Scotland, which removed the feelings of former rivalry. No renewal of the fierce and bloody contests between the two nations had, since the battle of Pinkie, and the subsequent war, exasperated the feelings of the English against the Scots. Those wars which had taken place during the reign of Mary, or shortly after her deposition, had been waged by the co-operation of the English forces with the Scots of the king's party, and had been uniformly successful; so that the personal recollections of the existing generation were of a description flattering to the prejudices of the more powerful nation, which had been engaged rather as an auxiliary than as a principal in such contests as had taken place. Since James had been in undisputed possession of the Scottish throne the actions which had occurred were generally mere border brawls, unpremeditated on either side, and which, though evincing to England that the Scottish spirit was unbroken, and their courage the same as their own, had upon each occasion been disowned by the Scottish government; the head of which, King James, had shown that, so far from being desirous to take exceptions, he was even anxious to concede more than could have been in justice demanded. It might be reasoning too finely to say that it was even happy that in these petty affairs, such as the battle of the Reedsquair, or the Raid of Carlisle, the advantage lying on the side of the Scots, gratified the pride of a nation peculiarly sensible to military fame, while the concessions made to England by the Scottish government argued an admission of the superior force of England. Each nation, therefore, retained a flattering sense of its own power. The Scots felt themselves in possession of the same determination and prowess which they had exercised in former days, while the English regarded with like complacency the unusual disposition of the Scots to remedy by excuses and concessions any casual breach of truce, paying thus a tribute to the national superiority of their neighbors in wealth, discipline, and numbers.

A contest, however long and inveterate, is at no period so likely to be brought to an amicable adjustment as when both parties are satisfied that they have maintained bravely their part of the quarrel, while each, at the same time, feels respect for the courage and force of their enemy.

The manner in which the mutual union was likely to be formed had also points in it agreeable to the feelings of both nations. If James, on the decease of Elizabeth, should succeed to her vacant throne, the Scottish nation must needs entertain a feeling of triumph for having on their part given a king of their ancient royal stock to the nation who, during so many centuries, had proposed to themselves to place over them an alien and a conqueror. The feelings of the English were also of a conciliatory nature, since, if they should accept the government of the Scottish king, it could not, in common sense, be regarded but as an act of their own free choice: James was the natural heir of Henry VII., their own king, who had succeeded to the throne by the unanimous consent of parliament and people, upon the extinction of the long and illustrious race of Plantagenets. It was easily to be understood that he was to reign over them as a natural English prince, fixing his seat of government in London, henceforth to be the metropolis of Britain, governing them by the direction of an English parliament and English laws, and acting in every respect as king of the whole island, but first and especially as monarch of England.

To the loss of their monarch, as a resident among them, the Scots might reconcile themselves, especially those who had some claim to James's favor, by the natural expectation that their prince's power of bestowing benefits upon his servants and countrymen would be more widely extended; and that, when he was himself promoted to a far more opulent and important dominion, they might naturally hope to benefit by the kind recollections which he must be supposed to entertain toward his native land, and the friends to whom he had been attached during his earlier and more limited sway. To this disposition of conciliation on both sides were added, on the part of the English, many hopes and expectations which the character of James, seen from a distance, were not ill qualified to inspire, although it might be that some of them were balanced by defects which were not obvious without closer scrutiny. The advantages possessed by James stood forth in broad light: his defects were thrown into shadow, or, to speak without a simile, he had only had an opportunity of displaying them in a very limited sphere.

The points in favor of the king of Scots, personally, we shall shortly notice.

In succeeding to a long female reign, the accession of a king was in itself desirable. While exhibiting the most brilliant success which could be recorded in history, the reign of Elizabeth was still that of a woman, and was marked in her domestic management with traits of unreasonable severity and arrogance of command, which men endure with more difficulty at the hand of a female, and which they are disposed to think would not be so apt to take place under a masculine ruler. But, in addition to this preference of the male sex in government, there appeared to be in James's personal character many advantageous circumstances upon which his future subjects might reckon with advantage.

He had shown himself in his government of Scotland a merciful and mild prince, ready to forgive injuries, and willing to remember benefits and services. In his personal contest with the Ruthvens he had displayed flashes of courage becoming his high descent; and upon other occasions, if he had not conducted armies, he had at least marched at their head; and though he might add little to it by his personal efforts, success had usually crowned his endeavors. The fidgeting and paltry instances of irresolution arising from the infirmity of his nerves were little seen, save by those who approached closely to his person; and during the reign of the Chancellor Maitland, and of Home, who succeeded him in favor, the steadiness of the ministers had supported what vacillation might be visible in the character of the prince. The spirit of profusion arising from good nature and indolence to which James was liable was a fault not likely to be discovered while the sovereign, having little revenue and no credit, possessed, in fact, nothing of which to be ostentatiously profuse. His spirit of favoritism, the principal blot of his character, was little seen in his Scottish reign after the fall of Arran; and his relaxing the reigns to that profligate and arrogant minister might, therefore, be well considered as a failing of youth. His learning, though it would in the present day have been qualified as pedantry, approached too near the taste of the times to receive so harsh a denomination. He had composed a work upon the education of his son, termed the *Basilicon Doron;* in which he argues with considerable ability upon the principles of government, and describes the duties by which a young prince ought to guide his reign. It was read in England with avidity; and the public in general received from the perusal of that work the same favorable sentiments with which Walsingham had been impressed by the conversation of James while yet a youth.

The religion of James was known to be steadily Protestant; and he had even drawn his pen in defence of the reformed religion, with the purpose of proving from the Book of Revelation that the Roman pontiff was the antichrist whose arrival is there denounced.

These various reasons were sufficient to gain the king of Scots a strong interest in England, certain to operate in his favor so soon as the throne should become vacant by the death of Elizabeth.

Enlightened men, and those gifted with powers of reflection, looked far more to the ultimate advantage which Britain must attain by the consolidation of its separate divisions than to the character of the existing king. It was enough on the latter point to know that he was no tyrant, was clement in his nature, inclined to peace and rational government, and likely to prove a good if not a heroic monarch.

But they considered with more interest the immense advantages likely to accrue to the island of Britain from the union of the two countries: they looked to the extensive and fertile countries on either side the border, long existing as a seat of constant war, and inhabited only by clans whose habits approached to those of banditti, and saw the probability of its being converted from a seat of eternal strife and rapine into the centre of a single kingdom, the habitation of peace and honorable industry. In the chronicles of ancient times they might read, that if England had been often the oppressor and the scourge of her northern neighbors, the vindictive retaliation of Scotland had been not less frequently or deeply felt. They might learn, that if France had been successful in many of her wars with England, it was generally owing to her being able to interest Scotland in her quarrel, and keep her frontiers open as a gate which the English must either guard at great expense, or expect sudden and dangerous invasion. They might remember, that of the numerous and bloody battles gained over their northern neighbors not one had been followed by a permanent result of conquest and humiliation. They might, therefore, from the most patriotic reasons, hail an event which promised, by a safe and easy remedy, to accomplish the cure of an ulcer which had for so many hundred, nay, thousand years, gnawed into the very vitals of the island.

The persons who may thus be supposed to take more general and enlightened views of the state of the country would not fail to remember the crisis in which Britain stood in the memorable year 1588. If Scotland had then, from a difference in religion or policy, or from national prejudice, favored the efforts of the ambitious Spaniard, he might, without hazarding his invincible armada, have wafted his troops from the Netherlands to the coast of Scotland by a short and easy passage, and laid England under the perilous necessity of contending for English liberty upon English ground. All these reflections could not fail, in the minds of reflecting persons, to give the utmost weight to the title of James, in his claim upon the English succession.

There was in England an oppressed yet powerful faction, to whom many of the reasons influencing other classes in England must rather have operated as disadvantageous in their eyes to the claims of the king of Scots. These were the Catholics of England, energetic in their zeal for religion, and, though sorely oppressed by the laws, still a body that was to be respected and feared. These, however, had their own hopes and expectations, separate, and in some points diametrically opposite, to those of the Protestants. King James, it was true, was a Protestant monarch; but it seemed evident that the bulk of the English nation had united to recognize his claim to the crown, and would unquestionably be still more unanimous in his favor against any Catholic candidate who could be proposed to them. The ambitious Philip had, by his vain pretensions of descent from the House of Lancaster, provoked the anger of the English nation, who bore him little goodwill for his conduct during the short time that he reigned over them by his marriage with Mary. His threats had roused general hatred, his defeat had occasioned that hatred to be changed into contempt. These angry feelings had extended to those of his own persuasion, for a body of Catholics were in arms to resist the armada.

Lastly, the claim of James seemed far preferable to any which could be stated in opposition. The king of France had made some vague pretence to the English crown, and in private had spoken of giving them a second conqueror from Normandy; but his pretensions were not of a kind to be acceptable by the English people. The Lady Arabella Stewart's hereditary claims were not superior to those of

James, and her power of making them good was incalculably less.

James, on the other hand, was likely to unite all votes in his favor, nor did policy recommend to the Catholics to make any general stand against his interest. On the contrary, his claim had, in their eyes, much to recommend it. He was son of that Mary whom, living, they acknowledged as the just heir of England, whose memory, when dead, they reverenced as that of a martyr in the Catholic cause. In consistence, therefore, with their general feelings, they were called upon to avow the right of King James, as lineal successor to the claims of his mother. Although of a different persuasion, strong hopes were entertained among them that he was at heart favorable to the Catholic religion. His conduct toward the Lords of Huntley, Angus, and Errol, who had embraced the Catholic faith and disturbed his kingdom with civil war, had been remarkably forbearing and merciful; that as his lenity had inflamed against him the resentment of the violent Protestants to a degree certainly unmerited, so in the like proportion it excited unfounded hopes in the minds of the Catholic party both in England and Scotland. That James would have adopted the religion in its present depressed state they did not and could not hope; but that he might and would considerably mitigate the heavy penalties under which they labored, was a point generally expected by the Roman Catholics of both kingdoms.

A singular incident which took place about this time, and which is not, perhaps, fully explained, confirmed the Catholics in their most extravagant hopes of receiving favor at James's hand. A dark story reached Queen Elizabeth, transmitted, as it was believed, by the banished Master of Gray, then residing in Italy, that her kinsman and ally, James, had been in actual correspondence of a friendly character with that pope of Rome whom he himself had endeavored to identify with antichrist. This produced an anxious and irritated remonstrance on the part of Elizabeth, to which James replied by an explicit denial of the fact. Gray, however, had been true in his report, although James was, apparently, no less sincere in his denial. The cause had arisen out of a voluntary but unauthorized measure which Elphinstone, Lord Balmerino, secretary of state to James, had taken in his master's name, but without his authority.

It afterward appeared, by Elphinstone's confession, that he had drawn up a letter from James to Pope Clement VIII., containing various expressions of regard for his holiness, and declaring his intention to treat the Roman Catholics with indulgence. The letter even went so far as to entreat a cardinal's cap for a Scotsman named Drummond, the bishop of Vaizon, in order to facilitate future communications between King James and the Holy See. This paper Elphinstone declared that he had shuffled in among other deeds to be signed, so that King James subscribed it in total ignorance of its contents. The secretary stated himself to have committed this unwarrantable action merely out of zeal for the king's welfare, and in order to secure to him an advantageous interest with the pope and the Catholics, by a mode which he knew his master would not have taken unless he had been deceived into it. This fraud was attended with evil consequences both to the king and to the secretary: the latter was tried for high treason and found guilty, but obtained a pardon. The former was accused of having induced Elphinstone to take upon himself the guilt of a measure in which he himself had been participant; and the confession of Elphinstone was looked upon only as an honorable artifice to save the character of the king. Some light might be gathered on the subject, if Drummond's relation to Elphinstone were known. His promotion is warmly recommended; and the Scottish men of that age were wont to go extraordinary lengths in behalf of those whom they called kith, kin, and ally.

Whether accessory to the device of his secretary or not James unquestionably courted the Catholics, and obtained the suffrage of the pope, and of many of the great English families of that persuasion.

Elizabeth, in the meantime, rendered by old age and discontent more irritable than she had yet been, watched the intrigues of James with the most jealous observation; although arrived at a period when neither health, spirits, nor the prospect of a much longer continuance in power, or in life, gave her the means of counteracting them.

The case, indeed, was strangely altered between Elizabeth and James. During his earlier reign, the English queen had been the chief means of supporting him upon the throne, and at a later period had alternately contributed to his comfort by increasing his revenue, or to his plague by stirring up intrigues in his court, and protecting the rebels who escaped to her frontiers. But she was now in the wane of human existence, and was doomed to feel those evils of foreign intrigue which she had formerly carried into the councils of Scotland now retaliated upon her own. They were, indeed, carried on by the Scottish monarch with a degree of moderation suited to his views and to his character. He had no purpose whatever of a violent nature, tending to disturb the queen's immediate government, or to shorten the period of a reign which was almost exhausted in the course of nature. His efforts were·limited to the very natural object of establishing such an interest in the bosom of the people of England as might induce all parties to be disposed to recognize his right of succession, whenever that right should open by nature. For this purpose he took occasion (using the phrase of the poet) to procure golden opinions from all sorts of men, and the state of the fluctuating parties of the English court were highly favorable to him in acquiring them. Events, which tended to overwhelm with clouds of despondency the setting beams of Queen Elizabeth's illustrious reign, served to prepare the way for the rise of her successor. These must be shortly noticed.

Through the whole of her reign Queen Elizabeth, pre-eminent as a sovereign, had never been able to forbear the exertion of her claims as a wit and a beauty. When verging to the extremity of life her mirror presented her with hair too gray and features too withered to reflect even in her own opinion the features of that Fairy Queen, of immortal youth and beauty, in which she had been painted by one of the most beautiful poets of that poetic age. She avenged herself by discontinuing the consultation of her looking-glass, which no longer flattered her principal failing of personal vanity, and exchanged that monitor of the toilet, which cannot flatter, for the more false, favorable, and pleasing, though less accurate, reports of the ladies who attended her. This indulgence of vanity brought, as usual, its own punishment. The young females who waited on the queen turned her pretensions into ridicule; and if the report of the times is true, ventured even to personal ridicule, by misplacing the cosmetics which she used for the repair of her faded charms.—In a report, or copy, by Sir Robert Sibbald, of the famous interview between Ben Jonson and Drummond of Hawthornden, the former is stated to have mentioned the fact of Queen Elizabeth renouncing the use of the looking-glass; and adds, that the tire-women, confident in their mistress's prejudice against a looking-glass, sometimes ventured to lay upon the royal nose the carmine which ought to have embellished the cheeks.

Yet in this state of old age Elizabeth's attention was still bent on attracting youthful admiration; and by a singular chance the person whom she fixed upon as the male favorite of the period held, in a remarkable degree, in spirit and action, the real character of a hero of chivalry, to which Leicester and Hatton, her former minions, had no other pretence than that of personal beauty, or accomplishment in the most trifling exercises. The former noble, even if we do not incline to credit the reports of enemies, who loaded him with the foulest crimes, was certainly a man of ambition, which he scrupled not to gratify by the most indirect means. Hatton raised himself to be keeper of the great seal principally by his grace in dancing; and neither the one nor the other had qualities, independently of a graceful form and presence, which ought to have attracted the favor of so wise a princess as Elizabeth.

But the Earl of Essex, who filled in her latter days the dubious situation of her favorite, was altogether of a different character. Brave as the bravest paladin of romance, he sought glory wherever it was to be found, and generous as brave, he was beloved by his followers for his frankness, liberality, and benevolence. The men of the sword, as they were then termed, those who had distinguished themselves by their feats in arms, were all strongly attached to his interest, and to his party.

Essex, from a love of justice, mingled, perhaps, with a regard to his own interest, in case of Elizabeth's death, early entered into communication with the king of Scotland, and, with his natural frankness, pledged himself to support James's claim as rightful heir of the English throne, when death should remove from it its benefactress, Elizabeth. But in all her attachments of this nature, however she might show the frailties of a woman, Queen Elizabeth maintained the wisdom of a queen; and while she on one hand lavished benefits, and conferred high power, upon those whom she thus favored, she failed not, upon the other, to maintain an intimate communication with those statesmen whose advice had led to the distinguished glories of her reign. Most of those were now, indeed, deceased; but the wisdom and experience of the celebrated Burleigh still survived in his son Robert Cecil, who headed in the court a party consisting of those who had risen to eminence by their wise conduct in civil affairs, and were, in the phrase of the times, termed gownsmen, in contradistinction to the men of the sword.

Cecil was in person ungraceful, and even deformed; but nature had implanted within a misshaped form a mind of the most profound capacity. It cannot be doubted that he had been deeply imbued with all the knowledge of state affairs which the experience of his father, Lord Burleigh, could teach a mind so peculiarly adapted to receive them. Cecil shunned any connection with the king of Scots, perhaps because he reserved himself to watch an opportunity in which he might charge such intercourse with James against Essex as a crime which, of all others, Elizabeth would be less likely to pardon. Cecil was followed and looked up to by the numerous party which, bred in the court, expected to rise by talents for civil business; and as the frequent starts of Essex's hasty and ill-governed temper brought him into a transient disgrace with the queen, Cecil, who governed every thought and expression so as best to suit her pleasure, was able to gain a steady and increasing advantage over his less cautious rival. It is also to be remembered that Cecil had not, like Essex, to support the difficult character of the respectful and devoted admirer of a capricious old woman, a character which the generous and open disposition of Essex often rendered it difficult for him to sustain. Thus, without pretending to any share in Elizabeth's affections, Cecil retained possession of a high share of her esteem, as a servant devoted to her interests, and without whom she could not hope to support that character for political sagacity which had raised her government so high in the general estimation of Europe.

But although Cecil did not acknowledge King James's title, he took especial heed not to involve himself with any other pretender to the crown. The king of France caused him to be sounded by an ambassador of great experience, who kindly pointed out to him the troubles to which he might be exposed, if King James's pretensions to the English throne should ever be realized. He represented that all the offences imputed to Lord Burleigh in the matter of Queen Mary were likely to be then remembered upon Sir Robert Cecil as his son, and that his condition could not in that case be either honorable or safe. In such an event he offered the protection of his master. Cecil lent a cold ear to this, replying that he was determined to do his duty

in the service of his sovereign, whatever might be the event
in a future reign, though, if he saw himself in peril of life,
he might flee to another city, and take the advantage of the
king of France's protection.   The Frenchman answered,
with great address, that he entirely agreed with Cecil's
principles, and that his master did not intend to interfere
with the king of Scotland's interest.   Cecil so far waived
his scruples as to send James notice of this dialogue, acquainting him, at the same time, that though he did not
choose to engage his reputation and his fortune before the
fitting time, yet in due season James should command his
active services.

Thus stood the contending parties in the court of Elizabeth; herself, probably, little displeased with their disunion,
which left her the mediator and arbitress between both.   Of
all the military men the only eminent person who adhered
to Cecil was the celebrated Sir Walter Raleigh.   He shone
distinguished as a soldier, a statesman, and a man of literature.   But moving with too hasty steps toward advancement
he had already more than once incurred the displeasure of
the queen, to whom his admirable qualities had highly
recommended him. He was in a bitter degree the enemy
of Essex, both from private and public reasons; of which,
perhaps, not the least was that he himself, by Elizabeth's
encouragement, made pretension to the kind of favor which
Essex enjoyed.   They were rivals, therefore, in power,
though certainly not in love.

While the parties were thus balanced in the court of England, the ill fate of Essex engaged him in irremediable misfortune.   The Irish war had been the plague of Elizabeth's
reign; occasioning a perpetual drain of men and money,
by the expenditure of which no adequate benefit had been
attained.   Confident in his own courage and conduct, Essex
rashly undertook to terminate that lingering warfare, and
obtained from his mistress the almost absolute command of
the army engaged against Tyrone, the principal rebel, as he
was termed, in that country. His success did not corre-

spond with the hopes he had held out; and he patched up a
convention with the rebel general, whom he was sent to subdue. To add to the jealousy of a princess so sensitive as
Queen Elizabeth where her authority was concerned, Essex,
during the celebrated expedition, made knights, and exercised other privileges of royalty, with which the queen was
highly offended. The rest of his story is well known: he returned hastily to throw himself at the queen's feet, but was
coldly received, and commanded for a time to retire to his
own house. Commissioners were appointed to try him; and
he was suspended from all his offices. Moderation and temper would have in time softened Elizabeth's displeasure; but
Essex, having only violent men around him, listened to their
rash counsels. He endeavored to spur the king of Scots
to an invasion of England, which he promised should be
seconded by the Irish army: he then advised him to insist
upon a declaration of his right of succession, and assured
him of his full support.

The pacific and prudent disposition of James resisted
these temptations: he saw that the fruit which he aimed
at, when come to maturity, must fall in his lap, and he
declined the perilous enterprise of hastening the possession
by shaking the tree. Essex, impelled by fate and bad counsellors, rushed into a wild species of rebellion, and was
taken prisoner in a frantic attempt to raise an insurrection
in the city of London. The queen of England hovered
between her deep feelings of resentment as a jealous sovereign, and those of a softer character, which, as a woman,
tempted her to spare the favorite, perhaps we may say the
beloved, object of her affection. It is well known how a
trifle turned the scale between these contending sensations.
In the days of Essex's favor Elizabeth had bestowed upon the
earl a ring, and desired him, upon any occasion of extremity,
to forward it to her as a pledge under which he claimed her
protection. The ring claiming her promise never appeared;
and the queen regarded this circumstance as a proof of the
inflexible and ungrateful obstinacy of her late favorite, who

would not claim safety itself at the price of humbling himself to ask it at his mistress's hands. She was mistaken: the ring had been sent, with a submissive letter, but, by mischance, it was delivered to the Countess of Nottingham, who suppressed both the letter and token. Elizabeth, therefore, gave way, late and reluctantly, to the execution of the sentence, which had been too justly pronounced upon the unfortunate earl. From this time a deep and profound melancholy sunk more fatally upon Elizabeth's constitution, and invaded the springs of life.

It had been part of Essex's plan to assert the right of succession in James's person. The king of Scots was grateful: he despatched two ambassadors, men of sagacity and talent, the Earl of Mar, and Bruce, abbot of Kinloss, to intercede in behalf of the unfortunate criminal. Ere they could reach London, Essex had suffered his doom, so that, with no hopes left of acting in his favor, the ambassadors confined themselves to a general compliment, addressed to the queen, on the suppression of Essex's sudden rebellion. The queen received the Scottish ambassadors well; and was glad to have it in her power to contradict, upon their authority, the rumors, industriously spread, that Essex had been condemned less on account of his rebellion than that he was supposed to be a favorer of the Scottish title of succession, which it was the object of Queen Elizabeth to cut off and destroy. She even listened to them upon a subject which, though often stated in the course of James's negotiations, had not as yet met with any attention on the part of Elizabeth. This respected the succession of James to the English estates of his grandmother Margaret, countess of Lennox, niece of Henry VIII., and mother of the unfortunate Darnley. Even now Elizabeth could not bring her mind to yield to the king of Scots the possession of lands in England, even as private property, but she consented to add two thousand pounds a year to the pension of her godson, in lieu of his grandmother's estates.

Since 1599, at least, the king of Scotland had maintained

James Sempill of Belltrees as a private agent for his affairs in London, in which, though his friends could be but scanty, it appears he did not neglect to distribute secret service money among his partisans. But he must have gained more by future promises than by immediate gifts. Agents of higher rank were now to enter the field.

Mar and Bruce, highly trusted by James, had a species of general commission (guarded by conditions which exacted the strictest prudence), to extend, as widely as possible, and to secure, by every means in their power, his majesty's interest among all the leaders of parties in England, and through the people in general. The tone to be adopted in such negotiations was in general that of the most sincere gratitude and respect, on the part of James, toward Elizabeth; they were to disclaim, on the part of King James, the slightest idea of interfering with or disturbing the government of the queen during her life, while, at the same time, they were to represent him as desirous to secure to himself, on her demise, the fulfilment of hopes which naturally arose out of his lawful right of succession. They were commissioned to say that those who might now contribute toward paving the way for his peaceful succession to the throne of England, upon the death of its present occupant, and those also who might throw obstacles in the way of his just pretensions, might reckon securely upon their good or evil will toward him being rewarded accordingly, should he ever reign in that country.

The Scottish ambassadors conducted this delicate negotiation with every attention to secrecy, and with the most consummate dexterity. They opened communications with various parties, each hating the other, and detested in their turn, and united the principal factions among them in the resolution to support the king of Scotland's title. These parties we shall briefly notice.

That of the late unhappy Essex, now without a leader, and thrown back from all hopes of preferment, were naturally soothed and consoled by the assurances which the am-

bassadors of King James transmitted to them, of the regret
he had felt for the death of their chief, and the sense he
expressed that the fatal catastrophe had taken place in a
hasty attempt to be of service to his claims. The party
likely to be affected by these protestations was formidable
in its character, including Lord Mountjoy, the principal
officers of the Irish army, and most of the distinguished
military men in England. It is but justice to say that
James kept his promise toward this class of men; and was
observed, during his whole reign, to show friendship to the
friends of Essex, and a prejudice, to say the least, against
the marked enemies of that gallant nobleman.

After these we must mention the Catholics of England,
still a numerous and respectable party, though oppressed by
penal laws and disqualifications. We have already mentioned that James was recommended to them by birth and
character, and by their inclination to hope, upon his accession to the throne, considerable relaxation in the penal code,
under which they now suffered. Their hopes on this subject
were so high that their disappointments in the succeeding
reign are supposed to have given rise to the gunpowder treason. At the period we treat of, these hopes were in full blos-
som; and the Earl of Northumberland, regarded as chief of
the Catholics, a nobleman of a high spirit and romantic
character, not only avowed himself a determined asserter
of King James's succession, but exhorted him to claim, as
a right, the instant acknowledgment of the title of succession even during Elizabeth's life, and boasted, should it be
necessary, to bring him in by the sword. James, in his answer to these violent proposals, calmly explained his determination to wait till the road should open through natural
means to the English throne. In the meanwhile, he was
assured of the whole party of Catholics, so soon as he should
desire their aid.

But a far more important accession to James's partisans
was that of Cecil himself. This sagacious statesman witnessed with anxious eyes the decay of Queen Elizabeth's

health, the extreme probability of James's succession, and the policy of acquiring the favor of the new monarch, and thus sheltering himself from the hatred which, like every prime minister, he was conscious he must have acquired while conducting the administration of his predecessor. He therefore, the master-key of Queen Elizabeth's cabinet, and who possessed the knowledge of its most secret recesses, engaged in intimate and secret correspondence with Mar and Bruce, in which he assured them of his devoted attachment to the rights of their master. At the same time, conscious of the delicate ground on which he stood, and that the least circumstance which would lead to discovery might cost him both his offices and his life, he endeavored to impress upon James and upon his ambassadors the absolute necessity of the strictest secrecy to be observed in their communication. The advice, which no one knew so well as Cecil how to give —the opportunities of assistance, which no one could use with such dexterity as this crafty politician—could only, he stated, be afforded under the strictest condition of secrecy. Like what is said of favors conferred by the fairy tribe, the disclosure of the source from whence they come would, he was careful to affirm, render those which were received of no value, and totally intercept the means of obtaining others. Lord Henry Howard, a person who had made himself distinguished by a book against pretended prophecies, was much employed by Cecil in the correspondence with the Scottish agents. The letters of this nobleman, and of Cecil himself (notwithstanding the importunity of the writers that they should be destroyed), still exist, and throw a curious light on these intrigues, imperfect, however, in particulars, owing to the enigmatical style in which they are written.

In one epistle (to give a specimen of this important correspondence) Lord Henry Howard boasts, on the part of Cecil, that he has saved the life of Southampton, and the reputation and credit of Lord Mountjoy (both adherents of Essex), on account of their professed affection to King James: "but this was not done," it is added, "without risk to himself;

for the queen hath passions against which whoever strives above the measure and proportion of state (*i.e.*, who exceeds in his remonstrances the limited bounds of a subject) shall be reputed a participant" (viz., in the offence of those for whom he pleads). A following sentence strongly expresses his desire that his services in such cases may be strictly kept silent, especially from the adherents of Essex. "Your majesty's rare virtue, wisdom, secrecy, and constancy, first warranted by those whom he (Cecil) durst credit, and after tasted from yourself, have moved him to give into adventures which neither this world nor any other world than eternity can make him do. So long as he is covered from these whose states, though safe, yet not fully satisfied, may press upon advantage by necessity, his plow shall walk as well to sow corn as to pluck up weeds; but from the time that either of these shall be able, out of knowledge, to conclude him to be your friend, he shall forever afterward prove a dumb oracle. It may be that either one or both may, before it be long, for the sounding of this passage, crave your letter, for their satisfaction in some degree; but whether the demand be great or small, avoid the motive as Charybdis; for one leak, upon the like occasion, might hazard as fair a vessel under sail as ever the winds blew upon." Sir Robert Cecil, in conducting this delicate correspondence, seems to have been principally afraid of some imprudence at the Scottish court, betraying the secret to one Nicolson, an agent whom Elizabeth had sent to reside there, and one of those characters whom she selected for such offices, prying, bustling, and intermeddling, all eyes, all ears, and to whom the discovery of a state secret, like that of Cecil's correspondence with James, would have appeared the foundation of a fortune. The secret, however, was carefully kept, although at one moment it was upon the verge of transpiring.

Queen Elizabeth was taking the air in a carriage where Cecil occupied a seat, when one of the royal posts passed them. "From whence?" the queen demanded; and the answer was, "From Scotland."—"Give me your packet," said

the queen. It was delivered accordingly.—"Open it," said she to Cecil, "and show me the contents." As the packet contained some part of Cecil's correspondence with the king of Scots, the command placed the crafty statesman within view of ruin and of the scaffold. To have attempted to suppress or subtract any of the papers which the packet contained would have been a hazardous experiment in the presence of the most sharp-sighted and jealous of sovereigns. Cecil's presence of mind found an expedient. "This packet," said he, as he pulled his knife out to cut the strings with which it was secured, "has an uncommon odor, and must have been in some filthy budgets." The queen was alarmed. She had been all her life delicate in the sense of smelling, and was apprehensive of poison, which the age believed could be communicated by that organ. "Take it," she said to Cecil, "and let it be aired before the contents are presented to us." The wily secretary obeyed her commands, and obtained the desired opportunity to withdraw such papers as he deemed it important to conceal.

We have, lastly, to mention those at Elizabeth's court and kingdom who were decided opponents to the accession of James. They were neither numerous nor powerful; for they could not easily form themselves into an ostensible party or agree upon a principle of union. The chief among them, a person of the highest ability, deep learning, fame in war, and renown in peace, was Sir Walter Raleigh, already mentioned. But his connection with the military men, with whom he ought naturally to have had most influence, was broken off by his deadly quarrel with Essex, the darling of the army. He had done all in his power to aid the prosecution of that earl to the death, and was said to have disgusted the people in general by witnessing the execution of his generous rival, and smoking tobacco (which herb he had introduced into England) during the time of the melancholy solemnity. Cecil, to whom Raleigh had attached himself, did not think it fit to intrust him with his own secret designs in favor of James; and Sir Walter, left to his own devices, employed his speculative imagination of an English commonwealth, with the exclusion of the Scottish king, or, failing that, upon some agreement with James which should place the regal authority upon a footing less absolute than it had been exercised by the race of Tudor. These were plans too vague and imaginative to suit the views of Cecil; nor had the wily statesman any intention to introduce into the king's good graces a rival who might prove an obstruction to his views of holding the same supreme authority under James which he had enjoyed under Elizabeth.

Excepting, therefore, Raleigh, and individuals like him, who might have their own separate political views, the parties in England, like rivers running to unite in the same channels, were all bending their course toward a joint object —the succession of King James to the throne of Britain. All this was afterward remembered to the advancement of Cecil, who became Earl of Salisbury, and prime minister under James's reign, and to the prejudice of Sir Walter Raleigh. In the meantime, the prospect that King James would soon be called to an increase of wealth and power had its usual effect in strengthening his sovereignty at home. He was yet under the management of statesmen of sagacity and experience, nor had he received into favor any of those beardless boys, to please whose perverse and peevish humors he was in the latter part of his reign too apt to sacrifice his dignity as a sovereign. The halcyon period of tranquillity in Scotland was usefully employed. The Catholic lords, so long restive under the authority of James, were compelled to submit to such terms of reconciliation with the Church as insured their remaining quiet subjects in future. Angus, who alone declined compliance with the conditions exacted, retired to Paris, to enjoy his religion in security, and there died. James's disputes with the clergy were also amicably terminated. The ministers of Edinburgh, who had been banished, were restored to their pulpits and congregations, and an unusual degree of union seemed to subsist between them and the crown.

While Scotland was enjoying an unwonted interval of tranquillity, England was in expectation of a great change. The life of Elizabeth was fast drawing to a close: the heavy melancholy which clogged the current of Elizabeth's blood, ever since the death of Essex, had assumed a deeper and darker hue. She ceased to smile, to talk cheerfully, to enjoy any species of diversion, or make use of any of her usual exercises or amusements.

The imputed cause is a remarkable one. The reader cannot have forgotten that the Countess of Nottingham had intercepted the delivery of a letter and ring sent to Elizabeth by Essex in extremity; and that the queen was chiefly induced to permit his execution under the idea that he was too obstinate to appeal to her favor. The truth was now to be discovered. The Countess of Nottingham, on her death-bed, felt herself no longer able to support the burden of the guilty secret, and confessed to Elizabeth in person her having retained the fatal token. The queen, in great agitation, replied, "God may forgive you, but I never will." The countess died a few days after she had made the fatal confession, and from that time the hand of death was on the queen, whose melancholy was changed into despair. She tasted no food; she took no medicines; she refused to go to bed, but remained upon a pile of cushions, with her eyes fixed on the ground. This could not last long. Her strength visibly declined, from lack of nourishment and total exhaustion. Her godson, Sir Robert Carey, who watched her dying moments with the purpose of being the first to carry the news to King James, describes her, in this state of stupor, as being only able to wring his hand, and repeat his name with a heavy sigh.

She is said to have replied to those statesmen who demanded her will concerning the succession, "That she would be succeeded by none but a king; and that the king of Scots, her cousin, should enjoy her throne." She died on the 24th of March, 1603, in the seventieth year of her age, and the forty-fourth year of her reign. On the third day after her death, Sir Robert Carey, travelling on horseback, with speed which was then accounted most extraordinary, arrived at Holyrood; obtained admission to the king's bed-chamber, and, kneeling by his bedside, hailed him King of England and Ireland, as well as Scotland. Sir Robert brought a token from a lady of quality, one of James's correspondents, in the form of a ring, which was to attest the truth of his message. As the information, however, was of a private nature, the subject of Carey's news was not made public till the arrival of Sir Charles Percy, brother of the Earl of Northumberland, and Thomas Somerset, son to the Earl of Worcester, with letters from the English privy council, acknowledging his right in its fullest extent, and acquainting him of their having caused his accession to be instantly proclaimed, and that the news had been received with the unanimous applause of the people.

James was now arrived at the pinnacle of his hopes, and seems to have enjoyed them with a good-natured complacency, which overflowed to all around him. He attended service in St. Giles's Church, and heard a sermon by Mr. Hall, upon the great mercy of Heaven in having thus accomplished his peaceable accession to a kingdom so long hostile to his own, without the stroke of sword or shedding of a drop of blood. He exhorted the sovereign to show his gratitude by his attention to the cause of religion, and his care for the people committed to his charge. After the exhortation, which the king took in very gracious part, he himself addressed the people, of whom he was now to take leave, in a warm and affectionate strain. He bid them adieu with much tenderness, promised to have them in his view and recollections during his absence, and often to visit them and communicate to them marks of his bounty when in foreign parts, as ample as any which he had been used to bestow when present with them. A mixture of approbation and weeping followed this speech; and the good-natured king wept plentifully himself at taking leave of his native subjects.

Wednesday, the 4th of April, 1603, James set forward to occupy the new kingdom, which after so many years of expectation had, like ripe fruit, dropped thus quietly into his lap. His train, from taste as well as policy, was rather gay and splendid than numerous and imposing. Two circumstances occurred on the morning of his departure, either of which would have seemed ominous to an ancient Roman.

As the king and his train approached the house of Seton the solemn funeral of a man of high rank, adorned with all the gloomy emblems of mortality, interrupted his passage: it was that of Lord Seton, who had been one of the best, most disinterested, and most faithful adherents among those who held up the banner of James's mother. The deceased lord had sustained a full share in Mary's misfortunes, being obliged to retire to Flanders, where he was reduced to subsist himself by driving a wagon, in which character and occupation he had himself painted on his restoration to his rank and fortune. The king halted his retinue and sat down upon a stone, long afterward shown, while the funeral of this faithful adherent of his family moved past. The sight was strikingly well qualified to impress upon James, in the moment that he was taking possession of such a high addition to his power, the recollection of the mutability of human affairs.

The other is a Jacobite tradition, but has been generally received as a real one. It is said that as the gentry and freeholders of the country came to wait upon the king on his departure toward England, and escort him a few miles upon his way, there was one aged gentleman, who, very different from the gay array and festival habits of those around him, appeared attired in the deepest mourning. Being asked the meaning of so unbecoming a dress on so happy an occasion: "I have known this road," he said, "to England; and have travelled it in my former days, as we now do, under the royal banner: I was then as well mounted and armed as became my fortune and quality; but we were then bent upon honorable war with

our national enemies: at present, when we come to transfer our king to the English, and yield up to a people who
could never conquer us in war the power of lording it over
us as a province, I come in sorrow for my country's lost
independence in a dress becoming one who waits upon the
funeral of a mother."

The speech was certainly rash and prejudiced, yet it was
not the less, in some sort, true; for many were the evils
which attended the first junction of the kingdoms into one,
and scarcely fewer those which attended the incorporating
union which followed at the interval of a century. These
disadvantages, indeed, were finally incalculably overbal-
anced by the subsequent benefits of these important events;
but the consideration would lead us much further than the
limits of this work permit. We shall, therefore, only say,
that King James entered the town of Berwick amid the
thunder of the cannon planted to defend that town against
his ancestors, and was received in the principal church by
the bishop of Durham, who performed a thanksgiving service upon the occasion; and with the sovereign's occupation
of a more wide dominion over a wealthier people, naturally
closes the history of Scotland as a free and independent
State.

CHAPTER XLII

SUPPLEMENTARY

I T will be observed that Sir Walter Scott's History of Scotland ends with the year 1603, when James VI. of that kingdom became James I. of England. No doubt a reader of the present day will expect to find added a summary of the more important events that have marked the ensuing three hundred years. The first consequence of the union of the two crowns upon one head was the cessation of the age-long border wars and of the English and French intrigues for ascendency at Edinburgh. On the other hand, Scotland ceased to have a court of its own, a loss not without some counterbalancing advantages, for it tended to promote the independence of the northern kingdom. It is, of course, well understood that the mere accession of James VI. of Scotland to the English throne did not bring about any change in the constitution, laws or National Church of North Britain. Although the Reformation had begotten a multitude of sects, Scotland, at this time, may be fairly described as Presbyterian, England as Episcopal, and Ireland as Papal. James himself desired to see his native land united with England, not only by a junction of the crowns, but also by a fusion of parliaments, and, at all events, by an ultimate, if not immediate consociation of the national churches. The latter desire could not be fulfilled, except by force, so deeply planted in Scotland was the love of the Presbyterian system of church government. Scarcely was James seated, however, upon the English throne before he began endeavors to this end. The first English parliament which convened under his reign appointed commissioners to treat with Scottish commissioners for an accommodation of religious, political, and legal differences. The commissioners met, but they could not agree, the English being determined not to permit freedom of trade, and the Scots being equally opposed to an acceptance of the laws of England. The only points upon which the commissioners could concur were that subjects of the common king, born in either country after the accession of James VI. to the English throne, should have in both kingdoms the privileges of subjects, and that those born before the accession should be capable of inheriting and acquiring land in England; though not of acquiring political rights or offices. The English parliament, however, refused to sanction the agreement, so far as those born after the accession of the Scottish king to the English throne were concerned, though it agreed not to treat Scotland as a foreign country, and to assent to covenants for the mutual extradition of criminals. Meanwhile, King James persisted in his determination to reintroduce episcopacy into Scotland, and the Scottish parliament of 1612 passed a law re-establishing episcopacy in the northern kingdom. At first, however, the bishops were not successful in introducing the same services which were followed in England, but, after the visit of James I. to his native country in 1617, the Scottish parliament tried to assure the desired conformity by enacting the so-called Five Articles of Perth. Three years later, these articles were confirmed by another parliament on the promise given by the royal commissioner that no further ecclesiastical innovations should be proposed. It was this parliament of 1621 which introduced a new mode of electing the so-called Lords of Articles, a species of committee by which all parliamentary business was initiated, and all power of introducing bills was taken away from private members. This law, practically, vested in the king the dual powers of initiative and of the veto. Other incidents in the reign of James I., which should be chronicled, were the ineffective attempt to colonize the Hebrides and the temporarily successful plantation of Ulster by Scottish farmers, the ancestors of the so-called Scotch-Irish. His efforts to colonize Nova Scotia, though they seemed almost abortive at the time, were to have, in the future, important consequences.

The sovereign who was known as James VI. in Scotland and James I. in England, died in 1625, and was succeeded by his son Charles I. During the subsequent eight years, no Scottish parliament did any business, though one was convoked in 1628, and adjourned annually without action until 1633. Neither was there, during this period, any general assembly of the Presbyterian Church; on the contrary, the restoration of episcopacy was steadily pressed by the exercise of the royal prerogative. Charles I. succeeded at this time in bringing about the resumption of tithes, for the benefit of the clergy, from the laymen who had appropriated them. In 1633 the Scottish parliament distinctly formulated the terms on which the tithes might be acquired by the parochial clergy, and, thereby, arrayed against the crown the nobles and landed gentry, who saw themselves threatened with the loss of all the gains they had derived from the Protestant reformation. Nevertheless, when Charles I. came to Edinburgh in 1633, there were no open signs of insubordination. On the contrary, the Scottish parliament passed thirty-one acts, almost all of which were regarded by contemporary Scotchmen as hurtful to the liberty of the subject. It was not until a twelvemonth after the departure of Charles from Scotland that the first impulse may be said to have been given to the Scottish revolution. In 1635, Lord Balmerino was tried on the charge of possessing a copy of a petition protesting against the acts carried in the parliament over which Charles had presided. Condemned to death, he was respited by the king, but the people of Scotland deeply resented the treatment of the possession of a petition for the redress of grievances as if it were a capital crime. In 1636, the Book of Canons, ratified by the king, was published, and, in the following year, the Liturgy enjoined by the said book was introduced in the service of St. Giles's Cathedral, Edinburgh. This was the beginning of a popular agitation which, in the end, proved fatal to Charles I. The vital difference between his situation and his father's was this, that James I. was so intimately acquainted with the temper of the Scottish people that he knew precisely when to stop short, and even to retrace his steps; his son, on the other hand, from a lack of similar experience, plunged headlong on a path which led him to a precipice. The riots which occurred all over Scotland in 1637 should have convinced him that he had gone too far. Instead of accepting the warning, however, he announced in the following year by a proclamation that he assumed the whole responsibility for the introduction of the hated Liturgy. Thereupon, the opponents of the innovations formed a powerful organization, in which not only the nobles and clergy, but the towns also, were represented, and a so-called Covenant was drawn up by several eminent ministers, and very generally signed. This covenant, while professing respect for the royal office, bound the subscribers to co-operate for the defence of the true reformed religion, and for the liberties and laws of the northern kingdom. Recognizing his inability to subdue by force the Covenanters, Charles I. now endeavored to arrive at a compromise with them. But the effort was a half-hearted one, and, evidently, came too late. An assembly which met at Glasgow failed to effect an accommodation, and it was, accordingly, dissolved by the king's commissioner. Notwithstanding its dissolution, it persisted in sitting, and proceeded to condemn the service-book, or so-called Book of Canons, ratified in 1636; it deposed the bishops, declared episcopacy illegal, and restored Presbyterian church government.

The lines were now sharply drawn between the king and the Scottish people. An appeal to arms was inevitable. On June 7, 1639, the Covenanters, under Alexander Leslie, who had been in the service of Gustavus Adolphus, confronted the royal troops at Dunse Law, and were so manifestly superior in quality that Charles gave way, and, by the pacification of Berwick, agreed that all ecclesiastical matters should be thenceforth regulated by assemblies, and all civil affairs by the Scottish parliament and other courts of law. In conformity with this agreement, an assembly was held which re-enacted the resolutions of the Glasgow assembly, above referred to, and ordered every one in authority to subscribe to the Covenant. The Scottish parliament also met and abolished episcopacy. This act of the Edinburgh parliament, however, was not approved by Charles I., who endeavored to secure from the English parliament sufficient funds for the coercion of Scotland. Once more the Scots appealed to arms, and a strong force under Leslie advanced southward and occupied Newcastle. Unable to obtain the money necessary for resisting the invasion, Charles was forced to accept a truce, and the English parliament, after impeaching the Earl of Strafford, the king's ablest supporter, not only refused to raise forces to be employed against the Scots, but actually voted three hundred thousand pounds by way of friendly assistance and relief for "our brethren in Scotland." In the following year, 1641, Charles I. came to Edinburgh, in the hope of creating by his personal influence a party favorable to his views. In the Scottish parliament which he summoned, he made large concessions, ratifying an act which substituted the Presbyterian for the Episcopal form of church government, and agreeing that the national legislature should be convoked every third year. These concessions failed to satisfy the Scots, who had no confidence in the king's sincerity, and, in November, Charles I. returned to London, where he had to face that opposition of the Long Parliament which, ultimately, brought him to the scaffold.

The part taken by the Scotch in the civil war can be quickly outlined. Toward the close of 1643, the English parliament sent to Edinburgh commissioners, who formally accepted the "Solemn League and Covenant," in consideration of which act they secured the alliance of the Scottish Covenanters. In the next year, 1644, while a Scotch force lay in the north of England, the Marquis of Montrose, who had accepted a commission from King Charles, made a diversion in the Highlands which was, at first, remarkably successful, but which, in September, was brought to naught by his defeat at the hands of Leslie. In 1645 Charles, whose cause was now ruined in England, ordered Montrose to lay down his arms, and himself took refuge with Leslie, whom he had created Earl of Leven. For some eight months Charles remained with the Scottish army, by the leaders of which an earnest but ineffectual attempt was made to induce him to accept the Covenant. His refusal destroyed his last chance of safety. On January 30, 1646, he was surrendered to the English commissioners by the Scots, who had received a few days previously two hundred thousand pounds sterling, and to whom an equal sum was paid a few days afterward. This transaction gave rise to the reproach, which royalists have never wearied of repeating, that the Scots, like Judas, sold their king for a certain number of pieces of silver.

By the execution of Charles I. the relations between England and Scotland were profoundly modified. In the former kingdom, the so-called Independents, headed by Cromwell, were now all-powerful, and, by a natural reaction against them, the majority of the Scottish Presbyterians decided to proclaim Charles II., and sent a mission to The Hague to invite the young king to assume the Scottish throne, on condition, however, that he should accept the Covenant and the Presbyterian system of church government. These terms being agreed upon, Charles II. landed in Scotland on June 23, 1650, but, within a month afterward, Cromwell had invaded Scotland, and on September 3 gained a victory over David Leslie at Dunbar, whereby the southern part of the Scottish kingdom fell into his hands. He was unable, however, to intercept the Scottish force under Charles II., which entered England and advanced as far as Worcester before Cromwell could overtake it. It is well known that the complete defeat of the royalists at Worcester was described by Cromwell as his "crowning mercy." General Monk, who had been left by Cromwell in Scotland, succeeded within three years in subjugating that kingdom, which, in 1654, was, practically, united with England. To the so-called Barebones Parliament, 1653, five Scottish members were summoned, and, in the parliament of 1654, twenty Scotchmen took part. On the death of Cromwell and the proclamation of his son Richard as his successor in both kingdoms, thirty Scotch members were returned to the new parliament, which, however, was presently dissolved. Before the Restoration was effected in England, Charles II. had already been proclaimed king in Scotland.

It might have been supposed that the deeply-rooted desire of Scotchmen for an independent Presbyterian Church would have found favor in the sight of Charles II., when he recalled their fidelity to him in the hour of his adversity. Such, however, was not the case. All he remembered was that Cromwell had succeeded in conquering Scotland, and in effecting a temporary union of that kingdom with the rest of Britain. The whole power of his government was, from the outset, concentrated on the task of suppressing the religious and civil liberties of Scotland. Argyle, who, in January, 1651, had placed the crown on the head of Charles II., was now tried and beheaded on a charge of treason, and leading clerical representatives of the more stalwart Presbyterians were hanged. A docile Scottish parliament annulled the acts passed by all preceding parliaments since 1640, and declared the Covenant no longer binding. In 1662, Charles announced his intention of restoring episcopacy, and the execution of this project provoked an insurrection, which, however, for a time, was quelled. In the next ten years, it is estimated that seventeen thousand persons suffered fines or imprisonment for attending conventicles, and not a few were put to death on the same charge. The retaliatory murder of Sharp, archbishop of St. Andrew's, by a small band of Covenanters in May, 1679, was followed by a new rebellion, which, after some successes, was put down, though only with extreme difficulty. The Cameronians, as the insurgents were called, were treated with the utmost cruelty. The last six years of the reign of Charles II. came to be known in Scotland as the "Killing Time." The accession of James II., in 1685, led to a still more rigorous enforcement of the law against conventicles, which was now extended to meetings held in private houses, provided five persons outside of the family attended domestic worship. A number of the Scottish nobles now became converts to the Catholic faith, and James II. offered to give Scotland free trade with England and an indemnity for political offences on condition that Catholics should be released from the test and penal laws. Then came the revolution of 1688, which had the effect of splitting Scotland into two divisions, the Catholics and Episcopalians clinging to James II., and forming the Jacobite party, while William and Mary were supported by the Presbyterians. Graham of Claverhouse, who commanded in Scotland for James II., beat William's general at Killiecrankie, on July 29, 1689, but his death at the moment of victory rendered it impossible to hold the Jacobites together, and the surrender of the principal fortresses kept Scotland quiet for the next two reigns. A convention parliament called at Edinburgh declared that James II. had forfeited the crown, and recognized William and Mary as king and queen of Scotland, providing, also, that, after Mary's death, the royal power should be exercised by William alone, and, in the event of his decease, by Anne of Denmark and her heirs. The Scottish parliament of 1690 put an end to the so-called Committee of Articles, which had monopolized the power of initiative in legislation, approved the Westminster Confession, re-established the Presbyterian Church, and restored all surviving Presbyterian ministers that had been deposed since 1661. In matters of free trade and navigation, however, the government of William and Mary discriminated against the Scots, believing that such discrimination was needed to persuade them to consent to a union with England. It was during this reign that the attempt of Scotchmen to find on the Isthmus of

Darien an independent outlet for colonization and investment ended in overwhelming disaster. The great achievement of the reign of Anne, so far as Scotland was concerned, was the final accomplishment of the union of that kingdom with England. Many obstacles had to be surmounted before the arrangement was effected. At one time, the Scottish parliament went so far as to exclude from the throne of Scotland, after the death of Anne, the successor to the English throne, except upon such conditions as would assure freedom of trade to Scotland. The refusal to grant this boon caused the failure of the joint commission, which sat from November, 1702, to February, 1705, for the purpose of bringing about a union. In the course of the last-named year, however, a new joint commission was appointed, which sat for some three months at Whitehall and framed a treaty of union, the chief articles of which were as follows: Both crowns were settled on Anne and her descendants, and, failing these, on the electress Sophia and the Hanoverian line; free trade was to exist between England and Scotland, and the Scotch were to have equal privileges, as regarded trade with other countries; the national debt and taxation were adjusted by imposing upon Scotland less than one-fifth of the land tax, and there was to be a uniform rate of customs and excise duties; finally, Scotland was to send forty-five members to the House of Commons and to elect from its peerage for each parliament sixteen representatives to the House of Lords. Considerable as were the concessions to Scotland, the treaty of union was, upon the whole, received with dissatisfaction in that country, and it was only with difficulty that it was ratified by the Edinburgh parliament. The act of union took effect on May 1, 1707, having received the royal assent on the preceding 6th of March. It is, of course, understood that, although, by this measure, Scotland lost its legislative independence, its Presbyterian church establishment was guaranteed, and it also retained its own system of judicature and laws. It also kept its national system of parish schools, burgh schools and universities.

We should further note that, up to 1746, the management of Scottish affairs in London was intrusted to a Secretary of State for Scotland, an office which has been revived in our own day.

It was late in the eighteenth century, however, before Scotland became reconciled to its loss of legislative independence. The people, moreover, felt themselves to be distinct from the English, and two rebellions attested their lingering devotion to the House of Stuart. Many of the Highland clans, the Catholics, and some of the Episcopalians, long considered that, after the death of Anne, their allegiance was due to the heirs male of James II. In 1715 they protested, in the name of James III., against the accession of the House of Brunswick, but their insurrection under the Earl of Mar was speedily quelled. Very different was the temporary outcome of their uprising, in 1745, on behalf of Charles, the son of the titular James III., and best known as the Young Pretender. An English force was defeated at Prestonpans, and, for a time, it looked as if the whole of Scotland would fall into Jacobite hands. At the head of a small army, largely composed of Highlanders, the Young Pretender advanced into England as far as Derby, and, for a moment, caused a species of panic in London. The Highlanders, however, refused to second Charles in his project of moving quickly on the British metropolis, and, a retreat being ordered, they managed to reach Glasgow within about two months after their southward departure from Edinburgh. They defeated at Falkirk an English force under General Hawley, which was attempting to raise the Jacobite siege of Stirling, but this was their last success. Driven back to Inverness, the supporters of Charles were utterly beaten by the Duke of Cumberland at Culloden in April, 1746, and the Pretender was compelled to seek safety in flight. After prolonged and romantic wanderings, which have been repeatedly depicted in verse and prose, he managed to escape to France, from which country, being eventually banished, he took refuge in Italy. After his death and that of his brother, Cardinal York, the direct male line of the House of Stuart became extinct. The suppression of this rebellion was followed by an act abolishing the use of the Highland dress and the right to carry arms, and the extinction of military tenures dealt a final blow to the feudal power of the northern chieftains. Within fifteen years, the Highlanders were induced to enlist in large numbers under the British colors, and, from that day to this, have rendered inestimable services to the English Crown in both hemispheres. After the accession of George III., the Scottish people gradually became reconciled to the new dynasty.

The intellectual development of Scotland began in the last half of the last century, and is memorable for the number of names eminent in literature, among which those of Adam Smith, David Hume, Robert Burns, Sir Walter Scott, Thomas Campbell, Dugald Stewart, and Sir William Hamilton may be particularly mentioned. Remarkable, also, has been the increase of capital, of commerce and of manufactures in the last hundred years. Scottish men of science were among the first to make practical applications of steam as a motive power. Skilful engineering has made the Clyde a competitor of the Thames and Glasgow one of the most populous cities in Great Britain. The population of Scotland, which, in 1801, barely exceeded one million six hundred thousand, is now upward of four million. It is noteworthy that the females considerably exceed the males, a result due to emigration, for the proportion of female births is smaller than that of male births. The percentage of illegitimate births is large, having amounted, in 1885, to nearly eight and a half per cent. Crime and pauperism have steadily declined during the last half century, not only in proportion to the population, but absolutely. From an agricultural viewpoint, Scotland is still a country of large proprietors. It is computed that, on an average, each landowner possesses in Scotland one hundred and forty-three acres against thirty-three acres owned by each landowner in England. Less than four per cent of the inhabitants of Scotland share in the ownership of the soil. The wholesale clearances of tenants carried out in many districts during the present century gave rise to the grievances of the so-called crofters, which have, in recent years, been the subject of remedial legislation. The skill with which farming is prosecuted in Scotland may be inferred from the fact that the average yield of wheat and barley is higher than it is in England. On the other hand, the yield of oats and potatoes is lower. The number of cattle and sheep per one thousand acres of cultivated land is much larger in Scotland than in England. According to the report of the crofters' commission, appointed in 1883, the area under deer forest in Scotland is nearly two million acres, or about one-fifth of the whole country. The grouse moors occupy a still more extensive superficies. Half a century ago the herring and deep-sea fisheries employed only about thirty thousand persons, but the number has been since more than trebled. The output of coal in Scotland has also trebled in forty years. On the other hand, the delivery of iron ore is now less than it was forty years ago. The woollen industry has rapidly expanded since 1850; on the other hand, the manufacture of linen has materially declined since 1867. The number of cotton factories is also smaller than it was fifty years ago. The number of gallons of whiskey produced in Scotland in 1824 was only about five million; sixty years later, it had risen to upward of twenty million. Of especial interest are the statistics relating to the shipping owned in Scotland. At the time of the union with England, in 1707, the number of vessels was two hundred and fifteen, having an aggregate capacity of less than fifteen thousand tons. In 1884, the number of vessels owned in Scotland was three thousand four hundred and sixty-eight, with a total tonnage of nearly one million seven hundred thousand. The tonnage of the coasting and foreign trade nearly trebled in the thirty years succeeding 1855. The value of the traffic increased during the same period from about thirty-six million dollars to one hundred and fifty-three million. It is true that, even now, the value of imports into Scotland is only about a tenth

as great as that of the imports into England, but it should
be remembered that large quantities of foreign products find
their way into Scotland from England by rail.

We have seen that, by the act of union in 1707, Scotland
was to be represented at Westminster by sixteen peers, to be
chosen by the Scottish peerage for each parliament, and by
forty-five members of the House of Commons. By the Reform act of 1832, the number of Scottish members in the
Commons was raised to fifty-three; by the Reform act of
1868, to sixty; and by the Seats act of 1885, to seventy-five.
It is since 1885, too, that the management of Scottish business in the British parliament has been confided to a Secretary for Scotland.

We have seen also, that, by the Act of Union, Presby-
terianism, which was professed by a large majority of the
Scottish people, was recognized as established in the northern
kingdom under the name of the Church of Scotland. There
were secessions from the Established Kirk in 1733 and 1751,
but these were insignificant compared with the great schism
which began in 1833 and ended ten years later with the ex-
odus which organized the so-called Free Church of Scotland.
The Free Church had, in 1885, two-thirds as many congregations as did the Established Church. Since 1874, patron-
age has been abolished even in the Established Church, and
the right of choosing parish ministers has been conferred
upon the congregations. We should add that, in 1885, the
Roman Catholic Church had three hundred and twenty-
seven churches or chapels, and that the population affiliated
to it was computed at over three hundred and forty thousand. The Episcopal Church in Scotland is still very weak,
possessing at the date last mentioned only about two hundred and fifty churches, and eighty thousand members of
all ages. Of Baptists and Methodists in Scotland there are
very few.

KINGS OF SCOTLAND.

Name.	Parentage.	Accession.		Death.		Contemporaries.	
		A.D.	Page	A.D.	Page	France.	England.
			v. i.		v. i.		
Malcolm III. Cean-mohr.	Duncan	1056	33	1093	37	Philip I.	Harold II. Wil. Conq. Wil. Rufus
Donald Bane	———	1093	38	1098	39	———	
Duncan II.	Malcolm III.	1094	39	1094-5	39	———	
Edgar	———	1098	39	1106	40	———	Henry I.
Alexander I.	———	1107	40	1124	40	Lewis VI.	
David I.		1124	40	1153	45	Lewis VII.	Stephen
Malcolm IV.	Grandson of David I.	1153	48	1165	50		Henry II.
William the Lion	———	1166	50	1214	56	Philip II.	Richard I. John
Alexander II.	William the Lion	1214	56	1249	57	Lewis VIII. IX.	Henry III.
Alexander III.	Alexander II.	1249	60	1285	63	Philip III. IV.	Edward I.
John Baliol	Devorgoil	1292	77	1296	81		
Robert Bruce	Grandson of Bruce, Baliol's competitor	1306	103	1329	180	Lewis X. John Philip V. Charles IV. Philip VI.	—— II. —— III.
David II.	Robert Bruce	1331	188	1370-1	233	John II. Charles V.	
Robert II.	Marjory Bruce	1371	237	1389	246	Charles VI.	Richard II.
Robert III.	Robert II.	1390	247	1406	251	———	Henry IV.
James I.	Robert III.	1406	260	1437	292		—— V. —— VI.
James II.	James I.	1437	293	1460	328	Charles VII	
James III.	James II.	1460	330	1488	346	——— Lewis XI. Charles VIII.	Edw. IV. —— V. Rich. III. Henry VII.
James IV.	James III.	1488	347	1513	365	Lewis XII.	Hen. VIII.
James V.	James IV.	1513	384 v. ii.	1542	406 v. ii.	Francis I. Henry II.	
Mary	James V.	1561	32	1586-7	252	Francis IX. Charles IX.	Edw. VI. Mary. Elizabeth.
James VI., and I. of England	Mary	1567	80, 110	1625	387	Henry III. Henry IV.	Elizabeth.

INDEX

8

INDEX

A

E